FAMILY SECRETS

LATINA/O SOCIOLOGY SERIES

General Editors: Pierrette Hondagneu-Sotelo and Victor M. Rios

Family Secrets: Stories of Incest and Sexual Violence in Mexico
Gloria González-López

Family Secrets

Stories of Incest and Sexual Violence in Mexico

Gloria González-López

NEW YORK UNIVERSITY PRESS
New York and London

NEW YORK UNIVERSITY PRESS
New York and London
www.nyupress.org

© 2015 by New York University
All rights reserved

References to Internet websites (URLs) were accurate at the time of writing. Neither the author nor New York University Press is responsible for URLs that may have expired or changed since the manuscript was prepared.

ISBN: (hardback) 978-1-4798-5559-9
ISBN: (paperback) 978-1-4798-6913-8

For Library of Congress Cataloging-in-Publication data, please contact the Library of Congress.

New York University Press books are printed on acid-free paper, and their binding materials are chosen for strength and durability. We strive to use environmentally responsible suppliers and materials to the greatest extent possible in publishing our books.

Manufactured in the United States of America

10 9 8 7 6 5 4 3 2 1

Also available as an ebook

La vida no es la que uno vivió,
sino la que uno recuerda
y cómo la recuerda para contarla.

Life is not what one lived,
but rather what one remembers
and how one remembers it in order to recount it.
—Gabriel García Márquez

*Dedico este libro a las 60 personas
que con profunda vulnerabilidad y generosidad
me compartieron sus vidas.*

For everyone keeping a similar story in the heart.

*A mi madre y a mi padre,
con mi más profundo amor y gratitud.*

CONTENTS

Acknowledgments / Con profunda gratitud — xi

1. *En familia*: Sex, Incest, and Violence in Mexican Families — 1

2. Conjugal Daughters and Marital Servants:
   The Sexual Functions of Daughters in Incestuous Families — 31

3. *A la prima se le arrima*: Sisters and Primas — 76

4. Nieces and Their Uncles — 125

5. Men's Life Stories — 180

6. Toward a Feminist Sociology of Incest in Mexico — 232

Appendix A. Study Participants — 263

Appendix B. Methodological Considerations — 267

Appendix C. Incest in 32 Mexican State Penal Codes — 271

Appendix D. Uncle-Niece Cases — 273

Notes — 275

References — 301

Index — 313

About the Author — 321

ACKNOWLEDGMENTS / CON PROFUNDA GRATITUD

First and foremost my most profound gratitude goes to the sixty women and men who opened up their hearts and souls to share the moving life stories that gave life to this work. I have done everything possible to write your stories in this book and other publications with the same heartfelt vulnerability, honesty, and respect with which you shared them with me.

In each city, my deepest gratitude goes to all of the following professionals, some of whom had been or became personal friends during this research journey. Some of you are no longer with us; *les llevo en el corazón.*

Ciudad Juárez: The late Esther Chávez Cano, *trascendiste a través de tu valiosa obra.* Irma Guadalupe Casas Franco, Claudia Heredia, Eva Moreno, Fernando Ornelas, Efraín Rodríguez, and Juan Vargas— *muchísimas gracias. Señora Socorro Gutiérrez de Lozoya gracias a usted y su familia por su hospitalidad y todas sus finas atenciones durante mi estancia en Ciudad Juárez.* Adela Lozoya Gutiérrez and Carmen Vásquez Sierrra, thank you for your loving and supportive friendship.

Guadalajara: Alejandra de Gante Casas and the late José Manuel López Schultz became my fortress and guiding light in the city. Alejandra, *querida* thank you for the kindness and generosity of your beautiful heart and friendship. The late Carmen Castañeda and Águeda Jiménez Pelayo, as well as Belinda Aceves, Gandhi Magaña, Nelly Ordaz, Patricia Peña y Marysol Soto—*gracias mil.*

Mexico City: Laura Martínez Rodríguez, *gracias por siempre, mujer de ardua lucha.* Miriam Valdéz Valerio, thank you for being there for me, especially as I consulted with you countless times after my fieldwork. Thank you for your presence and solidarity: Joaquín Aguilar, Sofía Almazán, José Barba Martín, Gloria Careaga Pérez, Patricia Duarte, Gerardo González Ascencio, Patria Jiménez, Alejandro Núñez, Alicia Elena Pérez Duarte y Noroña, Luciana Ramos Lira, and Patricia Ravelo Blancas. To the late Itziar Lozano: my gratitude for the encouragement and inspiration during that special conversation I will never forget.

Monterrey: Former senator María Elena Chapa Hernández, Marina Duque, and Martha Flores Cavazos, my gratitude for becoming a vital and unconditional presence. Elizabeth Aguilar Parra, Karina Castro, Ramona Gámez, Clara Beatriz León Hernández, Rafael Limones, María Aurora Mota, Antonio Nevárez, Silvia Puente, Maribel Sáenz, and Miguel Villegas Lozano—*muchísimas gracias*. Hortencia Rodríguez Castañeda and the Wong Rodríguez family: *agradezco su amistad y apoyo*. Gabriela Lozano de Pérez in Laredo, Texas: Thank you for your solidarity and support during my travels to Mexico. My special gratitude goes to my sister Olivia Guadalupe González López for her generosity, kindness, and hospitality during my various trips to Monterrey.

In these four cities, thank you to all of you, who organized, sponsored, and/or attended workshops and seminars where I presented my preliminary findings or related themes, prior to, during, and after my fieldwork. Thank you for helping me expand my professional networks, and for helping in so many ways, professionally and personally. Thank you to all of you who introduced me to each and every one of these remarkable sixty women and men, and to the many kind and generous people I met casually or very briefly in each city, people whose names are not included here but whose presence contributed to the completion of my fieldwork and later stages of this project—*muchísimas gracias*.

My deep gratitude goes to the faculty and clinical supervisors I met at the University of Southern California in the early 1990s: Constance Ahrons, Irving Borstein, Carlfred Broderick, Marcia Lasswell, and Alexander Taylor. I would not have been able to work on this project without the clinical and professional training you offered to me as a couples and family therapist; your wisdom and expertise became my best companion in the field.

I express my gratitude as well to all the people who worked as my research assistants. Ana Durini Romero in Mexico City: *Gracias de corazón por trabajar tantas horas de ardua labor conmigo*. At the University of Texas at Austin, thank you Paloma Díaz-Lobos for your professional support and for facilitating the presence of hardworking students:

Gloria Delgadillo, Allison Hollander, and Willa Staats. Thank you, Juan Ramón Portillo Soto and Brandon Andrew Robinson for your priceless help and support.

Thank you for the light of your friendship while I wrote this book: Sonya Grant Arreola, Marysol Asencio, Juan José Battle, Ari Chagoya, the late Elvira M. Cisneros, Beth Dart, Rafael Díaz, Patricia Emerson, Marcela Lagarde y de los Ríos, Ani Tenzin Lhamo, Lisa Moore, Lorena Porras, Sharmila Rudrappa, Pepper Schwartz, and Christine Williams. Thank you William Rodarmor for editing parts of this book, and for being a friend. Liliana Wilson: my deepest gratitude for your priceless friendship and commitment. Sylvia Flesner, Robyn E. McCarty, Dale Rishel, and Tony Ward: thank you for your healing presence.

This work was made possible thanks to support received from the Woodrow Wilson Career Enhancement Fellowship for Junior Faculty (2005–2006), and financial and professional support provided by the University of Texas at Austin through the Dean's Fellowship (Fall 2006), the Center for Mexican American Studies, the Department of Sociology, and the Teresa Lozano Long Institute of Latin American Studies. Thank you Peter Ward and the C. B. Smith Sr. Centennial Chair in US-Mexico Relations funds for your financial support. The Center for Women's and Gender Studies and Voices Against Violence: my gratitude for your professional support and feminist solidarity and inspiration.

Pierrette Hondagneu-Sotelo and Denise Segura, my gratitude goes to you for your insightful recommendations as I worked on the first draft of this book. Thank you Pierrette *querida* for the priceless support and professional solidarity of more than 20 years, and for believing once again in my work; thank you and Victor Rios for considering this book for the Latina/o Sociology series. Tomás Almaguer: thank you for your generous and kind spirit, and for your unconditional support when I needed it most. Cecilia Menjívar: Thank you for your gentle and kind heart, and your professional encouragement that knows no limits. Jodi O'Brien: Thank you for your generous and kind personal and professional support. My special gratitude goes to Caelyn Cobb and Alexia Traganas for their kindness, patience, and hard work. And to Ilene Kalish, executive editor at New York University Press, thank you for your commitment, hard work, and support, and for genuinely caring about this book—you became the answer to my prayers.

Venerable Kirti Tsenshab Rinpoche y Lama Thubten Zopa Rinpoche, los maestros de mi corazón, les ofrezco este libro y todo el trabajo y esfuerzo que le dieron vida. May these life stories contribute toward a better understanding, healing, and elimination of all forms of human suffering and pain, and their causes; may this book be endlessly beneficial to others.

Austin, Texas

Fall 2014

1

En familia

Sex, Incest, and Violence in Mexican Families

"My breasts stopped growing when my grandfather touched them," Elisa revealed in explaining her petite body, which has the appearance of a slender, flat-chested adolescent. Tearfully she described the sandpaper sensation of her maternal grandfather's hands on her tender skin, an aging man who in his eighties fondled her breasts from age seven to eleven. Back then Elisa's father's behavior was also confusing to her. After his night shift as a cab driver in Ciudad Juárez, Elisa and her mom would patiently listen over lunch as her father shared the horror stories and dangers he experienced at work and how blessed he felt to be back home after a long night in the frightening streets of the city. Then, after lunch, he would take Elisa by the hand to accompany him for a nap that never felt right.

"You must change, you must change, because if you don't, I kill you." Helián still recalls the words that his father would repeat consistently while using his thumb to penetrate his anus during his childhood from ages three to eight. At the time, Helián was an effeminate boy who suffered in pain and confusion, not understanding what his father was trying to tell him with these horrifying actions and death threats. "But change what?" he wondered. Why would his father kill him? Helián never asked; he was afraid. At the age of eight, his father penetrated him anally with his penis and left him bleeding on the bathroom floor. He received medical attention, but the tragic event was never discussed in the family. When I interviewed Helián, he was living legally as Heliana in Monterrey, a college-educated, bright, beloved, and popular school teacher in her forties who takes self-prescribed hormones and dresses modestly. "Have you ever watched *Tootsie*?" Heliana asked me in an animated tone of voice, as she explained that she was neither transgender nor transsexual and that Dustin Hoffman offered her years ago a creative and humane way to survive in homophobic Mexico, where, to be an effeminate gay man with a soft, gentle voice was a death sentence.

"Why the fuck my parents took so much care of me, if in their own house their own sons abused me, and they did not even know about it!" Renata exclaimed with tears of rage. Sobbing, she described the scattered but graphic memories she began to experience vividly and with shock and confusion after she and her husband attended a spiritual retreat the year before we met for her interview in Mexico City. In her memories, it became more and more clear that her oldest brother forced her to have sex with him when she was four or six and he was seventeen or nineteen. Raised in an upper-middle-class family concerned about the dangers of the outside world, Renata and all of her siblings completed college while enjoying a pampered life of comfort and privilege, private schools, and at least one vacation trip to Europe. Renata's parents, now deceased, will never know what she experienced with her brothers. Although she has told her sisters about it, she does not know if she will ever confront her brothers.

"Isn't your stepdaughter becoming pretty? Why don't you check her out?" Although Samuel felt confused by these questions asked by a woman he met through a chat room as he experimented with cyber-sex in his free time at a cybercafé in Guadalajara, the conversation also aroused his curiosity. Eventually he yielded to the temptation to en-gage in sexual activity with his eleven- or twelve-year-old stepdaughter. Carefully hiding his actions from his wife, he fondled her in her sleep and later undressed in front of her and kissed her deeply on the mouth. Eventually the guilt overcame him and he confessed to his wife about his cybersex activities and what he had done to the girl. His wife was devastated but appreciative of his honesty; together they sought profes-sional help.

* * *

You have begun to read a book that will be very difficult to get through. Needless to say, the entire project was an emotionally challenging endeavor. After listening to each one of the life stories, however, I believe it would have been even more painful for me not to give life to this book.

This book is about the life stories of sixty Mexican women and men who, like Elisa, Renata, Helián, and Samuel, honored me with their trust

and shared their most intimate and frequently untold stories of incestuous relationships and sexual violence in their families. I met and conducted in-depth interviews with these adult women and men in Ciudad
Juárez, Guadalajara, Mexico City, and Monterrey in 2005 and 2006, and
established contact with them through the generous support of activists, women's groups, community organizers, and other professionals.
I also include the insightful and thought-provoking lessons I learned
from interviews with thirty-five of these professionals.[1] Some of them
include activists whose names now appear in publications about Mexico
and human rights, policymaking, and laws aimed at protecting children
and women.[2]

Incest in Mexico

Why write a book about stories of incest and sexual violence in Mexican
families? As a Mexican feminist who identifies as a public sociologist
studying sexuality-related concerns and topics affecting the well-being
and living conditions of Mexican families, I realized in 2005 that it was
time for me to choose the subject for my next project. At the time, I was
interested in pursuing a project that would address the urgent needs
of a community that had been close to my heart for about four years:
Ciudad Juárez. Since 2001, I had been visiting this border city as a long-
distance volunteer to run workshops on violence against women and
gender inequality for community-based agencies in the city. I have a
background as a couples and family therapist working with Latina
immigrant women, including Central American women who were
raped during war. The experiences of these women moved me to organize the workshops, and in 2005, I asked local activists how I could be
of help as a researcher. "What kind of research is needed by the professionals who work with families that have experienced sexual violence?"
I consistently inquired in these conversations. I learned that while other
researchers were already highly involved in investigating the perverse
disappearance and violence against hundreds of women in the city,
other topics needed immediate attention, yet they had remained invisible and ignored. Through these informal conversations I learned that
girls and women who seek help from community-based agencies rarely
report that a stranger is the person exercising violence against them.

Rather, it is frequently someone *within* their families—not *outside* the family—who has sexually assaulted or molested them. Yet, life stories about the people who endure these experiences have not been examined and published. Incest and other sex acts within families, I learned, were the best-kept secrets of women and their families. This was an unexplored enigma for clinicians and professionals who had read little or nothing about incest or related topics in Mexico. Their limited knowledge was based on what they had recently learned from publications written and published in the United States, such as the influential work of sociologist David Finkelhor. As I did preliminary research, I learned that my activist friends in Ciudad Juárez were correct: the social sciences have been complicit in this silence. To this day, the few publications on incest-related concerns in Mexican society include personal accounts or autobiographies, descriptive statistical examinations, legal and judicial themes, and studies on popular culture in the humanities. However, there is no empirical research to date about incest, sexuality, violence, and family life in Mexican society.[3]

This book is a feminist informed, sociological study that documents and discusses the life stories of Mexican women and men who have experienced sexualized acts, interactions, and relationships within their families and contrasting urban patriarchal cultures and economies. In the book, I explore *why* and *how* sex, in varying forms, may be used against the will of children and women and as a complex form of power, control, and everyday family life. The women and men represented in these stories grew up in families where silence and confusion around sexuality were an unquestionable norm. I allow the stories to speak for themselves and avoid concepts such as survivor and perpetrator— concepts that some of these Mexicans actually perceived to be too pathological, foreign, or offensive to even capture the complexity of their lives; I use "victim" selectively. The stories also expose the ways in which the thrills of voluntary sex are lived within family cultures of secrets, betrayal, and lies, and the mysteries of love and romance.

Why is sexual violence in Mexican families so under-researched and under-examined? I gained some insight into this silence through my interviews. In general, the silence around sexual activity in Mexican families creates an atmosphere of ambivalence and ambiguity in which sexual secrets fester. These cultural ambiguities are reinforced by the double standards of morality that disadvantage women within both the family and society, and by family ethics promoting the idea that women should serve the men in their families—all of which makes girls and young women especially vulnerable. In a patriarchal society where women are trained to be sexually available to men, a girl or a young woman who is forced to have sex by her uncle, for example, may perceive it as "normal" and never talk about it. This woman's life may become an emotional labyrinth if these encounters become repetitive or seductive while she realizes that her uncle is loved by her own mother for being the generous source of economic support to her family. Some of the men that I interviewed who engaged in sex with other men of their same age group (for example, two adolescent male cousins) told me that it was difficult to know if their mutually consensual sexual encounters were always completely voluntary, or involuntary. They also explained that they were more distressed about the fact that they were having sex with another man than the fact that this man was a member of the family. The life stories that I gathered led me to question the very definitions of incest and to uncover deeper insights regarding the complex interplay of family, culture, and state that forms the backdrop of these sexual experiences. I also learned with certainty that Mexico is a profoundly sexist and homophobic society.

Studying Incest in Mexico: Writing about Mexican Families

Incest and sexual violence in families are prevalent in the history of many cultures and societies and are not exclusive to Mexican society. Incestuous activities have been identified in influential texts in Western and Westernized societies including but not limited to the Bible, and they have been examined across all academic disciplines covering human behavior. European and U.S. male intellectuals such as Émile Durkheim, Sigmund Freud, Claude Lévi-Strauss, Talcott Parsons, and Edvard Westermarck have theorized about incest from different historical periods, disciplinary perspectives, and cultural standpoints; anthropologists have offered groundbreaking revelations and examinations of these behaviors in different cultures, and psychiatrists, psychologists, and sociologists have looked at these patterns as well.

In the United States, pioneering books on incest include *Kiss Daddy Goodnight* (1978) by feminist writer and activist Louise Armstrong,

Father-Daughter Incest (1981) by Harvard psychiatrist Judith Herman, and *The Secret Trauma* (1986) by sociologist Diana Russell, who also conducted research on incest in South Africa.[4] Sociologist David Finkelhor (1994) identified sexual abuse of children as an "international problem" in an ambitious and comprehensive study of twenty countries (with the United States and other developed nations included), highlighting the prevalence of these incidents involving blood relatives as well as paternal figures such as stepparents and adoptive parents across a wide variety of cultures and nations.[5]

Thus, although my focus is on Mexico, it is important to emphasize: Incest is not *only* a problem for this nation. Incest and sexual violence within families is a phenomenon that occurs in many societies around the world, as does sexual abuse at large.

For the purposes of this book, I consider the definition-in-progress I have suggested in the past, which actually emerged from this study: "Incest refers to sexualized contact (involuntary and/or voluntary, and the gray area in-between) within the context of the family; this may take place between individuals sharing the same bloodline and/or within close emotional family relationships and involving vertical (i.e., relatives in authority positions and minors or younger women) or horizontal relationships (i.e., relatives close in age)."[6] Likewise, I am still working within the conceptual traps I discuss in this book and consider that *involuntary* incest takes place through a wide array of expressions of sexual violence.[7] Incest is in fact diverse and complex, and it may involve varying degrees and sophisticated types of coercion. In chapter 5 I incorporate the concept of *kinship sex* as I look at a complex, non-linear multidimensional continuum between coercion and consent. All concepts—incest, sexual violence, and kinship sex—are interconnected and examined within contexts of power and control dynamics, and relationships of gender inequality shaping family life.

The goal of *Secretos de familia* is to offer a close up view of *incest* and *sexual violence where they exist* in Mexican families while also zooming out the feminist sociological lens to provide a more structural analysis of these phenomena. In other words, this book is *neither* about Mexican families per se *nor* about family life in Mexican cultures. This book is *only* about the Mexican families where incestuous activities and sexual violence have become intricate labyrinths to be deciphered by the members of these families. Although the lines between non-incestuous families and incestuous families in Mexico may at times become fine and blurry, this book offers a critical perspective about the ways in which patriarchal beliefs and practices perceived as harmless and "normal" in mainstream, non-incestuous families may take perverse turns and create the nuanced and complex social conditions and circumstances that make girls, boys, and women vulnerable to the expressions of sexual violence I examine in this book. In other words, these Mexican-specific cases provide an opportunity to explore incest and sexual violence as sociological phenomena, rather than through an overly psychologized lens.

Because the book offers a contextual analysis, there are certain features of Mexican society that are significant in explaining incest and sexual violence at the social institutional level. As a social critic of the ways in which influential publications have promoted stereotypes about Mexican families, the book *The Children of Sánchez* comes to mind.

Repudiated by some and celebrated by others, *The Children of Sánchez* (1961) was first published in English by U.S. American anthropologist Oscar Lewis as an "autobiography" of a family living in Tepito, a working-class section located near the center of Mexico City. A movie based on the book was made years later, starring Anthony Quinn and other famous movie stars. I originally read the book in its Spanish version—*Los hijos de Sánchez*—as an undergraduate student in Monterrey. I had some form of ethnographic flashbacks of this book, especially when my informants shared detailed descriptions of crowded housing and *vecindades* (urban dwellings) in their recollections. At the end of my interviews, I also became aware of the sophistication of the life stories that women and men had shared with me with so much honesty. I thought about relevant methodological and conceptual concerns and limitations. For instance, the so-called concepts of the culture of poverty and machismo did not capture the complexity and richness of the stories I listened to for specific reasons.

First, Lewis suggests his controversial paradigm, the culture of poverty. From this perspective, people growing up in enduring poverty develop specific attitudes and behaviors, an entire value system that is reproduced and sustained across generations. That is, the poor trapped in vicious cycles of poverty develop a culture of their own—"poverty is inherent in the culture of the poor."[8] From a point of view that has been used to pathologize poor African American families as well, people who live in pervasive poverty end up being blamed for their own socio-economic marginality, society and culture are perceived as static and fixed, and thus any form of social intervention or change is practically impossible.[9]

And second, Lewis relied on machismo as a paradigm to explain patriarchy, men's lives, and masculinity, a concept that was useful to announce and make sense of gender inequality in Mexico in the late 1950s or early 1960s. Interestingly, machismo as an idea has gained popularity to this day; people use it in everyday life conversations to make sense of gender inequality, and scholars use it to discuss issues related to patriarchy in Mexican society (including myself, very early in my career). However, more than fifty years have passed already since this influential book was published, and new perspectives to examine gender inequality and manhood have emerged. According to some critical gender studies scholars, machismo as an idea and paradigm has become outdated, limited, and problematic, especially given the advances made in gender studies and men's and masculinity research with populations of Mexican origin in recent decades.[10]

Thus, I wrote this book with a keen awareness of the problems of over-generalizing and the dangers of perpetuating misleading cultural impressions. Sociologist Josie Méndez-Negrete has been accused of "reproducing a culture of poverty" or "a blame-the-victim" paradigm in her revealing book, *Las hijas de Juan: Daughters Betrayed*, a moving auto-ethnography of incest in the context of Mexican migration and family life in California. Her work has paved the way for me to honor the culturally based concerns raised by many of the professionals I interviewed, while also being mindful to not perpetuate damaging images about Mexican women and men and their families; her *testimonio* resonated deeply with the stories I listened to. With an open, receptive heart that embraces these intellectual responsibilities, I have written this book.

Beyond Culture Blaming

"*Nomás no me vengas con la misma historia de Los hijos de Sánchez* (Just don't come to me with the same story of *The Children of Sánchez*)," were the words that accompanied the stern warnings, pointing fingers, and rolling eyes I received from some of the professionals I interviewed.[11] These reactions became evident especially when I asked if they thought there was anything specific about Mexican society that may make girls, boys, and women vulnerable to sexual violence within the family. I reassured them about my interest in addressing the importance of challenging archetypal, stereotypical, and pathological images of Mexican children, women, men and their families as portrayed in the literature referring to a "Mexican culture," and stressed my interest in offering a sociological understanding of a complex phenomenon.

In these instances, attorneys, activists, and other professionals talked to me about the ways in which poverty and poor working-class families have been misrepresented and demonized in some publications about family life in Mexico, often referring to the book published by Oscar Lewis decades ago. Consuelo's words in this book illustrate the kind of family image these professionals were concerned about:

> Right after supper, everyone would go to bed. Marta in the big bed with her daughters; Mariquita, Conchita and I on my little bed; Alanes and Domingo and Roberto doubled over with cold on the floor; and now, the maid and her children, also on the floor. Night after night, this was the sad picture before my eyes. I tried to make it better, but by that time, I was almost afraid to speak up. (Lewis 1961, 417)

These professionals shared stories of incest and sexual violence in wealthy Mexican families, putting emphasis on the serious nature of this social problem for other countries and cultures. Some also reflected on the ways in which scandalous cases of sexual violence in poor families have been exploited and exposed by sensationalist newspapers preying on their fatal destiny, such as *Alarma!*[12] Poor families—unlike their upper- and middle-class counterparts—do not have the money and power needed to cover up their family tragedies and sorrows. Poor families are also the ones, they asserted, looking for professional help at NGOs or community agencies and public institutions, thus their cases usually become more visible and they become a statistic, and are frequently perceived as "the only ones" experiencing these complex and painful life experiences. In short, I was warned not to be *clasista*—classist—and oppress poor families even more.

In the end, the warning given to me by some of the professionals echoed anthropologist Matthew Gutmann's reflections from two decades ago about the impact of Lewis's work: "In their attempt to understand Mexican men, especially poor Mexican men, numerous writers have utilized specific data of Oscar Lewis's ethnographic studies to promote sensationalizing generalizations that go far beyond anything that Lewis ever wrote" (1994, 9).[13]

The voices of the professionals warning me against Oscar Lewis also confirm the life stories in this book: incest and sexual violence happen *across* and *within* all socioeconomic strata, with specific family contexts and social forces triggering the acts of sexual molestation or rape of a child. My goal is to offer a feminist sociological perspective to examine a complex social problem while taking into account (1) the historical evolution of laws on incest, sex, and sexual violence in the family, and children's and women's human rights in Mexican society while looking closely at their colonial and indigenous origins; (2) dominant cultural perceptions of sexuality, double standards of morality and family cultures promoting gender inequality, patriarchal religious practices and values, regional cultures, economies and ideologies, and pop culture; (3) social, political, and cultural perceptions of children as less-than-human, as extensions and property of their parents.

Methods

I conducted a total of sixty in-depth life history interviews with forty-five biological women and fifteen biological men; one of the men lived as a woman at the time of our interview (see Helián's story). They were born between the mid-1950s to the mid-1980s and were raised in a wide variety of socioeconomic backgrounds. The women and men I interviewed had a wide variety of skin colors and shades, as well as a rich expression and combination of phenotypic characteristics including but not limited to hair and eye color, hair texture, as well as height, and body size and structure. Only two of them (Otilia and Esmeralda) openly identified as "indigenous." All of them were able-bodied, with the exception of one informant who made a special request and asked me not to reveal that information anywhere in the study. Appendix A shows their demographic characteristics, including age, marital status, religion, education, and sexual and romantic history.

I met all of them for the first time in 2005 and 2006 as I conducted my fieldwork in the four cities that became my research sites (i.e., Ciudad Juárez, Guadalajara, Mexico City, and Monterrey). I met them through the help and support of many of the professionals I met in a wide variety of community-based and academic settings. As in my previous project with Mexican immigrants living in Los Angeles, I realized that informants selected themselves. That is, the people who agreed to be interviewed felt highly motivated to share their individual stories, with many of them being generous storytellers, reflecting their comfort with sharing life stories—*los relatos de vida*—a methodology successfully used in Mexico by social scientists.[14] Los relatos de vida are rich oral practices of traditional stories and anecdotes in Mexican families—*narraciones de cuentos tradicionales y anécdotas familiares*—reproduced from generation to generation and with roots in prehispanic societies.[15]

I collected the life stories presented in this book through in-depth individual interviews I conducted in a private safe space that was frequently provided by the organizations with whom I had established a relationship. My clinical background as a couples and family therapist gave me the necessary skills to engage in these conversations, to take care of myself, and also to support the individuals who were so generously sharing their difficult life stories. I was therefore shocked to realize that psychotherapy and research represent two completely different epistemological processes. For instance, immersing myself in the wounds of an interviewee with the purpose of conducting research soon revealed to me a state of consciousness I did not experience as a psychotherapist years ago, when I conducted clinical work with U.S. Latina immigrant women with histories of sexual violence. I discuss this theme in *Epistemologies of the Wound* (2006) and *Ethnographic Lessons* (2010a).

Listening to moving and frequently emotionally overwhelming interviews dramatically shaped the ways in which I decided to conduct my labor-intensive analysis, and eventually to write this book. I decided to present the storytelling approach of these life stories for specific reasons. First, the assertive methodological reflections of senior rape researcher Rebecca Campbell (2002) struck a cord with me. She states: "I question the emotional accuracy of academic research on rape. It now strikes me as too clean, too sanitized, and too distant from the emotional, lived experiences of rape survivors. What is the 'rape' portrayed in academic discourse? To the extent to which academic discourse frames rape as an individual problem of individual survivors, devoid of emotionality, it may miss the mark representing the problem of rape in women's lives and our society" (97).

Telling and writing the life stories as they were told to me, with painfully graphic details about their experiences, exposes these lived experiences *as is*, that is, without sanitizing them. This also resonated with the importance of addressing the messiness of human behavior in a wide variety of social contexts, as eloquently articulated by sociologist Jodi O'Brien (2009).

Second, as I listened to each one of the stories, I became aware of the political dimension of this project: I became a witness to a life story of sexual violence while conducting each interview; this was especially the case for people who were breaking their silence and talking about it for the first time. This also transformed the way I looked at these narratives and how I studied, analyzed, and presented the so-called data, something I discuss in more depth in *Ethnographic Lessons* (2010a).

Third and most important, I am telling stories about incest and sexual violence because the people who shared them with me did it with so much hope and with a sincere motivation: they re-lived their pain with the purpose of sharing a story of life so it could be *told* and thereby help others in similar circumstances. They felt motivated especially to know that their stories could be of help to a wide variety of professionals interested in creating social change. In short, telling a story is an ethical and political commitment I made with these sixty women and men.

Writing the stories became an ambitious and time-consuming intellectual journey. I read each individual interview transcript at least twice, developed a long list of thirty-plus categories of analysis so I would not miss anything in the organization of these stories, and then wrote each story without missing or distorting anything. The time spent was also a result of the ethical concern and care I felt for the people who had so generously shared their lives with me. Some stories are longer than others, and some are more graphic and detailed than others. Per their request, I had to omit specific aspects of their stories, as in the case of Otilia, which I published as a case study.[16] Regardless, I took great care to represent and include all the details as they were shared with me. Finally, not all of the stories of the sixty people I interviewed are included in this book in their entirety; a few have been (or will be) published elsewhere because of the specificity or the unique nature of their cases. All stories were usually united by the same family patterns I discuss in this book.

This study was conducted while following the same professional and institutional ethics and procedures that have guided my previous research with Mexican populations. I conducted my ethnographic work after I received IRB approval at the University of Texas at Austin in 2005. None of these subjects participated in any of the previous research that I conducted in the past, which was based on fieldwork I conducted in the 1990s in Los Angeles, California.

Appendix B discusses additional methodological and ethical dimensions of this study, which I have examined extensively in other publications. Working on these publications helped me make sense of what Rebecca Campbell identifies as "emotionally engaged research," an ethnographic journey that demanded a lot of emotional and intellectual work on a wide variety of methodological dimensions, something I had to do before I could even immerse myself in the emotionally overwhelming and intellectually abundant narratives so I could organize and analyze them and write this book. Finally, in order to protect the privacy of my informants, I use pseudonyms to identify the people who shared their life stories with me.

Shifting Definitions of Incest

"Do you want the legal definition of incest? Or do you want the clinical definition of incest?" professionals very frequently inquired as I asked them about what the concept "incest" meant to them. I soon learned that tension and contradiction have long existed around incest as a concept, historically and among legal and mental health professions.

As a nation that became independent in 1821, Mexico created its laws while still being influenced by the Catholic Church. For instance, a professor of law with extensive expertise in human rights explained that, following Judeo Christian religious and cultural traditions, these laws had to legally punish a taboo—incest. From other attorneys I also learned that the *Leyes de Reforma* (mid-1800s) were fundamental for a complete restructuring of Mexico's legal system and created the separation of Church and State. The legal system that experienced important changes with regard to family law in 1870, 1884, and 1917, however, has been historically patriarchal.[17] Laws that were later represented by state penal codes

> have traditionally and briefly identified incest as intercourse between blood-related "*ascendientes*," "*descendientes*," or siblings. Legally, incest is assumed to be voluntary sexual activity between equals who are blood-related. In general, in Mexico, the law punishes incest as sexual activity within the family but it overlooks issues of power, control, or abuse within families. Sexual violence within families is punished but as an aggravating factor of other crimes. For example, rape and child prostitution (among others) may receive a higher punishment if they go from "ascendiente" to "descendiente." Thus, incest per se (with all its complexities) is lost in these legal classifications, it is punished only indirectly and remains invisible.[18]

As of today, many state penal codes legally define incest as a "crime against the family." As of July 2013, more than half of the thirty-two penal codes follow such legal description, with five states associating incest with a violation of an individual's sexual freedom, sexual safety, or "normal" (meaning "healthy") psychosexual development. Tlaxcala and Puebla had no laws against incest when I conducted my fieldwork; "Maybe that is an oversight," commented a Mexico City attorney. Appendix C shows these contrasting patterns across the country. Additional research needs to be conducted to learn more about how these changes came into effect, and the changes in the making that some attorneys anticipated. As recently as 1980, in fact, a man who stole a cow received a more severe legal punishment than a man who raped a woman. In some states, these laws punishing what one attorney identified as *abigeato* (i.e., abigeat or theft of cattle) are still in effect to this day. "*¡Hay tanto por hacer!* There is still a long way to go!" became an expression I heard repeatedly in 2005 and 2006. Some professionals said they were optimistic about the future in a nation that has transitioned recently to becoming an urban society that is exposing new generations of Mexicans to high technology and information, and catching up (at least at the discourse level) with international treaties on issues affecting the well-being of women and children.

Through my interviews, I learned that incest was both more prevalent and more sophisticated than the outdated definitions the patriarchal Mexican state suggests. Interviewees did not always use the word *incesto* or *incestuoso* to identify their experiences of sex as violence in their families, which included a wide array of actions and nuanced expressions that range from the perverse and coercive experiences that Elisa, Helián, and Renata endured when they were children, to the voluntary and pleasurable sex that a young adolescent man enjoyed with a male cousin close in age. I also learned that *la familia* meant much more than the "father, mother and children" traditional image. Family included extended family members, men who become stepfathers at different stages in children's lives, in-laws and in-laws' blood relatives, and people who are emotionally and morally close to them as *amigos de la familia*— women and men who were "like family." Paradoxically, accepting others as family (for example, an aunt's new boyfriend or husband) may automatically grant people that mamá or papá barely know the moral authority to take care of children without even knowing if the person is emotionally or morally competent to be in charge of minors. In my conversations with two former seminarians who were sexually abused by controversial priest Marcial Maciel, I also learned that a young man may perceive a priest as a paternal figure and thus, being abused by him, meant being exposed to what one of them identified as "spiritual incest," meaning that the priest is also *el padre* who sexually abuses a "spiritual son" while also betraying *la madre iglesia*—the mother church.[19]

Catholicism is central to understanding incest and sexual violence in Mexican families with regard to issues involving the social organization of silence, secrets, complicity, and the confessional; double standards of sexual morality, guilt, and informants' interpretations of their experiences of abuse; Catholic-informed moral beliefs and practices affecting women and sexual and gender nonconformers; Catholic and other Christian religious leaders abusing children within and outside their families; and the contrasting views of sexualized violence in families offered by the Catholic priests I interviewed, all taking place in times of moral scandal of sexual abuse by priests and relevant transitions in

Catholic leadership. Beyond the Catholic faith, all of the above apply selectively to other informants raised in Christian-based religions in Mexico.

My intent is to contribute to conversations and dialogues about critical issues involving the human rights and well-being of children and women in Mexico, gender and sexuality studies, family studies with Mexican populations, and the prevention and elimination of all forms of violence. In particular, the stories and research in this book provide a culturally informed basis for understanding the interplay among family, culture, and state in perpetuating not only sexual violence within families, but also the structural conditions that foster this vulnerability and violence. My research strongly indicates the cultural specifics of these actions (including cultural practices that implicate priestly sex abuse as a form of incest) while also providing a framework for subsequent studies of incest across cultures.

Sexual Violence, Advocacy, and Other Interventions: Past and Present

Women as the target of violence exercised by men in what is known as Mexican territory goes back to prehispanic Mesoamerican times.[20] Indigenous women then became rape-able as part of the conquest: sexual violence was strategically used for political projects of invasion and colonization, involving at times some forms of reproductive coercion.[21] Colonial Mexican society witnessed additional sexualized secrets, including those that involved rape by a relative, as discovered and documented by historian Carmen Castañeda's revealing examinations of twenty-one confessions guides.[22] Priests used these religious texts to control the sex lives of indigenous populations in revealing ways: incest (or "sin" between people who were blood-related) was frequently identified as a sexual prohibition in these documents, and "(rape) forcing a woman, or corrupting a woman by force" is listed less often as such.[23] Loss of virginity and damage to the honor of her family was much more of a concern than a woman being raped. "The loss of virginity represented both a criminal and civil offense to a woman, but especially to her family."[24] *La dote*—the dowry—was demanded from rapists, and/or the obligation to marry her.[25] The penalty in the end was a way to reinforce a clear sexual norm: sexual relations must take place within marriage.[26] Elsewhere, I wrote, "Rape of a woman by a close relative showed how ineffective these legal measures and social prescriptions were, especially when girls and adolescent women were the victims. In such cases, judges were more concerned about protecting the families involved in these trials, which relegated women of all ages to a marginalized position in the legal processes" (2013a, 405).

Meticulous historical examinations of the ecclesiastical justice and the legal apparatus in colonial and independent Mexico have reflected the ambiguity of these incest laws, leaving as well unanswered questions.[27] In the meantime, women and children did not have rights as fully sentient, autonomous human beings, and nineteenth-century "legal commentators still warned that husbands and wives could not be equal because that would risk the 'continual mutiny of the subjects against the established authority,' and undermine the stability of the Mexican state."[28] A little known nineteenth-century feminist jurist, Genaro García, is a noteworthy exception to this patriarchal rule.[29] The most noticeable political and social changes were about to happen in the two centuries to come, and more specifically in more recent decades.

Although laws about incest have existed in some form of legal limbo since Mexico won its independence in 1821, near the end of the twentieth century, left-wing and women's groups and other advocates had made important strides to promote laws aimed at protecting children and women from different forms of sexual violence while addressing issues of power and control. Women's right to vote was established in 1953 and women and men become equal under the law according to Article 4, which passed in 1974 in anticipation of the International Woman's day to be celebrated in Mexico the following year.[30] Senior attorneys and human rights activists I listened to were consistent in their memory: CAMVAC (*Centro de Apoyo a Mujeres Violadas*) was established by a group of professionals in 1979 in Mexico City. CAMVAC offered psychological, legal, and medical attention to women who were raped, very likely the first organization of its kind in the nation. The brave groundbreaking pioneers who created CAMVAC experienced situations of danger and clandestine life, according to some of these senior professionals. COVAC (*Colectivo de Lucha contra la Violencia hacia las Mujeres*) in Mexico City and CAM (*Centro de Apoyo a la Mujer*) in the state of Colima were founded later, between the early and mid-1980s.[31] "This is what existed before starting to work more closely with the State," according to anthropologist Eli Bartra, reflecting about those times of transition (1992, 28). Since the late 1980s, according to González Ascencio (2007), a law professor in Mexico City, important changes were taking place at the State level:

> With regard to judicial practice, specialized agencies in sex crimes came into existence since 1989; *fiscalías* (equivalent to District Attorney's office) in that area of specialty; centers of professional attention and therapy; units to assist intrafamily violence and commissions of equity and gender in the different *secretarías de Estado* or government departments and the legislative branch; commissions for women at the state level also exist, as well as one *Instituto de las mujeres*—Institute for women—at the national level. In this way is culminated, in appearance, a long path of social and cultural transformations tending towards elevating the status of women and to recognize, based on the facts, her legal equality vis-à-vis the man. (78)

Before the end of the millennium, collective efforts facilitated the creation of other nongovernmental organizations exclusively concerned about issues related to sexual violence, such as the *Centro de Orientación y Prevención de la Agresión Sexual, A.C.* in Guadalajara, and ADIVAC in Mexico City.[32] By then, the Mexican masses had been exposed to a sexual abuse prevention campaign called *Cuídate a ti mismo* (Take care of yourself) produced by Televisa, an influential TV broadcasting company with wide national coverage. In the mid- or late 1980s, Televisa started to air commercials relying on the "*Ojo Mucho Ojo*" slogan to teach children to "watch out" for any risk of potential sexual abuse.[33] This campaign did have some impact in the population, as reported by some of the people I met and interviewed.[34] By then, the rise of psychology (officially established and recognized as a profession in the 1970s) and the role of feminism, and the long history of women's movements, had become strengthened. Shelters to protect women were established in the mid-1990s.[35]

At times in conversation with Mexico City and at times by themselves, Guadalajara and Monterrey by then had been following their own distinctive paths in their own efforts to offer professional services to children and women exposed to different forms of sexual violence from a variety of professional avenues, including but not limited to private practice, public institutions, and groups of clinicians and professors formally and informally addressing these issues at different private and public college spaces, in schools that taught nursing and public health, law school and criminology, social work, psychology, and psychiatry, among others.[36]

And finally, Ciudad Juárez exposed to Mexico—and then to the world—some of the most extreme and brutal expressions of sexual violence against women, which started to become documented in the early 1990s by the *Grupo 8 de Marzo*. This organization became the institutional ancestor of *Casa Amiga*, which opened its doors to the public in 1999. Casa Amiga became the first organization on the Mexican side of the U.S.-Mexico border to offer a wide variety of professional services to women seeking answers to a life without violence.[37]

By the first decade of the twenty-first century, the State had passed laws aimed at helping women achieve gender equality and a life free of violence, reflecting (at least on paper) a commitment to international treatises and agreements advocating for women's rights.[38] In a 2007 special report called *Delitos contra las mujeres* (Crimes against women), Olamendi explains that, "The consideration of incest as a crime has different arguments, some of which go from the concern that incestuous relationships may result in children with genetic problems, to those that have to do with social rejection toward this behavior" (48). The same report explains that, "Sexual abuse has not been established as such in any of the penal codes" (44), and offers an informative classification and analysis of all crimes identified under the *violencia sexual* category, state by state, as of that date. In this report, incest laws still echo colonial society.[39] Professionals working directly with people of all ages and genders with histories of different forms of sexualized violence frequently echoed research on rape in Mexico: "The risk of rape is greater with a relative, the partner, or a friend of the family," and clarified that any statistics of sexual violence within families is only "an estimate" of a social problem that can be difficult to assess with accuracy—incest is more prevalent than what we can imagine.[40]

Social networks of highly committed professionals concerned about violence related issues were already well established in all four cities when I conducted my fieldwork in 2005 and 2006. I frequently listened to some of them talking about *la cultura de la denuncia* (the culture of denunciation), which became evident as part of the campaign that was running during that time: *El que golpea a una, nos goplea a todas*—He who hits one (woman), hits all of us (women). Sponsored by the Instituto Nacional de las Mujeres, the TV commercial aired women celebrities showing faces with blood and bruises, inviting potential victims to report similar incidents. Professionals who used the concept of la cultura de la denuncia described the ways in which TV, radio, and public service announcements have encouraged citizens (especially women) to report physical and sexual abuse. They said this was part of a national and very public campaign against domestic and sexual violence, which has become visible in Mexico in recent years.[41] And two public institutions, the INEGI and the INMUJERES, in 2003 conducted and published the first national survey on family relationships, known as the ENDIREH, a landmark and a major reference according to the professionals I interviewed.[42] In 2005, the Supreme Court ruled that marital rape is a crime.

In the midst of these progressive changes, not far from Mexico City in May 2006, San Salvador Atenco witnessed events of intense police brutality and torture, including sexual violence against women. And sexual violence against indigenous girls and women (including but not limited to military related conflict and violence, and sexual trafficking) is not news, exposing the contradictions, paradoxes, and the long way still to go in correcting these injustices.[43]

Mexico is not only a cultural mosaic, but also a changing and unpredictable patriarchal collage. This fluid mosaic also validates the paradigm of "regional patriarchies" I proposed to examine contrasting patterns of hegemony and gender inequality in Mexican society.[44]

- A concept propelled by Mexican anthropologist Marcela Lagarde y de los Ríos, *feminicidio* is now part of everyday language and popular culture, and in 2014, the *Real Academia Española*—the Royal Spanish Academy—accepted the term as part of the new edition of their official dictionary.[45]
- A municipality that is part of Monterrey's metropolitan area, Apodaca has witnessed the disappearance of more than one hundred young poor women as cartels have become involved in a wide variety of criminal activi-

ties. This is only part of the pool of women who are vulnerable to sexual exploitation and human trafficking within and beyond Mexican territory.[46]

- *El bullying* is a concept Mexicans use these days as they talk about peer violence and the tragic news involving school children dying as a consequence of it; this concept has been used as well by President Peña Nieto and representatives of both the lower house and upper house of the Congress as they addressed their concerns about this social problem.

- In Guadalajara I met a teenager through an attorney working on her case. She was well advanced in her pregnancy by her father; she agreed to meet with me for a casual, informal conversation but later declined. Girls like her continue to be considered scandalous in the media, frequently provoking reactions about abortion-related debates and other concerns. Mayra Pérez Cruz, for instance, died in Tabasco at the age of twelve in May 2014; she was fourteen weeks pregnant as a consequence of rape by her stepfather, who was arrested.[47]

- In 2008, the government of Mexico City published the book, *Tu Futuro en Libertad* (Your Future in Freedom), a free publication for youth (available in hard copy and online). This is the most comprehensive and accessible publication of its kind, offering professionally informed, open, and candid discussions about topics related (but not limited) to sexuality and reproductive health; dating, love, and relationships; misogyny, relationship violence, and sexual violence; self-esteem and self-care friendship; sexual and gender diversity; sexual health, sexually transmitted diseases, contraceptive use, and pregnancy; drug use; and human rights and citizenship.

- The same week Mayra died, far away in Monterrey, a progressive activist held a poster that read, *Las ricas abortan. Las pobres mueres. ¡Basta de hipocresía!*—The rich have abortions. The poor die. Enough with hypocrisy! This was part of a heated confrontation between groups of women defending opposing views with regard to abortion, and the background surrounding local congress in Nuevo León approving the first of two rounds to pass a law that recognizes life from the moment of conception.

- Women's rights to a life without violence have become a central concern for INMUJERES (the Instituto Nacional de las Mujeres), an organization created by the federal government in 2001. INMUJERES has inspired the establishment of similar state-sponsored institutions in each state in the country.[48] In all the cities where I conducted my fieldwork, I met highly committed college-educated men working in a wide variety of violence prevention programs as well as support groups designed exclusively for men seeking help.

- I interviewed women and men who either witnessed or experienced personally the exchange of girls for sacks of corn or beans, or other goods, as young women were traded between families to provide sexual comfort and companionship to adult men who live alone in some parts in the country. Women and men directly witnessed this or experienced it within their own families and in different rural and urban communities of origin. One of my informants and her sister were sexually trafficked by her own parents, a pattern reported by researchers studying trafficking of women in Mexico.[49]
- In 2002, Mexico City passed a law to criminalize discrimination, and in 2003 the *Consejo Nacional para Prevenir la Discriminación* (CONAPRED) was created. A public institution, CONAPRED was established after a law to prevent and eliminate all forms of discrimination was approved by Congress.[50] Mexico City and its iconic *zócalo* continue to offer spaces for *manifestaciones y protestas* involving a wide variety of social justice related issues.

The juxtaposition of all of these images reflects the mixed feelings expressed by the professionals I met in these four cities. Many of them were highly involved in progressive activism and talked with optimism about the progress the country has made, yet they frequently talked about their skepticism and the long road ahead regarding laws involving the human rights of children and women in Mexico, and Latin America as well. For instance, the parallels and similarities uniting the lives of women living in two neighboring nations—Mexico and Guatemala—is illustrated by the stories I share in this book and the inspirational research that sociologist Cecilia Menjívar (2011) conducted with ladina women. Menjívar offers a paradigm that goes beyond "culture blaming" or the so-called machismo and exposes the complex forces that weave together inequality, everyday life, economic violence, and women's suffering.[51] My hope is that this book will contribute as well to these important ongoing conversations.

Toward a Feminist Sociology of Incestuous Families in Mexico: The Gender and Sexuality of Incest

The women and men I interviewed taught me important lessons about the social and cultural constructions of gender and sexuality that facilitate a variety of sexualized exchanges, from rape to voluntary sex, and the grey area in between, within families. First, women who reported the daughter-father incestuous arrangement exposed what I identify as *conjugal daughters*. The women who reported a wide variety of sexualized exchanges with their biological fathers may engage in a sexual function in their family and become the sexual partners of these men, at different stages of their lives and within contrasting family, class, and racial arrangements. A daughter becomes a conjugal daughter as a way to be of sexual service to a father because of (1) the ways in which girls are socialized to be of service to the men in their families (e.g., brothers and fathers), a process I identify as *gendered servitude*; and (2) patriarchal prescriptions that identify the marital arrangement as one that is established to satisfy the sexual needs of married men. A daughter becomes a sexual substitute for her mother (frequently absent, disempowered, or helpless as a mother and/or as a wife), who may also become jealous of her daughter. And a conjugal daughter may also openly serve both—a father as well as a complicit mother—for the sake of their marital relationship and thus become what I identify as a *marital servant*.

Conjugal daughters and marital servants exist because of the sexualization of the parental child, social codes of *honor* and *vergüenza* (honor and shame), a father's perception of the family as the symbolic hacienda (i.e., el derecho de pernada), kinship reassignments (i.e., a daughter as a wife, a wife as a daughter), idealized incestuous norms of heterosexual lifestyles of romantic love and sex in popular culture, visible and underground patriarchies, internalized sexism within the family and society at large, patriarchal notions of the paterfamilias and sexual slavery, and cultural rituals of misogyny. The patterns listed were identified mainly for biological fathers, although a stepfather may also engage in these arrangements.[52]

Second, sisters and *primas*—female cousins—of all sexual orientations and contrasting urban contexts may become the objects of sexual curiosity, initiation, experimentation, frustration, and other perverse sexual adventures of their biological brothers and male cousins. Their stories exemplify what I identify as *family sex surrogates*, that is, sisters and primas may temporarily satisfy the sexual needs of their brothers and primos under complex and nuanced forms of sexual violence.

Family sex surrogacy goes hand in hand with gendered servitude. Under specific family contexts and circumstances, gendered servitude makes brothers and primos believe that they are also entitled to sex as a service within the family. The fact that a man may experience a sense of entitlement while sexually objectifying the girls and women within the family (something women and men in their families learn to perceive as "normal") does not require that a man uses force to exercise this kind of privilege. It is no surprise then that many of these women described their brothers, for instance, as nonphysically violent, and at times affectionate, loving, and seductive as part of sexual coercion.

The sexual objectification of girls within the prima-primo relationship exposes the cultural validation of patriarchal entitlement of male relatives to have access to their sexualized bodies within extended families. This is illustrated by Mexican popular sayings such as *A la prima se le arrima* (You can get physically/sexually close to your female cousin) and *Entre primos y primores nacen los amores* (Between cousins and beauty, love is born). Although these relationships may include protagonists who are close in age, it exposes the ways in which sisters and primas are exposed to different expressions and levels of sexual violence within the confines of spaces that are perceived as familiar and safe but dangerous, including but not limited to their homes, their relatives' homes, and social spaces and contexts where family relationships, interactions, and exchanges of kinship take place. This becomes what I identify as *family sexual harassment,* a concept with the potential to make these practices visible. These everyday acts of misogyny within families usually take place in plain sight of adult women in positions of authority who ignore these forms of sexual objectification, who consider it a form of "gender helplessness." These adult women subscribe to two of the cultural translations of "Boys will be boys" in Mexico: "*Los muchachos nomás estaban jugando*—The young men were *just* playing," or "*Así son los muchachos, no les hagas caso*—That is the way young men are, ignore them." This in the end becomes a social corollary facilitating what Gavey (2005) identifies as the "cultural scaffolding of rape."

Gavey explains, "the discourses of sex and gender that produce forms of heterosex that set up the preconditions for rape—women's passive, acquiescing (a)sexuality and men's forthright, urgent pursuit of sexual 'release.'" (3). That is, Gavey problematizes "the whole domain of sexual taken-for-granteds" that become key in the formation of rape cultures. Similarly, I discovered that a cultural scaffolding of rape is created in these families: normative beliefs and practices with regard to boyhood, play, and the sexuality of children (as desexualized and innocent) all intersect to create what is perceived as "normal" and thus as harmless. These gender and sexual taken-for-granteds actually create the conditions for sexual harassment of girls and young women in families. This is only a microcosm of a larger ideological system that has socially organized different levels and degrees of sexual violence against girls and women in a wide variety of relationship contexts and other everyday life circumstances.

Third, one of the most relevant findings of the study involved the uncle-niece incestuous arrangement. Narratives describing an uncle exercising sexual coercion against his niece are the most frequently reported expression of violence in this study (more so than fathers or stepfathers, for example). As a group, women reported from highest to lowest frequency: uncles, fathers, brothers, stepfathers, cousins, and grandfathers.

Why are *los tíos* so frequently reported in this study? I incorporate three key concepts to explain this pattern: *family genealogies of incest*, the *feminization of incest*, and the internalization of sexism within the family. All of them are interrelated and explain why an uncle who sexually molested a niece does not become an isolated case, but rather one among a complex constellation of systematic and systemic multigenerational patterns promoting ideologies and practices of gender inequality that become fertile soil in the reproduction of *family cultures of rape*. Although rape in its most orthodox definition does not always happen in these families (i.e., penile vaginal penetration), family cultures of rape refer to the ideologies and practices that are conducive to rape, that is, family cultures that facilitate a wide variety of escalating expressions and degrees of sexually intrusive behaviors and attitudes that a family member may engage in (individually or collectively) vis-à-vis girls, boys, or men younger in age, and women within immediate and extended families (see also note 7).

The overrepresentation of maternal uncles (versus paternal uncles) in these uncle-niece reports illustrates the *feminization of incest*, which exists precisely because women have been devalued as authority figures and thus an uncle feels not only entitled but also safe to engage in these sexual transgressions. Frequently with similar histories of sexual violence themselves, adult women in these families have been socialized to internalize the same sexist beliefs that have oppressed them as women their entire lives yet use them to further punish and stigmatize a younger generation of girls, making them responsible as well for these unspeakable acts.

Fourth, men's stories challenge stereotypical ideas that associate sexual abuse of children with a culture of poverty: marginality and crowded housing, and the idea that "sexual abuse is only a problem of the poor." As a group, men reported from highest to lowest frequency: uncles, brothers, male cousins or *primos*, stepfathers, and fathers. Cases involving a grandfather were not reported by the men. Also, the maternal versus the paternal side is almost identical for uncles and primos, and only slightly higher toward the maternal side (an important contrast when compared to women).

I introduce the concept of *kinship sex* to examine men's narratives along a continuum between two extremes: consent and coercion, happening across all socioeconomic strata. These stories expose sexualized exchanges between boys during childhood or adolescence, which men may recall as seductive, voluntary, and playful. In contrast, narratives about coercive sex, especially with an older primo or an uncle, expose the dangerous dimension of the continuum. The continuum is neither flat nor unidimensional, but rather it is multilayered, nuanced, and complex. Some men experienced all of these possibilities of sexualized exchanges with one or more relatives.

Homophobic practices within the family and related issues of masculinity in the lives of effeminate and other gender nonconforming boys shape sexual vulnerability in these families, including the gay twist to the expression that objectifies male cousins: *Al primo me le arrimo*. Self-identified gay men more frequently reported homophobia as a precursor of sexual violence in the family than do self-identified lesbian women. I offer some reflections about this pattern, illustrating among other things the need to look at how gender inequality and prescriptions of masculinity, femininity, sexuality, secrets, and silence may shape distinctive patterns of vulnerability to hate crimes within families and society at large.

And fifth, in these incestuous families, all of the preceding gendered and sexualized processes are established and reproduced as part of everyday life. That is, incest is not an isolated event that happens in a social vacuum, incest is socially contextualized. Incest and other family sex acts are not isolated but reported to be a part of everyday life and daily family interactions. For example, incest takes place as protagonists cleverly decipher the geography of homes and arrangements of schedules and spaces to safely assail a child. Children in turn employ strategies of their own to anticipate and outsmart the act. In addition, incest becomes possible because of daily life pressures of hardworking yet absent parents who negotiate child care in ways that expose the child to abuse. I learned that socioeconomic forces may facilitate the conditions of sexual vulnerability in the lives of children, and that sexual violence might be reinvented as part of the U.S.-Mexico migration within transnational families.

All of the above are intricate and powerful social constructions, yet they have the potential to be contested and challenged, as illustrated by the women and men who taught me why and how human resilience and social change are still possible, beyond the most unbearable pain.

Organization of the Book

Because this book offers an emerging basis for future theorizing and research on sexual violence in Mexican families, I focus here on the ethnographic accounts provided through in-depth interviews. This book is significantly distinct from existing studies and first-person accounts on incest in that I do not focus on the psychology of trauma. Instead, the book invites readers to shift the focus and look through a critical feminist sociological lens at the family life processes and social, cultural, and economic forces that expose girls, boys, and women to sexualized violence in the first place.

The narratives in this book are purposely graphic. The intent is not to shock, but to fully engage the reader with the everyday contexts and their life-changing consequences for these women and men. My hope is that by offering an honest portrayal of these women's and men's testimonies, I will both honor the heartfelt openness of the experiences the interviewees shared with me and also invite future readers to conduct highly needed research on incest *within cultural contexts* in the social sciences, gender, and sexuality studies, Mexican family studies, and sexual violence. See appendix B for additional reflections about these methodological issues.

Although I describe these women's and men's experiences of violence in graphic detail—experiences that affected their emotional lives and the quality of their romantic and sexual relationships, usually leaving a wide variety of imprints on the heart—the book does not focus on examinations of the emotional trauma per se. However, I selectively and briefly incorporate a description of the emotional consequences of sexualized violence on both women and men (i.e., low self-esteem, depression, suicide attempts, relationship conflict, among others) in the four storytelling chapters. Women's and men's reports of the effect of sexual violence on their emotional, sexual, relationship, and family well-being are important issues that deserve subsequent in-depth examination, which is beyond the scope of this book.

Chapters 2 through 5 are storytelling. In these chapters I offer richly descriptive and graphic narratives of women and men within specific family relationships, arrangements, and experiences, and because I want the experiences of the interviewees to speak for themselves as much as possible, I focus on the narratives as the primary orientation and then include an analytical section at the end of each chapter. Each analytical section is designed to examine these stories of sexual violence within the family from a feminist informed sociological perspective. The analytical section includes the theoretical contributions made throughout this book, including but not limited to the incorporation and discussion of concepts such as conjugal daughter, marital servant, gendered servitude, family sex surrogate, family sexual harassment, family genealogies of incest, feminization of incest, kinship sex, among other concepts.

Chapter 2 explores the wide variety and nuanced sexual functions that girls and women—daughters in particular—play within patriarchal Mexican families, especially within the father-daughter arrangement, and within and across contrasting and complex social, cultural, and economic contexts. Chapter 3 examines the stories that expose the sophisticated ways in which—and the complex social, cultural, and economic reasons *why*—sisters and primas became sexually vulnerable to their brothers and primos, respectively. Chapter 4 examines the stories of women who are exposed to sexual violence at the hands of their uncles—*los tíos*. Chapters 2, 3, and 4 depict stories of daughters, sisters, primas, and nieces who are not passive victims, but who are women who fight back using the contextual means available and as they decipher ways to cope. These stories also expose the complex ways in which the men who exercised violence against these girls and women were at times reproducing the very same violence they were subjected to as little boys in their own families.

Chapter 5 includes the stories of men of different economic and family arrangements who were sexually abused as boys by a father, brother, older cousin, or an uncle, more so than by an older woman in the family. These stories expose the personal and family journeys the boys experience as they break their silence in their attempts to decipher their emotional turmoil. These stories also reveal the complex dynamics of an ethic of respect for the family, concern about the well-being of their mothers and the rest of the family, and a wide variety of family and economic pressures, as well as fears of homosexuality and homophobia and hate crimes in the family.

Chapter 6 revisits and summarizes the contributions based on the stories of incest discussed in the book, as well as the feminist informed examinations, and identifies the theoretical relevance, public sociology implications, and suggestions for future research.

Finally, as I revisit the findings and contributions of this study in the last chapter, I stress the importance of challenging archetypal, stereotypical, and pathological images of Mexican children, women, men and their families, while simultaneously offering a sociological understanding of a complex phenomenon. I learned, for instance: a mother or a trusted adult who believes and takes action when a child reveals experiences of abuse becomes a source of love and trust, which in turns helps the child to be stronger emotionally and resilient to whatever emotional impact he or she experienced. But, like life itself, resilience goes beyond childhood. From Itzel, Nydia, and other informants (women and men) I learned that children who share their painful experiences with other *fuentes de amor*—sources of love—may actually heal to an extent when they *trust in* and they are *believed by* family authority figures, teachers, partners, friends, siblings, including sisters, aunts, cousins, or others who were abused by the same relatives. This trust and love in connection to family justice may actually become a source of protection from potential trauma. As illustrated in some of the stories, this resonated with women who explained to me that an experience of sexual molestation or even the most horrifying rape experience had not been as painful as a family's reaction, which might have included additional harsh emotional and physical punishment that consequently promotes self-blame and deeply affects their emotional and personal well-being.

2

Conjugal Daughters and Marital Servants

The Sexual Functions of Daughters in Incestuous Families

—Delgadina, daughter of mine, I want you to be my mistress.
—Don't let it happen, my mother, nor you, all-powerful Virgin, for it is a sin against God and the perdition of my soul.
—"Come together, my eleven servants, and put Delgadina in prison; see that she is well locked up," said the king in great anger. "Fasten the padlocks securely so that no shrill voice is heard; and if she wishes to eat, do not give her any fine foods. If she wishes to drink, you will give her salty water, because I want to force her to become my sweetheart."

—An excerpt from "La Delgadina," a ballad that has existed in different versions and throughout many Spanish-speaking countries. The origins are frequently identified from colonial times in eighteenth-century Mexico.[1]

"So I just want to know, if you are no longer married and you are not having sex with anyone, and you had surgery and cannot be pregnant, why don't you and I have sexual relations?" Steaming with rage, Úrsula paraphrased her father's words as she recalled this Christmas Eve kitchen conversation. Úrsula was thirty-one years old and she had recently told her parents about her separation from her husband. Shocked and dumbfounded, she confronted her father about his offensive proposal, reproached him about his abuse from the past, and suggested that he look for a lover. Úrsula was in her mid-thirties when I interviewed her in Guadalajara, a few months after she had reconciled with her husband. He was the same man she ran away with at the age of eighteen as she tried to cope with the coercive sexualized encounters she had experienced with her father for about ten years.

"I was already twenty-three when I learned that my father did not see me like his daughter but like his lover, I told myself, this cannot be real, this cannot be happening to me!" Perla, born and raised in Mexico City in her mid-thirties and married with two children, experienced sexual encounters with her father from age twelve to twenty-three. While attending college at the UNAM, she unexpectedly learned through a consultation with a vocational counselor that these sexual exchanges of many years were not "normal" and became suicidal as a result.

The stories of Úrsula and Perla illustrate the ways in which women raised in incestuous families may become conjugal daughters, that is, the sexual partners of their fathers. In this chapter I examine the ways in which patriarchal moralities that assign specific sexual obligations to a married woman permeate these families and make a daughter vulnerable to become her mother's sexual substitute, especially in contexts where marital conflict and discord are present. For instance, a daughter who becomes the parental child (that is, the child who takes care of her siblings when a mother is not available) may also become the sexualized daughter who also takes care of her father's unmet sexual needs and urges.[2] A conjugal daughter who becomes "like a mother" to her siblings may also become "like a wife" to her father. In these incestuous arrangements, a daughter is expected to be sexually available to her father as part of a complex expression of sexualized violence, which may go from subtle and nuanced forms of affection to the use of extreme physical force and brutality. This form of sexual violence may happen at different stages of a woman's life within contrasting family, class, and racial arrangements, and as part of complex family dynamics surrounded by silence, secrecy, lies, and everyday life.

As a concept, conjugal daughter goes hand in hand with another dynamic revealed by women's life stories: gendered servitude. Gendered servitude refers to family ethics that promote values of servitude in girls and women (i.e., cleaning, cooking, doing chores for brothers, fathers, and other men in the family, among other housework-related tasks) which may result in blurred lines between nonsexualized and sexualized services and functions of girls and women within families. Gendered servitude has its roots in an ethics of care, which may promote disadvantages for girls and women living in contexts of gender inequality in patriarchal societies, as discussed in mainstream feminism and social science research with Mexican families.[3] These ethics take on a perverse tone in incestuous families, where daughters may become the sexual extensions of their mothers and thus be exposed to arrangements of sexual servitude. In addition to sexualized parental children and gendered servitude, I identify additional dynamics that contribute to a cultural construction of conjugal daughters and include: The family as a hacienda and el derecho de pernada; patriarchal kinship reassignments (i.e., daughters as wives, wives as daughters); normative models of heterosexual love and sex; and performative and underground patriarchies.

This chapter also discusses the rarely examined lives of daughters who become what I identify as "marital servants." Marital servant refers to a daughter who plays a sexual function or sexual service to both of her parents—her father and her mother. As a form of incest, a marital servant may serve specific sexual functions for her parents as a couple. In these dynamics, a father may seduce his daughter into coercive sex acts with the participation of a disempowered yet complicit wife/mother who experiences cultural and or economic pressure to see that her husband's sexual needs are satisfied. Interestingly, what all of them had in common was the presence of a religious, charismatic father who was involved in organized religion or some other kind of ritualistic practices— all of which played a role in the acts of sexual violence. In addition to some of the dynamics that explain the conjugal daughter arrangement, marital servants exist because of additional processes such as internalized sexism, paterfamilias and the sexual servitude of daughters, and sexualized rituals of patriarchy.

These are the stories of the women involved in these incestuous arrangements with their fathers, and I present them in two sections: conjugal daughters, and marital servants. The last section offers a conceptual framework to analyze their stories.

Conjugal Daughters

Ágata

"In the beginning my father fondled me, he only fondled me, later he started to penetrate me . . . but he always made sure my mother was sleeping, or made sure it was dark." Ágata described the experiences that began when she was eight or nine and her father was in his late thirties. This frequent routine stopped when she was fifteen or sixteen when a cousin invited her to move to Monterrey to explore job opportunities. With a deep sense of relief and gratitude, Ágata lived with her relatives in the big city while trying to leave behind the memories of the small ranch where she grew up and the sexual violence that took place through all of those years. Unfortunately, her sense of safety did not last more than a year. Her father made his way to Monterrey and forced her to go back to the ranch.

"He is a responsible man, I remember him that way, that is why I cannot understand why [he did it]," Ágata stated as she recalled a life of poverty that forced her hardworking father to explore the best ways to be a good provider while frequently migrating with his wife and children from ranch to ranch. Living in a rural landscape of harsh struggle, Ágata walked 6 kilometers each way to the closest elementary school, but dropped out after fourth grade and became a parental child. She said, "My mom would have her baby and I had to take care of the other one, I had to change his clothes, bathe him, take him to the restroom, cook for them, because . . . because we were many and I was the oldest one, and my mom, if she got sick, I assumed the responsibilities." Busy as she was working through her own struggles, including a deteriorating marital life involving physical and emotional violence, Ágata's mother never suspected that her daughter's responsibilities included satisfying her father's sex urges.

"Do not tell your mother, if you do, I kill her." Ágata recalled the terrifying whispered words that announced her father's frequent routine of sexual assaults. She decided to keep silent out of concern and love for her mother and siblings. "At times, he would threaten me with the gun," she explained, saying that she also felt confused by his contrasting behavior in other family and social circumstances. She said, "My father is a good person, he has lots of friends, very good friends, but he has like a double personality, like 'I am being correct before society,' before his friends." Behind doors, he was severe as he punished and disciplined his seven children. While struggling to understand their father's contradictory behavior, Ágata and her siblings developed a distant and fearful relationship with him. As they tried to avoid pain and search for a better life for themselves, they left the ranch, one by one and at different ages, to explore a larger city in Northern Mexico or somewhere in the United

States. Ágata had tried to do the same, but she found herself back in the ranch at the age of seventeen, where her controlling father did not allow her to go out with friends or to date.

"When my aunt, my father's sister told me, 'why don't you come to Monterrey?' she did not tell me twice!" exclaimed Ágata as she recalled a scene that became known within her immediate and extended family. In spite of her fears and her father's threats, she was able to hide and had a romantic relationship with a kind, young man from the ranch. However, when the respectful young boyfriend talked to her parents about formal plans to marry her some day, her father became enraged and blatantly said 'No!' Ágata broke up with her boyfriend and left immediately for the big city. She distanced herself from her family. As she became older, she only went back to visit her mother sporadically.

At the age of twenty, Ágata dated and married a hardworking man she had met in Monterrey; he held a stable and promising job. Although her sex life was painful and confusing earlier in the relationship (especially when flashbacks of the abuse came to mind while having sex), she decided not to tell her caring and patient husband about what her father had done to her. "Meeting him was a *golpe de suerte*—a stroke of luck," she said, as she explained that their marital relationship of almost twenty-five years has provided a comfortable lifestyle for her and their mostly adult children, one of whom attended college. As an adult, Ágata now feels safe while sharing a modest lifestyle that feels financially stable and respectful—a peaceful marital life, overall. Recently, however, a ghost of the past began to haunt her. As she worried more and more about her mother's deteriorating health, Ágata visited the ranch more frequently, at times by herself, at times with her children. When her daughter told her, "my grandpa has been touching me," Ágata cried helplessly and asked her daughter not to tell her father. She also promised her that she would never take her back for a visit to the ranch. But as she visited the ranch again to check on her mother, she learned that one of her two younger sisters and her daughter (Ágata's niece) had also been exposed to sexual violence at the hands of her father. Ágata no longer felt helpless and confronted her father. Her mother felt confused and depressed as these secrets came to light. Ágata's mother now lives with one of her adult children, while her father, who is sick, lives alone in the ranch located near a small town in Nuevo León. Ágata, who is in her mid-forties, is now trying to determine the best way to have an honest conversation with her husband without compromising their marital stability.

I interviewed Ágata in Monterrey a few months after her mother had learned about these family secrets. She had sought professional support at a family services organization and a therapist there introduced me to her.

Elisa

"He loved it when I went to bed with him, he loved to hold me in his arms, but I do not understand why he would put his tongue in my ear . . . he would put his hand in my private parts and push me. It hurt but I did not know. I thought that it was expression of love as a papá, but it bothered me." This is how Elisa described the "naps" she had with her father during her elementary school years. Elisa would arrive home from school at the same time as her exhausted father, a hardworking cab driver who was returning home after a night shift in Ciudad Juárez. Elisa and her parents would then enjoy lunch together, a daily ritual that included her father's frightening stories about the dangers of his job and how blessed he felt to be back home after a long night in the city streets. After these lunch horror stories, Elisa's father would then take her by the hand for a "nap." As she became more and more aware of the tension and distance between her parents, Elisa realized that she had become the marital substitute for her mother and that these "naps" provided a source of emotional and sexual comfort for her father.

When I asked Elisa if her mother or anyone in her family knew about what had happened to her with her father, she said that she did not tell anyone in part because "she justified her father's behavior." Elisa did not resist the naps with her father because she was moved by his dangerous job and the endless stories of horror she heard, including the tragedy of their own neighbor—also a taxi driver—who had been kidnapped and killed, and another cab driver her father knew who had also been a victim of cruel violence. Elisa said she did not "know how to defend herself from him" and although she felt ashamed, she was concerned about her father and so she kept the experience to herself. Her reasons for silence appeared further warranted when she learned that a neighbor had raped one of his sisters. The girl told her mother about it but she did not believe her. Elisa's relationship with her own mother is emotionally distant to this day.

Elisa's father died when she was twelve years old. Although she does not have clear memories about her parents' relationship, she explained that when he was not working as a cab driver, he often fought with her mother. Elisa is the fifth of six children and the youngest daughter. Her siblings are now in their mid-twenties and thirties. Now in her late twenties, she has never married, but when I met her she was in a relationship and raising her two sons while living on her earnings from a modest but stable administrative job in Ciudad Juárez.

Miriam

"He sobbed and sobbed," college-educated Miriam recalled while describing her father's reaction to a long-distance call she made to talk with her parents during her honeymoon trip. She was surprised because she had never seen him cry before. "I think he felt like someone had snatched something he had available to him . . . something that he wanted only for him," she said as she shared an excruciating experience of sexual violence that started when she was eleven or twelve and only decreased considerably when her boyfriend gave her an engagement ring at the age of twenty-four. For about thirteen years, Miriam said, "he tried everything," he made her masturbate him, kissed her on the mouth, touched her breasts and genitals, sexually assaulted her in her sleep, came into her room and assaulted her while she changed her clothes, and stalked her any time she was not alert, especially when nobody was around, for example, in the car or while taking a shower during expensive family vacation trips out of the country. She described these experiences as very frequent and always "repulsive."

As she became older and stronger, Miriam resisted her father's assaults more frequently, but he then became more selectively violent— either more physically aggressive, or more gentle and strategic. For example, he would tell her that she "was his favorite daughter . . . he said, 'I love you, my daughter, very much, you are my *consentida*, you are very pretty.'" But he also forced her to sit on his legs as a condition of going out with her friends, controlled the way she dressed, and forced her to quit a job where she was happy and instead come to work for fifteen years in his large, profitable business. In a scene that she described as "a horrible and humiliating day," he assaulted her violently when she was twenty-two or twenty-three as she got dressed for her cousin's wedding. Later that day she was forced by her family to dance with him at the reception.

Was Miriam silent about all of this? Not always. Immediately after the first incidents at the age of eleven or twelve, she told her mother about her father "touching her." Her mother believed her and gave him a warning. However, he did not stop and accused Miriam of being a *rajona*—a woman who backs out—and threatened to film her naked the next time. As the experiences of sexual violence continued, she said, "he threatened me not to tell anything because nobody would believe me. He would say, 'Do not even think about telling your mother.' He threatened me. I was always under the threat not to tell because something bad would happen." Miriam also kept silent as an attempt to protect her mother. Her parents had a volatile marital relationship that consisted of endless arguments and fights, and Miriam was afraid he might kill her mother. Miriam's father carries a gun, has a gun collection at home, and it is rumored that he is involved in drug dealing activities.

When I asked Miriam about her relationship with her mother, she said that she loved her and felt deep empathy for her, especially because of the volatile and violent relationship her mother had with her father. However, she was resentful toward her for being afraid of her husband, a fear that, she said, her mother "inculcated" in Miriam and her two younger sisters. For instance, Miriam described a daily mealtime scenario at home: "When he arrived home, all of us flew away, in other words, nobody wanted to be there. We never ate in the dining room, we took our plate to the bedroom."

Miriam married at the age of twenty-five and established a stable, satisfying relationship with a supportive man who knows about her experiences with her father; both are still working out ways for her to explore and eventually heal aspects of their emotional and sexual intimacy that remind her of her father. As a mother, Miriam says she has become increasingly confrontational and has given stern warnings to her father, especially when she sees her two children spending time and playing with him. Just when she thought that she had resolved and put her experiences of sexual violence in the past, the unexpected happened in her family.

A married woman in her late twenties at the time, Miriam's sister and the second of the three daughters, finally broke her own silence to announce that the father had also inflicted sexual violence on her while growing up. Then, the younger sister, a single woman a few years younger, decided to break her silence as well and described her own excruciating experiences with him. Miriam was in deep shock at learning about her sisters' experiences, but also felt validated and finally told her mother and her two sisters about the many years that she too had experienced sexual violence at the hands of the father. When they compared notes they realized that the sexual violence had started around the age of ten and included similar details of strategic, opportunistic sexual exploitation and manipulation by their father.

"They think we are lying," Miriam stated with an indignant tone as she described the reaction of his father's siblings and parents, relatives, and neighbors. People who have now heard the stories about the three daughters being the target of sexual violence by their father are inclined to disbelief. "Nobody knows about the double life that he has," Miriam exclaimed. She described her father as always impeccably dressed, a successful business man who drives a brand new truck, a devout man who spends long hours in a Catholic church and offers generous donations for the organization of spiritual retreats through a close relationship he has with a priest, the financially altruistic son and brother of his own family, and helpful neighbor who loves to be there for people in need of support in their colonia.

Miriam's depressed mother experienced an intense emotional reaction when she heard her three daughters' testimonies. She eventually decided to divorce her husband and was undergoing a strenuous legal process that was still unclear when I interviewed Miriam. I met Miriam when she was in her mid-thirties. A therapist that she, her mother, and sisters had recently sought out in Monterrey introduced me to Miriam.

Noelia

"I see him naked, completely naked on top of me, making movements [like thrusting]." This is how Noelia started to describe the memories of herself as a five- or six-year-old girl and her father, a young man in his thirties. A college-educated married woman when I met her, Noelia approached me in Monterrey and volunteered to share her story, which was a moving recollection of recent nightmares and blurry memories, but also vivid and clear images of sexual violence as a child. Some memories also reflect Noelia as a little girl frequently riding a horse with a father who sat her in front of him and stimulated himself, and touched her in ways that felt uncomfortable. These experiences began in her early years in elementary school and lasted many years, although she does not recall when they ended. Now in her late twenties, she recalls these events as painful. These episodes of being *la hija consentida*, the special daughter her father would defend and protect while punishing her brothers for something they did not do, are still a source of confusion for her.

Noelia described her father as a man who was "difficult to communicate with," but hardworking and the main source of economic support within the immediate and extended family. He raised his family in a modest colonia in the city where he had a small but successful business. He was generous in his support of his wife and children and his own parents, and offered financial support to his more than ten siblings and his in-laws. However, he also used this economic power to control and intimidate those who depended on his financial support. And as a ranch owner, he carried a gun and used it to discipline all of his children and to threaten his wife, with whom he had a highly contentious and emotionally distant marital relationship.

In the midst of family tension and conflict, Noelia became the family mediator, facilitating communication between her father and "anyone who wanted to talk with him," including brothers, relatives, friends, and her mother. And, as the second of six children and the oldest daughter, Noelia also "protected, took care of, bathed, changed the clothes, and fed" her siblings, and cooked, cleaned, and did the ironing as they grew up. Her frequently ill mother did not like doing house chores and struggled to take care of the family. When her father realized that Noelia was a bright student who was excellent with math, she was put in charge of the family money in her early teens. She helped her father with the accounting of his business, and became a generous friend who always had money to treat her school friends. Noelia also used the money to buy many things for herself, which is one of the ways she coped with the abuse.

As the paternal child and her father's "little wife," Noelia enjoyed a lot of power in the family. However, as she became older, her father used preferential treatment less and physical violence and threats more to exercise control over Noelia's comings and goings. He did not allow her to go out with friends or to date. *Eres una puta*, you are a whore, became a common expression her father used to discipline Noelia as he beat her up on the street in a colonia where "neighbors did not do or say anything" about it. She felt increasingly "ugly and unattractive" and morally devalued, and as a way of coping, she ran away from home twice, only to return both times. Feeling deeply confused, she accepted expensive gifts from her father: he gave her a horse on her eleventh birthday, a new motorcycle when she was fifteen years old, and a brand new truck when she was eighteen years old. But the violence also escalated. In her early twenties, she encountered her father fuming in rage and waiting for her outside the house as she made her way home near midnight after enjoying a party. He beat her intensely, left her bruised and bloody, and then kicked her out of the house.

Noelia left the family home, and with the help of a friend who told her about a place where she could make good money, she eventually made her way to a border city in the Northeast of Mexico and got a job as a *taibolera* (from the English "table dancer"), the Mexican version of a stripper. After changing her identity and wearing a wig, Noelia became a sex worker while "feeling terrible" but also reflecting, "I had nothing to lose, nothing, I have been exposed to everybody like that, like a whore . . . and I had been beaten up for no reason." She worked at an upscale club where she was shocked to learn that many of her coworkers were hardworking, college-educated, middle-class single and married women who were supporting families. She worked a 9 PM to 5 AM shift and witnessed a high rotation of women working at the club. Noelia survived on this job for about a year and felt fortunate to make an average of $500 U.S. per night on weekends. She said she overcame "many myths" about sex work as a result of the job.

When I asked Noelia about how her job as a stripper had affected her sex life, she explained, "Freedom, freedom to feel, freedom to expose myself, [before] I was unable to show my body to a partner." Later she elaborated, "It empowered me a lot. I felt . . . the place is as if you are on top and the men are down there, looking at you. So that makes you taller, [it places you] at a higher level." The image she had of herself as an "ugly, unattractive woman" became a thing of the past as she realized that she could sexually attract any man, as she "felt desired" by the lusty glances of men looking at her every night. Not everything was pleasure, however. She felt fearful as she listened to the horror stories of her coworkers who talked about clients who carried guns, men frequently involved in drug dealing activities who abused sex workers and then dropped them naked on the freeway. "That was the most dangerous aspect of the job," she explained. In addition, she had to drink "stupid amounts of alcohol" as part of the job, had to drink even more to be able to have sex with clients, and felt that she was raped by at least one of them, all of this while feeling ashamed as a well-educated woman "who worked there," frequently telling herself in silence, "It's impossible that I am doing this, I cannot be doing this!"[4] Noelia eventually returned to Monterrey permanently, where she dated and married a college-educated, supportive, and caring man. They currently have a happy, satisfying marital relationship. He does not know about what happened to her with her father, or about her life in the border city.

How was Noelia's relationship with her mother? "My mother saw me as a woman but not as a daughter," Noelia remarked, as she explained that her mother constantly blamed her for her marital problems and "was jealous" of her. Her mother also shaved Noelia's head and dressed her up with boys' pants and boots in an apparent attempt to make her less attractive to her father. "I think my mother thought that if I was ugly then, well, I could be a man and that was not as bad for her," Noelia said. As her father became increasingly violent, Noelia confronted her mother and asked her to protect her from her father's physical violence, but her mother reacted in unexpected ways. "She called me a puta," Noelia recalled as she explained that her mother used makeup to cover the bruises on her face so her father would not notice. As she became older, however, Noelia used her position as the one in charge of family finances to figure out ways to turn the tables: "I had a lot of power, and when my mother did not treat me right, I punished her and gave her less money than what she should have for her expenses."

At present, Noelia has an increasingly distant relationship with her parents. She never told her mother about being sexually molested by her father, and she has not confronted him either. Instead, when she left the family she did so thinking that, "this is the best for them as a couple," a realization she started to develop at the age of twelve, when she began running away from home.

Perla

"He would take me to bed, lay me down, lift up my arms like this, would get me undressed, unbutton my blouse, would touch my breast with his mouth or his hands, and would touch my vagina." Perla described the common routine she engaged in with her father from age twelve until age twenty-three. When she was twelve, he was in his mid-thirties. Now in her mid-thirties, the memories of some of these encounters are vivid and at times she experiences them along with sensations of genital pleasure, but some images of the past are unclear and blurry. For instance, she does not know if she had intercourse with her father, and she does not know how often these experiences happened, but she described the events as involuntary, taking place in the dark, frequently after going to sleep, and with a strong smell of alcohol on her father's breath.[5] In the midst of these uncertainties, she knows for sure that these coercive experiences were never physically violent, nor did her father tell her to be silent about it. So as she grew up, Perla assumed that sex between a father and a daughter was "normal."

As she came of age, Perla also learned from her mother and the Catholic Church about the importance of being a virgin at marriage. Accordingly, she refrained from sex with a potential husband and proudly wore white on her wedding day. She had intercourse for the first time at the age of twenty-seven with the man she married, her current husband and the only sexual partner she has had since. Although she experienced anxiety because she did not bleed the first time they had intercourse, she felt that she had offered her virginity "as a gift" to her husband on their wedding day.[6]

How does Perla reconcile these values with her involuntary sexual engagements with her father? When Perla talked about a boyfriend who attempted to sexually seduce her when she was twenty-one, she explained her rationale for resisting in terms of family: "It is because he was not part of the family. In other words, that is what I had realized, that in the end, the family could do with you whatever they wanted, but not people from outside—never. That is why I am telling you about my boyfriend, in other words, your father can do it to you but not your boyfriend." The message that Perla learned from her family became clear: "Virginity is lost with a stranger."

As Perla explained how the involuntary experiences with her father did not have an effect on her virginal status, she described in detail how vigilantly she safeguarded her body and limited her romantic exchanges with boyfriends to "hugging and kissing" until the day she married. She elaborated, "In fact, I had a boyfriend close to finishing college, who used to tell me, 'Let's make love.' And I used to tell him, 'No, wait, relax. I will wait until I walk down the aisle, after that, you can do with me whatever you want.' "

From her family, Perla also learned to be silent with regard to matters of sexuality, so she never discussed experiences of coercive sex by her father with her mother or anyone else. At age twenty-three, however, a college counselor she identified as a "psychologist" not only told her that these encounters were not "normal," he also asserted that perhaps "she was in love with her father." Feeling deeply confused and hurt, Perla took rat poison after her second session with the therapist. Fortunately, the poison did not have a major effect on her health, but she didn't return to the therapist and never again sought professional counseling. Thirteen years later, she joined a support group at the organization where we met in 2006. When I interviewed Perla, she had attended only a few sessions and had not yet shared her experience with the group. She says she is hopeful now and trusts that she may heal one day.

After the conversation with the college counselor, how did Perla's relationship with her father change? She avoided him and protected herself while the sexual violence of the past took new forms. From the day she married to 2005, he stalked her and sexually harassed her on the phone, gave her flowers and presents, complained about her mother, talked to her about her "sexual obligations" as a wife while inquiring about her sexual encounters with her husband, and told her in more than one way that "women are worthless." He also called Perla's husband to urge him to hit her if she did not comply with her "obligations as a wife." Her husband allied with her, as she had told him "something" about the sexual abuse. Perla felt frustrated and suicidal for the second time in her life, but the temptation did not last long and she decided to finally speak up. While her mother was on her deathbed battling cervical cancer and with her two sisters as witnesses, Perla broke her silence about the experiences of abuse she had endured for so many years. This conversation took place a few months before our interview. Her father did not deny it, her sisters remained silent, and she recalled her mother as saying, "I wished you had told me when I was healthy, now that I am sick, what for? There is nothing I can do."

Additional family secrets were revealed soon after. Perla learned from her oldest sister the reason why she had, for no apparent reason, taken her three-year-old daughter and left the family home years earlier. She recalled her sister's words: "You know what? I got away from home because papá gave me an engagement ring and gave me flowers and told me to stay, he told me that I was going to take the place of my mother." For many years, Perla's mother had been a full-time housewife, but she was chronically ill and, although the marriage was emotionally abusive, she was afraid of leaving her husband, who provided the family with middle-class comfort through an administrative job. Perla associated their deteriorated marital relationship with the fact that they slept in separate beds and her mother's fragile health, a consequence of apparent medical malpractice and health complications after her last pregnancy. In the meantime, Perla and her sister silently became conjugal daughters. Perla suspects that her niece—her sister's little daughter—is her father's child but nobody in the family talks about it. Perla's oldest sister is the only child from her mother's previous relationship. Perla is her mother's second child; she has four younger siblings.

Úrsula

"I love your breasts, I love them, I find you very attractive." Úrsula paraphrased with disgust the words of her father as he noticed that her body was maturing when she turned thirteen years old. At the time, he was in his mid-thirties and started forcing her to kiss him on the mouth "as if he was my boyfriend" and touching her breasts as a condition for allowing her to go out with her friends. Since then and continuing for about five years, he used coercive sex as a form of parental authority and control, while Úrsula associated these hurtful experiences with the fact that she was becoming more voluptuous and attractive than her mother. "My breasts became big, something my mom does not have, that is what got his attention," she explained.

Now in her mid-thirties, Úrsula said she does not believe that "her father was ever in love with her"; however, she explained that he was strongly sexually attracted to her in her adolescence. She realized that as she became a *señorita*, a young woman, the sexual molestation of the past was simply taking a different form. Úrsula was about eight years old when she experienced the very first incident that made her feel uncomfortable and confused. "Come, lay down here with me," her father would gently invite Úrsula to sit between him and her mother on the bed, cover all of them with a blanket, and watch TV. From age eight until age thirteen, a scene of apparent fun and entertainment became a family ritual that offered her father the opportunity to guide Úrsula's hand to masturbate him under the covers and in front of a wife who appeared unaware of what was happening. This activity went on more than twice a week for about five years.

In her adolescence she tried to resist and to stop the abuse by avoiding him and not talking with him. This was not always effective, however. Her father would push Úrsula into the bathroom to argue with her while fondling her. Initially she resisted and hoped that the privacy of the bathroom could offer a space to confront him and stop the abuse. Instead, however, over the next five years the bathroom became another space of sexual violence and threats where he told her repeatedly, "Do not tell anyone because nobody is going to believe you. They are going to believe more in me. In you, nobody is going to believe." Úrsula's father was never disrespectful or inappropriate in other family situations, but he did attempt to cultivate the reputation among other family members that she was a liar. Úrsula had an emotionally distant relationship with her mother, who would plead with her to work harder to promote family harmony: "Talk to your father! How is it possible that both of you get angry at each other?"

"When I realized that certain things should not be, in other words, when I became aware and knew that this kind of thing should not happen at home . . . that is what I felt. [I told myself] hey, wait a minute!" Úrsula exclaimed as she explained the state of keen awareness she experienced as an adolescent, as she figured out how to run away from home to escape the abuse that had gone on for about ten years. At the age of eighteen, she decided to tell her twenty-two-year-old boyfriend about what had happened to her with her father. He was supportive and together they planned to run away together. After she left the family home, Úrsula avoided all contact with her father and became even more distant with her mother. Úrsula and her friend and partner of almost twenty years are still together, raising their three children, even while experiencing some marital tension and a separation of a few years.

Úrsula kept silent in part because she grew up feeling confused about her father's behavior and had no one to talk to whom she could trust. Also, she felt obligated to protect her fragile mother, who suffered from seizures and had had a heart attack. Úrsula decided to never tell her about the abuse of many years and instead just kept her distance from her father, especially after she had two daughters of her own. She did not want them to be exposed to him—a red flag of danger in her mind. In the meantime, the price she paid for this silence was the constant accusations by her mother, who complained about not being able to see her grandchildren and blamed Úrsula for this.

For more than ten years, Úrsula felt safe from her father, but when she was thirty-one and visited her mother at Christmas, he suggested that she become his sexual partner. No longer helpless, Úrsula confronted him aggressively and told him to look for a lover. He replied, "No, I want to do it with you. I already convinced your mother that because of my diabetes I cannot have sex with her . . . your mother only wants to have sex in the same position, the one she learned from your grandmother." To this day, Úrsula's parents have shared the same bedroom in the large, nice house he had supported through his successful small business in Guadalajara. She described her parents' relationship as harmonious, free from any form of conflict or violence. She agreed with her father's sexual image of her mother. She described her mother as an "old-fashioned woman" who practiced "monotonous sex." She also identified her mother as a woman "without character," and a *borrega*, a sheep who always followed her husband's orders and was never "disrespected" by him in any way. Yet, she explained, her mother dressed up well, wore makeup, and had fun at fiestas and celebrations. When I asked her if she thought that the different forms of coercive sex she experienced with her father had helped in a way to maintain her parents' marital harmony, she said, "That was very likely the case."

As we wrapped up our interview, I asked Úrsula to think about why all of this had happened to her. She stated, "because I was the only daughter." Úrsula said that her parents "cared more" about their sons. She is the second in a family of four children; her three siblings are now adult men. She said she hoped to talk soon with her brothers because she is concerned about her nieces as she thinks of their visits to her parents' home.

Understanding Father-Daughter Incest

As illustrated, Ágata, Elisa, Miriam, Noelia, Perla, and Úrsula played a key sexual function as sexual and emotional substitutes for their biological mothers. Although each of these life stories is unique, they each point to common patterns and similar family dynamics. Some of these include the following.

Serial incest. A father may have one or more conjugal daughters. Daughters may alternatively become a father's conjugal daughter, especially as a girl experiences developmental changes and becomes older and sexualized, or as she escapes and migrates and other sisters or younger girls become new substitutes for the daughter who is no longer present and sexually available to her father. Judith Herman found similar patterns of serial father-daugther incest.[7] Serial incest also occurs in the brother-sister, primo-prima, and the uncle-niece incestuous relationships, as discussed later in this book.

Marital relationship. The father-mother relationship may vary with regard to the quality of the marital relationship. Although the marital relationships in theses cases usually involve couples that do not have a sexually satisfactory marital life, they vary in terms of emotional and domestic stability and conflict and also include couples with low or moderate levels of conflict, as well as couples with high conflict where the wife is exposed to emotional violence and/or physical violence involving a husband using a gun.[8]

Daughter-mother relationship. The daughter-mother relationship may have multiple emotional arrangements. Some daughters may identify high conflict and distrust, negligence and/or jealousy and rivalry, emotional distance and mixed feelings toward a helpless mother trapped in an abusive relationship, while other daughters may feel deep love and compassion for a mother who they feel is not to be blamed. Accordingly, the maternal figure is frequently emotionally disempowered and distant. Daughters often identified their mothers as physically fragile and with a history of health-related conditions and risks, including sexually symbolic illnesses such as cervical cancer.

Social images of the father. Fathers may hold positive images within their families and communities. Men may enjoy the social privileges of appearing as a morally idealized figure who is charismatic, responsible, and financially generous within their immediate and extended families and communities. In middle- and upper-middle-class families, fathers possessing financial power may use it as an instrument of sexual coercion and control over their daughters. These sophisticated and complex expressions of manhood (i.e., a father who is a good provider, nonviolent in other family contexts, and the generous son, husband, and neighbor) may exacerbate both confusion and silence in these women while their fathers strategically use the social image, ultimately protecting themselves while persisting in acts of sexualized violence.

Duration of incest. A father may have access to the sexualized body of his daughter for varying periods of time. At the extreme, a daughter is exposed to the sexual coercion for long periods of time, which is systematically sustained in some cases for more than ten years, taking insidious expressions especially after a daughter gets married. The acts of sexual coercion by a father may involve a wide array of behaviors, including the absence of physical force as well as the use of extreme forms of emotional and physical power and control—all happening while married to a wife, an adult woman that daughters perceive as emotionally absent, naïve, and clueless.

Birth order. Birth order placement in the family does not protect a daughter from the risk of becoming a conjugal daughter. Conjugal daughters may include the oldest daughter, the youngest daughter, the only daughter, or all daughters regardless of their birth order. And being the conjugal daughter does not protect her from being the target of sexual violence by other men in their families. As I discuss in detail in other chapters, some of these conjugal daughters were also the target of sexual violence exercised by (but not limited to) grandfathers, uncles, and cousins.

Silence. Women become silent about the sexual violence because of a complex web of interrelated factors, frequently related to fear. Although a young woman may be brave enough to share with a mother, ultimately she may remain silent because of threats and other forms of control such as emotional and physical force that become part of the sexualized violence. Silence may also be related to (1) feeling love and concern about a mother's reaction especially if she is sick or fragile, (2) experiencing fear of not being believed by a nontrusting maternal figure while also feeling helpless and ashamed, (3) having concern for the father and justifying his behavior, and (4) developing and believing a perception of sex between a father and daughter as "normal," especially if a father did not use threats to keep a daughter silent.

Beyond trauma. Women do not automatically become passive victims who accept sexually coercive experiences. Although a daughter may remain silent because of confusion, she is often still exploring ways to cope with and/or justify a father's behavior. In each case, the coping mechanisms are sophisticated and complex. Responses include severing the family relationship, running away from home, and migrating to another city within the country. A courageous daughter may eventually confront a father while keeping the secret in part out of love for a mother, while another may confront a father after a sister or female relative decides to break her own silence, or in front of a dying mother as the last opportunity to seek family justice only to learn later that an older sister had lived a similar experience in silence.

The personal experiences of Ágata, Elisa, Miriam, Noelia, Perla, and Úrsula are not isolated cases. Stories illustrating the conjugal daughter incestuous arrangement in families and communities of origin came up in many of my interviews with both the women and the men who shared their life stories as well as with the professionals. "Incest is very common in the ranch where my mother was born," Rosana said, for instance, as she explained that when her mother's sister died, her husband soon "took" his daughter to replace his wife. Besides her own family story, Rosana heard many other stories while growing up about her mother's Central Mexico ranch where "a father takes a daughter as his woman when the mother dies." A professional in Ciudad Juárez recalled two cases of women who migrated from rural areas in Central Mexico to the border city and who grew up believing that sex between fathers and daughters "was 'normal' and happened all over the world." Another professional in Monterrey recalled two shocking cases. The first was the story of a woman who pressed charges against her husband for systematically raping one of their daughters. While in prison, he frequently asked his family and wife to bring the girl he raped "to be with him" during his conjugal visits. The second case involved a mother raising four daughters: one daughter was in charge of grocery shopping, the second was in charge of cooking and organizing the kitchen, the third was responsible for cleaning the house, and the last one's job was to have sexual relations with her father. And last is the case of a middle-class woman who, out of confusion, sought the advice of another Monterrey professional: the very same day her mother died, her father told her that she was going to "replace" her. Professionals working in sexual violence prevention programs in Ciudad Juárez, Monterrey, Guadalajara, and Mexico City frequently recalled other shocking cases of daughters "substituting" for their mothers in ways that reflect dynamics very similar to the cases described in this chapter—all under a variety of complex social contexts and circumstances and across all socioeconomic strata.

Becoming a Conjugal Daughter

What are the social forces responsible for the conjugal daughter incestuous pattern? The following feminist-informed reflections offer potential answers.

The Sexualization of the Parental Child

As an expression of incest in Mexican society, conjugal daughters are the sexualized form of the "parental child." Unlike the parental child (who traditionally takes care of younger siblings when a mother is not available), the conjugal daughter takes care of the unmet sexual needs of her father when her mother is not sexually available to him. Therefore, this dynamic goes hand in hand with the patriarchal constructions of marriage discussed extensively in feminist literature and research with Mexican families. That is, men who are socially trained to believe that having sexual access to their wives is "normal" may automatically expect sex as an obligation that is part of the marital contract. However, when this is not possible, a man may feel entitled to have access to the sexualized body of one (or more than one) of his daughters. Thus, conjugal daughters exist, in part, as a consequence of a husband's patriarchal sense of sexual entitlement within marital relationships. Conjugal daughters who are the parental children not only become the second mother to their siblings (or the "little mother"), they also become the second wife to their fathers ("the little wife").[9] The concept of the little mother goes hand in hand with "role reversal," which I discuss later in the kinship reassignments section. Although not all conjugal daughters are parental children (and not all parental daughters become conjugal daughters), parental children like Ágata and Noelia become the conjugal daughters who play both maternal and conjugal functions.

Girls who are sexualized by their fathers are exposed to some form of "traumatic sexualization," which is not necessarily the result for all cases but may affect the healthy development of a woman's sex life.[10] For instance, interviewees talked about the negative consequences of these experiences on their attitudes and beliefs about sexuality, in particular, and their sexual health and well-being, in general. These are relevant issues that need further examination, which is beyond the scope of this book.

Gendered Servitude

Family ethics that promote values of being of service in girls and women so they can "serve" men in their families (brothers, fathers, uncles, grandfathers, cousins, among others) may create blurry lines between responsibilities traditionally assigned to women in their families (i.e., child care of siblings and a wide array of housework related activities) and sexualized functions traditionally assigned to women in patriarchal societies (i.e., serving as an outlet for men's sexual curiosity and urges). Gendered servitude became part of these women's lives as daughters who not only fulfill a sexual or emotional function within the marital relationship of the parents, but who also were socially trained that it is an obligation to serve the family. Family ethics that promote kindness and goodness while being of service to others within families may become genuine expressions of love, caring, and concern—all beneficial to the family members involved. However, beliefs and practices emerging out of legitimately good intentions may take perverse twists and turns in contexts of extreme inequality, power, and control in patriarchal families. For some conjugal daughters who are the parental child in middle- and upper-middle-class families (as in Noelia's case), these dynamics may create unexpected privileges and leverage for her within the family.

A father's sense of entitlement is instrumental in the construction of gendered servitude. Herman (2000) suggested the following: "Implicitly the incestuous father assumes that it is his prerogative to be waited upon at home, and that if his wife fails to provide satisfaction, he is entitled to use his daughter as a substitute. It is this attitude of entitlement—to love, to service, and to sex—that finally characterizes the incestuous father and his apologists" (49).

These ethics of entitlement to service in patriarchal families that place girls and women in opposition to boys and older men (i.e., girls and wives serving men, and brothers and fathers as deserving the services girls and women provide) are reflected in Mexican scholarship studying household work, domesticity and gender inequality, and major surveys.[11] The ethics of obedience and service imposed on girls and women has been documented throughout history as part of family life and formal education, and influenced by Catholic values.[12] These ethics were consolidated through the codes of *honor y vergüenza*—honor and shame—that defined rigid gender roles for women and men within colonial families, which implied that "Men were honorable if they acted with *hombría* (manliness) and exerted authority over their family."[13] But social privileges that favor men over women, as well as ethics of obedience and domesticity imposed on the latter, predate the Spanish invasion, as documented by historians and family studies scholars.[14] Thus, practices and ideologies promoting the idea of women serving men within a structure of gender inequality within the household have their historical roots in both societies—the Iberian peninsula and pre-Columbian Mexico.

The idea of women serving and being of "use" to their husbands is illustrated by the expression that one of the physicians and feminist activist I interviewed referred to: "*Mi esposo me usó*—my husband used me." The senior physician talked about the married women who sought her help in the 1960s and 1970s and used this expression during their consultations. This is an expression women of an older generation in Mexico may still use to refer to sexual intercourse with a husband, an expression I have similarly heard from women in many contexts and in different parts of the country.

The Family as a Hacienda: El Derecho de Pernada

"In Mexico, some fathers manage their families as if they were haciendas," said an attorney with a long history of human rights activism in Guadalajara. He asserted that it is not unusual to find "incestuous *pueblos* and *ranchos*" in Jalisco and that father-daughter incestuous relationships may have their origins in what he identified as *el derecho de pernada*. Other professionals in Ciudad Juárez, Monterrey, and Mexico City identified this dynamic as being responsible for the father-daughter incestuous relationship including situational, one-time, less frequent, and isolated events of sexualized violence exercised by a father against a daughter in rural as well as urban areas of the country. El derecho de pernada (or "pernada") refers to "first night rights" and identifies the landowner who has "relations with a new bride before her husband does."[15] This practice is a "remnant" of the conquest and colonization of Mexico, according to Mexican feminist intellectual Sylvia Marcos (1992). Marcos explains, "The Spaniards regarded, as part of their booty, the 'right' to sexually use all the female Indians in their territory. On the basis of this 'right,' landowners claimed the privilege of raping all virgin women on their plantations."[16] Thus, the family as a hacienda and part of the territory of *el señor*—the noble hacienda owner—is a paradigm that validates the idea of wife and children as a form of property, and, in the case of a daughter, grants a father the right to the first night, or to be the first man to use her sexually.[17]

The family that mimics an hacienda is not only a family dominated by the father but one that has a rigid division of labor: the mother is the caregiver of daughters and sons and the father is completely exempt from this responsibility.[18] Thus, although both parents have power over the children, the father has power over both the mother and the children. As the hacienda owner, he *owns* all of them. The idea of children as objects and possessions of the father was frequently highlighted by the professionals I interviewed, which resonates with Armstrong's reflections about an incestuous father's "perception of his children as possessions, as *objects*. He must see his children as there to meet his needs—rather than the other way around."[19] The attorney from Guadalajara who talked about the family as an hacienda explained,

For him, the father, he evidently believes that his daughter is an investment. So, if he has spent money to educate her, to take care of her, to buy
her clothes, so how is it possible that *un patán*—a jerk—who comes from
outside will come to enjoy his daughter first, before him?! So the father
takes his right as the *paterfamilia* to have that right, to be the first one to
use his daughter for the first time. And it is that way, because for them,
for these men, his daughter is used.

When I asked him to elaborate, he said, "They are their property, yes. The
hacienda owner had the property rights over his *campesinos*—his peasants.
El padre de familia has his property rights over his daughters, his family."

Some mothers may internalize this belief system, as indicated by
Marcos in her clinical work with Mexican mothers whose husbands
had raped a daughter, stating: "*son sus hijas y tiene derecho*—they are
their daughters and he has the right," as if, Marcos states, "we were talking about 'property' rights over the bodies of daughters."[20] Echoing
the same rationale, a Monterrey clinician shared the case of a father in
his early forties who began having sexual relations with his daughters
after his wife became sick, saying that he had "the right to have sex with
them." Other clinicians recalled hearing similar incestuous narratives.

Thus, because families living in rural and semi-industrialized locations are more likely than urban families to have been exposed to some
form of lifestyle as part of the hacienda system and its large landed es-
tates, the "family as an hacienda" model of fatherhood becomes an expression of "rural patriarchy," one of the expressions of patriarchy that
exist in contemporary Mexico.[21]

With regard to incest, what does this expression of patriarchy actually
look like? The Guadalajara attorney explained that he has heard from
at least one father who had been legally accused of sexually abusing a
daughter: "*Si me costó tanto, ¿por qué voy a dejar que otro la use primero?*" meaning, "If I spent so much money on her, how am I going to let
another man be the first one to use her?" From this perspective, does the
"family as an hacienda model" go beyond rural and semi-industrialized
areas? Does a wealthy incestuous father living in a large urban location
(who presumably spent a lot of money raising and educating a daughter)
have a stronger motivation to sexually use a daughter than a working-
class father? Potential answers to this question must be explored in fu-

ture research. Next I examine the revealing etymological roots of the words *familia* and *paterfamilias*.

Patriarchal Kinship Reassignments: Daughters as Wives, Wives as Daughters

"Why has society so stubbornly insisted in treating us, women, as if we were chronic minors?" This is a rhetorical question posed by a psychoanalyst and long-time advocate in violence prevention programs in Monterrey. She and other professionals have noted a recurring pattern among mothers who have sought professional support for dealing with father-daughter incestuous relationships: while a daughter may substitute for a mother in her sexual responsibilities, mothers in turn become infantilized, chronic children. In the conjugal daughter arrangement, both women have been reassigned in their kinship functions: the mother becomes the daughter while the daughter becomes the wife. As women, the conjugal daughter and her mother are both objects, and while the former is sexualized, the latter is desexualized. Thus, far from being a subject and an adult representing authority, the mother becomes an object and one more child in the family. In these kinship reassignments, the mother of a conjugal daughter becomes infantilized in more than one way: she becomes financially and emotionally dependent; fragile and needing protection if she is sick; may silently or overtly ask for love and protection from her children, especially if she feels trapped and helpless in an emotionally abusive marital relationship; and at times may also become jealous as she competes with a conjugal daughter for the attention and love of the father. In sum, a mother who becomes infantilized becomes disempowered and devalued as an authority figure, and thus she is emotionally and morally unavailable for a daughter who is the target of sexual violence. From her disempowered location, a mother may become complicit, especially if she is aware of the violence and does not intervene, a complex dynamic that takes other expressions and forms.[22]

Heterosexual Love as an Incestuous Lifestyle

"Women in this society are encouraged to commit incest as a way of life. As opposed to marrying our fathers, we marry men like our fathers, or in short, men who are older than us, have more money than us, more power than us, are taller than us, are stronger than us . . . our fathers," said feminist psychologist Phyllis Chesler.[23] More than a decade later, sociologist David Finkelhor reflected on the *"social-sexual attraction"* dimension that facilitates child sexual abuse in the family. From this perspective, he explains, "men are taught to be attracted to those smaller in stature, younger, and relatively powerless. To most men who adopt this cultural view, this means developing relationships with women who are shorter, younger, and economically dependent, but it also can lead to an attraction to their own daughters, who also meet those three criteria."[24]

In short, Chesler and Finkelhor expose the ways in which ideals of heterosexual love and romance that promote the idea of women "marrying up" (i.e., marrying a man of a higher social and economic status, also known as "hypergamy") may become more than a symbol mirroring incest between a daughter and her father. At its "best," marrying up has normalized a romantic and sexual lifestyle that is *only* symbolically incestuous; at its worst, marrying up has promoted ideologies and practices that actually make a girl vulnerable to be sexualized by her father.

These reflections echo the insightful analysis of a senior psychoanalyst with many years of clinical experience with incestuous cases in the Monterrey area, some of which involve upper- and upper-middle-class families. She expanded on how "marrying up" and incest may go hand in hand in Mexican society.

We have a social structure that sponsors the creation of men who have a particular style, you know, a personality that has a peculiar style: narcissistic, the man who is admired and admirable, and that looks for relationships where this admiration is fulfilled. And what becomes a very good complement for these men are infantile women. I am certain about this, at least in societies like ours, which is still conservative with regard to the education we give to girls and the ways we raise them. This society is oriented to producing women with those infantile personalities.

The Monterrey psychoanalyst further elaborated on how class and privilege shaped this view. She explained that women "become admired" through their husbands within these upper-middle-class and upper-class extended families and their social networks. "It seems as if the couple bonded originally on his need to be admired and her need to be admired through him. By herself she [feels like she] is worth nothing, but she acquires a lot of value when she is in his company. And this works as long as they have this game of admiration, and she admires him," she emphasized. From this perspective, she explained, when children are born, the couple is not able to have what she called "a humanized relationship," that is, one that is based on genuine love and caring from parents to children. Instead, parents perceive children as their "extensions that can be used" to satisfy their own needs. "And that is what allows the consummation of incestuous relationships," she stressed, while explaining that this has been the pattern of the many incestuous families she has worked with as a clinician.

Performing Hegemony: Privilege and Underground Patriarchies

"They come and we press legal charges but then they go and disappear," explained an attorney who has worked with women either living with or witnessing sexual violence within upper-middle and upper-class families in Monterrey. "Almost hiding, they look for help," she said, describing how adult women from these families who have broken their silence disguise themselves behind sunglasses, scarves, fictitious names, and park their cars far from her office out of "paralyzing fear." Another therapist working in Monterrey with affluent families recalled cases of courageous young women pressing legal charges against a father only to find out that a mother and other adult relatives, rather than being supportive, punish them and force them "to resolve" the case within the family. In the painful dramaturgy of incest, preventing a moral scandal within the family and protecting the public image of a family name and high standards of living (including but not limited to trips to Europe and exclusive private schools for the children) expose the visible social signifiers of privilege as well as Erving Goffman's (1959) classic sociological concepts such as social stigma, secrecy, compartmentalization of the self, and back stage and front stage where patriarchal hegemony is performed. The family contexts, situations, and everyday life experiences in which the hardworking, respectful, good provider husband performs his privileges through generous expressions of manhood for his grateful immediate and extended family relatives become part of the front stage. A father who socially presents a benevolent self (charismatic and/or religious at times) compartmentalizes part of this self while strategically assaulting or raping a daughter back stage—all articulated through secrecy and fear of family and social stigma. The families of Miriam and Noelia, for instance, illustrate these dynamics. In the case of Miriam, where the three daughters break their silence while facing social stigma and family rejection, hegemony is again performed back stage as a failed, corrupt, and inefficient legal system is bought with money and power.

* * *

I have thus far presented and examined stories of women I identify as "conjugal daughters," women who experienced complex forms of sexualized violence at the hands of their biological fathers while also sharing common everyday experiences of family life with them, their biological mothers, and the rest of the family, especially as they came of age and became adults. In the study, other women experienced other forms of sexual violence with their biological fathers, but these were isolated events taking place in contexts that involved physically and emotionally distant relationships with them. Regardless—in all cases—these experiences of sexual coercion happened *without* the apparent knowledge of these women's mothers.

Next, I share and examine the stories of the women who were exposed to sexual coercion by their fathers *with* the knowledge of their mothers; maternal figures who not only knew about but who also facilitated these experiences of sexual violence. I use the concept of "marital servants" to identify these incestuous arrangements which involve daughters who serve a sexual function as both parents cope with their sexual tensions and marital difficulties.

Marital Servants: Between Complicity and Disempowerment

In this study, the marital servant arrangement occurred in the lives of three women (Otilia, Maricruz, and Adelina), all of them daughters of charismatic men who are loved and worshipped in their communities because of their religious or spiritual responsibilities, such as Catholic priests, Protestant ministers, and men engaged in other forms of ritualistic practices, such as witchcraft.[25] I include the stories of Adelina and

Maricruz, and I refer to the story of Otilia—the daughter of a Catholic priest and his mistress, an indigenous woman.[26]

The sex lives of Mexican men who are leaders in Protestant religions and ritualistic practices such as witchcraft—and who sexually abuse their daughters—deserve special attention, as well as a more extensive analysis of the role of religion and the "supernatural" in those practices. Those examinations are beyond the scope of this book. However, I offer a general, brief reflection about these issues in the last section of this chapter. I hope the stories of Adelina and Maricruz and my analysis of their narratives will inspire and inform future research on these relevant concerns.

Adelina

"They would talk about it, my mother and my aunt used to say that his job was to rape *señoritas*, young women who have never had sex," Adelina remarked as she recalled the conversations she listened to in silence when she was about ten or eleven years old. Adelina did not understand what her mother and aunt really meant, but soon she learned that the man both adult women were referring to was her stepfather, a man in his mid- to late twenties who she identified as a *curandero brujo*, a healer warlock offering *curaciones* or healing services in a shantytown located in the outskirts of a city somewhere on the coast of the Gulf of Mexico. Adelina's mother, who was in her mid-thirties, had recently come through a difficult divorce and began a relationship with this man while working to put her life back together.

After an acrimonious divorce from a highly volatile marriage, Adelina's mother and her four daughters were living in extreme poverty in a house made of tin and cardboard. "My mother was alone, and she had no education," Adelina said. Her mother was determined to work hard and figure out a way to overcome such challenging living conditions, when tragedy befell their family. When Adelina was eight or nine, an accidental fire consumed the tin and cardboard house and killed the youngest of her sisters. As a result, Adelina's mother fell into an emotional state that Adelina described as "deeply, mentally disturbed," and out of despair and financial need established a relationship with a man she might have not chosen under other life circumstances. "And that is when it all started," Adelina said.

Adelina, her two sisters, and her mother moved in with the curandero and she soon started to identify him as her "stepfather." Needles plunged into cushions, bottles with solutions and potions for healings, a sharp machete, herbs, unusual noises announcing his state of trance, and *protecciones*, protections, located in different parts of the house soon became familiar to all of them. The curandero worked from the house, offering his services to his many clients, most frequently women from the same marginalized parts of the city. Apparently, he also had sex with some of his clients. Although he was neither physically nor verbally aggressive toward the three girls, Adelina realized that he and her mother had a volatile relationship that involved emotional blackmailing and manipulation. "My mother started to please him . . . He would stick the handle of the machete in the ground so the blade was straight up, and he said that if she did not obey him, he would kill himself," she said. Through tactics such as this, he was able to get Adelina's mother to do his bidding.

"He said that he needed *doncellas* (literally, "damsels," meaning "virgins")," Adelina said, as she recalled the first night her mother told her to come into the house and follow her stepfather's instructions. "This was his reward for all the divine knowledge he had," she said. Adelina's mother stayed by the door to ensure that no one would come in while the man raped Adelina. She was ten or eleven years old and she was raped on two or more occasions and under the same circumstances. He also fondled her at night while saying that she was attractive to "the spirits he worked with."

After Adelina was raped, her mother became concerned about her daughter becoming pregnant and did everything possible to avoid a pregnancy. She scrubbed Adelina's stomach vigorously with oil and herbs, causing intense pain, and forced her to carry heavy things in her attempts to provoke a miscarriage. Adelina said, "my mother . . . how ignorant. A woman cannot get pregnant if she has not had her period, and I was a girl who had not had her period yet."

Adelina's sisters (a few years older than she was) were subjected to the same practice. Their stepfather raped both under similar circumstances while her mother used the same procedures to avoid a pregnancy. Adelina's oldest sister did become pregnant when she was thirteen or fourteen and her mother gave her an herbal formula, which provoked an intense hemorrhage and a dangerous miscarriage. Adelina also heard stories of her stepfather traveling—while still in a relationship with her mother—and "staying with families where there were single mothers raising daughters." Adelina eventually learned that her stepfather's father—also a curandero—had trained him years earlier in the practice of raping virgin women. As far as she knows, none of these cases were ever made public.

Adelina's mother had a son with the stepfather, but the couple eventually separated and Adelina's mother found herself alone again with her children. As they became older, the daughters were able to work and earn money for the family. Adelina became a domestic worker while attending elementary school, and also sold fruit, chicken, iguanas, duck, and pozole on the busy streets of her coastal hometown as a way to help her mother. She was happy to be able to help her mother, who she knew had had such a rough life, but as she matured, she also experienced intense mixed feelings toward her. Adelina lost contact with her stepfather. She saw him once was when she was eighteen or nineteen and ran into him in town. They did not exchange a word, but she expressed her pain and anger as they exchanged intense glares in silence.

"Because of him [her stepfather], I never had a boyfriend, I never had a courtship relationship," she said. She then explained how the messages she received from her mother and aunt shaped her view of herself after being raped. "Since I had lost my virginity, a man was not going to love me, because I was no longer a virgin. [They said] that anyone who had a special interest in me, I was going to be worthless for that person. And so I devalued myself. That is what my mother and my aunt told me."

Adelina never dated as a teenager. She experienced tremendous unresolved resentment toward her mother and ran away from home when she was fourteen. She left the state and established a relationship with a man who was in his early thirties. Eventually, however, she escaped and went back to her mother. He had begun making comments about "her vagina being 'too big,' [meaning 'too loose']" and she realized that he was married and planned to exploit her sexually. Her mother introduced her to the son of one of her friends, a man who was more than ten years older than Adelina and who expressed a special interest in her.

Adelina dated and legally married the son of her mother's friend. He does not know about her experiences with her stepfather. Although she does not recall having flashbacks and described her sexual life with her husband as satisfying, she said she has also been in pain "morally." She has been living with the nostalgia of "the robbed dream" of a young adolescent who felt deeply devalued for losing her virginity by force and was thereby so undeserving of falling in love, voluntarily having sex for the first time, and feeling respected by a man. Her resentment toward her mother haunts her in a way that she does not know how to resolve. When in her early twenties, Adelina decided to confront her mother, which resulted in intense emotional exchanges, deep pain, and a deteriorated relationship.

I met Adelina in Monterrey in 2006 through a therapist with whom she had had only a few sessions prior to our interview. Because of his job, Adelina's husband migrated to Monterrey and she followed him shortly after. She does not love him anymore and does not know the future of their marital relationship; however, she "appreciates him as a human being" and as the father of her three children. In the meantime, Adelina has found joy in her children, school, and occasional paid employment. She felt proud after she completed her *secundaria* (equivalent to middle school; grades 7–9) and has enthusiastically made plans to continue with her studies. Adelina has also tried to nurture a renewed relationship with her two sisters, one of whom lives close to her in Monterrey while the other one migrated to the other end of the country. Each one of them is trying to heal in their own way, especially as they have grieved the loss of their mother, who had earlier been diagnosed with and ultimately died of uterine cancer.

Maricruz

So both of Lot's daughters became pregnant by their father.
The older daughter had a son, and she named him Moab; he
is the father of the Moabites today. —Genesis 19:36–38[27]

"They gave me the Bible, and I do not recall what book it was, but he said, 'Read this,' and so I did. And in that chapter it said that Jacob, but . . . I don't remember, or someone else who had had sex with his daughter because he did not want to sin with other women, so in order to avoid sinning, he had sex with his daughter. And I just looked at the Bible . . . I closed it and I went to sleep." Maricruz recalled the confusion she experienced the very first time her father told her—in her stepmother's presence—to read a biblical passage, which discussed sex between a father and his daughter. Three or four days later, Maricruz's father started to fondle her in her sleep, a routine that became frequent and eventually resulted in forced intercourse. He used other biblical passages in preparation for raping Maricruz again, for example, "God creating Adam and Eve because the man needed a woman." He raped her on different occasions with a knife in hand, threatening her to keep silent. Maricruz was twelve years old the first time she was raped. Her father was in his mid-fifties.

"After papá raped me, he did not let me get out of the house, and when he saw me talking with people of the same religion, he wanted to know what I talked about with them. He told me that he would kill me if I said anything about it," Maricruz reported. A charismatic community representative who was worshipped and respected by his congregation members, family, friends, and neighbors, Maricruz's father was a *predicador*, a preacher representing the Seventh-Day Adventist Church in Maricruz's town, located in central Mexico. He traveled in Mexico and internationally as part of his religious responsibilities. Maricruz traveled with him at times and he sexually assaulted her frequently in the hotel rooms they shared. "He used the Bible to give advice to people," she said as she explained that her father offered moral guidance to couples and families who approached him to find solutions to their personal and family problems.

"Because he was part of that religion, he was very strict, we could not do anything bad because he would hit us," Adelina explained, describing how her father disciplined her and her siblings. She dropped out of school in fifth grade because he would leave her bruised and she was afraid to go to school. "Bruises and blood, wounds, but nobody did anything. The pueblo was big but back then they were not concerned about children. I was afraid of my papá. Nobody intervened." Maricruz recalled how vulnerable all of the children in the family felt under the rule of a punishing father who also forced them to work to exhaustion.

Maricruz's father had at least ten children (mostly boys) of disparate ages and conceived by different women; Maricruz's biological mother had two children with him. After breaking up with him, the young mother left Maricruz in the care of her maternal grandfather, and *regaló* (literally, "gave as a gift" meaning "gave away") Maricruz's brother. But Maricruz's father showed up one day to claim his rights over the little girl and took her away. He and his new wife (who witnessed Maricruz's bedtime biblical readings on incest) raised Maricruz and some of his other children.

"My stepmother knew everything about it, because, because my stepmother told me that I should allow him to do it to me . . . she said that I had to do everything that he asked me to do." Maricruz recalled the conversation she had with her stepmother regarding her fear of getting pregnant, and also because she felt she could no longer withstand her father's sexual assaults. Maricruz was fearful of being killed by him but risked telling her, "Mamá, he touches my body and I do not like it. And she said, 'Well, you have to let him do it, stupid girl.' Because my father would touch me all over."

Maricruz then described an episode facilitated by her stepmother. "I tried to avoid my father but my stepmother forced me to sleep next to him. 'Sleep right there!' she said, but I did not want to sleep close to him. She laid me down to sleep in the middle of the bed and that was when he raped me again. So she was looking at what was happening." Maricruz did not give up in her attempts to make her mother understand her pain while being frequently raped. But then things became more and more clear to her:

> My mother told me that I had to let him touch me because "I am sick," she said. And I told her, "But no, because I am his daughter! He should not do anything to me because I am his daughter!" "It does not matter," [she said]. They did not have sex but she told me to let him touch me because, "I cannot do it, you must satisfy your father," she told me many times. When my father did it to me, I wanted her to listen to me, but she encouraged me to do it, to let him do it to me, many times. She was sick, she had a headache every day, but she was just in bed watching TV.

Maricruz always suspected that her older brothers knew all about it, she thought they were perhaps fearful and did not intervene. After a failed suicide attempt, Maricruz ran away when her stepmother was not around and while her father was on a trip. She went to her aunt's house pleading for help.

"So your sister was right," Maricruz paraphrased her aunt's words after she told her about the sexual violence she had experienced at the hands of her father and stepmother. About five years earlier, Maricruz's oldest sister—and the only other daughter of her father—was in her early twenties when she also ran away from home. Maricruz was eight or nine years old and did not know why her sister was suddenly gone. Maricruz's sister went to her aunt's house and told her that her father had raped her, but the aunt did not believe her. Instead, she kicked her out of the house and sent her back to her father. Her aunt told her that he had asked her sister "to kneel down and pray for lying." Shortly after, Maricruz's sister ran away and never returned. To this day, nobody knows where she is.

After Maricruz learned about her sister's story, she stayed with her aunt and felt protected from her father. She then learned from TV that men who rape could be legally prosecuted and talked to her aunt about it. Her aunt confided in a brother who had legal influence in town. Although her uncle did not believe Maricruz, he was willing to take her to a gynecologist for an exam to have proof and be able to proceed legally. A hopeful Maricruz enthusiastically waited for her uncle, but he never arrived to pick her up for the doctor's exam and subsequently did not visit her anymore. Her aunt became discouraged and Maricruz felt more and more afraid of being killed by her father, so she decided to run away again.

"To this day, I do not know how I did it to take such a big risk," Maricruz reflected in retrospect as she described her journey to a place far from home with her meager savings in hand. At the age of thirteen, Maricruz left the pueblo feeling helpless and neglected and took a bus heading for Monterrey. Upon arriving in the big city, she soon learned about the Alameda, a central plaza in the city and a location where immigrant women from different parts of the country gather to look for paid employment as household workers. With the help of women who later became her friends, she found a safe place to sleep the first night and eventually found a job.

Maricruz lost contact with her father and stepmother. She never went back, but she has heard shocking yet not surprising stories. One of Maricruz's aunts told the rest of the family about also being sexually molested by Maricruz's father, many years ago. And a woman who worked as a household worker for her father's family was also raped by him and became pregnant as a result. After people in the pueblo learned about Maricruz's case, some left her father's church. I met Maricruz in Monterrey at a family services organization where she had gone in 2006 to seek out therapy services. She was in her early twenties, had never been married, but she was in a stable relationship while raising her two children. She described her partner as a "respectable man," but she does not allow him to take care of her four-year-old daughter; the little girl accompanies Maricruz wherever she goes in Monterrey. Maricruz hopes to be able to trust him, and to completely heal some day.

Understanding Marital Servitude

As illustrated by Adelina and Maricruz, daughters who become marital servants are exposed to coercive sexualized experiences with a father *with* the knowledge and participation of a biological mother or a maternal figure (i.e., stepmother) who may endorse, approve of, encourage, and/or actively facilitate those encounters from positions that expose different levels of disempowerment and relationship tensions for heterosexual women. Even though daughters who become marital servants may share some commonalities with those who become conjugal daughters, their experiences share some unique and different patterns.

As revealed through my interview, first, the parental figures involved adult women and men who were not always the biological father or mother. Second, ritualistic abuse may involve a father who uses texts or discourses associated with patriarchal organized religions (i.e., the Bible) or other ritualistic practices and symbols as a way to frame and justify sexual violence against daughters, and/or as part of the context and circumstances in which he exercises sexual violence. Third, similar to the conjugal daughter incestuous arrangement, a father may have more than one daughter serving him as a marital servant. These patterns of serial marital servitude are the cause and result of what I identify as "family genealogies of incest," which illustrates the complex ways in which sexual violence within incestuous families involve not only one or two isolated cases, but more which are reproduced systematically and frequently within immediate and extended families, and across generations. (I examine these perplexing dynamics in greater depth in chapter 4.) And fourth, women who are marital servants did not take the sexual violence passively. Instead, women resisted actively and explored ways to cope with it, frequently running away from home or migrating with or without family support, even at a very early age.

As illustrated, in all cases, the same dynamics that explain the experiences of conjugal daughters explain, to an extent, the cultural construction of marital servants. Three additional processes help to explain these dynamics: internalized sexism, the paterfamilias, and sexualized rituals of patriarchy.

Internalized Sexism, Gender Inequality, and the Family

"How can we call for solidarity with our gender if we do not practice solidarity amongst ourselves [as women]?" This was the question posed by Marcela Lagarde y de los Ríos, a highly respected Mexican feminist anthropologist speaking at a conference in Madrid in 2006.[28] Lagarde's enthusiastic call for *sororidad* (equivalent to "feminist sisterhood") in her presentation reminds me of the sexual histories and stories of immigrant women born and raised in Mexico that I interviewed in the late 1990s. These women taught me about the insidious ways in which women learn to stigmatize and oppress other women (e.g., acquaintances and friends) through what I identified as "internalized sexism." This involves a process of "misrecognition" as women incorporate within themselves and reproduce the social structures that oppress them as women, which Cecilia Menjívar found in her study of women in Guatemala and that French sociologist Pierre Bourdieu theorized extensively (1996–1997, 2001).[29] As women participate in the social reproduction of beliefs and practices that oppress them as women, how does this take place *within* the family? How is that played out across generations of mothers and their daughters?

The mothers and stepmothers of young women who participate in the incestuous arrangement that I identify as marital servants are mothers who actively and purposefully facilitated the sexual violence perpetrated against their daughters when they were children, and at times, as they came of age. As I noted in an earlier publication,

> From a critical feminist perspective, however, many tensions and contradictions emerge as we become aware of the fine lines between responsibil-

ity and complicity vis-à-vis disempowerment and the fragility of women who live in marginalized communities within patriarchal societies. If we alternatively and carefully zoom in and out the critical lens of this kaleidoscope we see the intricate and complex patterns of persistent abuse.

When we zoom in the lens, we see a more complex illustration of a pattern a feminist law professor from Mexico City identified for me as she shared stories of the women she has worked with: "Mothers become *cómplices por omisión* when they cover up their eyes in front of these acts of aggression."[30]

A legal concept that has been examined by law specialists studying a mother's duty to protect her child in the United States, complicity by omission would very likely make the mothers of Adelina and Maricruz legally responsible and guilty for the acts of sexual violence they actively facilitated.[31]

If we zoom out the lens, however, we see how the image becomes more complex as it exposes the ways in which patriarchy reproduces itself to an extent through sexist paradigms of motherhood.[32] As we zoom out the lens and see closely and critically, we wonder about the extent to which each mother actively participated in the sexual victimization of their daughters precisely because (1) they have internalized (from society at large) ways to reproduce sexist beliefs and practices within the family by exercising sexual control over women in positions of disadvantage (in this case, a little girl within her family) yet they do so from their own social, economic, and cultural marginalities, and re-colonized indigenous bodies (as in the case of women like Otilia's mother); and (2) as marginalized women, they have learned self-oppressive ways to cope with their own disempowerment as adult women trapped in their own predicaments in these reportedly volatile and catastrophic heterosexual relationships. In sum, finding themselves collectively oppressed as women, these mothers oppress the younger women under their authority. "If, as mothers, they are responsible for these acts of sexual violence, to what extent are they innocent as women?" I have been asking myself after listening to these stories.[33] These are thought provoking, controversial issues, and far from taking sides—or exposing ways "to blame" mothers or "to justify" mothers for the actions that changed forever the hearts and lives of the women I interviewed—my goal above all as a feminist scholar is to uncover the perplexing complexities, tensions, and contradictions that are responsible for the organization of these expressions of sexual violence.

Paterfamilias: Daughters as Sexual Slaves

The moving stories of Adelina and Maricruz faithfully depict the Latin etymological root of the Spanish word *familia*. Historian Ramón Gutiérrez offers this revealing reflection:

> Nowadays, when we speak of *familia*, or family, we equate it with our immediate blood kin. That which is within the family is intimate, within the private walls of the home, and devoid of strangers. But if we focus carefully on the historical genealogy of the word *familia*, on its antique meanings, it was tied neither to kinship nor to a specific private space or house. Rather, what constituted *familia* was the relationship of authority that one person exercised over another, and more specifically, *familia* was imagined as the authority relationship of a master over slaves.[34]

Gutiérrez further explains that the etymological origin of the Spanish word familia is the Latin word familia. And he cites historian David Herlihy, "Roman grammarians believed that the word had entered Latin as a borrowing from the Oscan language. In Oscan *famel* meant 'slave'; the Latin word for slave was *famulus*." Gutiérrez then cites Ulpian, a second century AD Roman jurist: "We are accustomed to call staffs of slaves families . . . we call a family the several persons who by nature of law are placed under the authority of a single person."[35] Thus, family was in its origins a relationship with a clear power structure, placing one person over others, "most notably slaves, but in time, also over a wife, children, and retainers."[36] Critical examinations of the familia as an idea and a social institution with an oppressive structure have been at the core of such studies by late nineteenth-century intellectuals, such as social scientist and political theorist Friedrich Engels, and Genaro García, a feminist Mexican jurist who published about gender inequality and family life during the same period.

And the Latin word *pater* identified the father, who through the concept of *paterfamilias* eventually became the legal head of the family, as explained by the attorneys I interviewed. In contemporary Mexico, the word *famulla* is still used in a derogatory manner to refer to a woman who works as a domestic worker, and *padre de familia* is part of the common language used to identify a man (and at times a woman) raising children.[37] As a child growing up in Mexico in the 1960s and 1970s, I witnessed the use of padre de familia for both father and mother. A more gender-inclusive use of language in modern Mexico, however, would become *madre de familia* when applied to a mother.

As marital servants, Adelina and Maricruz were the sexual slaves in the incestuous exchanges they experienced. They became a sexual commodity as their parents explored ways to cope with the sexual frustrations, challenging health conditions, and unresolved conflict affecting their relationships. The sexualized bodies of these daughters not only became an object but also secondary in the midst of a sexualized encounter designed to help a mother satisfy the sexual urges and curiosities of a partner or as a stepmother to comply with her sexual obligations as a wife. All daughters became invisible and objectified within the context of late twentieth-century Mexican rural and urban families living on the margins of society in which a mother made use of the sexualized body of her daughter in order to resolve her own romantic, sexual, and relationship expectations and despairs. The syndrome of invisibility and dehumanization that made Adelina and Maricruz—and their respective sisters—sex objects also illustrates the colonial roots of contemporary perceptions of children and indigenous people as inferior, ignorant, and invisible—less-than-human.[38]

The most extreme form of marital complicity and sexual slavery was the case of Viridiana, the only person I interviewed who reported being sexually trafficked as a child by her parents. Viridiana recalled the day when she and one of her older sisters found themselves in El Paso, Texas, locked up in a strange place they shared with other children and young women who spoke an unfamiliar language that didn't sound like English. Soon Viridiana and her sister realized that their parents had sold them to a couple, apparently from the United States. Both girls successfully figured out a way to escape together and live on their own, surviving homelessness. But they soon took different paths, with Viridiana spending the rest of her life going back and forth between the U.S. Southwest and Ciudad Juárez, and her sister living far away in Mexico City.

Sexualized Rituals of Patriarchy: Ritualizing Misogyny

"Ritualistic abuse" (also "ritual abuse") is a form of abuse of children that takes place as part of "the invocation of religious, magical or supernatural symbols or activities" according to Finkelhor and collaborators.[39] Based on his extensive legal expertise with cases of ritual abuse, Lanning reflects on the social context that makes these ritualized activities even more dangerous for children: "A high potential of abuse exists for any children raised in a group isolated from the mainstream of society, especially if the group has a charismatic leader whose orders are blindly obeyed by the members."[40]

As illustrated by the stories of Adelina and Maricruz (and, reportedly, their sisters)—all exposed during childhood to patriarchal paternal figures who relied on these religious or magical belief systems, and lived in isolated social contexts—they exemplify the clinical literature examining ritualized sexual abuse of children. The rituals of sexual violence that Adelina and Maricruz described in their recollections of these paternal figures and their unspeakable acts are, however, more than a pathological behavior.

From a feminist perspective, these ritualistic behaviors are far from being isolated cases and exist as part of a larger patriarchal culture that has ritualized sexual violence against women in Mexico and elsewhere, within religious and nonreligious contexts.[41] Within religious contexts this is illustrated for instance by research conducted by Erdely and Argüelles, and Marcos, on the reported cases of ritualistic sexual abuse of minors by Samuel Joaquín, the charismatic religious leader of the controversial Christian denomination *La Luz del Mundo*—The Light of the World.

Erdely and Argüelles identify these patterns of sexual violence against minors at La Luz del Mundo as "the institutionalization of sexual abuse" facilitated by the "alleged divine status" of the religious leader.[42] Sexual abuse of minors involves a wide variety of sexual practices (including but not limited to sexual slavery), with sexual initiation taking place usually around or on the day relevant religious festivities are celebrated.[43] As in the stories told by Adelina and Maricruz, adult women may become complicit and facilitate these activities at La Luz del Mundo. A non-Catholic denomination, La Luz del Mundo has its international headquarters in Guadalajara, and has hundreds of followers in Mexico, the United States, and other countries.[44]

Although women like Adelina and Maricruz have been exposed to the same modus operandi or social process, whether extreme and lethal or less physically damaging,[45] these rituals are "symbolic representations of social relationships," according to Durkheim.[46] In this case, these relationships take place within marital and family contexts that rely on the sexual objectification of girls in order to satisfy the unmet sexual and emotional needs of adults who are practitioners of spiritual belief systems and rituals that make children vulnerable.

Rituals of misogyny exist as part of everyday life in urban social contexts conventionally perceived as safe, not only in the God-like or supernatural realms. The fathers of Adelina and Maricruz are part of the same group as the young U.S. college students who rape young women as part of rituals that place within some fraternities and the men who create ritualized cultures of "girl watching" to collectively objectify and sexually harass women at work, practices that may have some form of cultural equivalence in the Mexican context.[47]

At college or at work, some men engage in a wide range of sexually intrusive and violent behaviors to establish some expression of intimacy with other men, which rely on subtle or extreme forms of sexual objectification of women in the process. Thus I suggest that fathers like Adelina's or Maricruz's—who sexually targeted more than one daughter or stepdaughter in their families—rape a girl as a way to engage in some form of "interaction ritual" with their respective complicit marital partners.[48] And in doing so, these heterosexual couples establish some form of "social solidarity and symbolic significance," an expression of intimacy involving an adult woman who is not sexually available or one who is completely under a man's emotional control—or both.[49]

Besides exposing the pathological and aberrant nature of adult heterosexual relationships that rely on the sexual objectification and exploitation of a daughter, these stories expose the painful consequences in the sexual and emotional lives of women who are raped during childhood and thus who lost their virginity also as a *capital femenino, that is, virginity as a form of social endowment.* As illustrated by Adelina's story, some women rely on virginity as capital femenino in regions where gender inequality is severe. That is, women use an intact virginal hymen as a form of social capital they can exchange to secure financial stability and improve their living conditions. Virginity as capital femenino is in fact indispensable for women's survival in contexts of scarce educational or paid employment opportunities and rural regional patriarchies that promote extreme forms of gender inequality. This may become extreme, to the point that some Mexican women may request hymen reconstruction, a form of plastic surgery that "repairs" an intact hymen, and thus a woman can reclaim virginity as capital femenino.[50]

In the end, a father who is a religious leader and reads a biblical passage as a prelude to raping his daughter, or a stepfather who engages in misogynous rituals driven by a pernicious fascination with intact hymens, tight vaginas, and the fresh, youthful skin of girls and young women, exposes the symbolic value of virginity as well as some of the most extreme ritualized expressions of patriarchy within incestuous families and society at large.[51] It was no surprise to learn that virgin girls have been purposefully selected for the rituals of sexual abuse taking place in La Luz del Mundo, and that virginity was identified as a gift to the "Servant of God" in Amparo's story, one of the girls violently raped by the leader of this religious group.[52] Perla's story earlier in this chapter illustrated this perception of virginity as a "gift," a pattern I similarly found in my previous sexuality research with Mexican immigrants.[53]

Finally, the story of Maricruz and the scandalous cases of sexual violence against girls and boys in La Luz del Mundo evoke the national and international scandals of pedophile priests in the Catholic Church.[54] Clearly, the cultural values promoted by the Catholic Church as a patriarchal institution (especially with regard to the sex and family lives of priests) have extended to other Mexican men who are in positions of authority and power within non-Catholic religious institutions.[55] Even though Maricruz's father was not forced to practice chastity in his Adventist Church, he benefited from these double discourses of sexual morality that frequently elevate men like him to fictitious high positions within their families and communities.[56] A Ciudad Juárez clinician was familiar with cases of religious leaders within what she identified as a "Pentecostal church," men who for religious reasons engaged in marital celibacy in common agreement with a wife, but who sexually approached a daughter. Also, in their examinations of sexual abuse of minors in La Luz del Mundo, Erdely and Argüelles found that the "alleged ceremonial sexual abuse of young girls and some boys often appears to entail the blessing of the victim's parents."[57] The brother of Magdalena (a girl sexually abused by Samuel Joaquín) stated that his mother considered the sexual abuse of her daughter by the religious leader "a religious privilege."[58]

Finally, although Adelina's stepfather did not belong to a Christian-based organized religious group, as indicated, her story shared some commonalities with the Catholic priest and the Adventist preacher. A deeper analysis of the rape of virgin women by men involved in witchcraft and who are considered part of the family goes beyond the scope of this book, as those rituals require further analysis, especially as *brujos* or sorcerers involved in ritualized expressions of violence against women become increasingly identified in the literature and more visible in the press.[59]

* * *

In sum, the stories of women who have been involved in incestuous arrangements (either as conjugal daughters or marital servants) and my culturally situated feminist analyses expose the complexities of these dynamics. Sexual violence against a daughter becomes an intricate labyrinth when we become social critics of gender relations within the family, especially when we look at both *micro* and *macro* forces and processes articulating power, authority, and control in patriarchal societies. In fact, not all mothers of interviewees were disempowered or complicit; some actively engaged in inspiring acts of resilience and family justice. Chapter 6 offers these stories in dialog, with reflections about prevention, intervention, social justice, and gender equality within families.

In the next chapter, I examine the stories of women who were exposed as children to other expressions of sexual violence in their relationships with men they used to care about and love within their families: their brothers and cousins.

3

A la prima se le arrima

Sisters and Primas

Many rapes merely extend traditional heterosexual exchanges, in which masculine pursuit and feminine reticence are familiar and formalized. Although rape is a gross exaggeration of gender power, it contains the rules and rituals of heterosexual encounter, seduction and conquest.
—Lucy Gilbert and Paula Webster, *Bound by Love: The Sweet Trap of Daughterhood* (1982)

"'*Voy a cogerte* ('I am going to grab you,' and 'I am going to fuck you'),' whatever word they used. But right away, my brothers got on top of me. My mother could not leave [home] because it would happen, immediately! In other words, it was one of them first, and very quickly the next one would come in, just like that," said Maclovia, a woman in her early thirties, born and raised in a small pueblo in Central Mexico. Now a wife and mother living in Monterrey, Maclovia was six years old when her oldest brothers, seventeen and sixteen years old at that time, started to take turns sexually assaulting and raping her. The youngest brother stopped assaulting Maclovia when she was eleven years old or so, after he started dating young women; however, the experiences of sexual assault by the oldest brother continued. I interviewed Maclovia in Monterrey where she has lived since she was fifteen years old after running away from the ranch to escape from her oldest brother.

"I had to always be alert and watch my back and front," Esmeralda said while describing how, when she was ten or twelve, an older, adolescent primo, a male cousin, fondled her buttocks during an otherwise joyful family gathering at her paternal grandmother's house. "*Sentí tanta vergüenza*—I felt so ashamed," Esmeralda said as she recalled the laughter of the other primos who witnessed the event.[1] Her paternal tía was also within view but did not seem to be aware of what happened and did not intervene. These episodes continued for about four years whenever the family gathered at the grandmother's house, a place Esmeralda associated with love and tenderness, but also danger and fear. Born and raised in a town not far from Guadalajara, Esmeralda is an unmarried, college-educated woman in her early thirties. She said that the fondling episodes stopped when her primo started to have girlfriends.

As discussed in the previous chapter, father-daughter incestuous arrangements expose complex dynamics that may transform girls and women into the sex objects of the men in their families, and thus make them vulnerable to various forms of sexual violence. This chapter examines how and why, for women like Maclovia and Esmeralda, this patriarchal premise may acquire new expressions for young girls vis-à-vis their brothers and cousins. For instance, the concept of "gendered servitude" that transformed a girl into her father's conjugal daughter may similarly convert a girl into the object of countless forms of sexual curiosity, initiation, experimentation, frustration, and other perverse sexual adventures of biological brothers and/or male cousins. Although these kinship relationships are horizontal (i.e., between siblings or between cousins), the associations of Maclovia and Esmeralda and the other women discussed in this chapter are unequal because of age, gender, and body size and strength differences.

This chapter exposes the complex social and cultural forces responsible for the sister-brother and prima-primo incestuous arrangements. The stories of women subjected to sexual violence at the hands of their biological brothers expose two revealing patterns. First, in a patriarchal society where men are trained to believe that their sense of manhood can be compromised by a failed sexual performance, brothers may transform their sisters into what I term "family sex surrogates," that is, women within the family who become the safe temporary sex substitutes of a male relative's future sex partners. As such, sisters are used to satisfy the sexual needs of brothers before they start dating.[2] Second, as a sister becomes a family sex surrogate, a young man initiates himself into heterosexual manhood through sexualized rituals, acts, and behaviors that expose the ways in which sexual violence within families may become the most grotesque expression of how heterosexuality and heteromasculinities are constructed and lived in patriarchal societies.

In my analysis, I incorporate concepts such as the "continuum of sexual violence" and "patriarchal dividend" coined by sociologists Liz Kelly (1987) and R.W. Connell (2005), respectively. The continuum of sexual violence illustrates how and why pleasure and danger may become part of the same experience of sexual violence, suggesting that rape and patriarchal constructions of heterosexuality are deeply interconnected. As a young hetero-patriarch in training, a brother who harasses or rapes his younger sister may experience an early harvesting of patriarchal dividends, that is, a young man becomes aware of his potential to have power, control, and his "right to command" the women within his family and society.[3] These dynamics occur as a girl's feelings of love for a brother become tangled in a complex emotional web of confusion, guilt, shame, betrayal, and loss of trust. While women are not necessarily passive or helpless in these experiences, some women became aware of other women in their families living similar stories with the same or other men related to them, and/or learning about history of emotional, sexual, or physical violence within their immediate and extended families, across class differences and within influential religious contrasts.

While such dynamics may also be extended to prima-primo incestuous arrangements, two additional forces seem to be responsible for the experiences of the women that I interviewed. First, "sexual terrorism" explains why an adolescent primo may successfully use fear as a control mechanism that revolves around terror and ridicule as he harasses a younger prima in family life interactions and situations and as adult relatives who witness these events ignore, normalize, and trivialize them. A concept coined by Carole Sheffield (1989), sexual terrorism explains why different expressions of sexual violence become a sexual opportunity for a young primo to explore his sexual curiosity while practicing power and control of women within the extended family and as part of everyday life. And second, the acceptance and normalization of different forms of sexually intrusive behaviors of boys toward girls within their extended families has not only trivialized these forms of sexual violence, but has rendered them unproblematic, invisible, and unnamed. Thus, I suggest that making these experiences visible and naming them as "family sexual harassment" may offer possibilities to identify, label, intervene, and disrupt complex forms of intrusion and harm of women's bodies that occur at an early age. These are forms of nuanced violence that have been traditionally constructed as harmless within Mexican families. The normalization of cultural messages such as "*Así son los hombres, todos son iguales*" ("That is the way men are, all of them are the same") and *refranes* or popular sayings such as "*A la prima se le arrima*" (which literally means "You can get physically/sexually close to your female cousin") are two widely known expressions used to justify and trivialize multiple forms of sexual violence within extended families in Mexico where incestuous practices prevail.

The following are stories of women who reported a wide variety of sexual violence at the hands of their biological brothers and their male cousins or primos. The first section discusses brothers and the second looks at cousins.

Sister-Brother Stories

Alfonsina

"'Do you love me?' [He asked]. So I said, 'Yes! Because he is my brother!' [I thought] 'Well then it is not bad, if you love me it is not bad,' he said. But he also said, 'Do not tell our parents.'" Alfonsina recalled the confusion she experienced as her older brother showed her pornographic magazines and later started to get her naked and touch her. She was eight or nine and he was sixteen or seventeen years old the first time this happened. She is the youngest of three children. These episodes became increasingly frequent and he eventually penetrated Alfonsina when she was thirteen years old. She described herself as a reserved girl.

The confusion and fear she experienced when he raped her was exacerbated by his attitudes and behavior. "He always told me that he loved me very much . . . Always, after the abuse, he always gave me a gift," she said. He never used physical force as part of the sexual coercion, and in his attempts to "protect her" from becoming pregnant, always ejaculated outside. While touching her, he insisted that "it was not bad for him to touch her, but 'if you as a woman touch yourself, it is sinful.'" He knew the comings and goings of the rest of the family and was strategically savvy about the best time to assault her.

As she became older, he used pornographic movies and made comments about her body, telling her that "she looked hot" while also manipulating her, "if you do not want me to do anything to you, just let me look at you naked." Alfonsina noticed that when she turned sixteen and started to date young men, her brother coerced and assaulted her less frequently. In the meantime, he had married and had a child. However, one day, he caught her while she was having sex with her boyfriend at home when her parents were gone. "You are a puta," he told her. She confronted him:

> "I do not know why you are angry, if I am doing it with another person, and you did it with me." [tears, pause] He was silent and did not know what to say, but that time he still told me, "If you do not want me to tell mom and dad, you have to do it with me." [tears, pause] I accepted and did it just to make sure he would not tell our parents. [tears, pause] But that was the last time. From now on I said "no!" even if he wanted to tell our parents, he could tell them if he wanted to. He already had his son and he kept insisting a lot to me, and I already not, no, no more . . . I told him "no more" because I remember that I cried every time he wanted to touch me, or when I was alone at home and he arrived, and I felt so afraid. And I, crying, I would tell him I, that I did not want to, that he had to leave me alone. But he never, he never listened to me [tears, pause]. That was, that was the last time he did anything to me. But I was already twenty years old.

Alfonsina married in her mid-twenties while trying to understand why her brother became jealous and threatened her boyfriend if he did not treat her right. After she became a mother she noticed that the sexual violence slowed considerably, but not completely. Although he became "softer" after she started to babysit his son, and her own children developed strong feelings of love for him, he continued to harass her. She was shocked by this, especially because by then he had his second child—a little girl. Out of fear, she has never confronted him again directly. Recenlty, Alfonsina told her husband that she was "sexually abused as a child," and he responded with resentment for not telling him earlier. She did not tell him it was her brother.

As she reflected on the experience, Alfonsina said that she never "provoked" her brother, but always felt responsible for "allowing him to do it," especially as she eventually realized that "it was not right." She felt guilty for experiencing an orgasm and pleasure at least once with him when she was fourteen or fifteen, and for being silent and not being able to prevent it, especially as she confided in her oldest sister and learned that he had also sexually assaulted her, but she fought back aggressively and he never did it again. Although she grew up feeling loved by her hardworking parents and as her father's favorite child—his *consentida*—and surrounded by little or no physical violence in her household—she eventually learned about the many cases of sexual violence on both the maternal and paternal sides of her family.

"If the first time that my brother abused me, or when he started to touch me, my mother had been around, perhaps he would not have continued doing it," she said. Alfonsina described her mother as "selfish," "busy studying," or taking care of a business and thus absent when she was little, but she was also affectionate and supported her later in her professional development.

Raised in a working-class family in Mexico City, her mother sewed her children's clothes and figured out other ways to stretch the modest income of her hardworking husband. "*La pobreza hay que llevarla con dignidad*" (literally, One should bear poverty with dignity), Alfonsina repeated her mother's family mantra while explaining that her parents instilled middle-class values in their children. Both parents, for instance, saved money to take their children to a nice restaurant once a month. "Other people used to think that we had a lot of money, but it was never that way," she said.

In retrospect, Alfonsina primarily blamed her brother for what happened to her and her sister. Alfonsina identified him as "self-confident and easy going" but a "sick man" who "might have not had sexual contact" or who "lacked love" and therefore assaulted his sisters. Alfonsina characterized her sister as "stronger" than her and therefore able to resist the brother's attacks. Being able to talk openly about sexuality in the family as "something natural" might have also prevented this from happening in her family, she said.

Now a married woman in her early thirties raising children, she said, "Now I have the responsibility to be happy, and also, I have to take care of my children so they are happy as well." With her sister's supportive encouragement she sought professional help at the organization where I met her in Mexico City in 2006. She had attended a few sessions at a support group and was hoping to be able to share her experience with others and to heal some day.

Maclovia

"The first time I was abused I was six years old, so what was I supposed to say?" Maclovia said as she explained that her parents harshly punished or were completely silent toward her or her siblings when they made any comments having to do with sex, something she learned to perceive as "dirty" as she came of age. As explained in the introduction to this chapter, Maclovia was born and raised in a remote rural area of Central Mexico and became the target of her two oldest brothers' sexual curiosities and urges from an early age. Maclovia was six years old when her oldest brothers, seventeen and sixteen years old at that time, first sexually assaulted her. In her words: "I remember that at home, as soon as my mother left, all of them arrived, my brothers, and well, one of them right away came after me . . . immediately! Right at the moment when my mother left the house, my brother approached me and said, 'Let's do it, let's do *groserías* (vulgarities)'—that is the word they used, or '*Voy a cogerte.*'"

The second oldest daughter in a family of eleven children, Maclovia was raised on a small ranch with no water and no electricity. "It is a cruel life, there is no childhood over there," Maclova reflected in retrospect as she explained that things have not changed much to this day in her ranch. Children are forced to start working at a very early age, while formal education of girls is discouraged. "I remember I passed to fourth grade, and I was so excited, and I was told [by my father], 'you are no longer going to school so you can help your mother,'" she said.

Maclovia also had no sense of privacy in her modest home. "My father and my mother always had their oversights, it was one room and we were able to see," she said as she recalled feeling confused and running away every time she saw her parents having sexual relations. Maclovia had also observed three of her brothers looking at magazines that only made sense when she became older. And she had no doubt that some of her siblings had also witnessed their parents' sexual encounters. She then elaborated, "At that moment is when the *morbo* wakes up, the morbo of the youth, and young men who are older start buying pornographic magazines, and that is where they go, they wake up, and instead of looking for satisfaction in the street, look for it in the family, where they should not go."

Based on my own personal experience growing up in Mexico, "morbo" refers to morbid fascination, interest, or curiosity, which is usually associated with sex. This resonated with Maclovia's memories as she explained that her oldest brother undressed both her and himself when she was six, gave her instructions to bend down and move her body in a certain way, told her to never tell her mother or father about it, and "offered" her money. Maclovia recalled this happening repeatedly between the ages of six and fourteen with her oldest brother, someone she described as never being physically aggressive. Maclovia had similar experiences with her sixteen-year-old brother when she was six years old. Her brothers assaulted her individually and also together, while taking turns. However, the younger brother stopped assaulting her when she turned eleven or so. She explained why this happened: "He looked for girlfriends, and so he got away from there."

Although Maclovia does not remember specific details about these experiences with her brothers, she described these events as "her brothers having sex with her." These experiences were never physically or sexually pleasurable for her; however, they hid a vulnerable aspect of her emotional life as a child. "I felt nothing with my brothers, nothing . . . I felt, well, I think it was the lack of affection that they do not give you in the ranch. You feel like you are more loved. When they touch you, when they hold you, I felt that they gave me affection." She recalled the experiences with *vergüenza y rabia*—shame and rage—against her brothers and also against herself for not being able to do anything about it while growing up.

"In a ranch, the one who is responsible, the one to be blamed is always the woman. The man is never responsible for anything. In other words, in all of this, I was the responsible one," Maclovia said as she explained that her mother learned about what had happened to her with her brothers, but she used it against Maclovia and threatened to tell her father. Maclovia's mother never threatened any of her brothers.

In the midst of this family puzzle, Maclovia also worked hard to figure out ways to cope with the ongoing assaults from her oldest brother. She was fifteen years old when she decided that running away to Monterrey was the best option. She left the ranch, found a live-in job as a domestic worker with a "respectful family" where she always felt safe, even in the big city, and decided to never go back. In the meantime, her parents died of health-related problems.

After Maclovia left her small town, she learned about one of her younger sisters being eager to migrate. She followed Maclovia's steps, left for Monterrey, and eventually got a job in paid domestic work as well. Maclovia was saddened but not completely surprised when she learned that her sister had had identical experiences of sexual violence—and around the same ages—with her two brothers. "This is a chain, precisely a chain," Maclovia said assertively as she shared the shocking news she and her sister have gradually learned about their family, all taking place at her ranch:

- The oldest brother who assaulted Maclovia is now married and has two daughters. A neighbor raped one of the girls and he was initially prosecuted, but the legal process was discontinued after he paid a substantial amount of money to a corrupted legal system. Her father took her out of school to protect her from "strangers" and to keep her "safe" at home. One of Maclovia's younger brothers is in his thirties and lives now with them. At home, he is sexually assaulting his nieces (the girl who was raped and her sister) and offering them money. Maclovia's oldest brother—the father of the girls—does not seem to know.
- After Maclovia's father passed away, two of Maclovia's younger sisters told her that he raped them years ago. Maclovia's sisters are now in their twenties.
- Maclovia's paternal grandfather and his daughter (the sister of Maclovia's father) engaged in sexual relations and she had a daughter by him. Maclovia did not have any additional details about this case, apparently a conjugal daughter arrangement.
- Maclovia's uncle (her father's brother) lives with his niece as a couple.

Maclovia learned about these events while living in Monterrey and felt helpless to intervene, especially in the case of her two nieces. "The truth is that I feel so embarrassed to talk to my brother about it, because he was the one who had sex with me," she said. She also said that she had no money for an expensive and exhausting trip by bus. Her ranch is located about twelve hours away from Monterrey, which requires an additional two hours of walking from the bus station in the pueblo to the ranch.

Maclovia married the only man she dated after arriving in Monterrey. In spite of a challenging marital and sex life, they are still together because of their children. Because she fears being rejected, she has never told her husband about what happened to her with her brothers. Recently, Maclovia has experienced sexual interest and fantasies about women, and these feelings have caused her anguish and confusion. A psychologist introduced me to Maclovia at a family services center where she had very recently sought help in Monterrey. Maclovia was in her early thirties when she shared her story with me.[4]

Mariana

"When we were Catholic, we were a happy family," Mariana said as she recalled her childhood with nostalgia. Now in her early forties, she was born in Ciudad Juárez and lives there to this day. "Once my mother became a 'sister,' *híjole*, jeez, everything changed, everything," Mariana elaborated as she explained that her mother became involved with one of the largest religious groups in the country: the Jehovah's Witnesses.[5] Mariana was ten years old when her family experienced a religious conversion, which meant that she and her siblings had to join the new religion as well. This family transition eventually coincided with an unexpected change in Mariana's relationship with her oldest brother, a sixteen-year-old adolescent at the time.

"And that is when it started, the abuse with me, when he became a Jehovah's Witness," Mariana explained that not long after the conversion, her brother would jump into her bed every night, and although he never undressed her, he apparently tried to while "touching her all over." He engaged in this behavior for about six years, leading Mariana to use a heavy blanket even during hot weather. She was often afraid to sleep because she needed to defend herself from being assaulted. "If I was alert, if he heard that I was tossing around, nothing happened, do you understand? So . . . I tried to never sleep," Mariana said as she explained that her brother would stay in her bed and touch her, but as soon as she woke up, he would leave her immediately. Her mother and an aunt close to her noticed that Mariana started to take long naps during the day and that her school grades dropped. Her mother kept calling her *burra*, meaning that she was "stupid," and punishing her for doing poorly in school. Nobody inquired, however, why this was happening to her. She also grew up comparing herself with her primas, and she always felt "*gorda y fea*—ugly and fat."

"Why do you think he started to abuse you after he becomes a Jehovah's Witness?" I asked Mariana. She said, "Because I think that he had his life just like that, he started his sex life since he was very young. But there [the church] does not allow that. He used to have his *amigas* and everything. Because, that is what we talk about at home, about the way he used to be, he really changed! He used to be very rebellious."

Prior to religious conversion, Mariana's brother had long hair, played his electric guitar, loved the band Deep Purple, and smoked. She said, "He lived his *vida loca*, he went out with young women. He had girlfriends and everything. He was young. His girlfriends were also kind of crazy like him but he dated." Mariana's brother went to prison at least once for something that was not clear to her family, but reportedly took place in the context of group sex, *una orgía*—an orgy, she said. Prior to conversion, this same brother, with his long hair, electric guitar, and involved in sexual activities, was also a respectful and responsible brother who took care of Mariana and her two little siblings in their mother's absence.

"I do not know if it was the religion but you are so repressed in that church," Mariana reflected as she tried to make sense of her experience with her brother. Earlier in the interview, she stated passionately,

> Everything that happened to me happened right after we went to that church. So what I say is that that church made him [that way], because my brother, before he became a [Jehovah's] Witness, we were Catholic. My brother could go out, my brother could have a girlfriend, my brother could go out and dance. But when they stick that in my brother, about masturbation . . . in that church they tell you that it is bad. So I do not justify it, no. But I tell my mother, "in part all of this happened because you started to go to there [church]." And I do not blame God, no. I blame the fact that we are hypocrites when it comes to him. Do you know how I see that religion? It is like when you are coming in, you have this mask and you have to put it on before you come in. And when you leave, you leave it hanging on the wall and you behave differently outside. That is the way I see it. I was a Jehovah's Witness for many years.

Mariana, for instance, recalled her brother's testimony at the salón, the hall where people attending the congregation gathered and listened to him, now as a young man with short hair and morally transformed after giving up his promiscuous past life and embracing a new religion. Paradoxically, the same young man who regretted having an active sex life that also involved group sex was now sexually assaulting his younger sister at night.

"My brother never told me, 'Do not tell anyone,'" Mariana said as she explained that she loved him very much, and although she resented him, she did not develop feelings of hatred toward him. And as she became older, he would buy clothes for her. In addition to her strategies for coping at night, she purposefully spent her school summer vacation with her aunt in El Paso, so at times, she said, she felt safe. But when she was at home, and in spite of their apparently cordial relationship during the day, he consistently assaulted her at night. At the age of twelve or thirteen, Mariana gave her mother a detailed account about it. She told Mariana that she would talk to her brother about it but she never did.

"Why do you think your mother didn't talk to him about it?" I inquired. She said, "My mother always loved him very much. And also, everyone loved him. In the salón he was a very good son. My aunts . . . ¡Uy! [loved him], because he was a very good son. He helped my mother and everyone loved him." A live-in maid raising her four children as a single mother, Mariana's mother was deeply grateful to her son, a hardworking and responsible young man who represented the only additional and stable financial income in the family. Besides protecting her son's good image, Mariana believed, her mother was afraid of losing the financial support he represented for her and the entire family.

"I have to leave this house, I cannot stay here, my mother does not do anything about it!" Mariana recalled her past deliberations as she explained that at the age of sixteen she immediately accepted her boyfriend's marriage proposal and arranged her wedding in about a month. Mariana's brother never assaulted her again. A few years later, however, she had no words to explain what had just happened to her brother. Mariana had a disturbing dream that her brother was killed in an accident. In an effort to protect him, she told him about her dream, but that did not prevent the tragedy. Shortly after, when he was in his mid-twenties, he was killed in a work-related accident. To this day, Mariana feels responsible for his death.

Also a member of the Jehovah's Witnesses congregation, Mariana's husband eventually learned why she was so excited about marrying him when they were young, and he has been supportive of her. After more than twenty-five years of marriage, however, both are still working out emotionally exhausting tensions in their relationship and sex life, which has been adversely affected by Mariana's experience with her brother.

A few years ago, Mariana left the Jehovah's Witnesses congregation after her oldest son confided in her about the sexual violence that he experienced from the age of eight until he was fifteen years old at the hands of an *anciano*, a high-ranking representative known in English as an "elder". This authority figure within the Jehovah's Witnesses congregation happened to be the brother of Mariana's husband. In a recent casual family conversation, Mariana learned about her mother and her mother's sister being sexually abused many years ago by their oldest brother—something her aunt perceived as "normal." I met Mariana at a community-based organization in Ciudad Juárez where she sought professional help to understand why all of this had happened to her family.

Rocío

"There are two kinds of *abusadores* (men who abuse)—soft and violent. And those who are soft, they manipulate you, those who sweeten the pill to screw a victim. And those who are violent rely on the hard blow," Rocío from Guadalajara stated as she explained that her brother was the soft kind. She described him as an attentive and caring man who gave her gifts. He was also gentle, affectionate, and tender in his everyday interactions with her. She also identified her brother as a "schizophrenic man" who could be violent toward animals, but as someone who had a job. "I never saw him under the effect of alcohol or drugs, or out of control," she said. However, he "masturbated in excess" and frequently had to be chased out of brothels by their father who felt embarrassed by a son who spent lots of money on sex workers. Her brother had a relationship and made plans to marry one of them, but he broke up with her when his father threatened to disinherit him.

Born in an upper-class family that migrated from a pueblo to Guadalajara, Rocío described herself as the granddaughter of a wealthy hacienda owner and the daughter of a hardworking, successful businessman. A college-educated woman who attended private Catholic institutions since elementary school, she is the youngest child in a family of more than six children, and she was ten years old when her oldest brother was in his early thirties. In her memory, that is the age when she recalls a clearly unpleasant sensation of his warm body next to hers, touching her in her sleep especially right before waking up. Now in her early forties, she recalls the experience happening on different occasions between the ages of ten and fourteen, but she does not recall for how long or if anything else happened. She believes the experiences "opened up her sexuality," especially as she felt the need to explore and touch her own body. As an assertive girl who grew up feeling unafraid of "opening her mouth," she is certain that he never told her to not tell anyone. However, she grew up feeling "*sucia y confundida*—dirty and confused" and kept silent. As she came of age, she felt more encouraged to talk.

"We started to put two and two together," Rocío said as she explained that she was between twenty and twenty-two years old when she talked about it with her older sister closest to her in age. After her sister confirmed having similar experiences with him as well, both decided to talk to their mother, but she did not believe them. Later, Rocío was upset but not surprised to learn that her other three sisters have been similarly silent about their individual, coercive experiences with their brother. He had also touched them in their sleep, and he also spied on them while they took showers. Eventually, each one told their mother about these experiences. Their mother might have believed her five daughters to an extent, but she didn't seem to believe the degree of the "damage." Why?

"My sister so and so bled when she had sex for the first time, and my other sister, and my other sister. In other words, all of the daughters bled. And well, my other sister as well! Oh, my God!" Rocío said while laughing and explaining that she and the rest of the daughters in the family were "technical virgins" when they married—something her mother knew about. Rocío also said that she knew that her mother was in a predicament. She explained, "My mother never believed. Or she played dumb, I think. Frankly, I think my mother always knew about it but she was afraid that my father would kill my brother. My father was very violent." Rocío recalled episodes of her father "beating her up until he got tired" as she described the harsh physical punishment he used to discipline her as she grew up. Although Rocío's parents "fought silently," she recalls listening to her father calling her mother "dumb" and "illiterate." "They hurt each other psychologically," she said.

Rocío's oldest brother died in his early sixties from a series of health-related complications, a few years prior to our interview. Her father had already passed away years earlier. As Rocío and her sisters have finally tried to make sense of their experiences with their brother, another brother in the family has reminded them to be silent. "What happened is already in the past, and he is already dead," Rocío paraphrased his reaction when the topic has emerged in family conversations.

While Rocío believes that the experiences with her brother did not affect her sexually, she is concerned about the extent to which these have affected her relationship with her husband. She recently separated from him out of concern that he might be "sexually abusing" her five-year-old daughter. I met Rocío in Guadalajara through a professional who knew about her story.

Valeria

Valeria from Mexico City is the youngest of four children and the only daughter in a middle-class family. Now in her mid-twenties, she was four or five years old when her eleven-year-old brother (the second of the children) suddenly assaulted her. She recalled,

> That day they left us alone at home and my brother started to be very aggressive with me, started to pull me, he started to grab my hair, and started to hit me and started to tell me, to threaten me that if I tell anything of what was going to happen, well, I do not remember well what the threat was. But he hit me, hit me and hit me. There was never penetration, it was simply the touch, the touch of his penis in the middle of my legs. Well, finally, he finished and my oldest brother got home. My brother locked me up in the restroom and told my (oldest) brother that he had punished me for I do not know what reason. And I spent about two hours locked inside the bathroom. Time passed, I came out of the bathroom and well, later my mother got home, my dad got home, and they accused me of doing I do not know what. And I was with the fear of saying anything because he would hit me [teary voice] . . . and all of that I . . . Then a long time passed by, and he started doing the same thing again.

From the ages of four or five to eight, Valeria experienced similar versions of this scenario at the hands of her brother. When she was eight, her parents separated and she moved in with her grandmother while her brother stayed with her father and the violence stopped. However, she reported, "my brother would come to see me, he was always with us and with the intention of doing the same again. And as an excuse I would go to see my aunt or stay the entire time by my grandmother's side, I was glued to my grandmother." Her attentive and loving grandmother passed away when Valeria was about ten years old and she had no choice but to return to live with her father and her three brothers. The physical and sexual violence started all over again. Her brother's assaults ended when she turned thirteen years old. She said, "He stopped because I did not allow it anymore, the moment to, well, I felt more courage and if he hit me, I hit back." She clarified for me that prior to the first incident of violence her brother's behavior was close and affectionate. This made the onset of the first episode of sexual violence especially drastic and unexpected. After that, his engagement with her was never pleasurable and always involved physical and emotional aggression.

Valeria has never told her parents or anyone in her family about these experiences. "You tell anything and the worst is going to happen to you, puta!" Valeria mimicked her brother's harsh voice as she repeated the "threat that was recorded" in her mind since she was little. When her mother or father inquired about her bruises or cuts, she made up stories about falling on the floor. "What is the problem between both of you?" her father inquired frequently as they became older, but, out of fear, Valeria never said a word. At times she was tempted to break her silence, but she was always too afraid.

Over time, Valeria was able to distance herself from her brother when he left the family home in his early twenties. Valeria was stunned, however, when he returned later for a family visit and was supportive, loving, and generous, asking her if she needed a car, or anything, that he could buy it for her. "Like compensating for his guilt," Valeria said as she explained that she had rejected his proposals while witnessing how successful he had become as a salesman.

The relationship between her parents had involved emotional and physical violence on her father's part, and Valeria described her relationship with them as distant and lacking trust. After they separated and as she became older, her college-educated father became more loving and supportive toward her, while her relationship with her mother became "exhausting," especially as her mother coped with depression and struggled to keep stable paid employment. Valeria obtained her first job at the age of fourteen and began to take care of her mother and assumed financial responsibility for her. At the time of the interview, they still lived together.

"They were never at home, never," Valeria asserted as she explained that her parents' difficult relationship and their divorce—which was followed by "abandonment and carelessness"—were responsible for what her brother did to her. "Perhaps my brother found refuge in something, I do not know," she said. In addition, although her parents taught her openly about sex-related issues and reproductive health, ironically, they did not teach her "how to defend herself" from her brothers or other men.

Valeria has had dreams in which she has confronted her brother. Eventually, she said, she would like to heal and forgive him some day. Her sex life has been satisfying, although recently the quality has deteriorated. She said she would like to ask for professional help to explore both her sex life and the sexual violence she experienced with her brother. To this day, only her boyfriend of six years knows what happened to Valeria and he has been supportive of her.

* * *

The stories of Alfonsina, Maclovia, Mariana, Rocío, and Valeria are distinctive because of the length of time over which the abusive encounters were sustained, becoming part of a life stage, and leaving a deep imprint as a consequence. These women recalled experiences such as "he abused me from X age to Y age" as part of everyday life and family life.

In other cases, women described experiences of sexual violence that were less frequent. Although not less painful, they were not necessarily part of a life stage, and at times included sexual violence by more than one brother. Some women did not recall exact ages of these events, which at times were circumstantial or situational. What the events had in common was the absence of physical violence. Although their accounts are shorter in duration and less violent, they are informative and revealing.

Inés

"I do not know why it evokes this much pain," Inés said as she described an episode she experienced when she was five or six years old. Now in her early thirties, she recalled her underwear being down to her knees and lying on the bed in front of her nine-year-old brother, who also had his underwear down. "At that moment, I see one of my brothers coming in," she said, explaining that something was going to happen but it was interrupted by their older brother who walked in and threatened them, 'What are you doing? I am going to tell mom that you are doing bad things,' or something like that. And that was it. I recall that from that point on I lived with so much fear, fear that he would tell my mother." Although the experience she described happened only once, Inés grew up feeling "deeply damaged and very fearful," especially toward her mother.

Born and raised in Ciudad Júarez, Inés grew up in a family of seven children; she had four older brothers and the oldest child and youngest children were girls. When compared to her "pretty sister in the family," Inés described herself as a girl who was "ugly, dark skinned, and fat." A few years after the "incident" with her brother, Inés's younger sister confided that when she was four or five and he was twelve or so, she had a similar experience. Her sister told her, "That he wanted to touch her, in her vagina. She said, 'we are playing and he wants to touch me and I do not want to.'" Inés became protective of her sister. "*Somos muy unidas*," Inés said, meaning that she and her sister supported each other emotionally and morally as they grew up. They never told their mother or father about their personal experiences with their brother. Why? She explained,

> Fear of telling them about it . . . because they were going to react violently, but I do not know, fear that they are not going to believe in you. Fear of . . . fear . . . I felt guilty of it, as if I had provoked that. As if I had participated in this, and [fear of] what they were going to tell me. Because my brother walked in and saw, I was afraid of what they were going to say, that both of us did it. I do not know, like feeling guilt. Yes.

Inés described her mother as "a person with the problem of a very strong personality" who punished her harshly while growing up, especially with regard to issues pertaining to sexuality. She gave an example. "My mother told us that a girl she knew had put a stick inside her vagina . . . and then she said, 'if you do the same, they will take you to the police, they take you to jail for doing that.' And I . . . ay! I wanted to die! I said, how awful! I do not know why my mother said those things."

In comparison to her father, Inés described her mother thus: "She hit us. My dad was a saint, *un pan de Dios* (literally, "a bread of God"). We adored him. But my mother was violent, she became angry." Inés also stated that, "my mother was jealous of me, with regard to my father. Yes, my mother fought a lot with me because she said that my father loved me a lot, and that whatever I said he would listen to. Well . . . I do not know . . . kind of strange." Inés said that her father was attentive and concerned about his youngest two daughters—both girls were his *consentidas*—something their mother and brothers resented. Inés identified her father as an "excellent provider" and her mother as "absent from home for long periods of time to talk with neighbors." The latter, she said, triggered in her feelings of "being abandoned and disoriented" and the "lack of care, attention, and communication" from her mother toward her daughters as the main reasons why she thought her brother assaulted her and her sister.

Inés did not know about other cases of sexual violence in her family. However, she recalled two events. First, when one of her brothers became married, he moved in with his wife. Shortly after, Inés learned that another brother had "grabbed her sister-in-law from behind." "Because my family hides things," she said, "supposedly, my mother did her best so we did not learn about it." And second, her oldest sister was an adolescent when an unknown man broke into their house one night and sexually assaulted her. Her mother never talked with her directly about it. Instead, she asked someone close to her (a friend, or a relative, Inés did not recall who), to tell her sister "to put a little mirror down there to find out if something had happened to her." Inés never knew why her mother beat up her oldest sister so intensely, even more harshly in comparison with the way she treated her and her little sister.

I met Inés at the organization where she sought professional help to cope with a challenging divorce after her husband confessed about his extramarital relationships. And although apparently "nothing happened to her" and she does not have any other memories, Inés reported feeling deeply hurt by the experience with her brother. Other than her current partner, a supportive man, and me, she has told no one about her experience.

Juliana

"Let's go and play, ah . . . nothing is going to happen to you, ah . . . it is a nice game," Juliana from Guadalajara recalled as she imitated her oldest brother's voice. Now in her early thirties, she was nine years old and he was eleven or twelve when he used these seductive words to entice her into oral sex. She felt confused and manipulated by a brother who consistently told her "I love you very much" while also threatening her to remain silent. In the midst of these episodes, he eventually penetrated her vaginally. "Do not tell mom about this, if she learns about this, you are the one who is going to be punished, not me," or "Do not tell my mom, she would feel really bad, she would feel very sad." Juliana recalled the messages he gave her as she also learned a distinctive pattern in his behavior. He was never physically violent as long as she did not resist when he approached her sexually, but he hit her every time she defended herself and rejected him. "I would be thinking, 'I hope he is done soon, I hope he is done soon, I hope he is done soon, I hope this pain is over soon.'" This became Juliana's inner dialog as she learned to surrender in order to avoid physical violence. In the midst of these repeated episodes, Juliana experienced intense physical pain and could not walk or sit afterward, but was afraid to tell her mother.

About the same time, Juliana's younger brother started to imitate her oldest brother's behavior. He was a year or two younger than her when Juliana's oldest brother "induced" him to behave similarly. Very soon, he started to sexually assault and threaten Juliana. However, her younger brother also intervened and protected her when her oldest brother used physical violence. "I feel like my younger brother was also a victim. He was a victim because he did something out of obligation," Juliana said, as she was convinced that her younger brother had been forced by her oldest brother to behave that way. Although Juliana was not able to explain what exactly disrupted her brothers' behaviors of sexual violence, she noticed that these episodes did not last more than a year. Juliana was the second oldest child in a family of two sons and two daughters; her sister was the youngest in the family.

As Juliana grew up, she did not tell anyone about the abuse. Her silence was reinforced by her fear of being stigmatized and rejected, especially as she learned at her Catholic school about how "dirty this was because she was no longer a virgin" and "sex with anyone was a sin, a sin that you commit that causes pain, family pain." However, she could not keep her secret for too long. When Juliana resisted her mother's interest in enrolling her in a *secundaria técnica* (similar to trade school), her mother was curious about why she would not like to attend a school that is traditionally overrepresented by male students. Juliana finally revealed her secret to her parents in front of her two brothers. Her brothers blamed her and her father also accused her. With tears, she recalled her father's words, "You are the only one who is guilty of this, because you provoked them." Her mother was in shock initially, but she was eventually loving and supportive. She urged Juliana to seek professional help.

A divorced, college-educated woman raising children, Juliana did not know about other cases of sexual violence in her family, but she witnessed physical violence within her immediate family and from both sides of her extended family. "We had everything, the best toy, the best doll," she said while explaining that her upper-middle-class parents compensated for the emotional absence through expensive gifts and toys. During the same period of time when she was the target of her brothers' sexual violence, Juliana's maternal uncle used a doll to manipulate her, forcing her to masturbate him and give him hugs. He told her that "it was play" and to be silent about it; he was in his late teens. The abuse happened frequently, lasted for about a year, and stopped the day he became ill and died. She never told anyone about her uncle.

Ofelia

Now in her mid-forties and married with children, Ofelia grew up with her grandparents, an upper-middle-class, hardworking, business-driven couple from Mexico City. She was the youngest of the daughters in a family of origin consisting of seven children. Although she did not have frequent contact with her parents and siblings, occasional contact with her brothers at times involved sexual coercion. Of her four brothers, three of them actively maneuvered her into a variety of sexual activities, at different ages and in various circumstances:

- She was eight when her oldest brother, who was twelve or thirteen, induced her into caresses that eventually led to vaginal penetration. "You know what? This person did the same to me," Ofelia recalled telling her brother, explaining that she had confided to him about the many times that, for about a year, her grandfather's business assistant raped her when she was seven or eight. Her brother was surprised to learn about it. In retrospect, Ofelia is shocked that this news did not stop him. For about a month during school vacation, her brother actively looked for her and engaged her in these activities, which she thought of "like playing." She bled one time, and out of fear—she believed—her brother never sought her out again.
- When she was ten years old, another brother who was one year older than she also approached and fondled her. She "touched" him as well. These experiences happened on different occasions and, as with her oldest brother, she thought it was "like playing."
- "¡¿Otra vez?!—Again?!" Ofelia told herself in silence and with deep sadness when the youngest of her brothers stretched out his arms to hold her and gently rubbed his penis against her body. They were sharing the only bed available as the family tried to figure out how to accommodate their relatives who were visiting for a wedding. Ofelia got up immediately and left the scene. She was eighteen and he was fifteen.

"There was never violence, of any type, they never hit me, nothing . . . [but] . . . why did it happen so many times?! Why did I allow it?! I am realizing that . . . perhaps what I was looking for with these sexual relations was affection . . . Maybe, I do not know!" Ofelia said, enraged and confused as she explained that her uncle (one of her mother's first cousins) also coerced her into sexualized activities. In general, she said, none of them ever told her to be silent about it. The experience with her grandfather's business assistant affected her the most, she said. He was a trusted family friend who took care of her while her grandfather traveled. She thought that because her grandparents were absent, busy working hard and perhaps "too old" to take care of her, she had these experiences.

Ofelia's best friend—a woman who was also raped—is the only person who knows her full story. Some of her sisters and aunts know about what happened with her grandparents' friend.

Renata

As explained in the first pages of this book, Renata was the woman who sobbed with raging tears during our interview. In pain, she described the dispersed but clear and graphic memories she began to experience with shock and confusion after she and her husband attended a spiritual retreat the year before we met in Mexico City. She has no doubt that her oldest brother forced her to have sex with him when she was four or six and he was seventeen or nineteen. Now in her mid-thirties, she also has memories of another brother, who was thirteen or fourteen when she was six and who touched her in a way that did not feel right. According to her recollections, these were the only two episodes, one time with each brother. There may have been additional experiences with the same brothers, but she did not remember; she hopes that was not the case. She clearly recalls at least one occasion in which she experienced a physical response of pleasure. Although she had a closer and more meaningful relationship with the younger of her two brothers, they both used affectionate language with her, frequently calling her *chiquita*—the little one. As they grew into adolescence, both brothers were involved in (and eventually left) student activities involving organized violence, which are frequently identified in Mexico as *porros*.[6]

The youngest in a family of seven children, Renata was raised in an upper-middle-class family that was concerned about the threats and risks of the outside world. She and all of her siblings completed college while indulging in an urban lifestyle of affluence and comfort, private schools, and at least one family vacation to Europe. Renata's parents, now deceased, would have been shocked and heartbroken if they had only known what she experienced with her brothers, she said. She has told her sisters about it, yet she does not know if she will ever confront her brothers. In fact, she learned that a paternal uncle sexually abused one of Renata's sisters—a well-kept family secret that was revealed to her not long ago. Renata also shared that between ages four and six, her father's brother, a man in his forties who suffered from schizophrenia, fondled her. At the age of eight or nine, a male cousin who was older than she sexually assaulted her in the swimming pool.

How did Renata explain what happened to her with her brothers? "Everyday life, reality is bigger than you," she said as she explained that her parents' priority was to "give us a place to live, food to eat, and clothing to wear . . . there was no time to talk, to have a conversation." They were "invested," she said, in "their role as providers." Also, as a girl she felt especially vulnerable. "At home, I never felt seen," she said, as she explained that "sons were seen" and that genuine communication and trust were absent from family life. Earlier in the interview, she explained, "My mother had that mentality, you know, 'You have to pay attention to your brothers, you have to serve your brothers,' and with me, this was very strong. She had these things well-rooted in her mind," Renata said as she explained that, "it is shocking but very likely" that daughters are trained at home "to become objects and to not be seen. In Mexico, that happens a lot, a lot."

Bright, articulate, and college educated, Renata was in her mid-thirties when we met in Mexico City in 2006. She was happily married to a successful professional, college-educated man who has been kind and supportive in helping her to heal from the events she endured with her brothers.

Rosana

"He was an affectionate lover," said Rosana from Mexico City, referring to her oldest brother. Now in her mid-forties, she was eight years old and he was eighteen when an experience that she now vividly recalls took place: "He took me to a room where there was a bed and pulled down my underwear, pulled up my dress and touched my belly. Ah . . . he touched my vagina, in other words, he touched the vulva with his hand, and also with his mouth. He made me open my legs and touched me. He sat on a chair, with his pants on and rubbed me against him, in other words, [he rubbed himself against] my butt."

Rosana also explained why she thought her brother was "an affectionate lover." She said, "He took out his penis, and I almost had a heart attack, and he put it back inside and said, 'well, if you do not like it like this, well, I will be done soon.'" This experience happened at least twice, but he was never physically violent. He also gave her gifts.

The youngest daughter in a family of six children, Rosana was born and raised in Mexico City while listening to her mother saying that "she lived in sin." Rosana's mother ran away from a ranch located in Central Mexico in order to establish a permanent relationship with a married man with children—Rosana's father. Rosana identified her father as "absent," "not affectionate," and "weak" and her mother as "the one in charge, a bitch, devaluing my father—just like me." In her relationships, she behaved in similar ways to her mother, she said. "He was the good one, I was the bitch," she asserted, as she described the ways in which she emotionally "humiliated" a partner of twelve years she had broken up with recently.

Rosana's father lived with them and worked in full-time, low-income modest jobs while her mother also worked hard, full-time as a *comerciante*, buying and selling goods. In their absence, the oldest adolescent siblings took care of the younger children, Rosana's oldest sister substituted for her mother.

Although Rosana does not recall being exposed to any threats, her brother "locked her up" in the room where he sexually abused her. She recalled feeling intense fear but also a sensation of physical pleasure as part of the coercive experience. Shortly after, Rosana started to masturbate, an experience that she eventually associated with fear and guilt. "You are guilty of it, that is the reason why he is doing to you what he is doing to you! You are a *cabrona* (bitch)! You are a *pendeja* (dumbass)! You are *hija de la chingada* (a low-down bitch)!" Rosana recalled her mother's raging words the first time she caught her masturbating. Her mother also beat her up harshly and pulled her by the hair in an episode that was followed by her mother's persistent surveillance to make sure that Rosana did not "provoke" any of her brothers.

"That hurt me more than the abuse," Rosana said as she explained that her mother's punitive intervention might have protected her from her brother "abusing from her" in the future but left a deep impression on her. "And the truth is," she said, "there was always masculine domination in the home. We, the women, were second-class. We were always made to feel that way, to this day. And my brothers, whatever the fucking hell they did, they were always accepted."

After the first wife of Rosana's father passed away, Rosana's mother adopted the children from his previous relationship. "I saw strange things," Rosana said as she explained what she witnessed after her half-siblings moved in:

- Rosana's oldest half-brother and her oldest sister established a relationship, but it was difficult to know if it was sexually coercive and abusive or voluntary and romantic. Rosana also suspects he "sexually abused" his own biological sister.
- Another half-brother spied on Rosana's oldest sister when she took a shower. He used to call her sister "negra."
- "Her abuse hurts me more than my own," Rosana said as she explained that she wished she had intervened when she was ten years old and saw two of her teenage brothers "sexually molesting," one at a time, her four- or five-year-old niece. She was the daughter of Rosana's oldest sister who was raised by her parents. One of them also abused the youngest boy in the family.

"What happened with my brother hurt me a lot, but what hurt me even more was all of the things that were allowed, all of the things that this señora allowed," Rosana said as she explained that her mother was fully aware of what happened at home. "But she might have suffered, just like me," she clarified. As she referred to her mother, Rosana said, "At times I hate her, I feel disdain for her, at times I feel incredible love for her."

"I already forgave my brother, I do not know, [maybe] about ten years ago. He was not responsible. He was a product of a very strange family. He was born . . . he grew up seeing things. What else was he supposed to do?" Rosana said. She explained that her brother had to work hard on the busy streets of Mexico City when he was ten or eleven years old to contribute to the family; he worked late at night and sex workers of all ages became his companions. "I do not know what he went through as a child. Otherwise, he had not abused me," she said. She further elaborated, "My brother molested me because he was told that sex was bad and because he wanted to test whether it was bad. And how is it possible that what makes you feel so good is also bad? So he had to be taught about this with her, right? Because 'She' [me] was part of his own family. And because that is where the prohibition was, as Freud would say."[7]

Rosana identified herself as a *bulímica* and said "food has been my comfort" after what happened with her brother, a way to punish herself for the pleasure she experienced with him. She has attended group support sessions for people who use food to cope with emotional pain. Out of shame, however, she has never talked about the experiences with her brother in these meetings. A psychology major, Rosana completed college and eventually established a thriving learning center where she passionately promotes the human rights of children. By doing so, she feels she has finally reconciled in some way with the inner girl who was so deeply hurt. She has never been in therapy.

Other women who reported experiences of sexual violence by brothers identified them as isolated events. For some of these women, the experiences with their brothers did not represent the most relevant accounts of sexual violence in our interviews. However, these stories share some commonalities with the other stories discussed in this section.

Natalia

A married woman from Mexico City, Natalia explained that not long ago her oldest brother fondled her breasts "playfully." Now in her midthirties, she has always been afraid of confronting him because he is "closed-minded, arrogant, and irritable." Natalia and her oldest brother, and a younger sister, all share a common history: their uncle got them naked simultaneously and sexually abused them when they were children. The uncle was expected to care for them while their mother was absent, working long hours to support them. Natalia was also the target of sexual violence of other men in her family including her father, her mother's stepfather, and her father-in-law. Natalia also learned that her mother and her daughter were exposed to sexual violence within her family. "Most men are machistas, their word is the law, perhaps that is the reason why it happens so often," Natalia said as she explained that lack of parental attention, information, and "bad luck" were also responsible for what happened with her brother. In the next chapter I explore Natalia's story with her uncle in more depth.

Luisa

She was eight years old when her eighteen-year-old brother forced her to masturbate him several times. A mother of three children in her mid-forties and currently in a cohabiting relationship with a man in Ciudad Juárez, Luisa recalled the lack of privacy and vulnerability she experienced while growing up in a family where fifteen relatives from her immediate and extended family lived in her parents' house. Her parents had eleven children; the youngest five children were girls and she was in the middle. Luisa's parents generously welcomed at home some of their married children who were experiencing financial difficulties, which meant that a spouse and children automatically moved in as well. Luisa's parents had the privacy of their own bedroom and enjoyed a relationship of apparent mutual respect.

Besides her brother, Luisa experienced different forms of sexual violence with her brother-in-law and her nephew. Both molested Luisa's daughter and two of her nieces. Her brother-in-law exposed himself to and molested the children in the family and raped one of the boys, Luisa's nephew. When she reported all of these events to her parents, they did not believe her; she felt ignored. With regard to her brother-in-law assaulting her, her mother told her, "you want to destroy your sister's marriage." "¡A la jodida! We are in deep shit! How in the world am I going to put up with this!" Luisa exclaimed as she explained that the sexual violence stopped when she eventually moved out, a few years prior to our interview.

How did Luisa explain all of this, especially the experience with her brother? She said, "Because all of us were right there, tangled and everything. And people see things that they should not see. I put the blame on this." She also blamed her parents, especially her father, for not teaching the men to respect the women in the family. She also used the words *maniático*—maniac, and *mañoso*—sly, to refer to the men in their family who have assaulted her, men "who cannot be happy without touching a woman." As she considered why her brother-in-law sexually assaulted her, she said, "My sister did not give it [sex] to her husband so he was looking for it and in order to get a revenge or compensate, he came to me. But nothing ever happened. Why? Because I, by myself, I defended myself."

Understanding Brother-Sister Incest

As illustrated through these stories, the women I interviewed experienced complex forms of sexual violence at the hands of their biological brothers. As sisters and daughters, they had unique and different relationships with their brothers and their parents, respectively. However, these women share common patterns. Some of these include the following.

Sister-brother relationship. A sister-brother relationship may vary with regard to the quality of emotional relationship between siblings. Before their experiences of sexual violence, some women described loving, close, and emotionally meaningful relationships with their brothers, others had already experienced distance, conflict, and tension in these family connections, and others were somewhere in between these possibilities. Although some women reported feelings of love and concern for a brother (even after the experiences of sexual violence took place), the occurrence of sexual violence frequently damaged the quality of these family relationships.

Daughter-mother relationship. The daughter-mother relationship also had contrasting emotional arrangements and expressions, which included women's feelings and attitudes toward their mothers, as well as women's reports of their mothers' reactions toward them, especially after they learned about the abuse. The daughter-mother relationship reflected a wide emotional spectrum, ranging from a daughter who feels love, care, respect, and closeness toward the maternal figure, to a daughter who experiences fear, tension, and distance toward her. Women experienced emotional possibilities between both extremes, including, but not limited to, ambivalence or mixed feelings of love and rage toward a mother who is absent or disempowered. These feelings alternated and/or combined at different stages in their personal lives, especially depending on how a mother reacted when she learned about the experience of abuse. Women did not always tell the mother about their experiences with their brothers (and only a minority of mothers seemed to know about it). The responses of those who did learn about it ranged from blaming the daughter for "provoking" the brother and punishing her, to eventually becoming supportive of the daughter. In between, however, mothers reacted in unexpected ways, often leaving the daughter feeling neglected and unprotected. Some of those who had kept a secret were aware of a mother's potential predicament: a mother may feel emotionally divided and conflicted if she only knew that her son had sexually abused one of her daughters.

Daughter-father relationship. The daughter-father relationship of these women also had contrasting and complex possibilities; these reactions reflect the women's feelings toward their fathers, as well as their reports of their fathers' reactions toward them as daughters, especially after they learned about the abuse. Like the range of daughter-mother relationships, the daughter-father relationship reflected a continuum, which included feelings of love, care, respect, closeness, and at times idealization toward the father figure, to a daughter who grew up feeling fear and emotional distance toward a father who was perceived as emotionally and/or physically absent or weak. At times, women did not tell a father about their experiences out of fear of negative consequences, such as a father killing a brother. In the few cases where fathers learned about a son abusing a daughter, they either made the daughter responsible for it, or did not believe her or ignored her. Women who were raised by single mothers (or their grandparents) seemed to have feelings of nostalgia toward a father who was physically and emotionally absent.

Women's perceptions of their parents. Women develop specific perceptions of their mothers and fathers when they identify them as a couple and as parents, especially as they make sense of their experiences with their brothers. As a couple, parents are perceived as responsible for the sexual abuse, especially when they were physically or emotionally absent, unavailable, and clueless for a variety of reasons, including but not limited to divorce, conflict, a busy routine, work, and survival. Parents who are silent or secretive with regard to sexual matters and/or who associate sex with punishment and something "dirty" are also seen as responsible for the experience of sexual abuse. For women raised by parents in a traditional marital arrangement (i.e., the father is a full-time hardworking provider and the mother is a full-time housewife), the father may be perceived as ideal for working hard and supporting the family, while the mother is blamed for not "doing her job," that is, offering attention and care, and thus neglecting and not communicating with her children, especially her daughters. Regardless, a daughter may be critical of a father for not teaching sons to be men who should be respectful toward women. In all cases, women explained emotional, physical, or sexual violence as part of complex histories of sexual violence within and beyond their immediate families.

Women's interpretation of their experiences. Women interpret and make sense of their experiences of sexual violence as they try to explain a brother's behavior. Elements of these explanations include, first, a brother who sexually abuses a sister does so in response to external social forces including but not limited to (a) boys coming of age and being stimulated by pornography or sex activity in a home that lacks privacy; (b) boys becoming victims of the system, that is, being raised in a dysfunctional home, early exposure to commercial sex, and poverty; (c) young men being exposed to sexually repressive Christian religious discourses promoting double morality; and (d) boys using violence against a sister as an outlet to coping with challenging life experiences such as a parents' divorce. And second, perceiving a brother as a "helpless man" who, at best, is sexually curious but exploring sex in the wrong place, and at worst, is a "maniac" or a "sly" man who "needs to touch women," or "a sick man" with unmet emotional and sexual needs.

Expressions and patterns of sexual violence. Sexual violence occurs in multiple yet consistent expressions and patterns. First, sexual violence against a sister may last many years (sometimes more than ten years), or may be a one-time "incident" or experience. Regardless of the duration, the experience leaves a deep imprint in a girl's life, especially with regard to how a given life stage (i.e., childhood or adolescence), sexuality, and relationships are experienced. Second, coercive sex does not always involve physical force, and a brother may use expressions of affection and exquisite psychological manipulation as part of the experience that is presented as "play" or "a game," and at times including gifts and money. Third, a form of serial incest, the brother who exercised coercive sex against a sister may have tried the same with another sister; and, more than one brother may sexually assault a sister, an activity that is at times orchestrated collectively between brothers. In half of the cases, other men in the family also exercised violence against these women, including but not limited to fathers, cousins, uncles, grandfathers, in-laws, and *amigos de la familia*. Fourth, a girl is not always exposed to threats or told to be silent about the experience, which causes a myriad of mixed feelings, with confusion and fear at the core. Fifth, in most cases, women recall their experiences as painful and disgusting, and for the minority that identified feelings of physical pleasure, this is also associated with guilt and shame. Sixth, although half of the women were the youngest child or the youngest daughter in the family, women occupy other birth order placement in their families, such as the second to the oldest child, the oldest daughter, the one in the middle, or one of the youngest children, especially in large families. And finally, more than half of the cases reflect the image of a girl who is not older than ten years old and an adolescent brother when the first incident took place. Although in most cases brothers are considerably older than their sisters, the girls were not always passive but fought back, resisted, and explored ways to cope, especially as they became older and physically bigger and stronger.

How do we explain the experiences of these women with their brothers? Some of the dynamics responsible seem to have roots in the same processes that are responsible for conjugal daughters and marital servants. Gendered servitude, for example, may explain a brother's expectation to be "served" by a sister beyond the wide array of household activities traditionally assigned to girls and women in families, crossing a blurry and fine line to have some of his sexual needs and urges met by her as well. Beyond this general interpretation, I offer more specific, feminist informed reflections in the next section.

Family Sex Surrogacy

"Here in Mexico, men are expected to know about all of these things about sex, and it is also important that a man does not ridicule himself [sexually] with anyone. So, to prevent that, it is better for the man to learn about sex with a sister, right?" With a tone of sarcasm and while being harshly critical of what some people believe to be true, this is the assertion presented by a Mexico City psychotherapist with more than ten years of experience in prevention and treatment of sexual violence with women and their families. In her professional practice, she has learned, for instance, that women recall the onset of their complex histories of rape or sexual assault by a brother at specific ages in their lives, very frequently while the woman was attending elementary school and her brother was in his adolescent years, attending *secundaria*. "Why is that?" I asked. She explained, "Something is going on with the sex education of adolescent young men who do not dare to initiate their sex life with someone outside the house, and they do it with a sister, and in general, they take the little one in the family." She did not elaborate on the arguably complex reasons why the adolescent men she referred to may not take risks to explore sex outside of their families. Her insightful reflections, however, echo the testimonies of the women I interviewed and suggest the following interpretation of the incestuous arrangements: the wide array of expressions of sexualized violence by an older brother toward a younger sister (from isolated experiences to systematic coercive sex and rape) reveal the specific functions the latter may play vis-à-vis the former.[8] That is, as a sister becomes sexualized and sexually objectified by her brother in these incestuous families, she becomes the sex object who was also trained to engage in gendered servitude (i.e., serving others in her family), becoming, in the end, what I call a "family sex surrogate." As a family sex surrogate, a sister is the sex object who serves specific sexual functions for a brother, especially as he comes of age in a patriarchal family that is frequently silent, clueless, and/or punishing about matters related to sex, and the ultimate conduit to reproduce complex ideologies and practices that oppress women in larger society.

"A sister is like an inflatable doll," said a psychotherapist during a workshop discussion I facilitated in Monterrey in 2013. In her extensive expertise with cases of sexual abuse of girls, boys, and women, she recalled the case of a young man she worked with as a clinician who candidly confided, "*Tenía ganas y no sabía con quién*—I had a sexual urge and I did not know with whom." The young man sexually approached his younger sister.

Symbolically speaking, while Mexican society gives plastic dolls to girls to play with, to be socially trained with, and to engage in their early performances as mamá and papá in a heterosexual marriage, in these incestuous families, these same girls become the sex dolls of their brothers as these young men play, learn, and practice their first life lessons about heterosexuality, hegemonic masculinity, and patriarchy. A sister who becomes a family sex surrogate becomes the temporary sexual substitute, the sex doll of a sexually curious coming-of-age brother who may "use" her to discover and learn about the labyrinths of emotional manipulation, affection, seduction, secrecy, and adventure in relationships with women; to explore strategic ways to use pornographic material; and to engage in delicate and nuanced, as well as brutal and grotesque practices to control women, emotionally, sexually, and physically. A little sister who becomes a family sex surrogate offers an older brother the opportunity to explore his sex life in a relatively safe way from his gender, age, body size, and physical strength privileges. In these processes of sexualized violence, these young men become young hetero-patriarchs in training. In the words of radical feminist intellectual Catharine MacKinnon, "Male sexuality is apparently activated by violence against women and expresses itself in violence against women to a significant extent."[9]

Isaías is one of the men I interviewed and his story illustrates these dynamics. Now in his early twenties, Isaías is the only man in this study who reported engaging in sexual exchanges with a biological sister during a long, sustained period of time. The oldest child in a large working-class family from Guadalajara, he explained that he was about ten and his sister was seven years old when the sexualized exchanges between both started "like playing" and later became "an experience" for both of them. Both siblings started to touch one another, naked at night or when their parents were not at home during the day; these exchanges were sustained routinely and lasted for about eight years. However, by the time he was fifteen or sixteen, he was already becoming aware of something. "Well, I was already starting to have sexual relations with *la chava*, the young woman [I dated], so with my sister it was only *la carneada* as we call it, touching her body and that was it. But that was it because with the other women I was having a little bit more than kisses, vaginal penetration—everything. That was when I said, 'she is my sister and I better stop right here.'"

When I asked Isaías to elaborate further, he continued, "Well, like I said, when I started to touch *carnes de otro ganado* (literally, 'meat from another livestock'). And that is the way it started, I started to see, it is better to stop right here at home and start somewhere else." When I asked him to elaborate on the idea of "carne de otro ganado," he said, laughing, "Well, let's say that she is part of the family and I must respect the family as well."

I asked Isaías if he could explain whether he or both of them arrived at the decision to stop their sexual encounters. "It was my decision, because I have not even told her that I made the decision, but I told her that since I started to work and all of that [traveling out of Guadalajara], I said, we better stop right here. And I have noticed that she has not said anything about it, and I have not said anything about it either. And both of us are not worried about it."

Isaías began having *aventuras* with other women and traveled outside Guadalajara because of work, staying away from home for four or five months. The encounters with his sister became less frequent until they stopped completely when he was about eighteen years old, two years prior to our interview. How does Isaías look at it in retrospect? "I do not regret it but it hurts a little," he said.

Hetero-Patriarchs in Training: A Continuum of Sexual Violence

"The reason why sexual abuse happens is because men are allowed to do with their sexuality as they please, without limits," stated a senior attorney and legal consultant who had specialized in sexual abuse of children and family law for more than three decades in Monterrey. If men's sexuality under patriarchy has no sexual limits, I asked myself, what does empirical research suggest about mutually consensual sex, heterosexuality, and rape beyond radical feminism and other influential canonical texts? British sociologist, researcher, and activist Liz Kelly offers a potential answer through what she identifies as the "continuum of sexual violence," a concept that emerged from her research with women who had histories of sexual violence.[10] The continuum suggests that sexual violence exists in most women's lives in complex ways and expressions and that all women encounter some form of sexual violence at some given moment in their lives. All women in fact selectively reported being exposed to a wide variety of sexualized violence exercised by men of contrasting ages and within a broad range of relational and social contexts beyond the family, which included acquaintances, friends and romantic partners, classmates, school teachers and college professors, maintenance staff at school, priests and sacristans, co-workers and supervisors at work (including some high-profile public officials and a governor), physicians and psychologists, neighbors and strangers, street harassment, groping in public transportation and other social spaces (e.g., plazas and stores), and gang rape, among others.[11] Accordingly, separating and identifying some women as "victims" from the rest of the women is problematic.

Thus, the undercurrent or continuum that flows through a woman's unique subjective experience and all women's commonly shared experiences of sexual violence seems to suggest that consensual heterosexual sex and rape may have more in common than what one may want to accept. This is illustrated by the stories of sister-brother incestuous arrangements that some women, for example, recalled as physically pleasurable but also dangerous. For instance, Rosana was eight years old when her eighteen-year-old brother behaved with her as "an affectionate lover" who was never verbally or physically violent, did not pursue his apparent intentions to vaginally penetrate her when she became scared, and touched her in ways that felt physically stimulating—all while she was locked up and experiencing intense fear. Shortly after, when her mother caught her masturbating, Rosana was severely punished for stimulating herself and for "provoking" her brother.

In short, the gender inequality promoted through sexual silences, double standards of morality, a mother's internalized sexism and "misrecognition," and other sexist ideologies and practices regulating family life enhance the limitless possibilities a brother has to explore his sexuality with a sister as she deciphers a continuum of sexual violence. By taking a sister and raping her, some young men may both initiate themselves *safely* into heterosexuality and reaffirm their heterosexual manhood within the patriarchal microcosm of their incestuous families. As the performance of heterosexuality in its extreme expression, the act of rape may become a repetitive habit for a young man who may satisfy a sexual urge or fantasy while also validating his heterosexual identity and benefitting from his early harvesting of patriarchal privilege. He learns that a wide variety of expressions of sexualized violence and heteromasculinity go hand in hand as possible, permissible, and rewarding. Getting away with and feeling safe while engaging in these behaviors becomes part of a boy's emotional socialization within the family. Raping a sister may offer a brother some of the initial social training regarding the social profit men as a social group get from women, what R.W. Connell identified as a "patriarchal dividend," that is, "the advantage men in general gain from the overall subordination of women."[12]

Socioeconomic marginality and privilege selectively shape all of the above gendered processes in explicit and subtle ways. First, the sexual objectification of women hired for paid household work has been documented in Mexico.[13] These domestic workers—frequently poor and/or indigenous women—are the target of sexual coercion and harassment by their male employers, a tradition that exists throughout Latin America as well.[14] That is, a family that hires a domestic worker not only buys and exploits a poor woman's labor but may also obtain some form of "structural protection" for a daughter: a domestic worker will endure the potential sexual coercion that might have been directed at young women in the family. In incestuous families, this is aggravated by the fact that she may be perceived as if she was "part of the family."[15] In short, domestic workers who are exposed to different forms of sexual violence (from subtle harassment to rape) by the men of the families that hire them are taking on their shoulders a dangerous aspect of the gendered servitude expected from daughters. In extreme cases, however, the domestic worker *as well as* the daughters, for example, may become the target of a sexually violent father, as illustrated by Maricruz in the previous chapter. And a domestic worker may experience the above while being hired anywhere across the socioeconomic spectrum. Working-class families may hire poor women as domestic workers or as *nanas* and they may have the same risk of being exposed to men who may objectify them and sexually assault them, as in the story of Manuel, one of the children of Sánchez.[16]

In some upper, upper-middle, and middle-class families, however, buying the sexualized dimension of gendered servitude through a domestic worker does not mean that girls and young women will be automatically exempt from these dangers. Some upper-middle-class families have well-established "family genealogies of incest," a concept that I incorporate and discuss in the following chapter, which at times may overshadow class privilege. Renata, for instance, born and raised in an upper-middle-class family in Mexico City and sexually molested by her two brothers, reported the unraveling wave of sexual violence affecting her sister and some of her primas—*all* of them educated within the same privileged socioeconomic strata.[17]

For girls and women living in marginalized poverty—urban and rural—gendered servitude within families is potentially more intense, in part because the domestic worker as a "structural protection" is not present. Although poverty may have crude consequences for women living in marginalized urban contexts, the more brutal expressions of it can be found in financially depressed rural areas where the combined effect of lack of education and paid employment opportunities may have devastating consequences for girls and women. The vulnerability of women to intense forms of sexual objectification thus may become magnified in these rural socioeconomic contexts, especially where geographic isolation fosters lack of communication and transportation, and the legal apparatus is non-existent or poorly equipped when compared to the already flawed and corrupted legal system in the country. This multilayered combined effect of local socioeconomic forces and specific regional cultures that selectively compromise the living conditions and well-being of girls and women results in "rural patriarchies," one of the varieties of regional patriarchies that exist in contemporary Mexican society.[18] With a complex history of multiple cases of sexual violence against girls in her immediate and extended family, Maclovia's case best illustrated this process for women living in a rural town in Central Mexico. "It is very isolated, as people say, away from civilization," she said in describing her rancho. She elaborated, "It is a place where anywhere in the woods, anyone can grab a young woman and rape her and nobody would ever learn about it. It is a big ranch where something like seven families live, different families. And in all of those families, I can assure you that all of the women have been raped. There is no girl who has not been raped, by their same fathers, their same brothers."

Other informants and professionals familiar with similar cases shared stories taking place in ranchos and pueblos, involving as well what one professional identified as *endogamia* (literally, endogamy) as she spoke about marriage within extended family and more distant kin, which may involve consensual courtship and romance. These romantic arrangements existed in Colonial Mexico, and have been identified in contemporary society as well.[19]

A la prima se le arrima: Women and Their Primos

Elba

"During a family visit, my primo also abused me," recalled Elba who, as discussed in the next chapter, had a long history of sexual violence at the hands of her uncle. Now in her mid-thirties, Elba explained the event at her primo's house.

> We were on our way, traveling here in Mexico. And we stayed at their house to spend the night. And I recall that I liked a toy that he [primo]

had and I asked him if I could have it. And he said, "well, I let you have it with a condition," [silence] . . . and so he told me that the condition was to suck his penis . . . Initially, I said no but he insisted, "Just a little bit and then you can borrow it, you can play with it." I accepted. And well, when he left, he let me have the toy and then I left.

This one-time incident happened when Elba was about seven years old, and her cousin was sixteen or seventeen. She never told anyone about this event. However, in a casual conversation a prima also close in age made a comment to Elba about the same cousin. She exclaimed, "Ay, that primo is so nasty!" Elba felt validated as she learned about similar "acts and actions" that he had forced upon her prima. As both women exchanged their respective experiences with their primo, Elba recalled the expression they used to refer to him: "*Es un primo muy puerco—* The cousin is such a pig." He was the son of Elba's uncle, her mother's brother.

Esmeralda

As illustrated in the introduction to this chapter, Esmeralda is the college-educated woman who was sexually assaulted by her primos as all of them spent time as an extended family, frequently and for many years, at her paternal grandmother's house. Born and raised in Guadalajara, Esmeralda played the role of the parental child as her parents worked hard to support a large family. "There was never time for it [love]," she said as she explained that she developed an emotionally distant relationship with her hardworking, busy parents. In their absence, her paternal grandmother became Esmeralda's most important source of love. Esmeralda's grandmother's home became a symbol of love and comfort but also danger and confusion. Her grandmother's house was the favorite place for family reunions with the extended family—mainly primas and primos—and it did not always feel safe. Esmeralda soon realized that she had to be on constant surveillance and protect herself from her primos—one of them in particular. This began to occur when she was about ten years old and her adolescent primos were at least three or four years older than her. Esmeralda recalled with clarity many of the episodes that took place at her grandmother's house over a period of four years or so. Besides the primo who actively harassed her, two or three other primos were also involved in these events.

"I felt paralyzed," was Esmeralda's reaction when her primo came into one of the rooms in the house and grabbed her tender breasts. Frequently, he and other primos spied on her when she took a shower. He sexually assaulted her in other ways as well, and in the presence of primos who cheered, laughed, and made fun of her. "I felt guilty. I used to say, 'Why me? Why does he touch me?'" Esmeralda said as she recalled an incident in which he got on top of her and rubbed his genital area against her in her mother's presence. "¡*Mamá, mira!* – Mom, look!" she screamed begging for help, but her mother was busy sewing and apparently "that was not important for my mother," Esmeralda said. She elaborated, "Carelessness, negligence. My mother, as my father said, is very naïve." The paternal aunt who was within view when Esmeralda had some of these experiences with her cousins had a similar reaction.

Esmeralda never talked with anyone about these experiences. Why? "I had a foolish way of thinking," she said, explaining that she would have liked for her paternal tía to be aware and to intervene. At the same time, however, Esmeralda tried to make sure that her tía, other aunts on both sides of the family, her grandmother, and her parents did not learn about these events. She described her paternal tías as *cerradas*—close-minded. She did not receive information about reproductive health or hygiene from her parents. Her mother scolded her when she looked at her books on reproduction and she felt "*culpable y sucia*" ("guilty and dirty") about sex-related issues as she was growing up.

"I was worried about covering up all of this, because I certainly thought that if they were aware of it, I would be punished for it. Back then, I was wrong by thinking that way." Later, she elaborated, "I was afraid they would discipline me and say that I was the guilty one, the dirty one, the disgusting one." Although she felt loved and protected by her grandmother, Esmeralda never told her because she did not want "to make her feel bad." And out of shame, she did not tell her parents. In her silence, Esmeralda felt validated when she learned that her prima (a daughter of the sister of Esmeralda's father) had similar experiences when she was thirteen or even older, maybe sixteen. The oldest brother of the primo who assaulted Esmeralda similarly assaulted Esmeralda's oldest prima. Her aunt caught them when he was on top of her. Apparently, the incident had no negative consequences for the oldest primo.

"What else were they supposed to do? A small number of people lived there. It was a small pueblo, a small rancho, with very few people," Esmeralda said as she explained that marriage between women and men who were blood related was not uncommon in some of the towns near her own hometown in Jalisco. As she reflected on these issues, Esmeralda talked about some of the stories she has heard in her immediate and extended family. "I do not think it was abuse, I think it was incest," she said, as she explained that one of her primos had a child with his brother's daughter. She recalled the story of a woman and a man who are second cousins and who are currently married. And finally, she has heard rumors about her own father having sexual relations with the wife of Esmeralda's cousin.

"I think I already forgave him, I think so," Esmeralda admitted as she talked about the ways she has tried to make sense of the experiences she lived at her grandmother's house. "They were poorer than us and I believe he [primo] saw my aunt and uncle having sexual relations. They had no door. One bedroom and that's it. They slept in the dining room . . . or I do not know, maybe he liked my body. Or simply, he wanted to know how it felt to touch [a woman]," she elaborated and said that pornography and lack of information in the lives of adolescent men were perhaps the reasons why all of this happened to her. Eventually, Esmeralda's primo stopped assaulting her. How did that happen? She explained, "He had his amigas, or girlfriends at the secundaria he attended, because he went to school in another place. I think he had a girlfriend over there, or had sexual relationships with someone." Esmeralda then felt more at peace. However, these experiences left an imprint on her life. "It affected me a lot . . . I could not see myself at the mirror. I thought I was the most awful of all women . . . I felt like I did not deserve to let a man get close to me," she said as she explained that her sex life has been "promiscuous" because she has had sex with men without loving, affectionate bonding. Although she did not associate it with the experiences with her primos, both Esmeralda and her mother had uterine cysts that required surgery. Esmeralda has never experienced an orgasm, and was emphatic while saying, "many times, I feel like I have been used by men."

Esmeralda was in her mid-twenties when her maternal uncle strategically touched her genitals while they were in the back seat of the car and as the entire family traveled together. Esmeralda has been exposed to a lot of harassment on the street, at work, on the bus, and in the confessional booth by a priest who eventually was officially accused by many women of sexually molesting girls and women at the Catholic church where she attended religious services.

Like Esmeralda, other women in the study recalled incidents that had occurred with their primos. Unlike her, these women recalled these experiences as happening only once or twice and under specific family circumstances and contexts.

Nancy

"He fondled me with the hand, caressed my body, everywhere. But why me?! Why did this happen to me?! I always tried to explain that to myself and said, Why me?!" exclaimed Nancy from Ciudad Juárez as she described the experiences she had at the age of twelve or thirteen at the hands of a primo who was younger than she, maybe ten or so. A second primo that she identified as a "soldier" fondled her twice as well. After the second time, she told her grandmother, but reporting did not translate into an effective intervention or consequences for the men. She was about nine years old and he was in his early twenties. And not long before our interview, an adolescent primo, around thirteen or fourteen years old, assaulted her in her sleep. Now in her late twenties, she recalled,

> I was sleeping and he grabbed my breasts, and then I moved and I felt that he squeezed my nipple. So I pushed his hand away and I told myself, "Oh my Lord! ¡*Ay Señor!* Help me, what should I do?" In fact, next day I told my aunt. "You know what, tía? Your son did this and that, and he touched my breasts. And she said, '¡*Ay!* Maybe he was dreaming of his girlfriend, or he simply wanted to give you a hug.'"

Nancy eventually confronted her primo. He seemed remorseful and asked for forgiveness. These three men were sons of different aunts on the maternal side. Nancy also recalled an experience of sexual violence at the hands of her stepfather; she was seven or eight and he was thirty, and it happened one time.

Perla

As discussed earlier, Perla became the conjugal daughter of her father. Perla also described the experience she had with her primo when both were adolescents; she was fifteen and he was eighteen. He was the son of her mother's prima. She explained, "What I do remember is that he lay down, or I should say, I lay down in bed and he touched my breast and my vagina . . . yes, we were playing. In other words, I feel that we were playing because that was the reason why we visited our cousins. And then . . . well, I do not know. He might have taken me to the room to take a toy or something new that he had and right there is when it happened." When I asked Perla if the experience was voluntary, she asserted, "I felt it was normal, that this happened between cousins." "Why?" I inquired. She elaborated, "Because my father did it, so it is the same, because my father did it, in the end any primo or anyone of the opposite sex [in the family] could do it to me, no?"

This occurred only once and without being naked, Perla noted, as she described this experience as something that was not necessarily a "problem." "The problem," she said, "was to do this [sex] with someone outside the family." As she reflected on the extent to which this was against her will, she said, "Well, I say that it was voluntary because, in fact, I am telling you I knew that this was what people used to do and you had no choice. In other words, anyone [in the family] could do whatever they wanted to me." When this experience with her cousin happened, how did she live it? She said, "Well, indifferent, more than anything. I thought that it was that way, that that was normal. That all the family, all the primos went and did with their primas whatever they wanted to do . . . Now I feel that it should have not happened. And in fact, no . . . In other words, I feel that it should have not happened." In retrospect, Perla identified the experience as "*falta de respeto*" ("lack of respect") and "abuse" on the part of her primo.

Renata

As discussed earlier, Renata recalled the incidents she lived with her two brothers. In addition, she reported an experience with her primo when she was eight or nine years old. The event occurred as they played while visiting his family. She said,

It happened with my primos, it happened in the swimming pool and it made me feel so ashamed because he said, "If you let me touch you . . ." I do not recall what kind of deal. Anyway, the thing is that he said, "Let me touch you, or you touch me." But I did not want to, I said "No." He said, "If you say 'no' then I am going to tell your mother." So I said, "Go ahead and tell her." And he told her! And then my mother scolded me, and my sister scolded me, and I had this feeling of guilt, of being dirty. And well, like that, those are the memories I have of my childhood.

Renata was even more shocked by the family circumstances surrounding this event:

He talked about it at the table, while all of us were eating. And I made a face as if nothing had happened and his mother said, "So and so, shut up." [He insisted] "It is true!" And that was it. Later at the house of my other aunt, my sister told me, "Was that true?" And my mother was right there, "Was that true?" And I was just like this [meaning "silent"]. My face must have turned thousands of colors. My mother said, "That is really bad, you should not do that." And, well . . . [sigh]

Understanding Prima-Primo Incest

As illustrated, the narratives about women's experiences with their primos expose dynamics that are similar to the sister-brother testimonies. However, the prima-primo stories illustrate distinctive patterns.

Prima-primo relationships. When compared to the sister-brother incestuous stories, a prima-primo relationship reflected a more casual tone and less emotional closeness. Although at times experiences of sexual assault may last years (as in the case of Esmeralda), these events may also be situational and isolated occasions occurring once or twice. Nonetheless, they are still shocking and coercive in nature. Unlike the emotional damage women frequently reported when sexual violence was perpetrated by a brother, experiences of sexual assault by a primo was less likely to affect the emotional bonding between the parties involved. However, the impact of the experience is not less dramatic and may leave a deep imprint on the quality of the sexual and relationship experiences of a woman, especially as she comes of age.

Just play? Women reported a wide variety of sexualized experiences that took place within the *context of play* and constructed *as play*. The former refers to social contexts of everyday life as a girl and her frequently older primo play or engage in personal exchanges. The latter refers to an older primo actively and purposefully creating conditions to manipulate a younger prima (usually a girl) and sexually molest her or abuse her to make her believe that what they are doing is play and/or to use toys as part of the strategy to sexually molest her. These exchanges may happen on a one-on-one basis or in the context of collective interactions with more than one primo witnessing the event while allying with and supporting the primo actively assaulting a girl, a resemblance of the image of gang rape.

How do we explain these prima-primo testimonies? Why did these events happen? The two dynamics responsible for the brother-sister arrangement discussed in the previous section may arguably facilitate as well the primo-prima stories of sexual violence. No doubt, a prima may become the sex surrogate of a primo, and a continuum of sexual violence and patriarchal dividend may coincide in the lives of young men who learn about their sexual privileges within their extended families. Two additional dynamics seem to explain the testimonies of these women at the hands of their primos: Sexual terrorism and family life, and family sexual harassment.

Sexual Terrorism and Family Life

"Sexual terrorism is the system by which men and boys frighten, and by frightening, dominate and control women and girls. Sexual terrorism is manifested through both actual and implied violence," writes Carole Sheffield.[20] As an idea, sexual terrorism suggests that women, regardless of age or social status, are vulnerable to a wide variety of expressions of sexualized violence, which are part of everyday life.[21] Thus, the women I interviewed were vulnerable to experiences of sexual assault or molestation at the hands of their primos because some forms of sexual terrorism are allowed within extended families. Family sexual terrorism is disguised and trivialized by authority figures and the girls and young women themselves. In other words, sexual terrorism is normalized in these Mexican families. As girls, the women reported feeling discomfort and pain, yet felt confused and helpless while "getting used" to the sexual assaults or molestation. In the worst case scenario, women felt responsible for the experiences.

The family authority figures traditionally responsible for child care (i.e., mothers and aunts) seem to either ignore these sexual assaults or perceive them and interpret them as genuine play between children who are traditionally desexualized and/or invisible—as less-than-humans or asexual beings. In these configurations, adult women are not even expected to be "authority figures" in their families. As with the maternal figures in the previous chapter, these aunts and grandmothers similarly engage in the cognitive "misrecognition" which facilitates the normalization of these boys' behaviors. Sexually intrusive behaviors thus remain ignored and unquestioned, further reproducing a vicious cycle: oppressive family structures continue affecting girls and keep adult women disempowered. The family members witnessing these events may include adult women from the maternal and paternal sides of the family.

Sexual terrorism as part of everyday family life interactions and situations, especially within the extended families of the women sharing their life stories, illustrates Sheffield's argument: "These common experiences [of sexual intimidation], which include a range of verbal, visual, and physical intrusions, are the underpinning of sexual terrorism: they serve to remind women and girls that they are at risk and vulnerable to male aggression just because they are female."[22] As occurred in Esmeralda's case, women's bodies are a target of intrusion while other primos witness, laugh, and cheer, which may exacerbate the violence because, as Elizabeth Kissling explains, "ridicule thus becomes a tool of silencing, and both the ridicule and the silence support the system of sexual terrorism."[23]

This process exposes an additional dimension of the rituals of misogyny discussed in the previous chapter. Mexican boys who become involved in these practices fall into the same category as other young men who belong to some U.S. college fraternities and adult men who engage in "girl watching" at work: the sexual objectification and harassment of women becomes the founding principle of fun, entertainment, and intimacy among men.[24] This paradigm not only normalizes, for example, what Esmeralda's primos did to her, it may also remove any responsibility from them, as in "the boys were *just* playing." Or, as I have heard countless times in Spanish, "*Los muchachos nomás estaban jugando*."

The common Mexican *refrán* or proverb, "A la prima se le arrima," which literally means, "You can get physically/sexually close to your female cousin," validates the sexual objectification of primas who satiate the sexualized glances and curiosities of their primos raised in patriarchal families that ignore, allow, and/or normalize these intrusions. Sexual assault and sexual molestation become a safe sexual opportunity and also a way to exercise and practice privilege, power, and control between a young man and a younger woman within the extended family and as part of everyday life—"a fusion of dominance and sexuality."[25]

In addition, a young man may rely on the sexual objectification of a prima as he develops his self-perception of heteromasculinity in the context of friendship and camaraderie with other men close in age. A male informant from Ciudad Juárez, Valentín said, "This whole thing between prima and primo is like a tradition." He then explained that in some of his all-male group conversations he has heard on different occasions some of his amigos state with some form of pride, "*Yo le quité la virginidad a mi prima*," literally, "I stole my prima's virginity" as they share stories about their sexual adventures and conquests. This pattern resonates with the sexualized exchanges between primas and primos that anthropologist Isabel Vieyra discovered in her research on the first sexual experience of vaginal intercourse as reported by 320 women living in Mexico City.[26] In retrospect now I understand why some self-identified "sex educators" may perceive these practices as "normal"—one among many of the gender and sexual taken-for-granteds in Mexico.[27]

Family Sexual Harassment

"The first step in recognizing an act as a harm is the accurate construction of that act," asserts Deirdre Davis in her critical examinations of street harassment in the lives of African American women. Davis elaborates, "Once street harassment is constructed and understood to be a harm that plays a role in the sexual terrorism that governs women's lives by genderizing the street in order to perpetuate female subordination, street harassment becomes visible as a harm. In order to address, deconstruct, and eradicate a harm, we must give the harm a name."[28] Inspired by Deirdre Davis, I incorporate the concept of "family sexual harassment" to identify and give a name to the multiple nuanced, trivialized, and normalized expressions of sexual harassment affecting the lives of girls and women within Mexican families which are trivialized and seen as ordinary and "normal," and thus rarely questioned, challenged, or disrupted.

Although street harassment has been associated with the street as a "public" space and family as an institution has been traditionally perceived as a "private" space (and thus any forms of harassment within the family would be some sort of "private harassment"), I would like to provide some nuance to the private-public dichotomy.[29] One reason is because the family life experiences of the women I interviewed at times happened as part of family life interactions taking place in public contexts, thus challenging these more static private versus public distinctions. In addition, street harassment and family sexual harassment seem to share some parallels. First, like street harassment, family sexual harassment has multiple functions, one of them being "to produce an environment of sexual terrorism."[30] Second, like street harassment, family sexual harassment is not a consequence of sexually terroristic culture, but rather a force deeply engaged in the production of that culture.[31] Third, the fact that sexual violence within families has been examined frequently in its most extreme expressions (such as rape, including extreme force bruises and bleeding), more subtle, nuanced, and disguised expressions of harassment within families have become invisible in the literature and normalized by the people who experience it—and thus is neither studied nor reported. The cultural mantras that I heard repeatedly while growing up in Mexico, "*Así son los hombres, todos son iguales*" (That is the way men are, all of them are the same) and "*Así son los muchachos, no les hagas caso*" (That's the way young men are, ignore them) have a close cultural equivalent in English to "Boys will be boys." These expressions have promoted some kind of gender and cultural "helplessness" which has trivialized forms of intrusion upon the bodies of girls and women within their extended families, as in, "that is the way boys and men are, there is nothing I can do about it." This is aggravated by the "medicalization of rape," that is, women's perceptions of their brothers or primos as sick, maniac, or schizophrenic. This transforms a complex social problem into an individual problem, and makes sexist practices invisible; diagnostic labels reduce a social practice into an individual pathology.[32] The learned helplessness to explain incestuous behavior is not exclusive to Mexican society; it has been identified as well in the father-daughter incest literature in the United States.[33]

In sum, if we genderized Mexican families in their social contexts where multiple expressions of gender inequality traditionally have been normalized, we would be able to make visible under-reported and under-examined forms of sexual violence. As we remove the trivialized nature of some forms of apparently minor and non-offensive, traditionally ignored, innocuous forms of sexual harassment affecting the lives of girls and women, they would be more likely to be named and potentially prevented within their extended families. The concept of "family sexual harassment" may help us in this attempt at labeling, naming, and disrupting these expressions of violent intrusions upon the sexualized bodies of girls and women. Family sexual harassment is not limited to the prima-primo interaction, and it includes additional forms of kinship relationships such as women's experiences with their uncles, among other men identified by the women as part of their family. In the next chapter, I examine the testimonies of women exposed to violence at the hands of these men.

4

Nieces and Their Uncles

Reading these interviews over and over is taking me back to my childhood growing up in Mexico. I recall seeing those decals, stickers, or paper cards on the windows of my neighbors, and I think we had one in our house, a *"calcomanía"* reading with some religious pride: *"Este hogar es católico, no aceptamos propaganda protestante ni de otras sectas."* "This is a Catholic home, we don't accept propaganda from Protestants or other sects." Re-reading these uncle-niece narratives gave me nausea more than once. It also made me think of an invisible sticker by the doors of the women living in incestuous families who taught me so much about family life and the repetitive patterns of sexual violence across generations of women of all ages. It is as if their homes had an invisible decal, *"Este hogar es misógino: Aquí se viola a las mujeres."* "This home is misogynous: We rape women here."
—From my memo writing on el Día de la Vírgen de Guadalupe, Austin, Texas, 2012

"He locked the door the first time," said forty-year-old Bárbara from Guadalajara. She clearly remembers being eight the first time she found herself in the bedroom of her mother's brother. He removed her underwear, gave her oral sex, and touched her body and genitals while threatening her to "shut up and not to say anything." These episodes began as she cleaned, swept, and mopped her uncle's room, and made his bed, on her mother's orders. Bárbara's uncle was in his forties, and worked as a taxi driver.

Fear of her mother's reaction was a powerful reason to be silent about what her uncle did to her every time she went to clean his room, she said. "I was sure she would say, 'I don't believe you, you provoked him.'" According to Bárbara, her mother "always preferred her brothers." Bárbara's biggest fear was that her mother wouldn't defend her, she said. In the end, she never told either her mother or her father.

Itzel's story is similar. "It was like you feel someone is looking at you in an offensive way, in a lascivious way. So then he [her uncle] is looking at me that way. Then he gets closer and gives me a hug, and he grabs my butt. And I told him, ¡Ay canijo!—Oh, damn it! But I was shi-shi-shivering." Itzel was in her mid-twenties when I interviewed her in her native Ciudad Juárez. The episodes with her uncle happened twice when she was visiting her grandmother. She was sixteen at the time, and her uncle was in his early thirties. The second time, she assertively confronted him. It never happened again, and she never told her family.

Bárbara's and Itzel's experiences illustrate the complex ways women can become the targets of a variety of forms of sexual violence within the uncle-niece relationship. The stories of women who reported incidents of sexual violence perpetrated by men they identified as their tíos revealed similar patterns to those identified within the father-daughter, brother-sister, primo-prima contexts.

However, in this distinctive uncle-niece arrangement, additional complex dimensions of the social organization of gender inequality and sophisticated sexualized vulnerabilities emerged. As I read, organized, and analyzed the women's narratives of sexual violence in this study, the most revealing finding was how prevalent this family arrangement was. Uncle-niece incestuous violence was the most commonly reported by the women, and happened the most often, compared to all the other family patterns (i.e., father-daughter, brother-sister, or primo-prima arrangements), echoing research on sexual violence in Mexico.[1]

I also learned that an "uncle" can include the following family relationships: the biological brother or half-brother of a mother or father, a mother's or father's first cousin, the husband of a mother's or father's sister (identified as tío político), men related to them within extended family networks such as a great-uncle, and still other men they might call tío lejano, literally meaning "a distant uncle."

Beyond cultural differences of kinship relationships, Mexican women are not alone in this very common niece-uncle incestuous arrangement. Yet the pattern has received scant attention in the incest literature, which has traditionally centered on the nuclear family.[2] For instance, in their pioneering, large-scale sexuality research project conducted with almost

8,000 women in the United States, Alfred Kinsey and his professional team discovered that of the 609 "white non-prison females" who reported being sexually approached by an adult man during their pre-adolescence years, uncles were named most often, more than fathers, brothers, grandfathers, and other relatives.[3]

Similarly, sociologist Diana Russell found that uncles are "the most common perpetrators of incest," which is "slightly more common than fathers" in her groundbreaking research on incest conducted with 930 women from different racial and ethnic backgrounds in San Francisco, California.[4] "True, for most people the incest taboo is probably considerably stronger between father and daughter than uncle and niece," Russell writes. "Hence a complete and satisfactory explanation of father-daughter incest has to account for the overcoming of greater social and presumably internal inhibitions against acting out incestuous feelings by fathers than by uncles."[5]

Accordingly, the indirect blood connection and the distant emotional bonding with an uncle—which nearly all the women in my study reported existing prior to the abuse—might have contributed to making them targets of sexual violence. In analyzing these women's narratives, I also learned something paradoxical: despite emotional distance between both parties, an uncle might still have privileges over a niece.

For instance, while eight-year-old Bárbara was shorter than the broomstick she could barely hold, her mother still expected her to clean the room of a forty-year-old man. And this uncle molested her precisely when she engaged in what I earlier called "gendered servitude." Although in a patriarchal family the daughter "belongs to the father alone," an uncle may enjoy the same gender privileges that fathers (and older brothers, as illustrated earlier) may have over girls and women within their immediate families.[6] These complex entitlements emerge from an intricate web of family processes that create circumstances facilitating sexual access to girls and women within these extended families that are part of everyday family life, a dynamic I explain below.

In this chapter I examine the uncle-niece incestuous pattern by looking at family dynamics through three interconnected concepts:

(1) family genealogies of incest;
(2) the feminization of incest; and
(3) family politics of gender inequality: internalized sexism.

The concept of "family genealogies of incest" is informed by the work of Denise Segura's and Jennifer Pierce's examinations of Nancy Chodorow's classic and pioneering feminist examinations on gender inequality within nuclear families, family genealogy scholarship in sociology, as well as by feminist revisions of family therapy literature.

Sociologists Denise Segura and Jennifer Pierce (1993) explain that although the mother-daughter relationship in families of Mexican origin is of high emotional relevance, this is not the only emotionally meaningful bonding connection for a girl vis-à-vis other women in positions of authority in the family. For instance, a girl may develop strong and deep feelings toward her aunts, grandmothers, older sisters, and older primas. The girl may thus become an extension of her mother, but by virtue of these multiple and complex bonding connections, she may also become an extension of other women in her extended family.

A boy who learns to devalue women related to him within immediate and extended networks (for example, a sister or prima) can grow to become an uncle who automatically devalues the daughters of these women. Through a multiplying effect, he may similarly devalue other girls who have also become extensions of these and other women belonging to his kin. Thus, this magnified risk of vulnerability to sexual violence is explained in part by the fact that nieces are extensions of *all* adult women in their families. This complex and excessive effect results in systemic and systematic patterns of sexual violence against girls and women within these immediate and extended family networks. It facilitates the uncles' opportunistic and predatory habits of misogyny perversely reproduced in the lives of women of all ages and kinship networks across generations and as part of everyday family life and community engagement.

Finally, sexual molestation of girls was identified at times as part of local urban cultures. This includes daily life in *colonias* where rumors of sexual abuse of girls by adult men circulated but were rarely confronted or investigated at the collective level. Some of these uncles at times molested other girls, such as the daughters of friends and neighbors who had a relationship with these informants' families and communities.

Family genealogies of incest go hand in hand in establishing what I call the "feminization of incest." Feminization of incest refers to a special pattern in these accounts of uncle-niece narratives of incest: the overrepresentation of the maternal side of the family. That is, uncles who were related to the women via the maternal side were more frequently reported as the protagonists of acts of sexual assault, rape, molestation, and harassment of a niece.

Family genealogies of incest and the feminization of incest exist in part because of the ways in which women in positions of authority have internalized sexist ideologies they come to incorporate as part of family life. They may view their own experiences of sexual violence by a male relative when they were younger as "common" or "normal." Their learned perceptions of sexual objectification of girls and women within families are a key dimension of "family cultures of rape," a concept discussed earlier. This includes beliefs and practices that families reproduce with regard to sexuality *within* the family. These beliefs make girls and young women vulnerable to being sexualized by men within their kinship. The men may then move from subtle and nuanced forms of sexual harassment to more grotesque and violent expressions of sexual coercion. These family processes become more complicated, especially when the uncles are loved and respected within their families, and when men use seduction, affection, and manipulation rather than physical force as part of the sexual violence.

In the end, the adult women who reproduced practices affecting girls in their families might have experienced sexual violence themselves. Ironically, the same family processes that oppressed them as women decades earlier also kept a younger generation of women lost in fear and silence, or accused of lying when they finally took the risk to reveal a painful secret. The women I interviewed, however, were not necessarily passive as they actively figured out ways to make sense of and cope in creative ways with their excruciating journeys. Women recalled how they became resilient as they explored endless ingenious ways to resist and fight back at different stages of their lives.

In this study, twenty-one of the forty-five women reported a wide variety of experiences of sexualized violence by twenty-eight men they identified as uncles, men overwhelmingly related through the maternal side.[7] In this chapter I present twelve women's stories and classify them in five groups: maternal uncles, maternal tíos políticos, paternal uncles, paternal tíos políticos, and a paternal tío lejano (a paternal distant uncle).

It is important to mention that women's stories of sexual violence with their tíos are more fluid and complex than the above categories. For example, a woman might have been abused by a mother's brother and also by another tío. However, I chose a category for a story when the woman telling it identified it as the one lasting the longest period of time in her life, though not necessarily the one with the most negative consequences.

These twelve stories are about women who endured their experiences during sustained periods of time, sometimes identified as the years between certain ages. The other women reported experiences that were more intermittent. They were sometimes the "secondary" experience of sexual violence in their lives, or isolated events that the women clearly identified as opportunistic or situational "incidents" that happened once or twice with a mother's or a father's brother, and a mother's primo, and at times with more than one uncle. Some of these women were also exposed to sexual violence at the hands of other men in their families, beyond the uncle-niece arrangement. The intermittent, secondary, or incidental nature of the experiences does not undermine the relevance of their testimonies or the impact of these experiences on their lives; some of them creatively resisted or fought back. Because of the unique nature of these experiences, I will publish them elsewhere. Based on the pseudonyms I gave to each one of them, I present the twelve stories alphabetically in each section. My analysis is inclusive of *all* of the twenty-one women's narratives.

Maternal Uncles: Mothers' Biological Brothers

Bárbara

As I wrote in the introduction to this chapter, Bárbara was eight years old when her mother made her clean, sweep, mop, and make the bed of her mother's brother, a taxi driver in his forties. "I remember I would be crying, and crying, and crying, [and I would say], 'Oh my God, please make him take me down from the bed!'" Bárbara recalled how she experienced the abuse. She vividly remembered her uncle making himself comfortable in his bed, putting her next to him, removing her underwear, giving her oral sex, touching her body and genitals. "Don't tell your mother," he warned her.

Now in her early forties, Bárbara recalled that scenario happening at least six times, and it caused her feelings of confusion, fear, and physical pain. But she didn't take the abuse passively. She tried to sit up to resist. Also, she said, "I used to ask him about why he did it to me, and he would say, 'Shut up, don't say anything!' I would tell him, 'It hurts!' but he kept doing it." Bárbara says her genitals became swollen and painful as a result. She stopped going to clean her tío's room, but her mother scolded her. She also felt unsafe and scared when her uncle and some of his brothers spied on her while she took a shower. She recalled another experience with him and his brothers, weeping as she spoke.

> I grew up with fear, because I never [sobbing] told my mother. Always my uncles would be peeking at us [her and other girls in the family]. My mother would go out, but her brothers were there, and we had no doors or curtains, they would bend down, and by the time I would come out of taking a shower, and I would see them and say, ¡Ah chingao! Damn it! He would just [harass me] and I would be rude, I talked back, I confronted him. So he would report me to my mom, but he didn't tell her what he had done to me.

Bárbara soon realized that all these experiences were part of life in the *vecindad*, a working-class communal dwelling where her parents, aunts, and other relatives shared a common space as neighbors. Afraid of her uncle's reaction, Bárbara never told her mother. Her fears were validated when her mother didn't intervene when Bárbara's oldest brother beat her up. "I don't believe you, you provoked him," was her mother's response and a powerful reason to be silent about her uncle. "She always preferred her brothers." Her mother's brothers also took advantage of Bárbara's father, whom she described as a hardworking, caring man, and this in turn led to marital conflict. In her early teens, Bárbara was relieved when her parents and siblings moved out of the vecindad, and she no longer had to clean her uncle's room or be hypervigilant while taking a shower.

Today, Bárbara is happily raising her children as a full-time house-wife. Her husband is generally caring and kind, and her marriage is stable. But in their moments of sexual intimacy she is still haunted by feelings of *vergüenza* and experiences flashbacks of the abuse. She has not told her husband about this. She is afraid of his potential recrimination because she was not "technically" a virgin at marriage; she never told him about the experience with her uncle. But she was assertive and confrontational when she caught her husband spying on their fifteen-year-old daughter while she was taking a shower. He was remorseful and begged for forgiveness. Her daughter does not know about it, but Bárbara frequently tells her to "take care of herself" and to be alert, especially around her father. She has questioned her other children to find out if he has ever "touched" them or done anything that didn't feel right.

"The damage is done," Bárbara said, as she recalled her difficult relationship with her mother and the silence she had to endure while living in the vecindad. The uncle who abused her married a first cousin. Not long ago, he was found dead, with his body in an advanced state of decomposition. Bárbara never forgave him, but was moved by his tragic death. In retrospect, she thinks this was perhaps a way of life doing justice for her.

Eva

"I remember that we were at my grandparents' house, and my uncle would put his genitals against mine and stimulate me," said Eva, a woman from Guadalajara in her late twenties. Eva considers herself heterosexual and has never married. A smart and energetic factory worker, she attends college at night.

She said that the sexual encounters with her maternal uncle happened at their grandparents' house or other family gatherings. She was ten or eleven at the time; her tío was fourteen. These experiences happened frequently for about a year and a half. Eva recalls feeling *cosas chidas*—cool things—and physical pleasure while engaging in genital contact with her uncle. She also felt that these sexualized experiences were "normal" and part of "playing." Eva didn't actively resist her uncle, but she said she felt "manipulated" by him; at times, she "did it against her will."

As she got older, started menstruation, and learned about reproductive health, Eva became concerned. "What was I going to tell the world if I became pregnant by my tío?" she said. At that point, she started resisting him. They never engaged in these activities again, and he apparently never forced her. She experienced a deep sense of relief, especially given what she had gone through earlier at the hands of another man, her great-uncle.

Eva recalls an episode she wished she could erase from her life, a nightmare she still remembers with great detail. It happened at the hands of her great-uncle, her maternal grandmother's brother. "He wanted to touch me but I didn't want to, and then he put his fingers inside," she said. "I remember he inserted his finger inside my vagina. I wanted to start screaming and crying but he covered my mouth with his hand." Eva was about six years old, and she and her younger brother were spending the night at their grandmother's house. Her great-uncle, who was in his thirties, had come for a visit and spent the night with them. She recalls her grandmother telling her tío to take care of both children that night while she was gone for a few hours. In one of the most moving parts of her long recollection, she explains what happened when she and her little brother were in bed together, and her great-uncle came into the bedroom.

> I didn't want him to touch me, I was protecting . . . oh, the most important thing. And then again he tried to take my panties down and I put down one hand and tried to cover myself. And then he wanted to take off my hand and I didn't want to. He put his finger inside my mouth, the finger of the other hand. And then again, he wanted to touch me, and tried to take off my panties and touch me again and he just wanted to touch me. And I, I felt so much disgust, and pain, I started to cry. I could not believe it—he wouldn't leave me alone!

Eva fought her great-uncle, and he eventually gave up, especially as Eva's little brother kept moving in his sleep, which "threw him off," she said. "And all I remember is that I saw his shadow, he got up, zipped up his pants and left. I couldn't go back to sleep . . . It felt like the hours lasted forever, but I stayed awake to make sure he would not come back. And he didn't come back, as dawn brightened and the day broke."

The incident happened only once, and her great-uncle threatened to tell Eva's father if she said anything. Eva still has flashbacks of that terrifying night, and said that painful event is the reason she is afraid to be alone at home, and is the cause of her lack of self-confidence. She also feels deep hatred for her great-uncle.

During one of his visits years later, her affectionate grandmother said to her: "Eva, come and say hello to your tío and give him a hug." She remembers feeling disgusted. "I started to feel so much hatred and a lot of disgust and resentment," she said. "In fact, he is the person I hate the most in my life. I wished he was dead, I have wished that many, many times." She still feels deep pain when talking about the event. Eva's great-uncle has been accused of raping more than one woman in Guadalajara, but somehow has been able to get away with it. He remains a free man. Eva never told anyone in her family about her experiences at the hands of her uncle and great-uncle twenty years earlier. This is partly because of what happened when a girl cousin told her parents that she had been molested. "She told her parents about it and it led to huge chaos," said Eva, and did "psychological damage" on her family's maternal side.

Eva's *primita*—little female cousin—revealed a situation of apparent sexual molestation by one of her cousins. Eva says the girl's mother believed her, but out of *vergüenza* asked the girl not to share details with her relatives. This discouraged Eva from wanting to reveal her own experiences, she said, a feeling that was exacerbated by her own feelings of shame toward "my mother, my family, and society" for having had sex with a blood relative, her uncle.

Her tío's high status in the family was another reason Eva did not tell anyone about her experiences. "My uncle is someone they [my family] never see, and when they do, they feel so happy," she said. "So the love they have for him, and the fact that they would not believe me." The great-uncle who molested her was also popular, she said. "The family loved him very much."

Finally, Eva is herself at the center of a painful family secret. She grew up listening to family conversations, and at least once, she overheard one of her aunts asking her mother a strange question. "Who is Eva's father? Who is he?" Her aunt didn't realize that Eva was nearby, listening. "I heard, unfortunately, in a conversation that I was the consequence of rape," she said tearfully. She remains very curious about this, but her mother has always avoided her attempts to talk about it. With deep sadness Eva has become aware of her mother's own personal history of secrets and silence.

Ileana

Back then we used to have [family] reunions and I didn't want to go. My family used to take it the wrong way. And the few times I went he tried to harass me. One time he tried to kiss me by force. I screamed, and one of my tías said, "¿*Qué pasó*? What happened?! Ay! Nothing, nothing, you are just screaming for no reason. Please, don't be like that." That is what she used to say, and I left. I got away from there.

This experience was described by Ileana, a married housewife and mother in her early thirties who was born and raised in Guadalajara. The man in the story was Ileana's tío—a brother of her mother—who started to harass her when she was twelve and he was about nineteen. Her narrative illustrates a pattern I called "family sexual harassment" in the previous chapter, which exists because of the normalization of men's intrusions in girls' bodies within families at an early age, which is ignored by women in positions of authority, including these girls' aunts.

On different occasions, her tío pushed her onto her bed, undressed her, and touched her. In situations that felt less threatening, he would force her and tried to kiss her. He also started to harass her over the phone. She described the first time that happened:

> Ay!, and he would tell me that he had been with a woman who had a very nice pussy and that she had it like this and like that, and that he opened it and, 'I put my dick inside,' things like that. And I listened to that but I have never heard those things before. Then I had to investigate with a friend to find out what that was. She was the one who explained to me, and it made me feel sick. Since then I was not available to talk to him, so I hung up and said no more.

As Ileana began to understand and resist these experiences, she also experienced fear and confusion, especially after he successfully silenced her. She clearly remembered what he said. "'If you say anything, I'll come and get you at the *secundaria*. You aren't worth shit—*vales madre*,' he used to tell me. 'Yes, vales madre, because a moment will come when you will disappear and nobody will know where you are.' So I was terrified, I use to go to school by myself."

Ileana's uncle also threatened to kill her mother if she said anything. Ileana experienced this sexual terrorism for about three years. When she was fifteen, she was overjoyed to learn that her tío was leaving Mexico and migrating to the United States. Deeply relieved that her excruciating journey was over, she couldn't believe her luck.

Shockingly, the sexual harassment didn't end after her uncle migrated north. It simply took another form. Right after he migrated, the obscene local calls of the past simply became international phone calls across the U.S.-Mexico border. Phoning long distance, the uncle used family conversations with his sister and mother (Ileana's mother and grandmother) to continue harassing Ileana across the miles. A pattern that lasted more than fifteen years, he successfully established a form of long-distance "sexual terrorism" over the phone. Ileana felt threatened, torn, and in pain by these phone conversations (some lasting more than two hours), frequently taking place in the presence of her mother and grandmother (and at times her own husband) who were happy to receive news from him without ever suspecting Ileana's secret.

On one ocassion, her uncle had a tragic accident and called Ileana to ask for forgiveness. She felt, however, that the conversation was not genuine and hung up. Ileana eventually confronted her uncle over the phone and broke her silence and told her mother and grandmother about what he had done to her all those years before and after migrating, but they did not believe her and took her to a psychiatrist. He treated her with medication that did not help and only adversely affected Ileana. In an act of both resilience and resistance, she stopped seeing the clinician. Her uncle has not returned to Mexico, and Ileana has not talked to him since she broke her silence.

Ileana's story illustrates a complex expression of incest across and beyond borders that I call "transnational incest."[8] In addition to Ileana's experience with her immigrant uncle, other older adult men in the family also sexually harassed her: another maternal uncle (about five years older than her), a primo (her father's nephew), and a man she calls a *primo político* (the husband of her prima, the daughter of her father's sister). These isolated events happened within the two years before our interview as part of family religious celebrations (i.e., baptism of a child), fiestas, and other family gatherings. But Ileana says the experience with her immigrant tío was the one that affected her the most. As an adolescent, she used alcohol in a compulsive manner and attempted suicide three times. As an adult, she still occasionally has flashbacks.

Ileana married her first boyfriend, and eventually told him about her painful experiences. He hasn't always been sympathetic; he has used it against her in times of sexual conflict and tension. "Why do you play dumb if you enjoyed it when they touched you?" he has asked when she refuses to have sex with him. Ileana has never been in therapy, but a close mentoring relationship with a teacher from *preparatoria* (equivalent to high school), her love for her children, and a passion for reading about human behavior have all helped her to be resilient.

Natalia

"My uncle blackmailed us, and we very innocently did it," says thirty-five-year-old Natalia about the painful experience she and her two siblings had when she was about six. At the time, her mother was in her early twenties and worked full time. She would leave her son, Natalia, and a younger daughter under the supervision of her half-brother, a man about eighteen or twenty who worked part time as a mechanic and looked after the three children while their mother juggled multiple part-time jobs to make ends meet. Natalia was recently shocked to learn that this included working as a prostitute.

Born and raised in several vecindades in Mexico City, Natalia is the second child, the oldest daughter, and the parental child in a family of four children. Substituting while her mother worked, for example, she would feed her baby brother and wash his diapers. "My siblings always told me, 'You are my second mother.'" Natalia's parents had an unstable relationship and her father eventually left his wife and children. He was himself "thrown to the streets like a dog," Natalia said. An orphan who never met his parents, her father had a rough life, and Natalia doesn't blame him for not "knowing how to love us." But she feels that in abandoning the family by leaving, her father "left meat for the wolf." His leaving allowed her uncle to molest all the children.

> In the afternoon, because my mother wasn't coming home, he [uncle] told us, "You know what? You let me do *groserías* (vulgar behavior) with you, or I'll tell your mother." And practically, my siblings, when I went to the bunk beds, my siblings were already lying down in bed. My brother was there, my sister, and then me, close to the edge.

Natalia says her uncle undressed the children from the waist down, and "lined them up like *choricitos*—little sausages." He then "got his penis out" and "sexually molested" them. When Natalia's body developed, her uncle removed her clothes completely. The experience never gave Natalia physical pleasure. Instead, it fed a deep and lasting rage. This routine was accompanied by the uncle's threats of telling their mother. He knew this was highly effective, because the three siblings were afraid of her. "My mother was always angry, she always hit us," said Natalia. "She was always worried about us, she wanted to make sure we ate and went to school, but she then would hit us in front of our school friends. She used a whip to hit us, and if we used our hands [to protect ourselves] it was even worse." Natalia's school teachers called her mother in for a meeting when they noticed the cuts and bruises, but when the children got home, they were punished even more.

"On the one hand it was mother, on the other, it was my uncle," said Natalia. The children felt they were caught between a rock and a hard place. The violent routine took place almost daily for four or five years, to the point that Natalia said she saw it as "normal."

> The first time he did it, he covered our face with a pillow. If we didn't want to [or resisted], we were afraid of his threats, that he would tell my mother and then she would hit us. Then, the one who would hit us even more was my mother. And so, if we didn't accept [his abuse], that meant we had to accept my mother beating us up. In our innocence, we accepted that.

Although it seemed this would never end, things unexpectedly changed one day. Her mother was fired from one of her jobs and came home early, to catch her uncle penetrating Natalia's sister. "But when she discovered him, she wasn't only upset with him, but she also beat us," said Natalia—which was why they hadn't told her about it in the first place. Nor was her grandmother any help. "My grandmother came out and rescued my uncle," she said. "She told my mother, 'If you do anything to my son, you will be dead to me.'" The tío was her grandparents' favorite child.

Although the three children were usually alone, Natalia is convinced that her grandmother, grandfather, and the relatives who shared their modest home knew what her uncle was doing. Yet nobody ever intervened. "My grandfather sold *tacos de canasta*. Many times he came home after work and saw us lying in bed, and he never asked what was going on," said Natalia. "Practically everybody knew about it," she said. Because of the grandmother's stern warning, Natalia's mother didn't take more severe action. "She preferred her mother over her children," she said.

As the children became older, they figured out ways to cope, even using their poverty as an intelligent excuse to avoid their uncle. The older brother stayed away from home, washing cars on the streets. When Natalia was ten or eleven she started cleaning houses and selling *tortas* on the street. Her younger sister escaped completely. When the girl was about eleven, she started smuggling her clothes out of the house little by little without anyone noticing. Her sister then ran away with a boy of fourteen or fifteen, Natalia's first boyfriend.

In retrospect, Natalia said that what always hurt her the most was her family's reaction to the abuse, especially her mother's beatings. Now a married woman and mother of two girls, Natalia finally had a confrontational conversation with her mother a few years ago. "Have you ever thought about the huge damage that your brother did to us?" she asked. Natalia says that in their painful exchange, *le cayó el veinte a mamá*— everything finally "clicked" for her mother. Receptive and remorseful, her mother sought professional help shortly afterward, and eventually wrote Natalia a letter asking for forgiveness.

Not long ago, Natalia felt a deep need to have an overdue conversation with her uncle as well. Natalia bravely confronted him about what he did to her and her two siblings thirty years ago. Describing his demeanor of naiveté, she recalled his reaction: "I don't even know why, *mija*." She persisted, "Listen, tío, but why?!" She was shocked by his reply: "What I did to you was a way of taking revenge on your mother, because she hit me back when we were little."[9] Natalia's uncle is now in his late forties. He's a police officer in Mexico City and carries a gun.

Time has given Natalia perspective on her mother and uncle. "They are in bad shape," she said. "They share the damage." She has forgiven both. She claims not to hate her mother but feels deep rage for what happened. Of her mother, she said, "She feels very guilty these days, because she wasn't able to do anything about it." And of her uncle: "He lives alone. He has money and everything, but he lives like a dog, alone and sick." She calls him "a very sick person," and says she eventually learned about a big stack of pornographic magazines he had accumulated over the years.

In talking about her romantic and sex life, Natalia described her few and at times abusive relationships with men. Natalia was ten when she had her first kiss with a woman she identified as "her aunt's partner." Natalia has had same-sex fantasies and has seriously considered establishing a relationship with a woman. However, social stigma and the fear that her daughters might feel ashamed of her have never allowed her to pursue this possibility.

Natalia has never talked to anyone about the experience with her uncle. She said it has been difficult to revisit the experience and talk about it with her siblings. Her sister has memories of it, but she is reluctant to open up. She said her brother "blocked it out." This same brother made her feel very uncomfortable recently by "playfully" fondling her breasts.

Natalia has a long history of sexual harrasment by her male supervisors at work, including episodes of violent sexual assault by the son of her employer when she had a job as a domestic worker; she has lost her job every time she has confronted the men. She was kidnapped and raped by an armed stranger in her late teens, and survived a brutal gang rape in her late twenties. Not long ago, Natalia paid two visits to a psychiatrist to address her chronic depression, suicidal ideation, and a weight problem. She is now taking antidepressants. Natalia's husband is currently in a detoxification program after a long battle with alcoholism.

Maternal Tíos Políticos: Maternal Uncles-in-Law

Evangelina

"It happened over several years, and I must have been fifteen or so when he tried to do it for the last time," said Evangelina, a full-time housewife and mother in her late twenties cohabitating with a man in Monterrey. Born and raised in a vibrant working-class colonia, Evangelina says she was in elementary school when her uncle fondled her on top of her clothes, a situation that later involved direct physical contact and vaginal penetration with his fingers. The first time this happened, she was seven or eight, and he was between twenty-five and thirty. Her tío was the husband of her mother's younger sister. These experiences took place repeatedly, especially when nobody was around. "He claimed he loved me very much," she said, explaining that he never used threats or offensive language with her. In other circumstances he was respectful and nonviolent, and would talk to her as if nothing had happened. Regardless of the context, she never felt comfortable around him.

"In fact, he was the one who took away my virginity," said Evangelina. Her tío penetrated her vaginally with his fingers, causing her to bleed. She was about eight years old and remembers with almost photographic clarity an event surrounded by coincidences and chances. The day before her tío raped her, she'd been sent by her father to buy beer for him at the *depósito*, a beer storehouse in her colonia.[10] Her mother arrived at the depósito just as Evangelina was getting the beer, and saw the owner talking to the girl in a way that didn't feel right to her. It was rumored that the owner of the depósito, a man in his seventies at the time, had molested girls in the colonia. Her mother didn't think twice; within days she took Evangelina to a female doctor for an examination. The physician confirmed that she had been vaginally penetrated. Evangelina's mother blamed the depósito owner and repeatedly asked her daughter to say what he had done to her. Fearful and confused, Evangelina denied it but didn't elaborate, and remained silent. "I was afraid they wouldn't believe me, or would think I was the one provoking him," she said. She didn't have the courage to tell her mother about what her uncle had done to her. Her mother didn't pursue it further. The tío's abuse continued.

Although the man at the depósito hadn't done anything to Evangelina that day, he had fondled her on two or three previous occasions. As a way to cope, she decided to tell her mother that she would no longer buy beer for her alcoholic father. She remembers saying to her mother, "These are not errands for me to do. I can go buy a kilo of tortillas, but [to do this] for my father's vice, no." Where would an eight- or nine-year-old girl get this kind of awareness and courage? she wonders. From her third grade teacher, as it turned out. Evangelina explained: "My school teacher spent a lot of time with us [students], and he always said things like that, he would inculcate the idea that nobody should touch us. He talked a lot about these things; he always talked a lot about morality." As she grew up and succeeded in school, this teacher—a man who inspired respect and admiration—became her most important source of emotional support, self-esteem, and resilience. She was about twelve when she told her mother to leave her father, whose use of alcohol aggravated the abusive marital relationship, which included an attempt to kill her mother.

As she recalled the experiences with the man at the depósito, Evangelina said that the security guard—*el velador*—of a warehouse near her home had sexually molested her as well. On her way to do errands for her family and on several other occasions, the velador man stopped her, and fondled her and gave her oral sex. She was about eight years old and he was in his sixties. The security guard had a brother who lived nearby and became a protective figure for her, a caring man she calls her *abuelo*—grandfather. She never told him what his brother was doing to her, but he protected her. He would intervene if he saw an older child wanting to fight with her, for example. She said the experiences with the two men felt disgusting, and were never physically pleasurable.

It is very likely that Evangelina wasn't the only girl in the colonia being molested by the store owner and the security guard. Yet despite strong rumors of other cases of sexual molestation, none of her neighbors did anything about it, especially with regard to the man at the depósito. Evangelina thinks this was in part because of his connections to the local police: "I imagine people were kind of afraid because he seemed to have some kind of influence in his relationships with people in a position of authority," she said. The policemen in their police cars all used to go drink there.

Evangelina soon learned how to avoid the depósito owner and the security guard, but struggled to figure out ways to avoid her tío. She started to spend time with a girlfriend, and also had her first boyfriend. When her mother learned that she was having sex with him, she told Evangelina's father about it. He beat her up as a way to discipline her. She was fourteen at the time, and about to reach her limit. Her uncle, she said, "told me that nobody would believe me." That would soon change.

When Evangelina turned fifteen, she actively resisted her uncle's assaults, and said she was going to tell her mother about him. She also threatened to use physical force to resist or even kill him if he didn't stop, she said, "even if I had ended up in prison." Besides the positive influence of her teacher, where did she learn to resist with so much confidence? "I always urged my mother to leave my father," she said. Her heart ached to witness their constant fighting. This feeling intensified when she was fifteen or sixteen years old and accidently overheard her parents having sex. Her mother was sobbing and in so much pain that she felt confused, unsure if the sex was against her mother's will. She also told herself, "Here I am telling my mother to leave my father, so why am I letting [my uncle] abuse me? That's when I told myself, 'All right, that's it!'" Evangelina successfully put a stop to her uncle's behavior.

Around the same age, she was also figuring out how to stop being the parental child in her family. Her father was on disability after a tragic accident while her mother was away from home. Usually, her mother was working, but at times, she would go play cards with her friends. "I had to do everything," says Evangelina. "From the moment I woke up I did all the household chores. I washed the clothes, I did the ironing, I made sure my brother went to school. My little brother, the youngest one, was a baby and I had to change his diaper. I did everything. I felt as if I had a responsibility." In a way, she was already the woman of the house for her father. She recalled sarcastically challenging her mother when she was sixteen: "All I need now is to go and have sex with him, right?"

Evangelina finished secundaria highly motivated to go to college and become a physician, but her dreams vanished due to lack of family and economic support. Her parents eventually divorced. As she recalled the assertiveness she was developing in her adolescence, she shared another story that made her giggle and blush. "He was the most attractive guy in the entire barrio," said Evangelina with a glow on her face as she referred to another uncle, her mother's younger brother. *El tío guapo*—the good-looking uncle—inspired romantic fantasies in many teenage girls in the colonia.

"I'm going to have what nobody else can have," said Evangelina, remembering the kisses, hugs, and caresses she exchanged with him. She was about ten and he was about eighteen the first time these sexualized exchanges happened. Three years later, it happened again. He always took the initiative, and she described these experiences as voluntary on her part. The exchanges didn't involve vaginal penetration. When she became older, he approached her again, and when she said no, he didn't pursue it. "I think he saw it like that, you know, that thing about *a la prima se le arrima*, no? In other words, *un arrimón*—groping—and that's it. Maybe that is what he thought, back then," she said.[11]

But "un arrimón" didn't feel right, and by age seventeen, Evangelina was already telling herself: "I feel like I used him as revenge, because of the ways in which we women are used to please them [men]." She also said that she grew up feeling neglected by her parents and perceiving her older sister as the favorite child. So the experiences with her tío guapo made her feel like *la preferida*—the chosen one—who was "getting away" with something, although she didn't feel anything special physically or sexually with him. The experiences with him were never physically or verbally violent, and she never fell in love with him. Although she now perceives it as sexually abusive on his part because of the age difference, she feels that she "used" him emotionally. She somewhat regrets these experiences with him and believes that they happened because of her experiences with the men who sexually molested her when she was a girl.

Evangelina's experiences with the handsome tío remained their secret, but she suspected that other women in the family were having their own secret affairs with him. "I have always thought that he also had sexual relations with my sister," she said. Evangelina and her sister became jealous the day the tío was forced to marry a woman who was not *la novia de planta*—the official girlfriend—a woman with whom he had a sexual adventure and who claimed she had lost her virginity with him. Rumors circulated about the young woman's past sexual experiences with one of her uncles. El tío guapo and his wife eventually divorced.

Evangelina's romantic and sex life became a Pandora's box. She fell in love and had a child with a man and was amazed to later learn that he was the son of the security guard who molested her when she was in elementary school. Their relationship is perhaps the best one of all, and she is now a full-time housewife raising their children. These days, she lets her children go buy tortillas or milk for her, but never to run errands that might expose them to sexual abuse. She hopes that her children will succeed in school and benefit from the three encyclopedias she bought on installments for them.

Evangelina's third grade teacher has become the central character of the many stories and lessons of moral values that she teaches her children. She emulates him and actively talks to her children about sexual abuse, reproduction, and sex education. "He became the father I didn't have at home," she said, weeping. She dreams of finding him some day.

"I'm not afraid anymore," said Evangelina, as she looks back on her life. She has never been in therapy, and nobody knows about the three men who molested her. She isn't sure she will ever forgive the men who left her with such deep psychological scars, but she has silently witnessed the ways in which life has done justice for her. Her aunt left her uncle, who has had a hard life. The depósito man and the security guard were both abandoned and neglected by their families when they were facing terminal illnesses that eventually killed them.

Luz

> He got me naked and he got naked as well. He wanted me to touch him and vice versa. And I asked him "Why?" He said I was guilty of that, and that I shouldn't tell anyone because nobody would believe me, and that I was going to pay a high price if I talked to anyone. So I grew up believing that I had been guilty of it.

A college-educated woman from Guadalajara in her early twenties, Luz said that this episode happened once with her mother's cousin at his house. Luz was four or five and he was in his twenties. Luz used to visit him often to draw, especially on weekends. Her uncle owned a carpentry workshop that was full of things she enjoyed playing with. It was conveniently located across from her grandparents' house. She has an almost photographic memory of a damaging experience there.

> He touched me while he masturbated, and he wanted me to touch him as well. He grabbed my hands and made me touch him. He asked if I liked it and he told me, "You have to say 'yes.' I know that you like it, because if you didn't, you wouldn't be here. You would have not come." "You are guilty of this," he said, because I had provoked him.

Luz says our interview was the first time she has told anyone about this.

> I didn't even know what was happening. At that age I had no knowledge of any of that. But I was scared because of what he was telling me. When I arrived home, I was crying, and my mother asked me if there was anything wrong. I didn't tell her anything, and she went to see him and ask

him why I was crying, if he had done anything to me. And he said, "No, I didn't do anything." She kept asking me all afternoon, but I never told her anything.

Why was Luz silent? Partly because she was afraid he would do the same thing again, but partly—she wept as she said this—because of the way her family might have seen her, she said. She didn't know what her mother would have done had she known the truth. "I am even more afraid that people I know would know about it [the abuse] and I wouldn't be able to bear what they would say. Yes, that my family and people I know would know about it. I feel like they would see me differently, that they would treat me differently. So I prefer they never know about it."

During her childhood and adolescence, Luz never saw her uncle. He moved out of town; at times, as an adult, however, she has run into him when he visits Guadalajara on vacation. She has avoided any contact with him, and when they have met, she said "he behaves as if nothing had happened."

Luz also recalled two other experiences with another uncle, a tío político who was the husband of her mother's sister. The first time, this tío político was in his thirties when Luz was seven or eight, and he kissed and fondled her, but never undressed her. Sobbing, she said he always managed to make her feel like she was the guilty party. "He told me that he had done it like that because I excited him. Then, the second time, I had that firm idea in my mind that I was guilty, of what, of what [sobbing] and of what [pause], that is why I have not told anyone."

When I asked Luz if she recalled his actual words, she paraphrased them:

That I was guilty of what he was doing to me because he felt attracted to me. And if I wasn't the way I was then he wouldn't have done anything to me, and that I should not tell anything to anybody . . . Because if anyone knew about it, it was going to become a scandal in the family, and that many problems in the family would take place and therefore I was going to be guilty. And that if my aunt divorced him and the entire world was going to point the finger at him and that the family was going to come to an end because I . . . I didn't want to, that was the reason why I didn't say anything.

This occurred twice at Luz's uncle's home during family visits. As she became older, the sexual violence only changed in its expression. As she became of age, they occasionally ran into each other. "He would tell me that he was waiting for me to grow up," she said. "He would say that, and I realized he intended to do other kinds of things. He [would say] that I was not a girl anymore. And when I became an adolescent and my body changed and all those kinds of things, he said that he was alert to all of those changes in me."

A few months before our interview, Luz ran into the tío, who asked her if she was dating anyone. "I talk to him because I have to, but I don't like being alone with him," she said. "I don't like the way he talks to me, or the way he looks at me, so I try to avoid him." He has never used physical violence, but every time they meet he engages in these behaviors, especially when nobody is around. As with her first tío, when they are around family and other people, "he behaves as if nothing had ever happened," Luz said. To this day, neither her mother nor her tío político's wife know about her experiences with him.

Marina

"When the entire family is together, he is very kind, and he pretends to be very respectful," said Marina. "Nobody could ever imagine what he has done." Her relationship with her thirty-eight-year-old uncle was an excruciating journey that only ended the year before I interviewed her.

Marina's uncle—the husband of her mother's sister—started by fondling her when she was seven, as part of "playing with her." He strategically increased the tone of his sexual coercion and eventually raped her when she was eight. "He penetrated me so many, many times, I lost count," she said.

Born and raised in a working-class family in Guadalajara, Marina is now in her early twenties, and has two older sisters and a younger brother; the boy is the result of her mother's most recent relationship. Marina's mother divorced the father of her oldest children when Marina was young. Since then, her mother has had to work hard to support them, she said. Her mother struggled to pay the rent, for example. Marina's uncle and aunt didn't have a house, so they moved in with her, paying half the rent. Marina said her aunt and uncle's presence offered her mother financial relief.

As part of the family and the household, her uncle was seen as someone who could be trusted to take care of Marina while her mother and aunt were at work. But as he juggled different jobs, he also figured out the family schedule and exercised violence against Marina when nobody was at home. She feels pretty sure he didn't do anything to her older sisters, she said, "maybe because they went to school in the morning." Ironically, while the hardworking mother earned a living in her modest administrative job for a litigation law firm, her sister's husband was raping the youngest of her daughters.

Now an articulate college student, Marina clearly recalls her ages when those events of violence occurred. When she was seven and eight, he fondled Marina frequently, and raped her at age eight. Then Marina got a welcome break. For two years—from ages nine to eleven—Marina and her sisters went to a secular boarding school after qualifying for financial aid. These two years gave Marina a respite from her uncle and an exciting learning opportunity that she still recalls with joy. Unfortunately, when Marina was eleven, her mother decided the girls were "old enough," and brought them back home. From that moment until she was sixteen, her uncle became more and more strategic and opportunistic and raped her.

Marina was sixteen when a violent argument erupted between her aunt and uncle and her mother. It became a blessing in disguise, as Marina's mother and her three daughters were "kicked out of the house." However, when mother and aunt reconciled, the uncle visited them, and selectively harassed and raped Marina. She still avoids him to this day, she said. "For now, I go to the church choir or somewhere else," she said. "I am always out in the street to avoid being at home. If I know that nobody is going to be there, I leave."

"He became more aggressive, more brutal," she said. She explained that he wasn't physically violent in the beginning but started to use physical force especially as she became older, physically stronger, and resisted him more forcefully. "I made it very difficult for him once and—*me chingó*—he beat the fucking hell out of me." Bruises, cuts, bleeding, a twisted foot, and a limp were some of the consequences of Marina's increasing resistance to her uncle. When her curious and confrontational mother inquired about her bruises or wounds, she made up excuses, until she ran out. "I didn't know what else to come up with," she said. At some point she learned to become helpless, she said. "At some point I made the decision to not defend myself anymore, because that was even worse for me. I started to do nothing about it."

Meanwhile, her uncle bullied her into silence. She said he would say: "You tell your mother about it and I will tell her that it isn't true. You'll see, she won't believe you. Everyone is going to make fun of you." He said this so often after raping her that she eventually believed him. To this day, he calls her *niña*—little girl.

Marina has kept silent about the abuse, partly out of fear of what her mother might do to the uncle if she knew. "When my mother watches TV and sees something about abuse, she gets furious. I'm afraid she would kill him." Marina has never said anything to anyone in her family, also because of vergüenza. The encounters with the uncle were painful, never pleasurable.

While growing up, Marina never witnessed violence or heard stories of violence within her family. But she describes her family as *medio distraída*—they don't pay attention to what is truly happening at home. For example, she realizes that her uncle knew how to manipulate her mother and find ways to be alone with Marina. On one occasion, her uncle asked her (in front of her mother) to run some errands with him, and her mother insisted that she go. "I have no idea how he does it," she said.

As a teenager, Marina was plagued by nightmares and eating disorders, and tried three times to commit suicide. "I was never able to succeed, so I gave up," she said. "I once ended up at the hospital because of all the stress. First, I had an asthma attack, and then my body felt numb, and one time I had facial paralysis." Marina has suffered from asthma since she was young and gets sick frequently. She associates all of these issues with her uncle's violence against her.

Inspired by her hardworking mother, Marina went to work in a gift shop at age thirteen when she realized that her mother had no money to buy school materials for her. She has worked ever since. She now works full time and goes to college; her mother is recovering at home from a complicated surgery. Paradoxically, the mother's inability to work protects Marina from the uncle, who has stayed away from them. An optimistic Marina has dreams of buying a house for her mother some day. "Life is short, and I have to take advantage of it," she said.

Coping while remaining silent was possible because of her deep love for her mother, she said.

> Since the day my father left us, at times we didn't even have enough to eat. But my mother moved heaven and earth—*movía mar y tierra*—to give us everything. I'm alive because of her. Because I want her to be okay, I struggle, I strive, and I work hard. She is very happy that I am studying. She has given me an example, to teach me that I can make it, that I can move on. In other words, even if things are really bad, I can still make it.

To this day, a close friend, a college professor, and her gynecologist are the only people who know Marina's story. On her doctor's recommendation, she recently visited a psychologist. She finds him patient and relaxed, she said, but won't tell him about her uncle until she feels she can trust him completely.

Odalys

"I remember we were several children. But, for example, he would sit me by his side, and many times he would touch me, he would grab my hand and used it to masturbate at the movies. It happened many times," said Odalys, a middle-class, college-educated woman in her late forties. Born and raised in Monterrey, she and her family, including her maternal grandparents, were highly involved in an Evangelical church. When Odalys was ten or eleven, she was subjected to a wide variety of sexual experiences at the hand of her tío político, a man in his late thirties who was the husband of her mother's sister.

"When everyone in the family left to go out somewhere, most of the time he was the one who took care of us," said Odalys. Perceived by his relatives and other people as "a good person," the man often looked after Odalys, her primas, and other girls in her neighborhood, all of them about the same age. He would tell them stories or take them to the movies as a group. Odalys called him "a very astute person." "He had such a skill to touch you so nobody would suspect that he was touching you. In other words, if you got to look at something that was being exhibited, he would [be by your side and] touch your breast gently with his elbow, or if he put his hand down, he would gently touch your legs while doing it."

Before Odalys knew it, her uncle had seduced her into personal encounters that included getting her naked, touching her body, mutual masturbation, and attempting to penetrate her vaginally—all without using the slightest amount of physical force. "He was never violent," she said. "There was manipulation, perhaps seduction, curiosity, a series of things." She found herself experiencing a stimulating sensation of pleasure in these encounters. "He was a very, very skillful person," she said. He was also *atrevido*—daring. He would take the risk of seducing her when an adult relative was sleeping in the room next door. "I think he was one of those people who get excited by knowing that he could get caught." He would also show her pornographic magazines as part of these sexual encounters, or leave them in strategic parts of the house where she could see them.

Though Odalys experienced stimulating physical sensations with him, she said she felt "totally manipulated" in all the experiences. She may have been curious, but it felt as if "he took advantage of the moment," she said. "It was simple as that. The moment happened, he became aware of it, and he got away with it."

Odalys described herself as being rebellious and assertive from an early age, yet she never told anyone about the encounters. "He said that what was happening was a game between us, and that I couldn't talk [about it] with anyone else," she said, "and if anyone learned about it, he would kill my mother and my father." When she resisted, he would use these threats. At other times he would tell her that she was "special, his beloved girl," that he didn't treat all his nieces the same way, that "she was the best."

Odalys said she felt something wasn't "right" and was afraid of "going to hell" because of these "sinful" experiences, while also feeling good in her body. "I had no option," she said. "I am going to hell, but if I don't do it, he is going to kill my parents." In retrospect, Odalys wishes she had talked to an adult to protect others from similar experiences. Aside from the complex web of feelings and the fears her uncle's threats triggered in her, she was afraid she wouldn't be believed.

Right at the moment when I realized that my aunt [his wife] knew about what is going on and did nothing about it, from that moment on, believe me, I lost complete trust in the human being. I even had more love for my dog . . . [laughs] I couldn't believe she wasn't aware of what was happening, and that it wasn't the first time it happened. Because she wanted to keep her husband, she left me vulnerable, even given the fact that I was blood of her blood.

"I remember the way my tía looked at me and treated me as if I was her rival," she said. "I now realize that she was aware of what her husband was doing, right? And that I wasn't the only person he did it to." In fact, Odalys is positive she wasn't the only child enduring those experiences, and that her aunt ignored it. "*Mi tía se hacía güey*," she said, meaning that her aunt knew about what was happening but played dumb. Odalys didn't know how her aunt could live with someone who abused children.

One thing that convinced Odalys that he was abusing other children was a look she recognized in their eyes. "I feel like the same look with which we look at that person, I saw it in more than one person. The same look of rage, feeling you have been abused but without being able to say it, because you weren't able to talk about it. I saw that same look in more than one person, the same look that I had in my eyes when I looked at him." She later said that three of her primas openly avoided being alone with him or openly but silently rejected him.

Between the ages of ten and twelve, Odalys had a wide variety of experiences with him. By the time she was almost fifteen, he was still pursuing her. But by then she had learned the word *hostigamiento*— harassment. She confronted him and threatened to tell her parents. By then, she also had more information about reproduction and was afraid of getting pregnant. The harassment finally stopped completely when the tío and his wife left Monterrey. "Uffff!" she exclaimed in relief. "When they moved out of town, it was like releasing the escape valve of a pressure cooker," she said. "I finally rested." Her uncle died while still living out of town, when Odalys was in her mid-twenties. Other than her aunt, she thinks nobody in her family knows what happened to her.

Even though Odalys grew up feeling dirty and guilty about her experiences with her uncle, access to books about human sexuality and psychology have proved helpful. She found them at the house and in the company of one of her best amigas, and read them with deep curiosity. She was able to gradually overcome these feelings and understand that what had happened to her was not her fault. To this day, she has never been in therapy. In retrospect, she wished she had told her tío this:

¿Sabes qué? You know what? When I think of all the damage you might have caused me, I believe that, I forgive you. Because you were an adult and you knew what was happening and I was never aware of why that was happening, or what was actually happening. But I forgive you because you didn't scar me. I forgive you because you didn't damage my life. And I forgive you because, as a person, I am better than you.

Sabina

"I bled a lot, and he threw away two of the sheets," said Sabina, remembering being raped by her tío when she was eight. "My aunt was on her way home from work but she hadn't arrived yet." Now in her late twenties, Sabina vividly remembered that her aunt's twenty-one-year-old husband vaginally penetrated her by force. He was married to her mother's sister. "He got out the knife [to threaten me] because he saw me *desangrando*—draining of blood—and thought that I was going to tell about what had happened. He suddenly put his penis in my mouth, and then I felt kind of sleepy. He told me that it [bleeding] was normal because my menstruation was happening to me."

Born and raised in Ciudad Juárez, Sabina is the second child in a family of seven children. Her mother is now in her late forties and has worked full time for many years at a *maquiladora* (assembly plant), while frustrated at not being able to better provide for her family. Nor could she rely on her husband, morally or financially. "My father was always drunk," said Sabina. When her mother went to work, she said, she left us children at home alone, with the oldest taking care of the little ones. "*Nos criamos solos*," she said. "We were alone."

When Sabina was eight, her uncle decided to hire her as a nanny. "He asked my mother if he could *borrow me* [my emphasis] so I could take of their son." The uncle promised her mother money in exchange for Sabina being their nanny. Excited about the extra income, the young mother sent her daughter to live with the uncle's family during her school vacation. For the little girl, a nightmare was about to begin at her uncle's hands. "I arrived there from school, and he said, 'Come over here, so I can unbutton your skirt.' And I told him 'No,' that I wanted to sleep. Later I lay down on the floor, next to the door, it was summer time and I wanted to get some fresh air. I fell asleep."

Sabina doesn't recall how long she slept. To this day, however, she hasn't been able to forget what happened next.

When I woke up he was already on top of me. And he had already undressed me [without being aware]. And when I woke up, I covered myself with a bed sheet. And he started to tell me that he felt attracted to me, that I should be his, that he was going to give me the love my father never gave me. And then, he began to ask me to kiss him [his penis], many times. It lasted all night long, all night and I felt so ugly . . . and fear, because I didn't know what to do. Then, when he finished he told me that I was his, and that anytime he wanted to, he was going to have me. Then he pulled out a knife, he put it right here [pointing to her neck] and he told me that if I said anything, he was going to kill us . . . and that nobody would give us money, and that he would never give us money and that my mother would end up in jail. I felt so scared. I felt so much fear. I never said anything.

Sabina experienced more or less intense versions of the above scenario almost daily for two and a half months. Her uncle raped her vaginally and orally, and forced her to swallow his semen. She recalled her uncle's favorite words while raping her: "You're very hot." "When you grow up, you're going to be a great prostitute." The hemorrhage she had the first time she was raped was followed by chronic vaginal pain, which intensified both her fear and silence.

When her school vacation ended, Sabina went back home, but her uncle insisted that her mother send her over on the weekend. "I told my mother that I didn't want to go, but she forced me. My mother said, 'Go with him, you have to go because we need money.' She told me because 'you are going to go to school and we don't have money.' I didn't even have a pencil. So I had to go."

Sabina eventually told her mother why she didn't want to go to her uncle's house, but her mother didn't believe her. Sabina then became "very rebellious." She ran away from home and lived with a neighbor she calls a *señora prostituta*. A caring woman, she took Sabina to a doctor because of the intense vaginal pain, and protected her afterward. The doctor gave them what Sabina called a "certificate": written proof that she had been raped. With the document in hand, her neighbor confronted her mother, and Sabina had no choice but to run away from home again. Running away became Sabina's lifestyle. From age nine until she was about seventeen, Sabina moved from house to house and lived with at least ten different families. "I got older and I became more *maleada*"—into evil ways, corrupt. "I didn't let anyone mess with me." She protected herself from being sexually molested by at least one man in these households.

In her early twenties, Sabina worked at several cantinas and worked in commercial sex for three years "while feeling really bad about it." She "felt forced to do it out of need," to support her two daughters. They were born of a relationship Sabina had with a man who is now in prison, accused of robbery. Sabina today works at a maquiladora.[12]

Sabina has heard stories of her mother's brother "touching" her mother and her three aunts "all over." Yet when her grandmother learned about it, she never intervened. "What happened to me comes from there," she said. Her mother and aunts also experienced physical and verbal violence at the hands of their heterosexual partners. Of the women in her family, Sabina said, "All of them are weak. They've been taken advantage of, in every way. They've never defended themselves from anyone, ever." Sabina also learned that her uncle—the same man who repeatedly raped her when she was eight—also molested her oldest sister.

In her mid-twenties, Sabina ran into the uncle again, and he harassed her. This time, an assertive, empowered Sabina confronted him and threatened "to do something to his children" if he didn't stop. He never looked for her again. Sabina never lost contact with her mother, but she has struggled to relate to her because of her unresolved pain. After Sabina's own eight-year-old daughter told Sabina that her mother's partner had "put his finger inside" and threatened her to keep silent, Sabina told her mother about it. Her mother didn't believe that her partner—a man with a reputation as *muy buena gente*, a good person—could have done such a thing to her granddaughter. In addition, Sabina recently learned that her current partner's father refers to her two daughters as *prostitutas* and spies on them when they use the restroom.

I met Sabina at an organization where she sought professional help. Her heartfelt wish was to protect her daughters from the same fate, heal a damaged relationship with her mother, and eventually "forgive herself" for what happened with her uncle. She would like to overcome the difficulties she has experienced in her romantic and sex life, including a pattern of sexual involvement with married men, and to understand why she thinks she does not deserve to be happy.

Paternal Uncles: Fathers' Biological Brothers

Paloma

"He would jump into my bed and touch me, or try to kiss me," said Paloma, a mother in her early twenties living in a heterosexual cohabitation relationship in Monterrey. Born and raised in an upper-middle-class family she was trained to perceive as *la familia perfecta*, Paloma was in first grade when her tío (a younger brother of her father) started to harass her. He eventually got her naked and penetrated her vaginally with his fingers. Paloma used to share her bed with a brother who was a toddler. At times, her uncle raped her while the little boy was asleep.

Although in the beginning Paloma thought that what he did to her was "normal," she recalled these experiences as negative and never pleasurable. They took place frequently and lasted for about five years. This resulted in vaginal pain, blood, discharge, and infections that her mother neither took seriously nor investigated. Instead, she yelled at her and blamed her for it. To this day, Paloma resents her for this and for her emotional and physical absence.

Paloma lived these experiences almost daily, especially while her family lived in her paternal grandmother's big house. Her father had tried working in different parts of Mexico, but had to declare bankruptcy, which hit his business hard. Paloma was about ten when they moved out of her grandmother's house, but the abuse didn't stop. Her uncle was hired by Paloma's father, visited their home, and looked for her frequently. When she was six years old, her tío was about twelve or thirteen.

"Almost always, I would close my eyes," said Paloma. He would get on top of her "as if they were having sexual relations," with or without clothes, and she would "not pay attention" to what he was doing. As a way to cope, she would "check out" in her mind, she said. In her imagination she would go to the many nice places she visited during vacations with her parents.[13] This coping mechanism fell apart one day during a family vacation that involved her tío.

Paloma was eight or nine at the time, but remembered the experience in vivid detail. As her father drove his wife and children to visit a relative out of town, Paloma, her only brother, and her tío were in the back seat with their legs covered with a blanket that her mother had given them to protect them from the cold. As they drove, her adolescent tío kept his hand between Paloma's legs and fondled her. He then carefully fixed her skirt when they arrived at their aunt's home. As they settled at their relatives' home, her tío started to play rough with Paloma's brother. He wound up hitting the little boy harder than she could bear to witness without telling her parents. Her tío threatened her: "If you say anything, I will tell them where I had my hand during the car trip." At that moment, Paloma experienced a shocking realization. "That was how I became aware that this wasn't right," she said. "But I thought that I was guilty of it, that I was the one who was doing something wrong, not him."

From that day on, Paloma's tío established a system that allowed him to have access to her body while effectively keeping her silent. She explained, "Yes, I feel guilty because any time he wants to [do it], or I say 'no,' he would say, 'If you don't let me do it, I'll accuse you. I'll say that you let me do it in the past.'" He also threatened to "touch" her brother if she resisted. She felt helpless the day her brother complained of a skin irritation on his penis (which the mother did not investigate) while Paloma wondered in silence if her tío had molested him as well. Like the women in this study who became "conjugal daughters," Paloma played the role of the paternal child and learned to be receptive and attentive to her brother's needs.

Paloma was about eleven years old when she noticed with a deep sense of relief that her tío suddenly stopped chasing her or assaulting her. This happened right after he established a relationship with a woman a few years older than him who had a daughter and worked as a prostitute. The young couple established a relationship of breakups and makeups that survives to this day. After the couple broke up the first time, the uncle immediately started to harass Paloma again. She was sixteen years old then and was dating a young, working-class man from out of town who lived alone. Her family saw him as *un don nadie*—a nobody, someone not good enough for her. Paloma's tío, who was in his early twenties then, acted jealous and angry, and tried to convince her parents not to allow her to date. But shortly afterward the young tío reestablished the relationship with his girlfriend, and immediately stopped assaulting Paloma. Her tío was always kind and respectful when he and Paloma met at family get-togethers and events involving relatives or friends.

As Paloma became older, bigger, and stronger, she learned to protect herself. She either avoided her uncle completely, stayed around only if other family or friends were present, or left the house whenever he arrived. She ran away from home once to live with a close girlfriend. Later she spent long periods of time at her boyfriend's house, over her father's objections.

When she finally broke her silence and told her father that she went to her boyfriend's house after literally running, exhausted, from her tío who was chasing her, her father thought she was lying and using the story as an excuse to have sex with her boyfriend. He confronted the young couple and forced them to plan a marriage. But her father unexpectedly changed his mind and told them to live together for a year as a way to test the relationship.[14] They have lived together ever since, and Paloma decided it was "useless and stupid" for them to marry after all these years.

When I asked Paloma if she thought she had satisfied her uncle's sexual needs, she said, "I think that was the case." As she grew up, she learned about the stories of other women who had played a similar role in the family. By the time Paloma and her parents moved in with her grandmother, a prima about four years older who was being raised by the latter was preparing to move out to live with her father, who had recently remarried. "I substituted for her," Paloma says. While her prima was still living in the house—a period of six months or so—her tío never looked for her.

As adults, the two women have confided in and emotionally supported each other as they have talked about the similarity of their experiences with their tío, including their both being raped in the same bedroom and at around the same age. Paloma's prima became a successful college student who left for Europe to pursue her professional dreams and to put distance between herself and her painful past. As she shared other family stories, Paloma exclaimed, "¡Ahí se armó la revolución!" (And right there revolutionary turmoil flared up!) to describe the family revolt that emerged when her tío and one of his primas close in age openly developed a voluntary, romantic relationship, which was surrounded by family scandal and gossip. Paloma also recalled the story of a primo (the son of a brother of Paloma's father) who sexually assaulted his prima (the daughter of a sister of Paloma's father). The girl's mother intervened, but never told Paloma's father about it because she was afraid of losing financial support, Paloma said. Her father gives generous financial support to his sisters.

"I felt happy and I jumped up and down for joy!" Paloma said when she learned that her tío—now in his late twenties—was being prosecuted and on his way to prison outside Monterrey, in one of the state municipalities. The tío had established a relatively stable relationship with his partner of several years, but abused the girl who eventually became his stepdaughter. When the girl was twelve or thirteen, she accused him of sexual abuse, and was supported by her maternal grandmother.

By then, Paloma finally had the courage to tell her own story to both parents. They didn't believe her, and refused to let her confront her tío in front of them. They didn't believe the story of the tío's stepdaughter, either. "My father has money and my mother has *influencias,* people involved in politics and things like that," says Paloma. Her parents paid a lot of money to an attorney who managed to get her uncle out of prison while also making sure that the authorities destroyed any evidence of his criminal record. Her parents "had to do it," she said. The grandmother had an intense emotional reaction to these events and they felt they had to safeguard *las apariencias*—keep up appearances, the good image of the family. Paradoxically, if her family had been poor, it is likely that the tío would have remained in prison.

The day her uncle was freed, the entire family went on a vacation trip, says Paloma, "as if nothing had happened." She confronted him that day in front of her grandmother, who intervened and begged Paloma to be respectful toward her uncle. "And now he is on the loose, free and doing it to I don't know how many more," she said. Her tío and his partner of many years have reunited to raise their newborn child, but fresh rumors are circulating within and outside her family. "Now people are saying that he is having sex with his stepdaughter," she said.

Though born with a silver spoon in her mouth, Paloma is now a full-time mother and housewife living in a working-class colonia. She finished secundaria and pursued training in trade school. She is in an awkward position: she is the daughter of a successful businessman and supportive father who married a man who became one of her father's workers, making a modest income.

"I think I swallowed the pain," she said. "And that is why I became like this, cold and hard-hearted." A supportive teacher, a good friend, her prima, and the love for her children have helped her cope with her suicidal tendencies. She described her marital and sexual relationships as satisfactory and relatively stable; she and her husband love each other deeply. Still, he has complained that she wasn't a virgin the first time they had sex, and revisits the history of sexual abuse at times of tension and conflict in their relationship. She is concerned about his drinking habits as well. She hopes to find answers to these marital concerns at the organization where I met her, where she went to seek professional help for the first time.

Paternal Tíos Políticos: Paternal Uncles-in-Law

Regina

"He used to tell us that he loved us very much," said Regina, an attorney from Guadalajara in her mid-twenties who was molested by her uncle along with her little prima. "He said that we were like his daughters, that being with him we would never be poor, that we were what he loved the most. He always expressed a lot of love for us." As a nine-year-old in elementary school, Regina frequently visited her uncle's house on weekends to play with her prima, who was a couple of years younger. Her uncle was in his late thirties or early forties at the time and had recently married Regina's tía (the sister of her father). He became the two girls' caregiver while his hardworking wife was out tending to a family business or running errands.

Regina's mother died when she was a toddler. She was raised by her father and spent time with her father's sister. Regina described what her uncle used to do while the two girls were under his care:

> He used to play pornographic movies and he would get naked. One time he simply made us touch him, but he always made us watch those movies. At some point we no longer [did it], as we became older, not older in

years but more able to say no. We didn't like watching that, even though we didn't know what it meant or anything. We didn't feel pleasure or anything like that, because at that age you aren't even aware of what is happening. He also made us take showers, and the three of us would take a shower together.

The uncle had engaged in this routine ten times or more by the time Regina and her prima started to resist watching pornographic movies. While watching porn, he also asked them to touch him and masturbate him and used his finger to penetrate her prima vaginally. He attempted to do the same with Regina, but she resisted and he didn't insist. She said she always felt "uncomfortable" and confused around him, especially when he tried to hold them tight or as he tried to play horsey with them, one on each of his legs.

As Regina became older, he tried new tricks. Once when she was twelve, Regina, her tía, tío, and prima were all watching a movie at their home. Her aunt and prima got up to get the pizza that had just arrived at the same time as a kissing scene began in the movie. Her uncle then kissed Regina on the mouth in a way that didn't feel right. Regina felt fearful, confused, and paralyzed, and didn't know what to do. On a different occasion, he tried to kiss her again and Regina finally confronted him.

As Regina began to realize that her experiences with her uncle were not "correct," she started using her studies as an excuse to reject her aunt and uncle's invitations to come and play with her prima. "I went only sporadically," she said. But she worried about her fearful prima, who used to plead with her, "Please, please, stay!" when she was getting ready to say good-bye. "More than anything, I stayed because of her." Regina visited and stayed longer than she wanted to, because she didn't want to leave her prima alone.

"He never threatened or blackmailed us to make us not tell anyone," she said, but she never told. She still doesn't know why they never told anyone back then. Eventually, Regina stopped visiting her uncle and aunt and began to feel safe. But this lasted only for about six years. When she was eighteen, Regina began working as a secretary in the successful family business where all of them were employed—her brother, her aunt, and her uncle. Regina described what she experienced with her uncle at the office: "When my brother left for the day and went home, I was alone with him [my uncle] and he started to harass me." It brought back her childhood memories.

> I would be in my chair working on the computer, and my uncle would arrive and sit behind me, and would hold me from the back and touch my breasts. I would leave right away. I said, "¡Ay! Please stop!" I was so sick of it, because the harassment was very intense. Or he would tell me, "I had sex with so and so and my skin got irritated. Do you want to see where I have the irritation?" So he would do that type of thing.

In these exchanges, her uncle also claimed "to love" virgin women. He said he was in love with and obsessed with her, while insistently inquiring about her virginity. He also promised to buy her a house and a car, and said he dreamed of having a child with her. Regina said she was "never raped" by her uncle, but experienced different versions of the above scenario while becoming increasingly resistant and confrontational.

For about a year, Regina found ways to cope with these complex forms of harassment. But her prima found herself in psychotherapy after surviving a suicide attempt, depression, alcoholism, and a serious bulimic condition. Her prima broke her silence in therapy, and Regina finally had the opportunity to tell her own story to a supportive, understanding, and heartbroken aunt.

A few months before our conversation, Regina's father learned about the abuse through the aunt and expressed his support. But for fear of hurting her father's feelings, Regina didn't share any detailed information about her experiences with her uncle. She was also afraid of her father's impulsivity, believing that her father might kill him.

Regina's relationship with her father wasn't optimal, and she kept her distance from him. He used to call her *puta* when she was an adolescent and made her doubt her professional future. Now an attorney who is critical of the legal system in Mexico and the ways in which sexual violence is legally prosecuted, Regina is satisfied with her family's decision not to press charges against her uncle. After her aunt kicked him out of the house, he left the state. They never saw him again, and Regina experienced some degree of healing and relief.

Paternal Distant Uncle: El Tío Lejano

Elba

"I know that I have many memories that are blocked out," said Elba, a woman in her mid-thirties from Mexico City. What she called "the first images" she remembers while growing up and feeling that something was not right include an old man wearing a white laboratory coat undoing her clothes when she was a little girl. "In my memory, my mother is approaching, and that saved me." To this day, she doesn't know who this mysterious man was, said Elba with a sigh. But she has clear memories of another she recalled with sharp clarity: "I stood still, completely still. I didn't make a move. And when the situation was over, I fixed my clothes and went on with my life." This was an experience she repeatedly had at the hands of her tío lejano—a distant uncle on her father's side of the family who was married to her siblings' nanny.

Raised in a middle-class family, Elba is a polished, articulate woman finishing her last year in college. She grew up in comfort as the youngest daughter in a family of five children. A college-educated and professionally stable man, her father was "a tender husband" who provided for his children and his wife, a full-time housewife. The family didn't practice any religion.

Growing up, Elba witnessed neither aggression nor violence at home, but says her parents' marital and family life followed what she called the *esquema machista*—the sexist schema: an arrangement in which "she served, and he decided." A defiant Elba tended to rebel against this. "My father would come home and say, 'Please remove my socks.' And I would say, 'Why don't take you them off yourself?'" Their relationship was rather tense, and it has always been emotionally distant.

Her parents had a cordial marital relationship and very good communication as a couple, she said, and they rarely used physical violence to discipline their children. Elba's relationship with her mother was distant, but an older sister became her main source of emotional support. For Elba, life as a child felt fine, but things changed before she went to elementary school.

Elba's uncle used to visit her family only periodically, frequently staying for a few months with his wife and Elba's family. He must have been in his seventies or so and had a beard. He used to actively approach Elba when she was three or four years old. "I remember that he used tender words. He didn't use aggression, he didn't do it by force, never, no. The first time yes, the first time he did it because he used force to take down my panties, no? I didn't want to, but after that I didn't put up any obstacle. Then he didn't use any kind of force."

"You are so pretty, how beautiful you are, precious," were some of the expressions he used to seduce her. She then briefly described a scene she frequently experienced while he visited and spent time with her family. "He used to stimulate my genital area with his tongue, he touched it, he kissed me on the mouth, he kissed my body." While recalling these experiences, Elba says, "I don't know if I experienced pleasure. If you ask me now, in retrospect, I would say no. But I am unable to situate myself exactly in those moments." However, she said, "Being exposed to sexual abuse in my childhood, at such an early age, eroticized me. Therefore, it is a very fragile area in me." Elba started to masturbate frequently, and at times in a compulsive manner (and in specific stages in her life), something that took her by surprise with regard to her relationship with her younger brothers.

"There is an experience that is very painful for me because I still see it as abusive on my part," Elba said. When she was ten, she once asked her two younger brothers to do what her uncle used to do, that is, to stimulate her genital area with their mouths. Her brothers were three or four, the same age she was when her uncle molested her the first time. One of her brothers followed her instructions, and the other one refused. She neither forced them nor insisted, and it happened only once.

Elba doesn't recall what she felt at that moment. "I probably thought, 'What am I doing? What if my mother sees me?' Thank God, it never happened again." In her early twenties, Elba wrote a letter to her brothers asking for forgiveness. She has never received a response from them, and has never talked with them about it.

Elba was around ten when her uncle tried to penetrate her but he apparently ejaculated prematurely, spilling semen all over her pelvic area and terrifying her about the risk of pregnancy. From then on, she became more and more resistant to him, and he stopped insisting. Eventually, he stopped visiting her parents' house. As a teenager, however, she ran into him again. In his last attempt at seduction, he told her about feeling "very sad because she didn't want to do it anymore." She exclaimed: "¡Ay! That's blackmailing!"

In her childhood memories, Elba doesn't recall that her tío ever told her not to tell anyone. But an air of secrecy was there. "His attitude made me feel that it had to remain hidden," she said. "For example, he gave me money, and if we were in the kitchen and my mother was there, he gave it to me under the table." Aside from a couple of close friends, few people know Elba's story. Recently, when she told her sister, the woman warned Elba "to be careful and that she had read about something like *síndrome de falsa memoria*"—false memory syndrome. Elba also told three or four Catholic priests. The first of them "didn't give importance to it," she said. She noticed that none of these priests ever told her that what happened with her uncle was not her fault.

"The situation of people like us who have been sexually abused is very, very intense, severe. Therefore, I am not morally obliged to forgive, and I don't believe any woman is morally obliged to forgive," said Elba. "Without a process of recuperation of life, asking someone to forgive is very aggressive." Years ago, Elba spent about a year in therapy with a man who had a Catholic religious training. "Talking about it became a liberation," she said, but she doesn't feel completely recovered. "It is not difficult to believe that this can't be overcome," she said. "There is so much pain, a lot of pain." Of her therapy experience, she said: "He listened, but who is going to get me out of my doubts and my problems? So it was of help, but also not." Even though she knows that what happened wasn't her fault, Elba sometimes still feels guilty for what happened with her uncle.

Understanding Uncle-Niece Incest

As illustrated in these narratives, the women I interviewed experienced a wide variety of expressions of sexual violence at the hands of men they identified as their tíos—uncles. In general, these women rarely said they had an emotionally close relationship with their uncles before the reported incidents took place. Instead, women described their relationships with their uncles as casual, informal, and at times emotionally distant, even for men who used words of affection as part of the sexual violence. The experience of sexualized violence didn't necessarily damage an emotional relationship between the parties involved, but it shaped in different ways the women's perceptions of themselves as women, their sex and romantic lives, their bodies, their images of men, and their family relationships. In particular, the abuse affected their relationships with relatives close to them such as their mothers, especially after they reported the incidents. For instance, the emotional damage was not always a consequence of the act of sexual violence per se. It was sometimes caused by the negative reaction when these women reported the abuse to family members, including a mother, father, aunts, or grandmothers.

As demonstrated by their stories, the following patterns characterize these incestuous arrangements.

Maternal Side versus Paternal Side of the Family

More than two-thirds of the twenty-one women who reported the twenty-eight uncles identified them as men related on the maternal side of their families. In contrast, less than a third said the men were related by the paternal bloodline. Also, women who reported the occurrence of incidents with more than one uncle were women related to these men by the maternal bloodline; see appendix D. I use the concept of "feminization of incest" to identify these and other related patterns of overrepresentation of the maternal side of kinship networks in these uncle-niece incestuous arrangements.

Biological Uncles

Regardless of the side of the family—maternal or paternal—incidents that took place once or twice were reported by women who identified their uncles as the biological brother of a mother or a father. Consistent with the feminization of incest, this "once or twice" pattern exposed more cases of maternal than paternal uncles, which included a mother's biological brother and a mother's first cousin. As illustrated, the fact that it happened "only" once or twice doesn't mean that the intensity or the damage of the experience was less serious. That is, some of these isolated events could be what Evangelina called *un arrimón,* a common expression in Mexico meaning groping, while others could be more physically intrusive and violent or emotionally abusive. But all were damaging in distinctively unique and contrasting ways for each woman. The women all recalled with crystal clarity the number of these incidents, events resulting frequently because of opportunity. A wide variety of family contexts and interactions surrounded these events. While the typical scenario was of a girl alone, sexual assault also happened in the presence of parents, grandparents, and other adult relatives.

Tíos Políticos

Sexual assault by tíos políticos and distant uncles (i.e., uncles who were not directly blood related but connected by family affiliation) all had specific characteristics: (1) The women were sexually molested or raped over a sustained period of time; the abuse lasted months or years and happened frequently, at times until very recently when I interviewed them; (2) The experiences sometimes involved the most intense and brutal expressions of physical violence: blood and bruises, injured internal and external sexual organs, and bodies in deep pain.

However, this doesn't mean that uncles directly related by blood didn't exercise extreme physical violence or exercise violence for sustained periods of time. Frequently but not exclusively, other cases of long sustained violence and / or extreme use of physical violence involved a mother's brother.

Uncles who were identified as caregivers of an informant during her childhood engaged in behaviors of sexual molestation of more than one child at the same time while they were supposedly taking care of the children. That is, the informants reported that molestation didn't happen to them alone, but they also witnessed some form of collective child molestation targeting other children related to them (e.g., primas) who were also under the custody of these men. These uncles who were caregivers were tíos políticos on both sides of the family, and in one case included the half-brother of an informant's mother.

Adolescent Uncles: Almost a Primo

Some women who identified uncles who were close to them in age (for example, men who were in their adolescent years when informants were in elementary school) reported sexually violent behaviors that resembled the ways in which a prima would be sexually harassed by a primo. Similar to the primos who harassed their primas, these adolescent uncle-niece arrangements exposed specific patterns. First, a woman experienced molestation as part of play and at times perceived it as something "normal." Second, a girl might not necessarily resist and might have had physically pleasurable experiences, while feeling that she was being manipulated emotionally. This was especially true of encounters where the lines between "voluntary" and "involuntary" might have been blurry. Third, a woman might realize later in life that she had been a sex surrogate in a young man's life, and might learn that other sisters or primas had played the same role. Fourth, a woman's memories of her childhood include images of adult women in positions of authority in her family as ignoring or not paying attention to what was happening to the girls, or normalizing the assaults as they deciphered different forms of family sexual harassment and sexual terrorism. The men involved were frequently related to informants on the maternal side. These incestuous arrangements at times lasted for long periods of time, but also were occasional or isolated events.

How do we explain these patterns? Why do these forms of sexual violence happen? Why are these uncle-nieces the most common expressions of incestuous sexual violence in the study? Three paradigms offer potential answers: family genealogies of incest, the feminization of incest, and family politics of gender inequality.

Family Genealogies of Incest

The brothers and primos who grow up in incestuous families are socialized to perceive different expressions of family sexual harassment—the sexual objectification and intrusions of girls' and young women's bodies by their male relatives, such as brothers and male cousins—as common and normal. As these young boys and men grow up, these sisters and primas (who are presumably heterosexual) may marry men and have children, and thus their young brothers and primos become uncles themselves. As adult men, they have been exposed to different forms of the normalization of sexual harassment of sisters and primas within their families. Therefore, the daughters of these now adult women automatically become exposed to the risk of being objectified by the very fact that they are women themselves.

If a brother or a primo devalued his sister or prima within the same horizontal location in the family relationship (that is, a sister by a brother, a prima by a primo), this risk becomes exacerbated when her own daughter is placed in a lower location within the vertical axis of the hierarchies within a family. In other words, as an extension of the daughter of a sister or a prima who had been devalued and sexually objectified in the past, a niece may become similarly objectified and become an easy target of sexual harassment for her uncle and arguably for other men in what then become incestuous extended families.

This cultural prescription of sexism is aggravated because of the hierarchies within families that place children in positions of dependency and marginality within families because of generation or age difference and body size and structure, as well as by adults' perceptions of children as not fully human or as property of their parents in patriarchal societies, as reported by the professionals I interviewed, the incest literature, and auto-ethnographies on incest in families of Mexican origin.[15]

For Mexican women, this vertical process of sexual objectification across generations has more layers because of the ways in which women establish emotional connections with other women in the family, as examined by Segura and Pierce. In their insightful critique of Nancy Chodorow's seminal feminist reflections of nuclear families and gender inequality, Segura and Pierce explain and illustrate the ways in which the presence of multiple women in positions of authority in families of Mexican origin may give life to a wide variety of emotional arrangements between women across generations, beyond the mother-daughter dyad of the nuclear family. That is, the mother is not the only and/or the most relevant authority figure or source of love and emotional support for a daughter. For example, a girl may develop an equally important bonding connection with her aunts, older primas, and grandmothers. In this and the two previous chapters, this was illustrated by the stories of women who confided their experiences of violence to an aunt, grandmother, an older sister, or older prima rather than their mother, or who received more emotional and moral support from these women than their own mothers. Thus, a daughter may not only be perceived as a vertical extension of her mother, she may also become an extension of other older women within multiple family arrangements across generations and within a wide variety of diagonal and intersected lines going in multiform directions.

In some regions in Mexico, such as parts of Guerrero and Chiapas, for example, an aunt is identified as "*mamá*" and "*mamita*" ("mom" and "mommy"), illustrating the complex ways in which language and terms of endearment are used as these gendered connections are established and reproduced within extended families.[16]

Thus, I suggest that these complex and manifold connections between women across generations similarly create a complex web of relationships of gender inequality in incestuous families. For example, an uncle who as a boy learned to devalue women in his immediate family (for example, a sister or prima) and who as an adult may automatically devalue the daughters of these women, may similarly devalue other girls who have also become extensions of these and other women belonging to his kin. In other words, an uncle may not only devalue his niece through the linear process I explained earlier, but he may also devalue a more extended network of girls in his kin—an entire younger generation of women may become objectified by virtue of this multiplying effect.

I use the concept of "family genealogies of incest" to identify the process by which incestuous extended families orchestrate multiple forms of domination of Mexican girls and women across generations. This promotes their vulnerability of being exposed to a wide array of expressions of sexual violence, as illustrated by the women's life stories in this chapter.

Family genealogies of incest as a paradigm is inspired and informed by family genealogy scholarship in sociology, feminist revisions of family therapy, and examinations of multigenerational family histories through the use of genograms. Family genealogy may become "a vehicle for the sociological imagination that links personal biography to social–historical contexts across generations."[17] Family genealogy illuminates the interconnections among family histories, memories, storytelling, and legacies of traditions, as well as social inequalities and injustices reproduced within kinship and inherited from generation to generation.[18] Feminist family therapists conducting research on incestuous families in the United States emphasize the relevance of understanding power asymmetry affecting daughters and mothers and the need for equalizing these power imbalances in family life as a goal of treatment.[19]

From this perspective, family genealogies of incest are both systemic and systematic. Family genealogies of incest are *systemic* because they affect the lives of girls and women across and within generations while being reproduced as part of family life within immediate and extended families, which is interwoven with transgenerational negligence and permissiveness, and other unresolved issues across generations. Family genealogies of incest are *systematic* because they are established through patterns of repetition in cyclical fashion that result in habits of misogyny for uncles who sexually assault more than one niece and other girls in their families with no negative consequences for these men. These incestuous family legacies are shaped by *generation* (e.g., a form of "serial incest" where one girl substitutes for another when the latter is no longer available), *everyday life circumstances of opportunity* (e.g., exposure to the uncle as in an apparently harmless family interaction), and *context* (e.g., care-giving that facilitates and conceals collective abuse of more than one child).

Thus, these family genealogies of incest describe kinship patterns and reveal why (1) an uncle sexually molested or raped not only the women I interviewed but also other girls (and sometimes boys) in their respective immediate and extended families; (2) the women were frequently the target of sexual violence of more than one man in the family; and (3) women are exposed to multigenerational patterns of sexual violence within their families of origin. According to the latter, family genealogies of incest was illustrated by the unraveling of endless stories of sexual violence that these women shared with me when they talked about the lives of sisters, mothers, female cousins, and aunts, among other women who were exposed to sexual violence by other men within their immediate and extended families, and previous and younger generations.

I also suggest that sexual violence reported by a girl or a woman within the uncle-niece arrangement is a red flag, a predictor of sexual violence within a family. If a niece is being sexually molested or harassed by her uncle, it is very likely that other girls, women, and boys have been abused by him, or by other men within the immediate or extended family.[20] As I explain in the next chapter, girls and women are not alone at risk within their families, men fit into these family genealogies of incest in distinctive ways. Men also recalled their stories as boys who were sexually molested or raped by their uncles, the relative reported with the highest frequency as well. In a pattern that was less frequently reported but deserves special attention, Elba's story illustrates how and why a pre-adolescent girl may engage in behaviors that are potentially harmful to her preschool brothers as a consequence of what she experienced at her uncle's hands.

In sum, a wide range of expressions of sexual violence against a girl, a young adolescent, or an adult woman within the context of family is not an isolated incident but only part of a complex and widespread organization of sexual violence against women (and at times boys or younger men) within the family, a gendered pattern that is reproduced systematically and systemically across generations and within immediate and extended kin, intertwined with family legacies of negligence and permissiveness. Figures 4.1 and 4.2 illustrate these complicated family patterns across generations. The former shows the three groups with the highest frequency (uncles, biological fathers, and biological brothers), and the latter is Maclovia's family genogram.

Figure 4.1. Family Genealogies of Incest

	Uncles of the 45 Women Interviewed
〰〰〰〰〰〰〰〰〰〰〰〰	21 reported an uncle
〰〰〰〰〰〰〰〰〰〰〰	19 of them reported histories of sexual violence in the lives of one or more female relatives (e.g., mothers, sisters, daughters, aunts, primas, grandmothers, stepsisters), and male relatives (e.g., sons, brothers, fathers, mainly during childhood); incidents involved men older in age within a wide variety of kinship relationships
〰〰〰〰〰〰〰〰〰	17 of them were sexually assaulted by other men in the family (e.g., fathers, other uncles, brothers, cousins, grandfathers, among others)
〰〰〰〰	8 of them reported that the same uncle assaulted another family member (e.g., sister, niece, cousin, little brother)
	Biological Fathers
〰〰〰〰〰〰〰	13 reported a biological father
〰〰〰〰〰	9 of them reported being assaulted by other family members, with maternal uncles having the highest incidence (*)
	Biological Brothers
〰〰〰〰〰〰	12 reported biological brother(s)
〰〰〰	6 of them reported being sexually assaulted by other family members, particularly uncles and grandfathers
〰〰	4 of them reported being sexually assaulted by more than one biological brother

(*) As well as, from higher to lower incidence: biological mothers (frequently as accomplice), paternal uncles and maternal grandparents, brothers and cousins, and stepfathers.

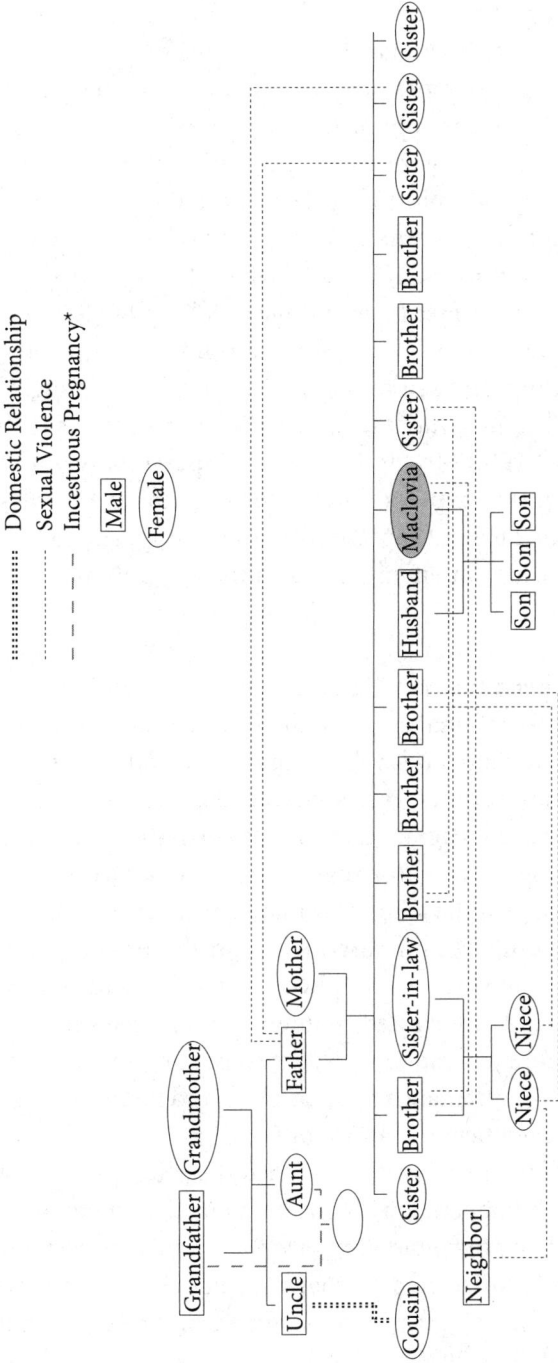

Figure 4.2. Maclovia's Family Genogram

Domestic Relationship
Sexual Violence
Incestuous Pregnancy*

Male
Female

*apparent conjugal daughter case

173

Socioeconomic class and marginality further shape the above. Two examples illustrate how marginality and privilege selectively complicate the family genealogies of incest, creating at times paradoxical situations. First, if Bárbara's poor family had had the means, they would have hired a domestic worker to clean her uncle's room. However, it is very likely that the domestic worker—probably a minor—would have been the target of his sexually violent behavior.[21] "The majority start in this occupation [domestic work] when they are girls, from 12 or 14, and in the states at times from the age of 8," explained a representative of an organization advocating for the rights of domestic workers in Mexico.[22] A domestic worker's sexual vulnerability is aggravated if she is perceived "*como si fuera de la familia*," meaning "as if she was part of the family." While living in Mexico, I personally witnessed some families using this expression to refer to a domestic worker. An expression of endearment represents vulnerability: she may become one more among the women entangled in these family patterns of gender inequality.[23]

And second, Paloma's upper-middle-class status made her believe that she had been born in "la familia perfecta" which was more concerned about social image and status—the so-called *apariencias*—than the safety, protection, and well-being of girls and young women in the family. Paloma's parents were able to bribe attorneys and successfully maneuver a flawed legal system to free her father's younger brother, a man with a long history of sexual molestation of girls within the family who was also able to have his criminal record destroyed.

Although complex and paradoxical, in these family genealogies of incest, women don't necessarily become passive and simply accept the sexual violence. As illustrated, women may become keenly aware of the ways in which they can identify a context of risk, survive, challenge, contest, and even manipulate a situation to avoid being sexually assaulted, especially as they become aware of the high prevalence of sexual violence in their own families. Ofelia illustrates a unique case of resilience. She recalled: "It happened with one of my uncles when I was fifteen and we were preparing my *fiesta de quince años*. My uncle came to my grandparents' house and started to chat with me about my dress and stuff. And the same old things started to happen, and he touched me. But this time I thought, 'Now it's my turn!'"

As described in chapter 3, Ofelia had suffered a long history of sexual molestation by her three brothers and one of her grandfather's most trusted friends. But by the time of her *quinceañera,* she'd become astute about her vulnerability and determined not to let the men prey on her. So when her uncle, a man in his late forties, said he wanted to have sex with her in the back of the house, a secluded place outside, she decided to make a fool of him.

> I thought, "He's crazy. How in the world can he believe that I'm going to have intercourse and all?" But I told him, "Yes, fine, tío!" [laughs] So he got his stuff and went to the back of the house. I went to the dining room where my grandfather, my grandmother, my uncles, and my aunts all were. I went to the kitchen, got my soup, and sat down to eat with them. I just left him waiting for me.

Of her trick, Ofelia said, "I took great delight, a deep joy." She silently told her uncle, "You wait right there. Let's see long you can wait." "Finally he came in the house to the dining room, because he was tired of waiting. And I just looked at him, laughing. Oh my God, no, no, no! That was my *malicia*! Do you understand? And that was it. I remember all those things so well, and I remember this with pleasure, because I didn't fall prey to him."

For Ofelia, the trick was a small revenge for the three times he had touched her body and forced her to masturbate him. What Ofelia called *la malicia* was her skill in coping with her uncle's intentions. He was her mother's first cousin, a man she called *dejado*—abandoned by his wife—and "irresponsible" with his children. For Ofelia, that joyous day was a major turning point. "After that, absolutely nothing happened again," she said. "He never touched me or did anything to me ever again."

Feminization of Incest

These family genealogies of incest expose what could be called the "feminization of incest," a concept I incorporate in this study to identify the disproportionate representation of the maternal side of the family in these Mexican women's narratives of uncle-niece incestuous sexual violence. The feminization of incest was illustrated by the following patterns: (1) The most common pattern of uncle-niece was that of women who were exposed to sexual violence by a biological brother of her mother (more than twice as frequent when compared to a father's biological brother). (2) The next most frequent pattern, by maternal tíos políticos, was much more frequently reported than a paternal tío político.

Why does this happen? Although gender inequality may happen within both maternal and paternal sides of a woman's family, the feminization of incest accentuates the family patterns of incest more on the maternal side; the women I interviewed were more frequently objectified by their uncles within the maternal kinship networks.

When I presented these findings at a workshop with professionals who specialized in sexual violence in Mexico City, participants suggested that the maternal side was overrepresented in this uncle-niece pattern because women may rely on their families of origin to take care of their daughters and thus sexual molestation is situational and may happen due to exposure to these men in this context. Interestingly, in this study, the cases of sexual molestation by a caregiver were a minority, and in only one case was a mother's brother. Instead, I suggest that while a father's brother may objectify women within his extended family (within extended families where genealogies of incest prevail), within these patriarchal families, a woman who is a mother is at risk of being devalued and disrespected as an authority figure, and thus an uncle may exercise sexual violence against the daughter of his sister, prima, or sister-in-law without fear of discipline or punishment. Why? The uncle who is now an adult man used to be a boy who learned that his first object of love—his mother—and the extensions of her (e.g., his sisters and nieces) are inferior within the family and society at large. This goes hand in hand with the emotional socialization of a boy who is raised to suppress anything that is associated with femininity, and consequently, as Herman states, "His capacity for nurturance and for affectionate identification with women is therefore systematically suppressed."[24] Thus, a man's perception of his sister as devalued and unworthy of empathy is a well-rooted lifetime family process, one that may facilitate all types of sexually abusive behavior in uncles, fearlessly and mercilessly. This is also exacerbated by the fact that in spite of feminist gains, laws and the judicial system are still flawed, inefficient, and corrupt, as illustrated by Paloma's story.

How can we explain cases of women who are raped by paternal uncles? Interestingly, the father-daughter relationship was seriously deteriorated and/or emotionally damaged in cases of women raped by a paternal uncle, which reinforced the family genealogies of incest.[25] This is further complicated by the fact that women in positions of authority may actively participate in silencing or punishing the women.

Family Politics of Gender Inequality

Sexual violence exercised by uncles against girls relied in part on the internalized sexism of women in positions of authority in these families. This pattern is similar to the father-daughter incest stories, as discussed earlier in this book. As illustrated in these niece-uncle narratives, although some women in positions of authority within immediate and extended families may become emotionally and morally supportive when they learn about their daughters' reports of sexual violence, other women engage in behaviors and attitudes that were oppressive to a younger generation of women within their kin networks. This is further exacerbated by the experiences of sexual violence that women experienced earlier in life. Reportedly, when the mothers, aunts, and grandmothers of some of these women learned about the incidents of sexual violence, they engaged in a wide variety of expressions of internalized sexism, some of which resembled the attitudes these same adult figures exhibited when a brother or primo harassed a girl, as discussed in the previous chapter.

In the niece-uncle arrangement, these forms of internalized sexism included the adult woman being indifferent or not intervening; not believing when the girl reported an incident of sexual violence and therefore not stopping the violence, especially when the uncle had a good image in the family; punishing a girl or making her feel responsible for the abuse; defending or advocating for the uncle who exercised violence, and thus becoming the "enemy"; and, being dismissive or negligent of the girl's well-being, which becomes secondary to the "good image" of the family.[26]

The adult women who expressed this internalized sexism sometimes had a history of sexual abuse themselves. As discussed earlier in this book, these patterns were also exhibited in the father-daughter, brother-sister, and primo-prima arrangements. Within the labyrinth of gender inequality in these incestuous families, some of these women in positions of authority had experienced violence themselves in their lives, and some were disempowered as adult women within their families. In the end, the cognitive "misrecognition" of patriarchal gender scripts that are oppressive to them and women of all ages in their families has facilitated the naturalization and legitimation of their own disempowerment as adult women, a process of cognition and gendered socialization that other women living in patriarchal societies may experience beyond Latin American territories or U.S. Spanish-speaking communities.[27] The women that I interviewed seem to be keenly aware of such "misrecognition" and worked hard during the interviews to make sense of it.[28]

If an aunt or a grandmother was raped, and then engages in internalized sexism, is she complicit or responsible as an adult but innocent as a woman? This resonates with the complex question I presented in chapter 2, and it also requires a sophisticated answer. In the process, I have similarly decided that, rather than taking sides, my goal as a feminist scholar is to precisely expose these tensions, contradictions, and paradoxes as I try to make sense of women's stories of incestuous sexual violence.

Last, some women told me they were shocked and surprised by the negative reactions of their adult women relatives, reactions that at times were even more painful or traumatic than the experiences of sexual violence per se. Some women reported that they had decided to remain silent precisely because they had anticipated a negative reaction on their mothers' part. Frequently, women were aware of family politics of gender inequality in their families. When some finally spoke to them about the abuse, their original fears were validated. Internalized sexism facilitates in part the creation and reproduction of family cultures of rape. These complex webs of gendered and sexualized forces interacted to create these and other forms of sexual violence in families, and all are rooted in a sophisticated social organization of silence and secrets as part of family life.

Finally, it is beyond the scope of this study to compare the psychological impact for women who were sexually abused by an uncle vis-à-vis the effects for women abused by a father, brother, or cousin. A clear-cut comparison may be hard to make for various reasons: (1) some women were the sexual target of more than one man within a wide array of kinship arrangements, and (2) as indicated earlier, the family's reaction at times was even more traumatic than the rape per se, for example. Regardless, the life of a woman who is sexually abused by an uncle may be deeply damaged by the experience.[29]

5

Men's Life Stories

Mexico is the country with the second-highest rate of homophobic hate crimes in Latin America, with Brazil in the leading position.
—*Informe de crímenes de odio por homofobia, México 1995–2008*

One use of the *puto*, *joto*, and *maricón* labels is to discipline young boys so that they will conform to the cultural ideals of Mexican masculinity. For example, a father may correct his small crying son by saying, "*¿Qué no eres hombre? ¡Pareces maricón!*" ("Aren't you a man? You seem like a sissy!"—i.e., homosexual); or a maid may try to quiet a three-year-old boy by saying "*¡Cállate, maricón!*" ("Shut up, sissy!"). During my years of travel in Mexico, I have often heard small children tease each other with the labels *joto* and *puto*; and when walking through neighborhoods of all social classes, it was not unusual to see *puto* and *joto* scribbled on walls.
—Joseph Carrier, *De los otros: Intimacy and Homosexuality among Mexican Men* (1995)

When Leonardo, Matías, and Pablo repeated more than once that the male relative who had sexually assaulted, raped, or molested them when they were boys was a gay man, I felt confronted and haunted by ethical concerns and dilemmas. My head started to spin. Should I include that in the book or not? How could this further reinforce homophobic discourses that identify gay men as pedophiles and child molesters? Could that be potentially used against LGBTQ communities in Mexico, and potentially in U.S. Latino communities? Would this be cited out of context? If so, by whom, how, and when? I have reflected and published about some of the ethical dilemmas I have encountered in the sexuality research I have conducted in the past, and I have learned that the process of writing about this struggle *actually* validates the ethical concern and/or dilemma and also offers a space to disclose controversial and/or sensitive findings that may push us intellectually beyond being politically correct and safe—all with the intention to help us advance our knowledge in any given topic.[1] While embracing both the need to be ethically transparent and to explore possibilities for intellectual growth beyond my comfort zone, I disclosed these findings out of respect for my informants as well. My ethical responsibility is toward Leonardo, Matías, and Pablo, who like all of my informants shared their life histories and stories with so much honesty and trust, hoping their stories could be of benefit to future readers and professionals concerned about boys and men still looking for answers to painful questions that left deep imprints in their lives. I have the same trust in the process of intellectual maturity and professional growth that is based on being truthful to my sixty interlocutors, future readers, and me as well. This is a long intellectual process and I am still learning.

* * *

"The primo says, '*Ay, voy a calarme,*' as we say over here. 'I am going to test myself and see if I like it.' It was the first time the primo had sex with a man," said Zacarías with a laugh. A bright man in his early twenties, he is a self-identified gay man born and raised in Mexico City. He was reflecting about the group conversations he has had with his five friends, also gay men close in age. Zacarías engaged in these conversations with his friends out of concern. He didn't know if he was "the only weird one" and felt the need to share with them about the experience he had with his primo years before.

Zacarías was twelve years old when his primo of the same age gave him a kiss on the mouth, and they wound up having sex, an event Zacarías called his "first sexual experience." As his friends talked about their own personal experiences, his friends didn't tell Zacarías who had *actually* initiated the sexual encounter (either Zacarías's friend or the friend's primo, or how the encounters had been negotiated); these men reassured him that what happened to him was "normal." In their case, it had been a one-time experience under the same premise: a young man who assumes himself to be heterosexual—but "he isn't 100 percent sure" of it yet—sexually approaches the primo who he thinks "for sure" is gay. Zacarías explained that for the young man who approaches a primo suspected of being gay, the sexual encounter becomes *la prueba* or the test to find out "*qué tan machín soy*—to what extent I am a *machín*."

In Mexico I have often heard people use the word "machín" as a diminutive of "macho," and as synonymous with being brave, strong, or a "real man," which may also have a sexual connotation.[2] "Well, in the case of my primo, it seems like the test lasted four years!" said Zacarías, laughing. Secretly, they had a long-term, voluntary romantic relationship that involved frequent sex. As he reflected about these conversations with his friends, Zacarías used the expression "*Al primo me le arrimo*," putting a gay spin on the expression that has been traditionally associated with primos getting sexually close to primas, as discussed earlier in this book.

* * *

"After all these things happened to me, I used to look at other children and I wanted to do the same, I wanted to do the same to them, and I wanted to tell them to touch my penis," said Valentín as he explained that he "wanted to try to abuse children" and forced younger, smaller children to touch his genitals. A single self-identified heterosexual man in his early twenties who works at a maquiladora in Ciudad Juárez, Valentín did not recall the exact number of children he approached, but has memories of these children either becoming angry or resisting. These children were directly related as cousins or nephews to two tíos políticos who sexually assaulted Valentín since he was a boy. His uncles and other men in the family used homophobic bullying to harass him and call him "gay" and *maricón*, frequently blaming him for their own actions. Both tíos were in their late teens and Valentín was seven years old when the first incident took place. Like Valentín, the children he approached used to spend time within the extended family as well. "It was like revenge, that is the way I see it, I feel like I look at these experiences that way," said Valentín while explaining that he was about nine years old and felt "enraged" when he started to engage in these experiences. "Later," he explained, "after I was ten years old it came back to me again, but then it happened with my cousins, and from then on . . . With my primas, I started to fondle them, to do all those things." Valentín described these experiences as part of playing *a las escondidas*—hide-and-seek.

This chapter analyzes the stories of the men who volunteered to be interviewed for this study. They frequently reported complex histories of sexual experiences with other men, exposing among other things the high incidence of sexual violence in the childhood of adult men who identify themselves as gay and/or bisexual.[3] Zacarías's and Valentín's stories illustrate the sophisticated and nuanced ways boys and young men experience this, exposing the multigenerational and cyclical patterns of sexual violence within their immediate and extended families, as well as the many forms of sexual coercion and molestation against girls, boys, and younger men. This chapter offers the stories of men who illustrate two related family processes: the continuum of sexual consent and coercion, and kinship sexuality.

Men's stories of sexualized encounters within the family expose a continuum between the two extremes of *consent* and *coercion*. On the one hand, some men recalled voluntary sexualized encounters with relatives close in age (e.g., primos) that involved mutual seduction, play, and curiosity. Others reported experiences with relatives who were considerably older (e.g., fathers, tíos, older brothers, older primos) that occurred against their will, and involved control, fear, and at times extreme violence. However, this continuum is neither flat nor unidimensional. A wide, gray area of nuanced expressions of pleasure and danger, seduction and fear, may exist between the extremes. This became evident through the two dimensions that emerged from these men's stories, namely, interpersonal and intrapersonal.

At the *interpersonal* level, a man may have had both types of experiences at different stages of his life, for example, being raped or sexually molested as a boy by an older brother or an uncle, but voluntarily engaging in pleasurable same-sex experiences with a primo close in age, later in life as an adolescent. And at the *intrapersonal* level, at times there isn't always a clear line between coercion and desire as part of the same lived experience. Based on the men's recollections, coercion by an older male relative didn't always involve physical violence but rather gentle seduction, and a boy or young adolescent didn't feel compelled to resist, and in fact experienced feelings of pleasure. For a boy, this pattern was reproduced through a routine of encounters that were established and repeated in the midst of both curiosity and confusion, and through different yet nuanced degrees of coercion and consent. In the vast majority of these cases, men reported other male relatives as the ones with whom they had these experiences.

With its roots in codes of honor and shame established in colonial Mexico, gendered prescriptions of sexuality within patriarchal families may grant boys and young men—more so than girls and young women—some license to explore bodily desire and to follow this sexual curiosity *within* their families.[4] This influences how a boy might perceive a wide variety of sexualized situations with a male relative. The sexualized encounters taking place at the extreme that involves the highest level of consent (which may include some form of mutual seduction and play between the parties involved, frequently boys and young men) to explore sexuality and the erotic among their kin exposes what I call *kinship sex*. In this study, men more frequently than women reported experiences of kinship sex, which involved same-sex rather than heterosexual encounters. This pattern was especially evident for men who through these experiences discovered their same-sex sexual interest and who later in life came out as gay. Accordingly, the consent–coercion continuum was practically nonexistent for the women in the study; for them, the coercion extreme was overrepresented.[5]

Two related processes further shape the consent–coercion continuum and kinship sexuality: heteronormative compliance and the "Al primo me le arrimo" paradigm. Heteronormative compliance refers to beliefs and practices of obedience established by parents, siblings, and other relatives with the purpose of policing and reproducing heterosexuality as the norm within families and society at large. A parent or sibling may feel entitled to exercise emotional, verbal, and bodily intrusion against boys and young men who are perceived as "less of a man" (i.e., effeminate) and who therefore need to be corrected or "fixed." The homophobic discourse (i.e., being called *maricón, joto,* or *puto*) is used strategically as part of these forms of sexual violence exercised by fathers, brothers, tíos, primos, or other men against boys within immediate and extended families. Although this is magnified for a queer or effeminate boy, the homophobic discourse is used strategically to exercise power and control over *any* boy or young man, regardless of his gender expression or sexual identity, as illustrated by Valentín's story.

As illustrated by Zacarías, "Al primo me le arrimo" refers to the ways in which young men who are suspected to be gay may become sexual targets of other primos close in age. These young men who may not be sure of their sexual orientation will sexually approach them to "test" their sexuality and prove to themselves that they are not gay and embrace with confidence the sexual norm of heteromasculinity. "Al primo me le arrimo" is complex and fluid and may also include the experiences of men who have their first sexual encounters or erotic adventures with primos. These experiences are not necessarily coercive or painful. They may in fact be voluntary and pleasurable as young men create their own sexual cultures kept in secret, contributing in the end in positive ways to their sexual socialization as gay men *within* the family.

Finally, men's narratives expand on the continuum of sexual violence previously discussed in the chapter on sisters and primas.[6] Men illustrate their own experiences of sexual coercion and also come full circle to confirm women's reports: a man can be a sexual subject, a man can also be a sex object, and at times he can be both. In addition, men's narratives expose the complex multigenerational nature of family genealogies of incest and of a family continuum of sexual violence. These selectively affect both girls and women, and boys and young men, marginalizing and making vulnerable those who experience gender and sexual inequality as part of family life in Mexican society.

This chapter includes nine stories of men who lived these complex experiences as boys or young men along the consent–coercion continuum in kinship relationships that includes father-son, brothers, cousins, and uncle-nephew.[7] I present the men's stories in three sections: (1) men who recalled different and contrasting patterns, from kinship sex to coercive sex, as well as incidents that blur the lines in between; (2) men who only reported instances that took place against their will during their childhood, situations that involved different forms of emotional manipulation, rough play, and/or physical force at the hands of pre-adolescent or adolescent primos and uncles; and (3) men who described the most sexually violent events, with a father at the center of their stories.

As with the stories in the previous chapter, men's stories are at times more fluid and complex than the patterns just described. For example, a man might have been abused by his father and also by his tío. I chose a category for a story when the man described it as the one lasting the longest in his life, though not necessarily the one with the most negative consequences. The last section of the chapter offers an analysis of these narratives.

Kinship Sex and Beyond
Matías

> That tío always got my attention back when he used to give me that kiss
> on the mouth . . . His big mustache, and the smell of that lotion and ciga-
> rette . . . I always loved that tío. And that Navidad (Christmas), I came out
> to the gate, and he was loaded with presents for his family. He grabbed
> me and gave me a kiss, and it was totally like a discovery, like "Wow!" I
> rose into the air. I went up into a different level. I stopped being myself.
> And that is the way it started.

This was Matías's recollection of a life-changing moment when he was
eight or nine. His uncle was the husband of the sister of Matías's father.
The tío was in his mid-forties at the time, a well-educated professional
with a high income, said Matías. His tío was "very, very, very intelligent
to be able to inspire trust in the family," even in Matías's mother, who
was usually mistrustful and very protective of her children. "He used to
train me so they would not find out about it at home. He trained me a lot
about that. [As in] 'Make sure your mother does not see this, make sure
your mother does not see that.' But that day, after that kiss, I kept trembling. Trembling, trembling, trembling. Totally. But before I had a sexual
relationship with him, he did it a lot, introducing the idea of 'Make sure
your father does not see this, or if your father asked you about this, you
tell him so and so.'"After that kiss, which Matías still recalls vividly, he
found himself being seduced sexually and romantically by his tío, individually or as part of a triangle that involved another primo, a boy close
in age.

A college-educated man in his early forties, Matías was born and
raised in an upper-middle-class urban family. Matías said that his uncle
could have written the *manual total del pedófilo*—the complete manual
of the pedophile.

> *¡Uy!* He was very, very, very, very skillful, extremely skillful. So skillful
> that he trained us how to be sexual beings: How to be sexually pleasing,
> what we had to do to be more sexually pleasing, how to have oral sex with
> the penis and the anus, how to caress, how to play with the tits. All the
> spots in the body, he started to show me what is the most exciting thing

to do, how you can create a situation, to what point you can handle a situation of the person. In other words, all the information, *información en vivo*, because it got to the point where, he took me to the sauna so I could learn how to be able to provoke sexuality in someone else, but without touching me because I belonged only to him. He was very excited by the fact that other potential pedophiles became crazy about me but in the end I ended up being with him. So it was a very strange game that thank God stopped, because if that boy had continued to be trained by him . . . He taught me how to go to the movies and provoke a sexual reaction in an adult, and how to consummate a sexual relationship. He made me into a person who knows how to please others. He taught me all the tricks that have existed and that will ever exist to be sexually pleasing to others.

Matías explained that his uncle "made him to fall in love with him" and trained him to become a "machine of pleasure" to everyone, except himself, Matías. "Any adult that looked for me, I took him to bed. I became a *perro machuchero*, an old skillful dog who knew how to handle an adult sexually . . . In movie theaters, buses, the street, everywhere. From ages ten to fifteen, I think I did it at least once a week." He said he usually felt "disgusted" afterward.

"Since I was a boy, I was also very intelligent with regard to how to manipulate things," he said. "When he didn't want to see me, I still ended up seeing him because I manipulated things, with la tía or los primos. I manipulated things to be able to be with him, which got him very excited." Matías explained that although he might have physically enjoyed the sexual exchanges with his tío, he had a contrasting emotional reaction, such as taking vengeance and stealing money from his uncle. Soon he developed what he called "a double morality." "[I became] the boy who was cool and well behaved at home and the boy who went to the movies looking for an adult man, or the boy who opened the purses of my tía, or the boy who started to fondle his primos. I became a child who was an abuser and I started to have sexuality with my primos."

These behaviors developed when Matías was in fifth grade and he was becoming what he called a "sexually compulsive" boy. Between the ages of ten and fifteen, Matías made sexual advances to primos close in age. "I approached many primos and many primos looked for me," he said. Apparently, his primos marked him as gay or heard stories about him. He never approached a prima, he said, with the exception of a two-year-old prima he gave a "deep kiss" to when he was fifteen or sixteen as a way to "investigate" why men like his tío enjoyed kissing children on the mouth. Matías explained that he "never forced" his primos because by then he was already a *perro cuerero*, "an astute, skillful old dog with all the sexual experience in the world." In learning how to be seductive, he had gone to a "great school": his tío. Matías identified ten different primos he had sexual exchanges with back then, in a variety of family situations and circumstances, including vacations.

"How long did the experiences with your tío last?" I asked.

"That's the painful part: until I grew up," said Matías. "By the time I became fifteen years old, I stopped being attractive, and to no longer be attractive to someone I was hooked on gave me a lot of emotional problems." His uncle ignored Matías's calls and avoided him in family reunions. "I stopped being a child," he said. "I stopped being a child and I was no longer attractive."

Matías was always silent about the wide variety of complex sexual experiences with his uncle, including what he was shocked to discover about a year before their breakup: that his tío was part of a group of men that shared young boys for sex.

> I think they were more than ten men, many more. Based on the conversations that they had with him [tío], there were many more. And many of them were upper middle class, or upper class. But there were also some truck drivers who would bring things and stuff. Those were the ones who brought the boys. These truck drivers were like the vehicle they used to bring the boys. And each one of these men had their specific boys, and among them, I was one of them. The boys they kept, protected, the boys they shared amongst themselves.

When Matías realized that his tío was going to let his friends "borrow" him so he could have sex with the adult men of this group, he resisted. In retrospect, he realized, the game of power and control between him and his tío became debilitated and broke. "I didn't allow it, I was in panic, it excited me a lot but I felt a lot of fear. In other words, at that moment his control had not been that much," said Matías. Apparently child pornography didn't seem to be involved in these adult men's networks. "Fortunately, there were neither digital cameras nor any of that," he said.[8]

When Matías was eighteen or nineteen, he finally told his mother and father about what had happened with his tío. His mother was very empathetic. "She wanted to know everything and I told her everything," he said. After his parents learned about it, his relationship with them became closer, more loving and protective. "My tío never set foot in our home again," he said. "He never came back to our home, ever."

Matías felt deeply loved and supported by his parents, but he was deeply shocked by the response of his extended family to what he said about his tío. "His children, his wife, the nephews he abused, everyone . . . they set up a squadron around him. Everyone. The entire world knew about the story, and they saw me as the boy who went to rape the poor uncle. *¡Pobrecito del tío!* That is my rage that I have inside, very startling." Matías actively talked to adults, teenagers, and children within the extended family to alert them about his uncle. He recalled:

> Every time I left my hometown and asked, "Where is primo so and so?"—
> "He is with el tío in the ranch,"—*¡Hijo de su madre!* That motherfucker!
> I would feel sick to my stomach, because I knew what they were doing. I
> talked to the little primos and one in particular. I would ask him, 'What's
> happening? What's up with *el tío*? What's going on?' I tried to help him a
> lot. I tried to make sure he would be very open with me. But all I found
> was the same little monster I used to be: a boy who tried to seduce me.

Matías refused him. Matías was about twenty at the time, and his fourteen-year-old primo was his tío's "favorite nephew."

Frustrated and in pain, Matías also looked for legal advice to see if he could press charges against his tío, but he couldn't find any professional support and gave up. In the meantime, he said, "The entire family took sides. In other words, he is the one who is abused because I continued harassing him. The boy who looked for revenge is the devil. The other, *pobrecito*, I am accusing him of something, in other words, the roles were exchanged." Since then, Matías said, his uncle has been treated within the large extended family that knows all about it "as if nothing had happened." Matías elaborated, "They are the classic upper-middle-class family that resolves everything with a priest. In other words, all those conversations ended up with talks by priests about acceptance and support to the spirit." Distrustful of Catholicism, Matías has kept his distance from the church most of his life; as an adult he has actively explored spirituality in another Christian congregation.

Matías tried to calculate how many nephews, sons, and grandsons of his tío he knew had been similarly exposed to what he had experienced with him. "Based on my counting of the cases I know about, easily about thirty," he said. He has also heard stories of older primos sexually harassing or raping primas in at least two cases. "In fact, when I was already an adult I had sexual relations with his son. That was the way I took revenge on my tío," he said. Matías didn't take pride in this. The primos he had sex with were close in age and he didn't "force them," but he now knows that he was an "emotional abuser."

For instance, he clarified, "I never considered myself being raped, because there was neither force nor threats; absolutely not. However, I was violated as a child. In my mentality, in my way of being, in my development, in all of that, it was a very invasive violation, very painful, very penetrating, very disturbing, very castrating." This is what Matías told one psychotherapist, in trying to explain that he wasn't "sexually raped" but rather "emotionally raped" by his uncle. "Thank God, I am not a pedophile and I have never been interested in that. So I broke the pattern of the abused who abuses, thank God!"

"Without that kiss, it would have not happened," underlined Matías as we wrapped up our interview. He also wanted to make sure that I understood that, "The first sexual experience I had with that tío, he didn't look for me. I was the one who looked for him; it was me." When I asked him to elaborate, he explained that by then he had previously had sexualized contact with an adolescent man. "*Quiero más*"—I want more—he told himself back then. "It was not curiosity," he emphasized for me. Prior to the life-changing kiss with his tío, Matías had developed romantic feelings for a man he identified as *amigo de la familia*, a man who was in his late teens when Matías was seven or eight years old. Matías explained that he was *enamoradísimo*, deeply in love with him, and had sexualized exchanges with him that he enjoyed, and which he never felt were the result of manipulation or obligation. Matías ran into him decades later and they became good friends. His friend, who is married to a woman and raising children, felt deep guilt when Matías told him that he was gay. Matías also explained that he eventually learned that his tío was gay and his wife of many years was a lesbian. They were never open about it, he said. "They decided to play the game and get married."

Loved and supported by parents and siblings as a gay man, he came out to them when he was about eighteen. Now an activist for more than twenty years, Matías has worked with LGBTQ communities and drug abuse prevention programs. He now lives and works in Monterrey, where he shared his story with me.

Uriel

When Uriel was a little boy, his half-brother raped him every time his family had overnight visitors. His mother and father had no idea this was going on.

A witty and engaging young man in his mid-twenties, Uriel grew up in an upper-class family in Northern Mexico. His family had close emotional connections to relatives within the extended family. The big, fancy family home had space for almost twenty beds, he said, and for good reason: "It's a large family, because there are many children. And now imagine plus the sisters [aunts], plus the brothers-in-law, plus the brothers [uncles], plus the godchildren, plus the primos lejanos . . . There are a lot of us!"

So when a relative visited their hometown overnight, Uriel had to give up his bedroom and go sleep with the boy he calls his "brother," though he is his mother's son by a man who is not Uriel's father. Uriel said that he "neither loved nor hated him," and he felt only "minimal affection" for him. "Give your bedroom to so-and-so and go to sleep with your brother," his parents would say. "And that's when it happened, the abuse ¡Chíngale!—fuck him!" He said.

Uriel recalled what his brother forced him to do between the ages of four and six: perform oral sex, swallow his semen, and masturbate him. The adolescent boy also performed anal sex on Uriel, which included penetration with a carrot. He described the experiences as painful, never pleasurable. His brother was about fourteen years old when the first incident took place, and Uriel soon developed an uncontrollable fear of him. The teen increased his threats, emotional control, blackmail, and physical force that left blood, bruises, and wounds, but Uriel lied about all of them when his mother inquired.

A family trip shortly after brought a brief reprieve. "Back then my father was working for the government and he had an official assignment overseas," he said. "My mother, sister, and I went for a visit. I don't know how many days. It was such a long time that I had to go to school there." Uriel was five when he came back to Mexico, and didn't want to go home because he was afraid. "I was in fear until I was six or so, because the abuse continued," he said. "I felt panic just being with him alone at home, and panic. When we came back from overseas, I experienced a huge panic."

Uriel said his brother not only abused him while they had guests, he started to abuse him during the day when nobody was at home. Uriel started to look for excuses to be away from home and avoided being alone with him. Uriel suffered from enuresis (incontinence). This disappeared when his brother left home, but the symptoms came back later, especially when his brother visited the parents.

The abuse finally stopped when the brother left home to study out of town; a relationship of "mutual indifference" only became more distant and painful. Years later his brother survived a near-fatal accident and spent a long time in a coma. When he came home, he was disabled and needy. For Uriel, the tables had finally turned. "I am very kind and very docile, but in matters of revenge, I am poisonous," he said. When the brother came home, Uriel was an older and stronger adolescent, and got into violent fistfights with him. "I didn't care, and I beat him up. He could not defend himself because of his disability, so I won."

In his early twenties, Uriel finally shared his story with his best friend, who then told Uriel's mother. "It became *la revolución*," said Uriel as he talked about the family revolt that resulted after his mother confronted his brother in front of him, three years before our interview. That was the first and last time the issue was brought up in the family. His mother attended individual psychotherapy afterwards. His father never learned about the abuse.

"When my father said that I was neither the first one nor the last one, I said, '¡*Ay!* Are more [gay men] out there?'" said Uriel with a big laugh as he shared his "coming out" conversations with his parents and siblings months before he turned thirteen. Tension, rejection, endless arguments, and lack of communication emerged between Uriel and his parents. Eventually, both accepted him, and Uriel's adult brothers and sisters were supportive as well. Out of love and concern, a brother or a sister accompanied him to his first same-sex love dates when he was a teenager. The brother who raped Uriel, in the meantime, used homophobic bullying to harass him verbally.

Uriel said he'd had special feelings for men from an early age, emotions of tenderness he had no name for. He experienced these feelings even prior to the first incident with his brother. Being an effeminate boy was no doubt the reason why his brother raped him. Uriel never confronted him about this, but he became assertive, with zero tolerance when his schoolmates bullied him with homophobic harassment in school. "I was being trained to use books at the library and one time I prepared a speech that I went and read to the school principal." He was ten at the time. "I told her that I wanted to be respected," he recalled.

A popular leader and an activist in the making, Uriel nurtured his intellectual curiosity by reading books at the library. These taught him about "homosexuality, lesbianism, hermaphrodites, and bisexuality," and helped him eventually come out to his family.

Uriel's first voluntary sexual experience and erotic adventure with a primo was pleasant. He was about twelve, and his primo—the son of his father's brother—fifteen. It first happened as "play" while the boys were out riding, dealing with an incident with one of their horses on the family ranch. "It was by mutual agreement and there were no feelings involved, so there was no way to hurt anyone. He enjoyed it, I enjoyed it, and there was no commitment."

"Did anyone in the family learn about it?" I inquired. "Yes, another primo—and we included him!" replied Uriel, laughing. The trio of primos engaged in a threesome that soon evolved: "And then my first primo invited his amigo, and since I liked his amigo, I stayed with the amigo, and my other primo kept my primo." Apparently, nobody in the family suspected these encounters. The primo he had sex with at the ranch maintained a relationship with a girlfriend while also having frequent sex with Uriel. "In fact he just got married," said Uriel, "and we have an awesome relationship, as if nothing happened."

Uriel recalled the sexual encounters he actively pursued at the age of eighteen or nineteen with a different paternal primo. Mutual seduction might have started years earlier when both were lying in bed watching TV and his primo put his head on Uriel's lap but ended up grabbing his butt.

Uriel said he didn't fall in love with his primos, but felt *cariño muy selectivo*—very selective affection—for them, more than for primos he hadn't had sex with. He had a number of same-sex experiences with primos close in age. "I have had sex with primos on my father's side that I know are not gay. They're married, but just like to have sex with men." He does not know about any primos married to primas within his large extended family. However, he has heard stories about his late maternal grandfather re-marrying as an older man to a niece with the exclusive purpose of being taken care of by her.

Uriel doesn't know if his half-brother raped anyone else in his family. And other than his own experience, he has not heard of any other cases of children or women sexually abused by a relative within his immediate or extended family. He said, however, he has heard a story rarely discussed in the family about the brother who raped him: his paternal grandmother found the boy drunk, naked, and in pain after being gang-raped near home when he was eleven years old.

Of his extended family, Uriel said that one of his tíos—a highly respected Catholic priest—was once in a car accident. After inspecting the vehicle, the police found pornography, sex toys, videos, and sexually explicit photos of minors. "He bribed the newspaper, he bought everything, because he is highly respected, he bought everything, they didn't do anything to him," said Uriel. The priest continued working with his congregation and was never prosecuted.

The big house, the family ranch, expensive private schools, fancy birthday parties, clothing and trips, name-dropping of influential politicians in family conversations, loyal service workers, gourmet meals and desserts at the snap of a finger at home all made Uriel aware of the social and economic privileges of his upper-class family between the ages of four and six, the same ages he was abused.

Uriel's father was a businessman and rancher who was also involved in politics. His mother was a dynamic businesswoman with a stressful daily routine orchestrated around family commercial transactions and charity events. Uriel described his relationship with his father as *magnífica*, a superb connection that was supportive and loving, though not emotionally expressive on his father's part. He also loved his mother dearly, but the relationship wasn't always close or easy. Uriel remembered his father emotionally abusing his mother, a pattern that vanished the day she received a generous inheritance. His parents relied on a tía and a *nana* to take care of Uriel when he was a boy. Of his nana of many years, Uriel said, "She loves me so much, I don't want her to feel rage toward my brother. There are many things I never told her."

Uriel has never been in therapy but said that he has relied on a renewed Christian faith to heal past wounds while distancing himself from the Catholic and Muslim faiths he was exposed to in his family. The grandson of a former senator, Uriel graduated from college in Mexico City and was living in Monterrey when our interview took place.

Pablo

> This tío was married, and he actually used to take me into his wife's bed to have sexual relationships with him. I must have been twenty-four. He would ask me things, and I would tell him that I had met a young man and that we had had sex for example. And then he asked me [animatedly], "Did you like it and everything?" I understand now that he became excited when I talked to him about [these experiences], and then he would do it to me.

This was Pablo's recollection of one of his last sexual encounters with one of his mother's brothers, who is seven or eight years older than him.

A shy man in his early fifties, Pablo was the oldest of all the people I interviewed in this study. He was also the one who reported sexualized exchanges in the family that were sustained for the longest periods, from early childhood to adulthood, and the one who most struggled to say whether they were coercive or not.

"With my tío, I don't know if it was voluntary and I don't know at what age it all started," said Pablo, trying to recall the first time his uncle approached him sexually. His best guess is that he was seven years old, and said he feared that it might have started earlier, when he was three or four.

However, Pablo clearly remembered what he used to do to him in the beginning: "When I was a little boy, he didn't penetrate me. I think that only started to happen when I was older. When I was a boy he only made me give him oral sex and I let him touch me," he said. "It happened when nobody was around or at night, at least once a week." An older brother and another maternal uncle exposed Pablo to similar yet less frequent sexualized experiences since childhood.

Born in a small town not far from Mexico City, Pablo moved with his mother and siblings to the big city when he was a little boy. In the early 1960s, Pablo's father left one day and never came back home. A woman in her mid-twenties at the time, Pablo's mother sought her family's support. Soon they all moved in with Pablo's maternal grandmother, who lovingly and unconditionally took them in. "My mother was a very good mother," said Pablo. "She worked to send us to school and made sure we had everything, although at the same time she would leave us alone." Ten blood relatives ended up living at his grandmother's home, including the brother and two uncles who abused him.

Pablo said that the frequent experiences with his uncle went from being one-on-one to being shared with one of his maternal primos. "My tío would make us get naked, and then made us to caress one another, and then to have oral sex, me with my primo and then my primo with me. Afterwards my tío would participate." His primo is two years younger than Pablo. "It must have been when I was thirteen and he was eleven, or maybe I was fifteen and he was thirteen." The sex among the primos and their tío happened many times, over a four-year period. Pablo's primo told him about his tío raping him when he visited his parents, and about getting angry at his stepfather for letting his tío share his bed when staying overnight.

Pablo was ten or twelve when a brother who was four or five years older assaulted and raped him. Pablo was always silent with his brother about these experiences, with the exception of one conversation. He said, "Well, finally, my brother asked me why I let my uncle do things to me. That is all he said, but I didn't say anything. But I did think about it, 'Well, but you did it to me.' I did think about it, I remember that I did think, 'Well, I don't know why he is in so much shock if he did it to me [as well].'" These experiences happened on different occasions, but less often than with his tío, said Pablo. The brothers used to share the same bed.

Pablo also remembered incidents with a younger tío, another of his mother's brothers, who was four or five years older than Pablo, when he was in elementary school. "With my other tío, I used to come home from school and would be changing out of my uniform. When I was in my underwear, he would grab me as if he were playing. He would lay me down and take his hand and fondle me and I laughed, I laughed. When the opportunity arose, both of us would lay down together in bed and he said, 'Turn over.' Or he would ask me to do oral sex to him, and then he would say 'Turn over again' and then that was it." Pablo's brother and two uncles behaved "as if nothing had happened" after they had approached him sexually; they behaved in the same way in other everyday life interactions.

In retrospect, Pablo said he had "sensations of pleasure" with his brother and younger uncle, which made the experiences "less abusive." He felt similar physical sensations of excitement with his older uncle, but that tío came across as more manipulative and controlling, Pablo said. He was "more abusive" than the other two. He developed feelings of distrust and emotional distance toward the three men; his individual experiences with each one of them got lost in silence. Pablo's relatives all eventually married women and had children.

Near the end of our interview, Pablo admitted something that made him shake and cry. "There is another situation that I haven't told you about," he said. "I abused a boy. I abused a boy." The boy was the son of his mother's close friend, also a single mother, who found support and emotional closeness with her. They used to take their children for walks and to play together outdoors. "We were very close, almost as if we were related," said Pablo. "I remember that we had fun together. So I don't even know how I could have done this to this boy." By now, he was weeping.

> I think I was thirteen or fourteen and he was maybe seven or eight. And that boy used to look up to me a lot. One day, my uncle left a [porn] magazine around, and I told the boy to come over and I showed it to him. I think that is what my uncle used to do. "Let's see, show me, let me touch you," I told this boy. And I penetrated him. I have always remembered that boy, very much, and I have thought about the damage I may have done to him.

Pablo explained that he was "used to these kinds of things" at the time, and didn't think anything was going to happen. But he became worried when the boy told him—the same day or the day after, he didn't remember—that he was bleeding. Pablo was afraid the boy's mother would complain to his mother about it. "But that didn't happen," he said. "The boy did what I did as a boy, he was silent about it as well."

As he recalled the experiences with this boy, Pablo exclaimed, "¡Ahhh! The tío of this boy actually tried to abuse me. The same. He was older than me, well not much, maybe four or five years older than me . . . I was fourteen or fifteen." Pablo explained why this was not consummated: "When he was going to penetrate me, I remember that I didn't let him do it because I thought, 'Why should I? He is going to tell everyone about it!' I pulled up my pants and ran out of there."

By then, Pablo had experienced many similar situations with his two uncles and his brother. He wasn't afraid of others learning about it, or its potential negative consequences. However, he said he always felt "very confused" about these exchanges.

"What caused the confusion?" I asked.

"The fact that we were both of the same sex, even though I know that I am gay."

I probed, asking, "More than the fact that you were related?"

"Well, yes," he said. "Later I even ended up thinking that it was normal. To the point, maybe, that I felt fortunate to have an uncle like that."

Pablo laughed when he said he didn't think he ever felt "fortunate" because of the sexualized experiences with his brother and uncles. But he started perceiving activities as "sinful" and became fearful in two ways. "I was afraid I would be punished by God," he said, "and afraid of becoming aware that I liked men, to accept myself [as gay]." Pablo was raised as a Catholic, and left the church as a teenager, feeling conflicted by many issues, including its teachings on sexuality, double standards of morality, and sexual abuse by priests. He felt validated in his decision by something that happened when he was about twenty: a man who actively seduced Pablo on the street turned out to be a Catholic priest in charge of a mass service to honor a quinceañera celebration he attended some months later.

"I don't know how to explain why I let him do all that to me," he said, weeping, referring to his oldest tío. "I don't know if as a boy people could tell, that I was effeminate or something. I just don't know how it happened, I don't know," he said. "I think I got used to it, and didn't wonder whether it was abusive or not until recently. He used to show me [porn] magazines and tell that I was a pretty boy, and I got used to that."

Pablo didn't think he would be able to forgive his uncle for what he did. His tío never used physical or verbal violence to sexually approach him and Pablo felt "loved and accepted by him." But he never developed any feelings of respect or affection for his uncle. "Okay, I'm gay, but I should have lived my childhood with innocence," he said. "He stole my innocence and that is difficult."

Pablo said that he started to "voluntarily" approach his older tío sexually when he was thirteen or fifteen. In general, however, Pablo said: "I think that he was always abusive. Even when I was twenty-four, he used to climb into my bed. I think that he was always abusive," especially when he assaulted Pablo while he slept, as a boy or in his early twenties.[9] By age twenty-four, Pablo had a stable romantic and sexual relationship with a young man close in age. One day, he realized that he had never felt any kind of special attraction toward his tío, and left him. "I think my tío is gay," he said. "He married for the same reason I considered doing it. If he was bisexual, he would enjoy sex with his wife, but he once he told me that he didn't," said Pablo. To this day, he said, "I believe, he would still want [to do it with me] if I accepted him."

"In fact I saw that he [the same, oldest tío] was lying down and my sister, younger than me, I believed he had an erection and he made my sister touch him. I think I told my mother about it, but she didn't do anything. I don't know if he abused my sister," said Pablo. Pablo was fourteen or fifteen and his sister was about seven at the time. He also heard stories about another sister being raped by a neighbor; she was six and he was in his sixties. When Pablo heard rumors about it when he was a teenager and asked his mom with deep concern, "*¡¿Qué pasó mamá?!* What happened?!" She simply replied, "No, *nada, nada*"—nothing.

The fact that nothing was done or said about his sisters' experiences was one reason Pablo never talked to his mother or another adult about his abuse. "I knew that nobody would do anything to him, but I would be punished [instead]," he said. Pablo has been similarly silent with his gay friends who have confided about experiences of sexual violence by a relative as children. "My primo is also gay and I told him, 'You go to therapy because you want to justify why you are gay, you are blaming him [uncle] for being gay, but we were born that way.'" Pablo's primo has encouraged him to seek professional help, but other than the few conversations with his primo about what the oldest uncle did to them, our interview was the first time Pablo shared his story with anyone.

"I always knew that I liked men, maybe since I was inside my mother's womb," he said. Fear of being rejected, however, has not allowed him to be "out" to his family or at work. "I think that my family knows intuitively," but "don't ask, don't tell" is the rule at home. At work, he is exposed to homophobic jokes and remarks that he ignores, too frightened to even talk back. He hasn't been in a romantic relationship or had a sexual relationship in a long time, but deep in his heart, he hopes he will find the right man some day.

Pablo finished preparatoria and for many years has worked in the same modest but stable administrative job in Mexico City. He shares his home with an aging relative. Of all the men I interviewed, Pablo expressed the most visible reactions of emotional pain and confusion, sobbing inconsolably while telling about the boy he raped.

Lies, Rough Play, and Pain

Saúl

"I don't feel like he forced me. I feel like he lied to me," said Saúl. "He treated the situation as if it was play." A college-educated man in his early forties and one of the youngest in a large middle-class family in Monterrey, Saúl described what happened one day when he was six and his primo was twelve.

> The abuse started with the lie that we were going to play over by the big tires behind a trailer, a big one. We came in and he unzipped my pants, and unzipped his. He started to caress me, then sat me on his legs and penetrated me. Then he told me to give him a kiss, and I didn't want to. And basically that is what the abuse consisted of.

Although Saúl said he felt "physical pleasure," he made sure I understood this event was abusive, because of the age difference. "If he had been twelve and I had been twelve, there is no problem," he said. "If I'm six and he's six, there's no problem. The fact that both sexes were the same, there is no problem either. The abuse is because my brain hadn't developed enough to handle those emotions." Saúl's primo was twelve, and was already developed, he said.

> Ah, I felt confused anyway, because you feel physical pleasure but at the same time in my mind I was afraid, I felt that what I was doing was not right. Especially when he told me to kiss him, and I said no. I wanted to give him a kiss, something in me said it wasn't right. Then, what you feel is confusion; emotional confusion. Because it was many things. There was physical pleasure, but also mixed feelings that "this isn't right," and "someone might catch us." There were mixed feelings.

Saúl thinks his primo may have told him not to tell anyone, "but not under any threat," he said. Shortly after that first experience, his primo invited him to do it again. An assertive six year old, Saúl said "no." His rationale? "Because I am going to end up being gay," he said.

Here is what Saúl learned at the age of six:

> I would listen to other boys, like my brother, who is about four years older than me. He told me once, "Don't let anyone do that to you, because then you become homosexual, you become a *joto*, a faggot." I heard those comments and I told myself, "Well, I did it already, but if I don't do it anymore, it might stop and I won't be homosexual. But if I keep doing it with my primo, if I accept his invitation, in the future I won't be able to stop it. It will be inevitable."

Saúl said he grew up feeling "very worried about being gay," not only because of what he had learned from his older brother and friends, but because of something else his primo told him when he penetrated him anally. He described it with difficulty and sadness.

> I've only talked about this once, and I'm struggling to talk it about for the second time because it sounds so ugly, so sick in the mind, on his part. He told me that when I grew up I was going to be a woman and that in order for that to happen I had to put my genitals between my legs every time I went to bed to sleep. He said the day was going to come when I would no longer have my masculine genitals; that I was going to have feminine genitals.

Saúl said his primo told him that exactly at the moment when he abused him. "I'm embarrassed to say so, but I feel shame on his behalf," he said with a giggle. "Now I say, 'My poor primo, the psychopath.'"

Saúl felt guilt and resentment following this incident because he felt he had been lied to and deceived. "I don't know if I knew the word or not, but it felt like a stolen innocence, like it wasn't the moment for me to experience that. I'd been comfortable the way I was, with tranquility, but I experimented too early. I had mixed feelings; depression and sadness. I started to eat more than I should and to bite my nails, and my grades dropped. I felt completely confused."

After the experience with his primo, Saúl's older sister noticed something unusual in him and inquired about it. He struggled to talk to her about it, while trying to make sense of it himself. She reacted in a way that made him feel "scolded." Saúl kept silent about it, growing up with damaged self-esteem and an inner struggle, especially as he discovered the special feelings he had toward boys. He grew up feeling confused not knowing if these feelings were caused by the abuse. He was always reserved and shy about his feelings toward boys, and preferred to spend time with girls; he felt safer with them. He grew up feeling enraged and frustrated, hoping his feelings would change one day.

"I think I was effeminate but I'm not sure," Saúl said. In secundaria, his classmates called him *maricón* and *joto*, and harassed him constantly. But at some point, these men unexpectedly became friendly with Saúl and invited him to join them to watch pornographic movies at a theater. He declined. "I already knew they could abuse me," he said, "I anticipated they would abuse me right there at the movies."

Saúl does not know if his primo abused anyone else in the family. He reflected,

Before he abused me, when I was still six years old, it was that same year, and my prima, his sister, was five years old. Outside my house was this beat-up old car. We got inside, we got undressed, we took off whatever we were wearing and there was touching. In other words, there was some kind of exploration. What is normal, I touched her, I touched her part and she touched me. And at that moment, my primo, the one who [later] abused me looked through the window and saw us. He said, "*¡Ah! ¡Van* *a ver!* I am going to tell my mother!" So a week or two later, I don't quite recall, the abuse happened.

Apparently, the families had experienced some tension in the past. When in his early twenties, Saúl eventually told his mother what had happened when he was six. She was so enraged, he was afraid she would kill his primo. After things settled down, Saúl, his parents, and his siblings had a conversation about what had happened with his primo. They all reached the same conclusion. "We thought that because my tía and her husband are kind of Machiavellian, they came up with the idea of the abuse [by the primo] because they thought I was abusing my prima," he said. "They didn't see that she and I were just exploring each other, which was normal. In their ignorance, they saw it as if I was abusing her. So my primo abused me for revenge."

Saúl doesn't know if his primo molested anyone else in the family, and he never had a follow-up conversation with the prima involved in the incident described earlier. However, one of Saúl's older brothers sexually molested his sister, the one who had "scolded" him. Saúl's sister was eight and his brother was fourteen when it happened. A remorseful father told Saúl not long ago, "I feel like I wasn't a good father," as they discussed the reasons why neither father nor mother intervened when they learned about Saúl's sister.

Saúl had his first stable and formal romantic relationship with a man in his late twenties, years after he gave up a heterosexual relationship that felt sexually frustrating and untruthful as a man. About that time, he "came out" to his parents and siblings. His father and mother were both supportive, but Saúl was concerned about his mother. To reassure her, he said that "nobody was guilty of it and that [he] had come out of the factory like this"—meaning "irregular." If you do not come out "straight," you come out of the factory *chueco,* a factory defect. His older sister used the same "scolding" tone of many years ago, while insisting that Saúl was gay because of what happened with his primo.

Saúl's primo eventually married a woman; Saúl has had only sporadic contact with him. Born and raised in a Catholic family, Saúl left the church as an adolescent. He tried other Christian churches, hoping he could find answers to his inner struggle. He said he used to be "obsessed in his wish to change his sexuality." Although Saúl said that "God helped him forgive" his primo, he wished he could have confronted him about the abuse. Saúl was in psychotherapy and taking antidepressants when I interviewed him.

Anselmo

"I was the son of one of my tías, and then ... because of the problem I had, I became the son of another tía," said Anselmo, a young man who was about to turn twenty when I interviewed him. When he was a little boy, he was shuttled between his relatives, and while living at an older tía's house was abused three times by his aunt's teenage son, two of those times violently.

Anselmo was born and raised in Mexico City, and told me he had exciting plans to attend college. Growing up, both his parents worked long hours to provide for their children, and relied on the adults in their extended family to take care of them, including his father's older sister, the first tía. "When her son, my primo, abused me, I started to tell my parents, 'I don't want to stay with my tía anymore.' But I didn't tell them *why*." Anselmo said his father didn't inquire about it, and simply replied, "Oh well, I'll take you to my youngest sister's house then."

Anselmo's oldest tía was a hardworking woman with a full-time job. While she was at work, she trusted her son, who was seventeen or eighteen, to take care of Anselmo, who was between six and eight.

Anselmo remembered what happened to him the first time.

> That time, I recall, it was my primo's turn to clean the house. Every day, he was supposed to clean the house, mop the floors, then I, in the meantime, I recall that everyday at the time of house chores I used to go to my tía's room, she had *Cablevisión* and I watched TV. It was a small room, those were small apartments, and I stayed there. But I recall that one time my primo, I don't recall how exactly this happened because afterwards you feel enraged, no? I was lying down in front of the TV and he got there and lay down next to me, wearing his white T-shirt, the T-shirts that give me emotional trauma, maybe that is the reason why I wear black so much. So he got there and lay down next to me. He removed his T-shirt, something that I thought was normal at the moment, I didn't expect less from the

family. So he then removed his T-shirt and then his pants, he was wearing only his underwear. I kept watching TV and he kept watching TV as well. He hugged me and started to caress me. Something that perhaps, at that moment the first time didn't see it as bad, the second time he started to tell me things. He started to caress me and said, "I know what kind of game we are going to play" and obviously, I was a child and I was *¡Ujjuuu!* Yay!

Anselmo thought he was going to have fun with his primo. Instead, life took an unexpected turn that day.

Then that was when he grabbed me and said, "Turn over" and I said, "Good!" Then I turned over and lay down. Then, but I saw it as normal, no? In other words, I didn't perceive anything, nothing that was not normal, until he took off my little T-shirt. I didn't see it, I don't know, I didn't know why I didn't feel anything, In other words, I don't know why my body didn't tell me "*¡Aguas!* Watch out!" And then he pulled down my pants and my underwear and I felt that he was playing with my butt. But well, he made me feel very ticklish. That is something I cannot forget, I was ticklish and I was laughing and laughing, "ha, ha, ha!" laughing and laughing, I was so happy and then suddenly he got on top of me and then I said, "Hey, get off me, you are heavy!" And he moved to the side and then that was when he opened me up and penetrated me. It was a terribly strong pain. It was such a strong pain, to this day, still at times, until recently I talked to the group therapist about it, it is an instant in which I didn't remember what had happened before or after. In other words, I recall that moment, period. Those three minutes that were, because just imagine I felt immense pain but the first time, it hurt me so bad. He pulled it out and then again, put it inside, and I felt terribly worse.

Anselmo got up and started to run naked all over the house screaming, "*¡Me duele, me duele, me duele!* It hurts, it hurts, it hurts!" Then his primo got dressed and went on cleaning the house.

Similar versions of this scenario were repeated twice more in the same month. The second time occurred as Anselmo and his primo were roughhousing. Anselmo ended up being raped again, this time running naked all over the house, screaming in terror, "*¡Sangre! ¡sangre! ¡sangre!* Blood!

blood! blood!" After this incident, Anselmo said, "My primo acted as if nothing had happened. He went to my tía's bedroom to watch TV." Anselmo locked himself in the bathroom until his tía arrived and asked what was going on. "I cried with her but I didn't tell her anything," he said.

Anselmo remembered that before the last incident, his primo said roughly this: "Remember what happened the other day? We are going to do it once again and then we will never do it again, I promise. Just this time, and that's it." But Anselmo firmly said no. "He tried to take off my T-shirt, but he couldn't, because I was pulling back," he said. "I remember feeling some kind of fear, that hit me very strongly, and that was the moment I started to resist. I didn't give him a chance." Anselmo's primo never approached him again.

Although his primo never told Anselmo to be silent about these three incidents, he never told anyone, and he never explained why he refused to go back to that tía's house. "I feel that if my father had asked me, 'Why don't you want to be there?' I would have told him," he said. "But he never asked me, or at least I don't recall if he ever did."

Anselmo was silent about the abuse until recently, but as he grew up, he became very assertive, in situations that were potentially abusive. "I believe that all my strength to defend myself and stop suffering from abuse comes from the pain," Anselmo said. For example, when he was eleven or twelve he fought off a neighbor who approached him to "play doctor." Later, he beat up a Catholic priest who sexually assaulted him and his friend at a retreat a few years before our interview. He never went back to the church.

Although Anselmo didn't feel guilt or responsibility for what happened to him with his primo, he felt remorse about the ways he tried to cope with it. He used marijuana, cocaine, and crack. He also engaged in promiscuous sex with both women and men he met casually at fiestas or *antros*—bars and nightclubs. When I asked him about how he identified himself with regard to his sexual identity, he said, "Homosexual or not, I don't know yet." He did have stable and romantic and sexual monogamous relationships with a woman and a man. "You suffer so much, I would not be able to cause that much pain," Anselmo said that the idea of "touching" a child has never crossed his mind. His own experience as a child has made him overprotective now that he takes care of a younger brother who attends elementary school.

"I had everything to be a happy boy," said Anselmo. His parents were a happy couple, and supportive and loving parents when they were available. They provided a life of comfort for everyone at home. Anselmo grew up feeling similarly loved by all the paternal tías who took care of him. Although Anselmo resents them for being "too ambitious"—working too hard and not spending enough time with him and his siblings as they grew up—his relationship with both his parents was one of the most genuinely caring, loving, and supportive parent-child relationships I encountered in this entire study.

Interestingly, Anselmo only recently told his father about the abuse by his primo as part of a conversation about why he wasn't doing well in school. His father offered unconditional loving support to Anselmo, reacted with pain and rage, confronted his primo, and thought about taking legal action. His mother reacted similarly. Although Anselmo doesn't think he will ever be able to forgive his primo for damaging him so much, he kept his parents from pressing charges and potentially sending his primo to prison.

As he tried to make sense of the three incidents, he said that before them, their relationship as cousins had been "very good." His primo had spoiled and pampered him as a child. Anselmo lost contact with his cousin after the last time he tried to rape him. But after all these years he ran into him a few days before our interview. Anselmo confronted him in front of the family, and the encounter ended in a fistfight.

Apparently, sexual violence was not news in his otherwise caring and supportive immediate and extended family. Anselmo learned, for instance, that his father's uncle sexually assaulted one of his beloved paternal tías when she was about twenty. Anselmo was beginning to explore these issues as part of a support group he had joined in Mexico City shortly before we talked.

Valentín

"I remember he pulled down my shorts. He made me bend down, but I didn't know why. It was like a shock inside of me, because I didn't even know what had happened, it was very quick. It was kind of a shock, I don't know what had happened, and it happened." Valentín was anally penetrated when he was seven by a man about eighteen years old he identified as his "tío"—the brother of the wife of his mother's brother. "Later, the next day, he told my uncle [mother's brother] that I had told him I was gay and I liked doing this and that. That way, he got rid of the problem."

Now in his early twenties, Valentín works at a maquiladora in Ciudad Juárez and goes to school at night. "When he told my uncle [mother's brother] that I was gay, he made fun of me, and didn't believe me," he said. "That's why I told myself that nobody would believe me, and I was afraid, for sure." Valentín didn't feel safe or confident enough to tell anyone about this and the other experiences that happened within his extended family. For instance, the tío who raped him the first time was soon joined in abusing him by a seventeen-year-old young man (also related to an in-law of his mother). Valentín called the two *parientes políticos*, "I see it as some kind of abuse because [later] there was no penetration but the first time it happened there was. They forced me like this, to do things to them. Or they would grab me from behind and start to do it. These buddies had their penis erected, and they would put it [their penis] close to me and I could not defend myself. I did my best to be strong, and they used to do all these things to me."

Valentín used to spend time at both his maternal uncle's home and his maternal grandmother's home, and encountered his tíos políticos there. Ironically, Valentín went there to escape his mother's harsh corporal punishment. As a way to cope with her physical punishment, he also ran away and recalled sleeping as a child on the streets of his hometown, a small pueblo on the Gulf of Mexico coast where he was born and raised before migrating to Ciudad Juárez as a teenager.[10]

The instances of sexual violence exercised by his uncles were situational, occurring when the oldest of them spent the night at the maternal uncle's house or as part of other events that might have appeared to be safe family gatherings and fun for the rest of the family. Valentín recalled other instances of sexual assault with the older boys when he was on the verge of adolescence. "They made me touch their penis, and this happened in the river, when we were swimming," he said. "They told me to grab their penis by the force. They were older and bigger than me, and if I didn't, they tried to drown me."

Thinking back, Valentín said, "They treated me like a maricón, as if I was gay. They used to see me like that, I don't know why. They saw me like that, and they were mean to me." As he became older and stronger, the violence eventually stopped.

But living at home with his mother and stepfather wasn't sexually safe either. From the ages of seven to ten, Valentín's stepfather fondled him at night. "At times he would be affectionate," he said. "But he wouldn't say anything. Simply, he took advantage of . . . He pretended to think I was sleeping or something, but actually I was awake. I didn't say anything, I don't know why I never said anything." Why didn't he say anything? I asked. He said, "The only person who knew about this was my uncle, and he made fun of me. That didn't give me the courage to tell anyone else, because I was afraid that my mother would say the same thing, tell me that I was gay. I was afraid. My mother wasn't treating me well, and if I told her this on top of it, I felt like my mother would love me even less."

Homophobic bullying came up constantly in my interview with Valentín, who said his uncle and other men in the family would frequently harass him and call him gay and maricón. "I feel like if they had not said those things to me, perhaps it would not be affecting me." Valentín felt that the homophobic terrorism left a deep imprint in his heart as a boy. But he didn't take the pain passively. He even plotted to kill his uncle when he was eight: "I wanted to kill my uncle for making fun of me and not believing me. Back in my hometown, people use machetes and I was going to kill him *a machetazos*—I was going to slash him with a machete."

Said Valentín: "I was seven or eight when I started watching porn movies. We had a neighbor who lived nearby and he would watch adult movies with the entire family, in broad daylight. He left the window open and then all of us, boys and friends would get together to watch." Valentín described what he recalled doing twice when he was seven or eight: "There were some girls at a daycare near where my mother used to rent a space. I started to want to do the same [things to them] that I saw in the movies. We would kiss and I think my penis was already erect. It would come out of my pant fly, and I tried to put it through their skirts."

These experiences didn't feel right at times because of discomfort he associated with the Catholic religion, but he was also excited to be "experimenting something new." Back then he was becoming exposed to older adolescent boys in his neighborhood who masturbated in front of him. "I think they were trying to teach me to do it," he said. He was eighteen years old when had his first sexual encounter with a neighbor, an older woman who visited his home and flirted and seduced him frequently. As part of these exchanges, he recalled an incident: "I feel like she forced me . . . it lasted at most two minutes. I just wanted to ejaculate and go back home."

"I have become closer to God, I used to go to church a lot. I did things like that. Perhaps that is from where I learned to forget about these things and try to forgive. And my childhood, well . . . I never had a childhood, there was never a childhood for me," he said.

As Valentín came of age, he attempted suicide once and tried everything to soothe himself emotionally: alcohol, pills, thinner, cement, cocaine, glue, and marijuana. He became sober at some point, but he was devastated after his girlfriend confided and told him about her own experience of sexual molestation by her brother. Valentín then told her his own past as a way to offer his support to her, but she started to call him "gay" in times of tension and conflict. The addictions of the past returned. The idea that he might be homosexual has deeply affected him. Valentín decided to seek professional help at the organization where we met in Ciudad Juárez.

In the Name of the Father
Leonardo

> I was sent to sleep with my uncle, who was going to be sleeping alone. So [my mother] sent me to sleep with him. She was already asleep, and I felt when he stuck it [his penis] in me. Well, he got clo[ser] . . . well, he stuck it in me. And he said "Do you like it?" And I said "No" and he said, "Ah!" and continued as if he was having sexual relations. He then said, "Don't say anything," and I said "No." And he kept on going and going.

This was Leonardo's recollection of the first time his paternal uncle sexually abused him—Leonardo was six and the uncle was fourteen. Leonardo's relatives were visiting for a quinceañera celebration and the house was full. His parents figured that the best way to accommodate everyone spending the night was to ask their children to share a bed with older children of the same gender.

Leonardo endured a similar experience with the same uncle twice more. He was always in a state of shock, and it was never pleasurable. Afraid that his uncle would punish him, Leonardo didn't resist after the first time. He has always felt guilty for not telling his mother after the first incident.

Born and raised in Mexico City, Leonardo is the oldest child in his family and the only son. Now a single man in his early twenties, he finished trade school and studies *preparatoria abierta* (open university preparatory system) while figuring out life without paid employment. Leonardo's parents are a young working-class couple who got married when they were adolescents.

Soon after these experiences, he said, Leonardo's father noticed something "strange" about his son and questioned him persistently. Eventually, he broke his silence and said what had happened. "He became furious," said Leonardo, and stormed off to confront his brother.

Meanwhile, the six-year-old boy encountered a painful reaction from his father's sisters: they called him a liar and hit him. But his mother was supportive, and remains Leonardo's most important source of love to this day. She believed the boy, and confronted the paternal aunts, who were afraid that their furious older brother would kill his younger brother. To this day, neither Leonardo nor his mother knows if his father ever confronted the uncle. But for Leonardo, life began to take an unexpected turn. "My father used to beat me up hard, a lot," he said. "Also, he used to call me a maricón, a faggot. 'You're a maricón, you are this and that!' And I cried and well, he used to hit me. I recall my father dragging me out of the house, bleeding. He would beat me up and say, 'Get out of this house, I don't want to see you anymore!'"

His father had called him *afeminado*—effeminate—since he was a little boy and used corporal punishment to teach him how to walk and move his body in "a more masculine way." Mother and sisters weren't physically violent, but forced him to do the same—the entire family monitored Leonardo's body movements. The way he walked and moved his body, and his high voice, became the topic of long family conversations. The intention was to help Leonardo change "for his own good," efforts that Leonardo has endured many times since early childhood. "I hate being alive," an anguished fourteen-year-old Leonardo once told his father during one of the most violent beatings. He asked his father to kill him. A couple of years later, when Leonardo started working and contributing in a significant way to the family income, he noticed that his father hit him less frequently.[11]

When he was seventeen, he remembered his mother asking him if he was homosexual. "I said 'No'. She said, 'Tell me, really, tell me,' and I said 'No'. That was it. That was my first conversation with her about it."

One of the most dramatic events in Leonardo's life with his family occurred after he was taken to the emergency room for a stay at a Seguro Social clinic a year before our interview.[12] He had a persistent fever, and the medical staff couldn't explain it. Said Leonardo: "This person, presumably a doctor, said I probably had HIV."[13] He told his mother this after he was released, and she then told his father—without anticipating the shocking consequences. "My father kicked me three or four times and I didn't fight back. He kicked me three or four times and told me that I was rotten inside, that I was a walking dead person, that I had ruined my life, he was crying. He said he was ashamed of me because of who I was, for what I have been." Days later, when he was finally tested for HIV and the result came back negative, the entire family felt relieved.

Leonardo identified his father as a *machista*, an alcoholic who was violent toward his mother and sisters. Still, the violence toward the women was less intense than what Leonardo endured; Leonardo said he wished he had been a woman so his father didn't hit him so hard. His father stopped drinking and became less violent after he became involved in a Jehovah's Witnesses church; Leonardo's parents were Catholic when they married.

Leonardo's experiences with his family have become part of a larger labyrinth of sexual violence that he has been trying to make sense of his entire life. When still in preschool—years before his uncle abused him—Leonardo was already wondering why his classmates and friends bullied him—even in front of his sister, who lovingly defended him and encouraged him to fight back.[14] As a boy, he preferred to spend time and play with girls rather than boys, and cried easily. Throughout his adolescence he gave oral sex to other men, mainly classmates and friends close in age; these were casual encounters that felt voluntary but which he rarely enjoyed.

In his early twenties today, he is sexually harassed daily in the busy streets of Mexico City. This especially involves groping in public transportation, including *el metro*—the subway system—which working-class gay men use as a place to hook up.[15]

Leonardo said, "I have met certain people [men] who sexually harassed me so much that I said, 'Well, if that is what you want, let's do it, ¡órale! Let's do it! If you'll leave me alone if I give you what you want, let's do it!'" He feels responsible for the harassment. "I contribute to it," he said. "I don't like my body." About a third of the sexual encounters he has had with men happened under this kind of coercion, in a variety of social contexts and circumstances. Leonardo includes these experiences among the sexual partners he has had so far: fifteen men and two women, all close to his age. The men were mostly *hombres masculinos*—masculine-looking, he said. He has later run into some of these men, and learned that they are often married with children. The sex with the women happened when he was about twenty; the young women were his coworkers.

"I didn't know I was effeminate," Leonardo said about his childhood. He eventually learned that the uncle who sexually molested him was gay, and said he'd abused him because he "thought that I was the same way, and in the end I was going to be homosexual . . . That I was following his same path." Because of the experiences with his uncle, Leonardo called himself "bisexual." Lately, however, he has felt "undecided" about how he identifies himself sexually. He thinks that marrying a woman and having children would be the ideal for a permanent relationship. Interestingly, his father has never told him or suggested that "he is maricón" because of the abuse.

Leonardo has a large circle of more than thirty gay friends—young men between their teens and mid-twenties—and his conversations with them have felt personally validating. "Of the 100 percent who are gay," he said, "99 percent" have told him that an uncle, primo, father, or friend has sexually abused them.

As a young adult, Leonardo has run into his uncle at their grandparents' home. A successful, college-educated man, his uncle is always respectful and friendly toward Leonardo; he has never touched him or seduced him from the time Leonardo was six. An assertive, empowered Leonardo confronted his father recently about the pain of the past, but his father always reacts with silence. "He can't express love spontaneously toward men," Leonardo said. "Because he never had his father's love, he does not know how to give. Maybe in other ways he is asking for forgiveness, ways that perhaps I don't understand."

Leonardo realized that he was "afraid of abusing" a boy himself when he was thirteen or fourteen, but said he didn't feel sexual attraction or curiosity for children. He said he has actually "pushed away" boys who attend his same church and who sit playfully on his lap or give him hugs. "At my age, I'm too mature to do these kind of stupid things," he said. He is a fervent believer in "Jehová," and wouldn't do anything "that God wouldn't approve of."

Becoming aware of his own pain as a boy has been good protection from abusing a minor, not to mention the potential legal and family consequences. Leonardo grew up in a state he called a *coma emocional*—an emotional coma—accompanied by depression, fatigue, social isolation, poor grades, frequent illness, eating disorders, and several suicide attempts.

Leonardo presented himself with an effeminate gender expression—body movements and voice conventionally associated with femininity—during our interview and talked about the ways he is often read as "gay" in many social situations. For instance, a year prior to our interview, Leonardo was officially expelled from the Jehovah's Witnesses congregation "for being homosexual." Although he openly told me about his same-sex erotic exchanges, he seemed to be struggling to accept his desires for men. Leonardo said he had never been in love with a man. In spite of his ideal of marrying a woman, he would like to have a romantic relationship with a man one day. He recently sought professional help for the first time, at the organization where we met.

Alberto

For Alberto, the abuse was all wrapped up with riding the bus driven by his stepfather. "I loved riding that bus so much," he said. "And he would say, 'Okay, we'll ride the bus, but we need to spend the night over there, in the ranch,' where we used to stay. I think that was the way he used to blackmail me."

Alberto explained that when he was a boy, traveling with his stepfather always involved sharing the same bed and being exposed to experiences he didn't have a name for. Alberto was six years old at the time, and his stepfather was a man in his early thirties, a bus driver who enjoyed transporting passengers along the dusty roads connecting the pueblos, ranchos, and *rancherías* or collection of ranchos. Now in his early forties, Alberto is married, a father, and lives in Ciudad Juárez. He still remembers the bus rides with nostalgia. "He would grab me and take me to wherever he wanted to go," he said. "I think that is the reason why it happened, because I used to sleep with him."

> In the beginning, he would grab my hand and made me touch his [private] parts. It started that way; it was like that for a while. I believe that . . . well, now I understand, that he masturbated. Later, he started to put his parts and did it to the point that he did penetrate me, and he did that many times . . . In the beginning when he wanted me to touch his parts, he put his part in my mouth, many times, and he would say, "Do it like this."

Similar versions of that scenario used to happen after an exciting bus ride, a routine that took place from the ages of about six to nine. Eventually, his stepfather penetrated Alberto anally on several occasions. In retrospect Alberto realized that attending school protected him from these painful experiences. However, bus rides followed by sexual molestation at night became a daily routine during his summer vacation.

Alberto has clear memories of these experiences, which happened while he was awake, and also while he was asleep, he is convinced. "I thought it was normal," he said. "Probably at that moment I had no idea of what was going on in my head because I told myself, 'I have to be with him and that is the way it should be.' I thought that was the way it had to be." But Alberto suspected that something wasn't right the first time his stepfather warned him, "Don't ever tell your mother, because she won't believe you anyway." Silence was soon joined by fear and confusion, especially later, he said. "He used to say that I should never tell my mother about what was happening, because if anything happened to my mother, I was going to be guilty of it and I didn't want to lose my mother." Said Alberto: "There are many things I am grateful for, because of him I work, he taught me to work, and now I am who I am. But there are many things I will always reproach him right to his face."

As it happens, Alberto today has a job that requires a lot of driving. Working at an early age became a family obligation for all the children. It was a collective effort to survive in the small towns where they grew up, many years before they migrated to Ciudad Juárez or the United States. But if hard work at an early age was a blessing for him, it was a curse for his sisters. Alberto was at work and away when his stepfather began to molest Alberto's younger sisters. His stepfather also molested both girls at night, he said.

> I don't know exactly what he did to them when he went into their room. We [children] only saw that he would go in their room. We pretended to be sleeping, we used to sleep that way, and he would go into their room while my mother was also sleeping, and he would go and do things to them.

As a boy, Alberto was still making sense of his own experiences with his stepfather, and he was far from knowing how to intervene on his sisters' behalf. As he became older, however, tension in the relationship with his stepfather eventually erupted in intense fights and confrontation, especially as Alberto saw his parents fighting. "I put the gun to his head," he remembered, in an intense quarrel that took place shortly before he turned twelve and was trying to defend his mother. He was a physically strong boy and used to carry the gun he had access to at the dispatching company where he worked.

Alberto and his siblings were exposed to harsh corporal punishment, which both parents used to discipline them. Mother and stepfather worked hard, full-time and they took turns caring for the children. When their mother was not around, however, their stepfather was more punitive with everyone and threatened them if they ever said a word to her. Through conversations about the physical violence they all shared, Alberto and his sisters eventually told each other about their experiences of sexual abuse, he said, though without "any details."

His sisters tried to cope without telling their mother about the abuse; they just left. "As soon as they could, they left home," Alberto said. A few years before our interview, the sisters told their mother about the abuse, and Alberto said they were shocked by her reaction. "My mother said we hadn't told her because we liked it. And she said, 'Do you want me to kick him out? Do you want me to be alone?'"

In a large family of step-siblings from two different marriages, Alberto came of age convinced that he and his two sisters were the only children sharing a common history of sexual abuse at the hands of their stepfather. They all hoped that being away from the man, becoming adults and getting married and having their own families, might erase the pain of the past. A few years ago, Alberto and his sisters were shocked but not surprised when their younger sister—a woman now in her twenties—told them that she too was being abused. They decided to get her out of their hometown, he said. "I told my sisters, 'Let's help her so she can go to *el otro lado*, to the U.S. side, let's help her come over here. Once all of us are over here, and she is with the children, we will start acting against him.'" Alberto and his sisters helped the adolescent girl cross to the United States to live with a relative. She then told them openly about her own experience with her father.

This incident took place as Alberto learned about his stepfather's attempts to also molest one of Alberto's nephews. Carrying a gun and in front of some of his brothers and his stepfather's sons, Alberto confronted his stepfather about sexually abusing him, his three sisters, and his nephew. The man was terrified and apparently remorseful. As Alberto described: "He said, 'I swear on my mother, who just passed away, I swear on her that I will never do it again.'" Alberto was raised Catholic, and blames the church for some of the sexual abuse. "Now I understand why there are so many cases of priests who have raped people or children," he said. "The Catholic church is so rigid." His stepfather was a former seminarian, never used drugs, rarely drank alcohol, and wasn't violent toward his wife early in their relationship.

Alberto converted from Catholicism to another Christian religion not long ago; he said that religious conversion has helped him cope with the abuse. "I fear God, because I know that God is good but he is also tough." At the organization where I met him, Alberto said that fear of God is one of the things that has stopped him from abusing children himself, but in a tone of concern and sadness, he admitted he had once thought of "touching" one of his stepdaughters. Temptation got the best of him and he acted on it, but he said that something—"I don't know what it was"—helped him realize that "it wasn't right." But, he said, "I have never done anything I would be ashamed of."

He explained that not long ago he had actually touched his step-daughter once again, this time on top of her clothes when she was on his lap. When it happened, he said he experienced a sensation that felt good but uncomfortable, and he stopped. "You know what, *mija*? Why don't you go outside?" Alberto explained that he said this to his stepdaughter, who was attending elementary school, as a way to cope with what seemed to be both a concern and temptation.

"So what exactly stopped you at that moment?" I asked.

"Because of what happened to me, I think that at that moment, I felt like it was being done to me."

"Have you ever had similar experiences with your biological children?"

"No, I never did it," he said.

When I asked him to elaborate, he said: "To our own [flesh and] blood, we would never do that, I don't think so. Even though there are fathers who have done. But I wouldn't do it. In fact, with my own daughters, I would not even get close to them physically. If there is anything I regret is the fact that I never told them, 'My daughter, I love you very much.'" Remorseful, he admitted that he has used physical punishment to discipline the girls.

Alberto doesn't know if his mother was sexually molested as a child, or had a history of sexual violence. But his current wife and a former partner both told him that they had been sexually abused by a stepfather and an uncle, respectively. As we wrapped up our interview at the organization where he recently started family sessions, he said weeping: "I would like to give closure to this in my life, and for the well-being of all my children."

Helián

"*Tienes que cambiar, tienes que cambiar, porque si no, te mato,*" became the deafening echo of pain and anxiety in the boy's heart. "You must change, you must change, because if you don't, I kill you," were the words his father constantly repeated while using his thumb to penetrate Helián's anus. His father had a long, sharp thumbnail, which aggravated the pain. This happened when he was between the ages of three to eight. An effeminate boy at the time, Helián was confused by what his father was trying to tell him and horrified by his death threats. But change what? Helián wondered. And why would his father kill him?

Helián never asked; he lived in fear. And because he was afraid of being punished, he didn't tell his mother about the abuse. His father gave him a stern warning as well when he was a little boy. Of gay men, his father used to say, "Those people don't have the right to cry. So if you cry, do it alone." When Helián was eight years old, his father penetrated him anally with his penis and left him bleeding on the bathroom floor. The boy received medical attention, but the tragic event was never discussed in the family; he has suffered from serious rectal conditions since. His father then stopped the abuse, "perhaps he realized that it wasn't right."

As Helián came of age and became aware of his attraction to men, the realization of what his father had meant all along hit him hard. It became more evident the day Helián became the target of gay bullying; in his early teens, he was gang-raped more than once by the same group of young men. In his late teens, the painful clarity became terror when he learned of a cousin's tragic fate: when they learned he was gay, Helián's father and uncles arranged to kill him. They took the young man out on a boat, threw him overboard in a deep part of the ocean, and made sure the sharks ate him. They were never prosecuted.

Hearing that, Helián then understood that his father's abuse was his poor attempt to "protect" him from the same fate; he attempted suicide twice as an adolescent. Helián was also shocked but not surprised when he learned that his father had also sexually abused at least one of his sisters. When one of the girls became pregnant by his father, her pregnancy became a secret in the family. Helián's mother was aware of what had happened to him and his sisters, but did nothing about it—silence and fear about anything related to sex was the rule at home. Eventually, however, she supported her daughters and her husband was sent to prison, though he was released later. Helián remembered her as a "super-heroine," a hardworking mother he loved and admired but also hated, especially when she used harsh corporal punishment to discipline them. She died when Helián was a teenager.

"The first person I talked to about all this was a college professor," Helián told me in our interview. "I cried and cried. You have no idea of how much I cried. I had so much anger and resentment. And especially, I asked myself, Why were they so cruel? Why did they humiliate me that way?"

A few years ago, Helián finally confronted his father in a telephone conversation. Now an aging alcoholic, his father was deeply pained, and he asked for forgiveness. "I cried as well, and you have no idea of how much he cried," he said. "If you ever write my story, please don't portray my father as a bad person, because he wasn't. He loved me, and he wanted to protect me," Helián said. "He wasn't bad, he simply didn't have the words to explain to me why I was supposed to change," he said. "My father and his brothers weren't well educated. He was taught to be *machista*."

I conducted this interview in Monterrey in 2006, many years after Helián left his home on the Mexican Gulf coast to make a life for himself that would be new in many ways. He'd felt emotionally wounded, but motivated to try his luck in another part of the country with hopes of healing and starting a new life. He succeeded to an unexpected degree.

When we met, "Helián" was a memory of the past: he had already legally become Heliana, a college-educated, bright, beloved, and popular schoolteacher in her forties who takes self-prescribed hormones and dresses modestly.[16] She is also a respected community leader in her working-class colonia. Other than the one-time conversation many years earlier with her college professor, she has never sought any type of professional help.

As Heliana, she identifies herself as a heterosexual woman, a devout Christian *creyente*—a believer—who daily prays that no one will discover that she was born a man. At the time of our interview, she was in a stable cohabitation relationship of many years with a hardworking, supportive man, the only person who knows about her past. But she said that every second of life is like "walking on the edge of a cliff," worrying about people discovering the truth about her life. She was terrified of losing it all: the socially respected identity as a woman, her gratifying and well-paid job, and the house she now owns.

Heliana has only a distant relationship with her family of origin; she has never had contact in person with the relatives that she left behind back home—as Helián. "I continue to be a question mark to myself," Heliana said. She explained, "To this day I believe that I don't even know what I want. To this day I don't even know who I am. I feel like nothing but a mannequin living in a strange body that isn't mine."

As we concluded what was the most emotionally exhausting and moving interview of my career, Heliana gave me a smile and lightly asked if I had seen the movie *Tootsie*. She wanted to be sure I understood that she was neither transgender nor transsexual. Years ago, Dustin Hoffman had offered her a creative and humane way to survive the intricate labyrinths of social discrimination in Mexico. As an effeminate gay man, Helián never experienced a mismatch between his birth-assigned biological sex and his gender identity. As Helián, he *forced* himself to become Heliana. He became Heliana with the exclusive purpose of surviving in homophobic Mexico.

As a fervent advocate of women's rights, Heliana is afraid of being raped, yet feels protected as a woman. She feels safer as a woman than as an effeminate gay man. But she won't attend LGBTQ-related events, for fear of people thinking she is a lesbian. She has survived, and on her own terms. The effeminate gay man with the soft, gentle voice who was humiliated, spat on, beaten up, and stepped on as he walked down the street, by now—the man she used to be—he would be dead, asserted Heliana.[17]

Understanding Men's Stories of Incest

As I listened to and later analyzed the men's stories, four specific themes united their unique yet commonly shared experiences: (1) the relationship with the person who exercised violence, (2) the mother-son and father-son relationships, (3) religion, and (4) reactions to the experiences of abuse.

First, the father-son relationship might have been damaged by pain and anger; the emotional bond, however, may become a complex emotional web that may also include feelings of respect and understanding toward a father, especially as the latter becomes an aging man asking for forgiveness. Within the brother and primo relationship, in contrast, the emotional bond might have been close and loving prior to the incidents of sexual violence; consistently, however, the relationship became seriously damaged, frequently characterized by distance, tension, and conflict. And within the uncle-nephew context, love and respect toward the authority figure may exist prior to the first incident of sexual violence, especially when the former is an adult. However, for the uncle and nephew who are relatively close in age, the emotional bonding might have a more casual tone of informality and distance. Regardless, the connection between both parties results in emotional pain and distance as a consequence of experiences of sexual violence, especially when adults and/or the family system blame the victim.

Second, for men in all arrangements, the relationship with the maternal figure is not uniform: the son-mother relationship might be positive, close, and loving (before and/or after she learned about what a son might have experienced), but these relationships may also expose a maternal figure who was viewed as disempowered and impotent as a parent, and/or punishing and/or neglecting of a son and other children, who might also have been abused in the family. This pattern resonates with women's stories and research on father-daughter incest, wherein a mother's complicity, if present, may become "a measure of maternal powerlessness."[18]

The father-son relationship in all arrangements followed similarly contrasting patterns vis-à-vis the mother-son relationship. Some men described the father-son relationship as loving and emotionally close but not always expressive, which may improve after a son confided the experience of abuse by an uncle or an older primo. Other men lamented the absence of a paternal presence while growing up while also sharing the pain of having a stepfather they may initially trust when they were young, but later learned to fear and reject after the first incidence of child sexual molestation took place. The latter was aggravated in the case of a stepfather sexually targeting more than one child in the family. In the most extreme cases, the relationship with a biological father was distant and tense in the beginning and deteriorated considerably after the paternal figure became sexually violent or abusive. As indicated above, an adult man may eventually forgive an aging, sick father.

Third, for the father-son arrangement, all men were Catholic at different stages of their lives but converted to a different Christian religion; they reported that religion helped to cope and/or to develop some form of self-control and prevented them from exercising sexual violence against others, mainly children. Research with Mexican men has identified a similar pattern: some Mexican men may use Catholic religion or conversion to a different Christian religion (e.g., Protestantism) as a way to cope with alcoholism, marital conflict, chronic illness, and sexual dysfunction.[19] For men with stories involving their brothers and primos, all of the men were similarly raised in families where the Catholic faith had an important presence. They converted or left the Church, however, for different reasons, including the moral contradictions they have witnessed or personally experienced, such as stories of being seduced or sexually assaulted by priests. Men who reported an uncle similarly reflected upon the same issues, and one of them illustrated the ways in which adults who exercise sexual violence against a child and/or become complicit may use religious interventions to silence those involved and keep incidents of sexual violence unresolved within the family.

And fourth, a son does not take his father's sexual violence passively in perpetual silence; he may use emotional or physical violence to confront his father at contrasting stages in life, especially as he learns that more than one child has become the sexual target of his father. Similarly, within the brother and primo arrangement, a young man may hit back emotionally and physically in intense ways, becoming resentful and aggressive in the most extreme case. A young man may have a similar reaction within the uncle-nephew context: he may have a desire to kill his uncle. In the most brave and admirable possibility, a young man may become a passionate and vocal advocate for himself and other primos similarly targeted by an uncle, yet he may receive poor support from the extended family, the victims, and a flawed legal system. Men, in general, were more likely to use all forms of violence (physical, emotional, verbal) as a way to react to and confront a father, brother, cousin, or uncle more frequently when compared to the women I interviewed. Boys are socialized to rely on aggression as a key dimension defining manhood in patriarchal societies and as a default response to a wide variety of emotional states, a trait that may become a strategic coping skill for a boy who is navigating these painful predicaments.[20] This may also resonate with the scandal regarding sexual abuse of children by Catholic priests, wherein men have become more visible and vocal than women who have experienced these unspeakable acts.[21]

Although the preceding four aspects of their experiences are relevant, heteronormativity and homophobia were the additional dimensions that were deeply and selectively interwoven as part of a vicious cycle that included the cause, the process, and the effect of their experiences of coercive sex. This was illustrated, for instance, by Helián and Leonardo, who recalled being effeminate boys who were the targets of their biological fathers and realized later in life they were not heterosexual. Both men recalled wanting to be girls during childhood, so they would be more protected within their families. Similarly, being effeminate during childhood made a boy an easy target of sexual violence by a brother or a primo, as illustrated by Uriel and Saúl, gay-identified men who recalled the use of homophobic language or stigma during or after the painful episodes. In the most extreme of the cases, one or more uncles who individually or collectively sexually assault and harass a boy may use homophobia as a way to silence and blame him, as was the case of Valentín, a young heterosexual man.

As discussed earlier, kinship sex (or kinship sexuality) is used to identify different forms of voluntary sexual activity within the family (or voluntary incest), and it may include same-sex or heterosexual exchanges. In this study, men more frequently than women reported experiences of kinship sex, which involved same-sex rather than heterosexual encounters. The latter included few reports by men who talked about a reportedly voluntary romantic relationship with a prima or a sexual adventure with a tía, which was kept secret from the rest of the family.[22] Kinship sex may become damaging as the age difference and body size and structure increase, and as levels of consent decrease between the parties involved. Figure 5.1 illustrates this conceptual framework.

I next examine two related processes to determine *how* and *why* the consent-coercion continuum and kinship sexuality are organized within Mexican families. The first dynamic refers to heteronormative compliance; the second identifies the "Al primo me le arrimo" paradigm. And finally, I discuss some reflections about the family continuum of sexual violence.

Heteronormative Compliance

Heteronormative compliance in the family refers to beliefs and practices of obedience established by parents, siblings, and other relatives within the immediate and extended family and the entitlement they may assume to apply the corresponding sexualized disciplinary interventions to establish, reinforce, and reproduce heterosexuality as the expression of sexual supremacy within families and society at large. In this way, parents, siblings, and extended family members of boys who do not comply with normative gender expectations of hetero-masculinity— and who are suspected of being homosexual, for example, effeminate and/or gender-queer boys—are exposed to a wide variety of corrective measures used to intervene, discipline, and/or "fix" them, even at a

Figure 5.1. Continuum of Sexual Consent and Coercion

Kinship sexuality	← →	Coercive sexuality
Sexual play	← →	Sexual abuse
Seduction	← →	Force
Voluntary	← →	Involuntary

very early age. Heteronormative compliance within the family has two dimensions: (a) the emotional and verbal violence commonly associated with homophobia, as reported by my informants and research with gay men in Mexico;[23] and (b) the behavioral or corrective dimension used to "fix" what sociologist Peter Hennen identifies as *kinesthetic effeminacy*, that is, body movements and voice associated with femininity.[24] Accordingly, a parent, a sibling, or other relatives feel entitled to exercise different forms of bodily intrusion to correct or "straighten up" a boy's body to make sure the latter complies with heteromasculine ways of corporal expression including but not limited to facial gestures, body movement, and tone of voice.[25] This is illustrated by some of the gay Mexican men anthropologist Guillermo Núñez Noriega (2013) has interviewed who recalled being forced as a boy to take a shower early in the morning; being kicked, slapped, and/or pushed while receiving messages such as "move and walk the right way, behave like a man"; and being exposed to some form of the so-called conversion or reparative therapy (i.e., hormonal treatment). These gay men endured these experiences in the 1960s and 1970s.[26] Although progressive discourses in urban social contexts may potentially disrupt homophobic beliefs and practices, these family practices are still present for a younger generation of men, as illustrated by Leonardo's story.[27]

Heteronormative compliance may rely on extreme expressions of sexual violence, as illustrated by Helián's case. He was an effeminate boy whose father raped him anally while insisting that he "change," words that made no sense to the toddler.

In sum, these bodily intrusions normalize, justify, and become the vehicle to exercise sexual violence against boys who do not comply with heteronormative expressions of gender and sexuality. Sexual violence may become an expression of moral panic and gender and sexual cleansing within families in Mexico, a country where lesbian women and gay men are not always welcome at home, as indicated by a large-scale national study on sexual diversity and discrimination.[28]

Although both father and mother may become complicit in affirming heteronormativity, a father may have a special investment in heterosexual compliance. As illustrated by sociological research on parenting and gender nonconformity, a heterosexual father may feel responsible for raising sons who embrace the appropriate masculinity, and as a consequence he sees himself as a father who has "failed" if a son turns out to be gay.[29] Thus, I suggest that a heterosexual Mexican father who may "suspect" a son's different sexual orientation may use sexual violence as a corrective measure to prevent a son from becoming gay, not only for the supposed "good" of a son being raised in a homophobic society, but also for his own as a father and a man living in a patriarchal culture. I suggest that the brutal nature and compulsive repetition of the unspeakable actions that queer boys like Helián or Leonardo endured at the hands of their fathers are to an extent a reflection of a father's own terrifying fear to fail as a man who was not able to raise a son who can be a "real" man, especially if the boy is the oldest child or his only son.

Al primo me le arrimo

The expression that objectifies primas within families—*A la prima se le arrima*—seems to have its equivalent within the world of boys and young men within families: *Al primo me le arrimo*, meaning, You can get physically/sexually close to your primo. The latter is different than the former, becoming more sophisticated for boys if we look at this from the pleasure–danger paradigm I discovered in my previous research with Mexican immigrants and sexuality.[30] On the pleasure side we find what Núñez Noriega discovered in his more than two decades of research on gay men: sexual exploration between primos is very common during childhood, especially as a way to learn and engage in some form of sexual socialization.[31] Núñez Noriega's informants identified the latter as *juegos eróticos*—erotic play—that may include heterosexual and non-heterosexual primos, a pattern that may vary across generations.[32] These sexualized exchanges taking place within families may allow self-identified gay men like Uriel to explore same-sex sexuality in a safe, gratifying, mutually negotiated fashion with primos who are close in age during adolescence.[33] Although two or more primos may voluntarily engage in these exchanges, these arrangements may include a primo involved in a primary relationship with a woman, a pattern that does not seem to be isolated. This was also reported by self-identified gay men like Zacarías, Uriel, and Elías, as well as by other men in a study by Carrillo and Fontdevila of gay and bisexual men raised in Mexico.[34]

As a paradigm, Al primo me le arrimo has a contrasting and more dangerous expression, which goes hand in hand with homophobia and gender inequality. Gender nonconforming boys—who are automatically "suspected" of being gay—are hypersexualized and their bodies become vulnerable and perceived as available to other men in their families so the latter can test their sexual identity and sense of manhood. In other words, queer boys may become "the test" for primos who want to prove to themselves that they are *not* gay. Like "A la prima se le arrima," which validates and normalizes the perception of primas as sex objects within families, "Al primo me le arrimo" exposes the other side of heteronormativity and family life. Compulsory heterosexuality not only relies on the availability of a woman's body to reproduce itself, it also relies on a young man's access to the body of a boy or adolescent man who is perceived as "less of a man." The age difference and degrees of coercion and violence make this pattern starkly different when compared to the sex play of boys close in age.

Echoing C. J. Pascoe's research on "fag discourse" in a California high school, queer boys in Mexico may become the "abject" within their families, that is, the one to be repudiated and rejected by other men who rely on them to "test" their own sense of heteromasculinity and virility. Men's studies scholars explain that men define their sense of manhood not based on what they are, but rather on what *they are not*: what they are socially trained to reject—femininity and anything associated with it.[35] The homophobic discourse (i.e., *maricón*—and its derivatives such as *marica* and *mariquita, joto*, and *puto*) is widely used across urban and urbanized regions of Mexico to discipline boys within families. Boys and adolescent men use this homophobic language as part of the sexualized cultures they actively create and reproduce within and outside their families. These social groups may include older primos and adult uncles (as well as friends and neighbors) who use it strategically to label little primos and nephews as such, and then justify, normalize, and gain sexual access to their bodies.[36] Boys and adolescent men also use the homophobic discourse in many situations of power and control among peers, social contexts that may have nothing to do with same-sex desire.[37]

Last, I suggest that family sexual cultures that sexualize a primo may similarly sexualize a boy within the uncle-nephew relationship, a family pattern rarely examined in the literature, with a few exceptions.[38] Within the context of a relationship that involves authority and power, extreme cases of sexual coercion may resemble the uncle-niece arrangement, including the vulnerability that may arise because a nephew is only indirectly an uncle's "own blood" (Alberto's rationale). That is, family genealogies of incest may place a nephew in a lower location within the hierarchy of the extended family, which makes him also sexually vulnerable, especially if he is effeminate and thus "less of a man." A hierarchy of masculinities within the family genealogies of incest makes this possible: it places boys at the margins because of kinship, age, and body size and structure. Thus, homophobia is both cause and effect of the gendered family processes discussed in the previous chapter. These legacies of incest rely on hierarchies of masculinity that marginalize boys vis-à-vis adolescent and adult men, placing queer and effeminate boys at the bottom of a family structure they selectively share with girls and women.[39] A contrasting dynamic emerges in cases where uncle and nephew are close in age, body size, and structure, arrangements that would be shaped as well by degree of consent on the nephew's part and his actual desire or interest in sex.

Boys and young men do not react passively to sexual violence within the family; a boy may resist or fight back. In the case of Matías and Pablo, both tíos were married to women and had children, and engaged in an enhanced exercise of power and control: each one had sexual access to two nephews at a time, for many years. Matías and Pablo talked about their family histories of more than one child being sexually molested by the same uncle. In the extreme and complex case of Matías, he identified as victims some thirty nephews, sons, and grandsons. His uncle was a wealthy, well-educated, and charismatic man of power within the family and his community; he was also a member of a network of sexual trafficking of children beyond the family context. Matías and Pablo identified themselves as gay men who might have sexually enjoyed these encounters as boys or younger men, yet they were in deep emotional pain as they discovered the emotional control and power exercised by their tíos. "I was not sexually raped," emphasized Matías. "*Mi tío me violó el corazón*—my uncle raped my heart."[40]

As illustrated by these men's stories, the extent to which boys and young men identify the sexual experiences they shared with me as completely voluntary or involuntary may become blurry. As noted previously, this is also shaped in part by a young man's awareness of his own sexual curiosity and desire, age difference, and body size and structure of the parties involved, and many other circumstances. This may become complicated in cases of relatives who are "like primos," as in the case of uncles and nephews close in age and body size and structure. Regardless, I suggest that family sexual cultures that sexualize boys and young men within the extended family (i.e., primos and nephews) may be responsible for the fact that two-thirds of the men I interviewed reported a wide range of sexualized experiences (voluntary, involuntary, and in between) with primos and uncles—both straight and gay. This pattern deserves further research given the revealing results of recent studies on sexual abuse of children in Mexico.[41]

The Family Continuum of Sexual Violence

The concept of "family continuum of sexual violence" is inspired in the "continuum of sexual violence" coined by sociologist Liz Kelly (1987), as discussed in chapter 3 on sisters and primas.[42] This perspective expands on Kelly's paradigm to illustrate the following patterns I found in this study. First, men's narratives expand on the continuum of sexual violence—at times as subjects, at times as objects, at times both—in a wide variety of kinship arrangements with both women and men of all ages within their families. Although not all women informants knew if a father, brother, cousin, uncle, or other relatives in their stories had been sexually abused earlier in life, the men who candidly reported being the one sexually approaching a child reported histories of incestuous sexual abuse during childhood. However, not all men who were sexually abused as children reproduced the same behaviors later in life.[43]

Second, men's stories come full circle to expose and confirm (a) the other side of stories of sexual violence that women reported and (b) the complex multigenerational nature of family genealogies of incest, which at times may include a man's heterosexual partners. And third, the family continuum of sexual violence suggests that boys and men, and not only girls and women, may be directly or indirectly affected by sexual violence within patriarchal families. The latter selectively hurts girls and women, and boys and young men as well, marginalizing those who experience gender and sexual inequality as part of family life. Alberto's family genogram illustrates these dynamics (see figure 5.2).

And finally, men's narratives complete and expand on the culturally specific map of gender inequality and sexuality of Mexican families. Boys and men—straight and gay—safeguard in subtle ways the boundaries of gender and enforce sexual access to girls and young women, and boys and young men as well.[44] This selective process of affirmation of manhood and virility reflects the paradigm of gender relations originally established through the codes of honor and shame in colonial Mexico, a cultural blueprint still present in Mexican families today.[45] It is a key component of the "sexual scripts" shaping the cultural, interpersonal, and intrapsychic dimensions of sexuality, as illustrated by the moving stories of the women and men I interviewed.[46]

Figure 5.2. Alberto's Family Genogram

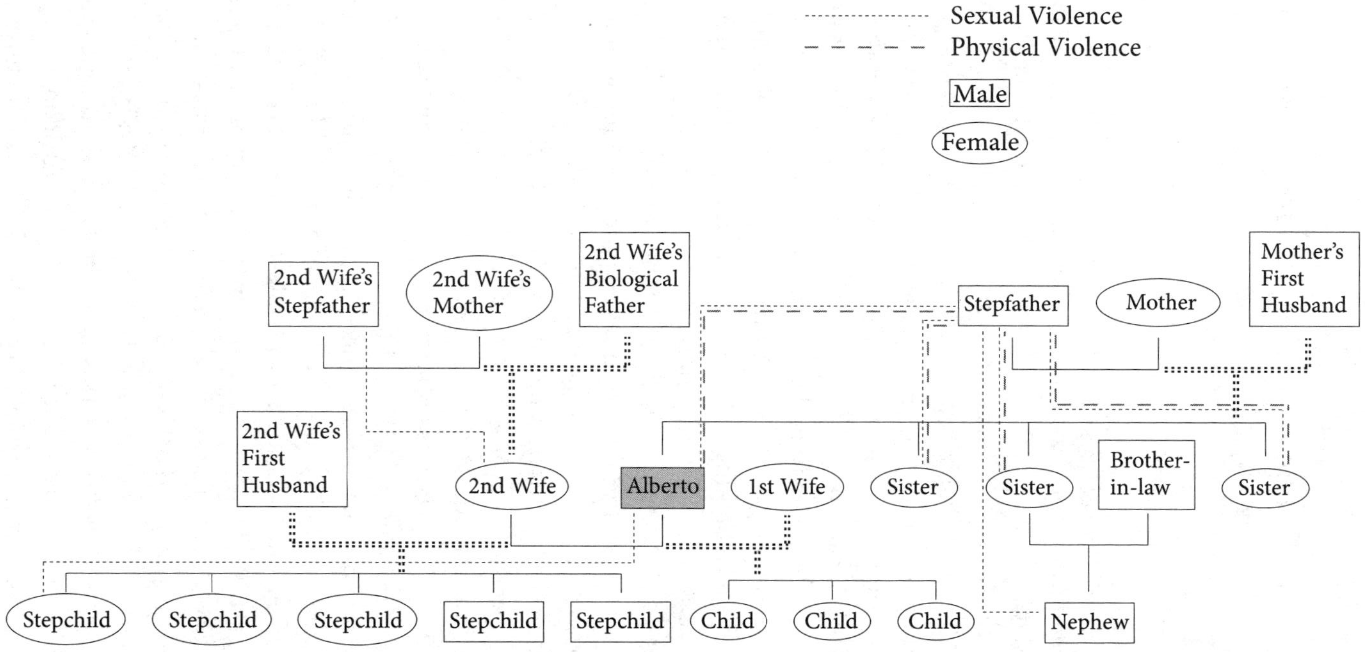

6

Toward a Feminist Sociology of Incest in Mexico

"*Mexicanos, al grito de guerra.*" I can recall vividly the first words of *el Himno Nacional Mexicano*, the Mexican National Anthem I was taught to sing with so much fervor as a student at the *Escuela* Presidente Adolfo López Mateos, a public elementary school at the colonia Independencia in Monterrey. "Mexicans, at the cry of war" is not only the translation of the words announcing an anthem that glorifies war, but also the state of fear now surrounding the lives of the residents of the working-class colonia I learned to love and respect as a child. More than four decades have passed already, and the same colonia where I lived has become an icon of poverty, social stigma, danger, crime, and violence as a result of the drug trafficking–related activities that have placed Monterrey and the entire country under siege.

As I finished the fieldwork that gave life to this book, the brutal violence affecting countless women in Ciudad Juárez and other parts of the country continued unchecked. Violence associated with drug-related activities became a national concern, selectively affecting specific locations, moving through different cities and regions of the country. Statistics vary, from an estimate of 50,000 to at the very least 100,000 victims of homicides resulting from drug-related activities of the so-called War on Drugs that unfolded under the Calderón presidency (2006–2012); these figures do not include the thousands of adults and children who have been reported missing as well as the hundreds of thousands of people who have been forcibly displaced as part of the same wave of crime and violence.[1] The nonstop discovery of *narcofosas*—mass graves of dead bodies connected to drug lord criminal activities—and other horrific evidence of massacres in different parts of the country do not take Mexicans by surprise anymore. And as I wrote this last chapter, the disappearance of forty-three students from a teachers' college in Ayotzinapa, Guerrero—one of Mexico's poorest states—resulted in collective outrage, large mass

demonstrations in Mexico City and other parts of the country, exposing a state in chaos, digging its own grave.

Thus, I wrote this book immersed in some form of split consciousness. On the one hand, I was shocked and in pain by the repeating news
reports about the drug cartel–related violence taking place in Mexico,
and I tried to make sense of it myself. On the other hand, I struggled
to stay focused to work hard and not get distracted while keeping this
book a priority. I kept wondering—was there a connection between the
extreme violence affecting Mexico since 2006–2007 and incest and sexual violence in the family? I asked myself an existential question more
than once: Is it worth it to work on this incest project while many are
experiencing these cruel forms of violence and dying? I thought immediately of Elisa's story, one of the women I interviewed in Ciudad Juárez.
After her father returned home from his night shift as a cab driver in
Ciudad Juárez, Elisa and her mom would patiently listen over lunch as
her father shared the horror stories and dangers he experienced at work
and how blessed he felt to be back home after a long night in the frightening streets of the city. Then, after lunch he would take Elisa by the
hand to accompany him for a nap. Back then Elisa was in elementary
school. Now, as an adult, Elisa reflected about the ways her father held
her body close to his during those naps: it never felt right. He embraced
her in a fetal position, kissed her ear with his tongue, and put his hand
in her genitals, pushing her against his body. These "naps" occurred on
different occasions, as she became the conjugal daughter in a marital
relationship characterized by distance and tension. In retrospect she realized that her father had used her body as a way to cope while living
and working in fear.

The relationship between the current wave of violence in Mexico and
incest and sexual violence in families has yet to be explored in depth,
and it is beyond the scope of this book. I hope, however, that the stories I collected during a period of time of contrasting social climate in
the country as a whole will contribute to the ongoing conversations on
sexuality and gender research, family studies, and prevention of sexual
violence against children, women, and people embracing gender and
sexual diversity.

This final chapter includes two major sections. The first highlights
the contributions of the study with regard to (a) theorizing on gender,

sexuality, and family life for a better understanding of incest in Mexican society; and (b) law and policy–related issues and concerns. The second section offers additional reflections and outlines some suggestions for future research, with the hope that they will inspire similarly concerned researchers and facilitate social justice and change.

Sexual Cultures of Incestuous Families

Gendered servitude and family sexual obligations. The stories about the father-daughter incestuous arrangement that I listened to expose the complex ways in which a daughter (of practically any age) may become sexualized, as well as a wife's exhausted helplessness and sophisticated complicity. "*Hija, sírvele a tu papá*"—a mother's request to her daughter to "serve" her father is a normalized part of everyday language for the average Mexican family. In the sexual cultures of families where incest and sexualized coercion are part of everyday life, *servir*—to serve— has devastating sexual meanings for a daughter. For the women who illustrated the conjugal daughter or marital servant arrangement, *servir* reflects both linguistic and social meanings. "*Estar al servicio de alguien*—to be at someone's service" or "*Estar sujeto a alguien por cualquier motivo haciendo lo que él quiere o dispone*—To be subjected to someone else for any reason doing whatever he wants or decides" are the top two among the nineteen revealing meanings of *servir* in Spanish, according to the Real Academia Española.[2]

From a feminist sociological perspective of incest, a daughter who is of sexual service to a father (and at times a mother, frequently helpless), has learned these forms of gendered servitude within the following interconnected family processes: the parental child arrangement, family and social codes of *honor y vergüenza*, the family as the symbolic hacienda (i.e., el derecho de pernada), kinship reassignments (i.e., a daughter as a wife, a wife as a daughter), heterosexual incestuous lifestyles of romantic love and sex, visible and underground patriarchies, politics of gender inequality within the family and society at large, historical constructions of the paterfamilias and sexual slavery, and cultural rituals of misogyny. These dynamics resonate with the historical genealogy, mythology, and romanticized image of *familia* as an idea and a social institution, one that originally involved the authority relationship of a master over slaves. This theme has been examined since the time of social scientist and political theorist Friedrich Engels in the late 1800s up through historian Ramón Gutiérrez in the late 1990s. *Family Secrets,* however, is the first book to expose *how* and *why* these historical and social constructions of the family actually become lived realities for Mexican children, youth, and women experiencing a wide array of expressions of incestuous injustice in their own hearts and flesh.

Sisters and primas do not escape from these patriarchal conjugations of gendered servitude and other family sexual scripts. New forms of sexualization within kinship with similar inflections of *servir* shape the lives of a sister or a prima who is sexually approached by a brother or a primo, respectively. *Servir* also means *"Aprovechar, valer, ser de utilidad*—To take advantage of, or make the most of, to be good for, to be of use."[3] A sister becomes a family sex surrogate, the symbolic sex doll of a brother who sexualizes her as he learns his first lessons of hegemonic masculinity, heterosexuality, manhood, and male privilege. A young sister is exposed in this way to her first extreme experiences within the continuum of sexual violence, a common experience for many women living in patriarchal societies, further shaped by socioeconomic marginality.[4] For instance, *la sirvienta* (traditionally exposed to sexual objectification and different forms of sexual harassment as part of her work) may potentially offer some form of "protection" to a daughter in the family. All families are potentially dangerous for a domestic worker, with incestuous families becoming even more of a threat for her, especially if she is considered to be "part of the family" and thus is automatically incorporated as an extension of women in position of authority within the family genealogies of incest.

A prima who is exposed to a wide variety of sexualized behaviors and attitudes at the hands of one or more primos has lived in the flesh a cultural saying—*a la prima se le arrima*—you can get physically/sexually close to your female cousin. Sexual terrorism may become part of everyday life within the context of family engagements, enabled by women in positions of family authority who have been socially trained across generations to turn a blind eye to a primo's sexual harassment. Incorporating and using concepts such as "family sexual harassment" as part of our vocabulary may give a name and visibility to these practices normalizing the sexual objectification and harassment of girls within extended families. This may expose one among many of the gender and sexual taken-for-granteds in Mexico and disarm "the cultural scaffolding of rape" which actively facilitates the establishment and reproduction of the family cultures of rape examined in this book.[5]

"*Los muchachos nomás estaban jugando*"—"The young men were *just* playing," or "*Así son los muchachos, no les hagas caso*"—"That is the way young men are, ignore them" reflect the sexual cultures based on patriarchal constructions of "fun" and "play" that boys collectively create, and expose a social problem: these cultural scripts make girls and women vulnerable to a wide array of sexualized violence in families. Giving a name to what has been socially trivialized and accepted as "normal" for boys and men may challenge and disrupt the reproduction of these culturally learned, pernicious expressions of "gender helplessness." These have normalized the habitual, socially learned sexual behavior of men as part of their *nature*, as in the social myth that "men by nature cannot control their sexual urges." Like the women Menjívar (2011) interviewed in Guatemala, a mother, an aunt, or any woman in a position of authority in the family may internalize the structures that oppress them as women with their families, and remain unaware of them at the cognitive level, socially reproducing oppressive beliefs and practices and affecting their nieces, daughters, or other younger women related to them in the process. This process of "misrecognition" and masculine domination extensively theorized by French sociologist Pierre Bourdieu (1996–1997, 2001) is not unique to Latin American or U.S. Latina women.

Family cultures of rape. The gendered beliefs and practices that are conducive to rape within the family have specific characteristics. First, the families of the women and men I interviewed perceived girls and boys as desexualized beings. Boys and older teenage siblings (or an adult) who are blood related are believed to be able to share a bed without any sign of sexual danger or red flag. An older (male) relative (or anyone who becomes "part of" or "like" family) is similarly desexualized, making the person automatically morally equipped to take care of a child. But when sexual activity takes place and becomes visible, a child—regardless of her or his age—is to blame. That is, children are desexualized, innocent, and not fully developed human beings yet, but when sexual activity is exposed (even if it is abusive), children suddenly become sexual transgressors.[6] If children do not report these acts during childhood and do not talk about them until later in life, it is because "they liked it" and thus they are blamed for the acts, and for being silent about them.[7]

And second, these beliefs and practices exist within the context of larger and more complex processes, which are responsible for the sexual objectification and the sexual violence against girls and women of all ages in Mexico. That is, as a supposed sexual transgressor, a girl who is raped automatically becomes an adult woman, and thus, the same patriarchal norms that define women's sexuality are applied to her. A girl is exposed to this abusive sexualization in two directions: from the authority figures in her family (e.g., typically a mother, but also a father), and from the man who exercised sexual violence against her. From her mother, she is judged and punished as if she was already an adult woman. She is to be blamed for being *provocativa*, sexually seductive, for "provoking men." Shockingly, this is the case even if the relative (frequently male) sexually approaching her was considerably older—an adolescent or an adult. And from the man who raped the girl: she is exposed to the same heterosexual mechanisms of power and control adult men use with adult women, as in, "You excite me, I find you very attractive," "You provoked me," or "You would not be here if you would not like it." In short, men sexualize girls through the language of emotional abuse and as part of the sexual violence, making violence even more effective within a hierarchical relationship of contrasting age difference and body size. Sexual violence reinvents itself to become unmitigated and it does not have to become physically violent. For a girl, being blamed for her own victimization becomes part of the abuse itself, magnifying any potentially negative impact as well.

In a society where women are responsible for their own sexual behavior as well as that of others (i.e., men), women who are raped or exposed to other expressions of sexual violence are perceived as responsible for their own victimization.[8] This blame-the-victim paradigm—frequently cited in the vast literature produced by scholars based in English-speaking countries who study sexual violence in the lives of women—is consolidated in Mexico through a long legacy of sexual socialization based on a sexual morality revolving around temptation and guilt, and the view of sex as sinful and dirty. Even though Mexican women raised in the Catholic faith may not automatically follow its mandates, biblical texts remain an influential cultural blueprint shaping ideas about sexual morality in a nation strongly influenced by Christian moral values.[9] Starting with Eva in the Bible, women are held accountable for the sexual behavior of men, even if it is abusive.[10] These belief systems selectively shape the lives of people embracing other non-Catholic Christian denominations. The clinicians I interviewed shared stories illustrating this pattern, as in the case of an adult woman who told a psychologist I interviewed in Monterrey: "rape was God's punishment" for wearing a dress she was convinced had provoked her father to sexually assault her when she was only eight years old. Blaming the victim gets twisted within families, as indicated by the Monterrey psychoanalyst working with the family where the father goes to prison for raping one of his daughters when she was nine or ten years old; the girl is blamed by the rest of the family for "sending" her father to prison and for no longer having a father. This same man then asked his wife to bring the girl "to be with him" during his conjugal visits while in prison.

Confession as a religious ritual may exacerbate feelings of guilt and self-blame in girls and women who have been raped in a predominantly Catholic nation, unless they are fortunate enough to find progressive priests like the one I interviewed in one of the cities where I conducted my fieldwork.[11] A Catholic priest self-identified with liberation theology and left-wing socially progressive agendas, and working with *colonias populares* for many years, said that he was shocked by the stories of sexual harassment, coercion, or other forms of sexualized violence (rarely of "complete rape") that women have shared with him in the confessional booth throughout the years. He shared women's reactions during confession: women assumed guilt and responsibility for these acts (frequently experienced during childhood at the hands of a male relative), asking for forgiveness through confession. A priest who genuinely came across as passionate and concerned about women's issues and gender inequality, he shared what he has found himself telling them during confession: the sexual aggressor (frequently identified as a stepfather or an uncle and occasionally an older brother) was the one who actually needed confession and who should be blamed. A Guadalajara attorney identified a contrasting pattern in his work with Catholic women who reported an incestuous father during confession: they encountered a priest who scolded them for "judging" their father, with women choosing silence about it within the family afterwards. And a pro-feminist male psychologist working in Monterrey with men's groups said some priests reprimanded him for promoting women's rights and gender equality in his work with men. Thus, the masculinity of priests seems to be as complex and diverse as that of secular men.[12]

In sum, like other Latin American women exposed to different forms of violence, Mexican women may effectively learn to blame themselves for their own sexualized suffering precisely, as Menjívar states, "because the cognitive frameworks through which they understand the world around them are shaped by the same social order that produces the inequalities and suffering in their lives."[13] In the end, incestuous sexual violence against girls and women is not a result of gender inequality but an active factor in creating it.

Family cultures of rape may have different expressions, including but not limited to:

(1) family cultures as "*el hogar como la tierra de nadie*"—"the home as nobody's land" where parental or adult authority and supervision are fragile or non-existent;

(2) family cultures of obedience, further reinforced by the Catholic Church and other religions, as in "*obedecerás a tu padre y a tu madre*"—"you shall obey your father and mother," which are imposed on children who give in to coercive sex while complying with the ethics of obeying an authority figure despite feelings of confusion, betrayal, and pain. Being good is confused with being obedient, and being respectful is confused with the need to surrender to those in positions of power. These cultures go hand in hand with the *cultura de confianza* or cultures of trust within the family that inhibit critical thinking and any questioning of authority figures within the family; and

(3) *el castillo de la pureza syndrome* inspired by a classic Mexican film of the same name, refers to parents who construct the outside world as dangerous and the home as safe—a castle of purity.[14] This was the case of Renata and Miriam, from socioeconomically privileged families. These families may paradoxically create conditions of collective denial as a social process within family life (e.g., not talking about it means that it does not exist or it is not happening). This may also result in self-contained families that strategi-

cally control and alienate their members from outside family interactions, with fathers at times living a double life. In the case of Miriam and her two sisters, their controlling father raped all of them. He was a beloved, generous, religious man of power, social connections, and money who was also suspected in their colonia in Monterrey of being involved in drug trafficking. An attorney familiar with legal cases of wealthy families described incestuous families where a father was able to get away with serious sexual offenses by hiring powerful attorneys who strategically maneuvered their professional networks within a corrupt, patriarchal legal system, resonating with the story of Paloma.

Family genealogies of incest and the feminization of incest. The uncle-niece incestuous arrangement exposed one of the most relevant, unexpected, and revealing findings in this study. This pattern has received little attention in the literature, yet is the one that was reported with the highest frequency by the women I interviewed, echoing similar patterns in influential sexuality and incest research studies in the United States.[15]

Why is this uncle-niece pattern so frequent? First, I discovered a family process that I identify as "family genealogies of incest," which are established based on the emotional bonding that girls and women establish with other women within their immediate and extended kin, relationships of love and support that go beyond the nuclear family for women of Mexican origin.[16] Through this process, girls become extensions of *all* the adult women they connect with through these relationships of love and trust (e.g., older sisters and primas, aunts, grandmothers). Thus, a boy who has learned to devalue and sexually objectify women within his immediate and extended family (e.g., a sister or a prima) may potentially become the uncle who will automatically devalue *all* girls who have become extensions of these women because of a magnified multiplying effect. This facilitates the systemic and systematic patterns of misogyny of all varieties and expressions exercised by men that informants identified as their *tíos*—uncles. Men engage in predatory and opportunistic habits taking place as part of everyday life and family engagements, and in sophisticated ways that are not necessarily physically violent.

In addition, these genealogies of incest exist in concert with what I identify as "the feminization of incest." This refers to the overrepresentation of the maternal side in these women's reports of incidents perpetrated by an uncle. In families where girls are devalued and adult women in positions of authority are not respected, an uncle may easily cross a boundary without fear of being punished, thus creating a revealing collective pattern. This is aggravated by the ways in which women have internalized and "misrecognized" the very same sexist ideologies and practices that have oppressed them as women, facilitating in this way the establishment of patriarchal cultures promoting sexual vulnerability of girls and women within these families.[17] This process of cognitive "misrecognition" as part of gender socialization shapes women's lives in other patriarchal societies as well, that is, it is not exclusive of Latin American nations or U.S. Latina/o communities.[18]

In all incestuous arrangements involving a girl and an older man within kinship—a father, a brother, a primo, or an uncle—may become jealous and possessive toward her, claiming in this way his unconditional property rights over her body. In cases of serial incest, the bodies of girls and women are disposable: a girl can be sexually used, disposed of, and replaced with the body of another girl or woman within the family and across generations.

Girls and young women become *selectively* vulnerable in these incestuous families, a process that is shaped by many factors, including but not limited to her age, and age and body structure differences between the parties involved, multigenerational family patterns of gender inequality, individual and family histories of violence in the lives of women across generations, and social context. Thus, incestuous sexual violence, gender-based violence, and family violence share common intersections; one may be contained by the other, partially or in its entirety, at the conceptual and experiential levels.

Although stories involving stepfathers and grandfathers were less frequently reported in this study, this does not mean these arrangements are less prevalent or relevant. Nevertheless, I hope my reflections on incestuous arrangements involving a father, brother, cousin, or uncle inform future research exploring those as well as additional kinship relationships.

In this study, the overwhelming majority of the stories of sexual violence I listened to identified a man—not a woman—as the one who sexually approached a minor, contact that was orchestrated through a wide array of power and control dynamics and taking place in a rich variety of contexts and circumstances.[19] How can we explain this pattern? Feminist psychiatrist Judith Herman (2000) has articulated a comprehensive analysis of this gender asymmetry based on her research of the father-daughter incestuous arrangement in the United States. Her arguments convincingly apply to Mexicans living in nuclear family arrangements: the problem (and the potential solution) is at the core of gender inequality, socialization, and family life.[20] A family where the father dominates, the mother takes care of the children (and the father does not), and the sexual division of labor is characterized by rigidity results in contrasting differences in the socialization of girls and boys. In this patriarchal arrangement mothers also have tremendous power over children (and thus could arguably unleash their own incestuous desires); however, it is not power alone that is responsible for the father-daughter incest. Instead, Herman argues, "It is the sexual division of labor, with its resultant profound differences in male and female socialization, which determines in mothers a greater capacity for self-restraint, and in fathers a greater propensity for sexually exploitative behavior."[21] From this perspective, a mother who takes care of and nurtures a child has the potential to develop feelings of love, concern, and empathy inspired by the minor she is socialized to care *for* and care *about*, all of which may help her refrain from sexually abusive behavior to begin with. In the Mexican case, this process takes place within a larger social context where the woman who becomes a mother was socialized to refrain from freely pursuing her sexual curiosities. Sexually abusing the one she is expected to care for (and who is younger in age) would not only mean that she has failed in her family duty as a woman, she would become both a sexual and a moral transgressor. As explained by feminist psychoanalytic theorists, scripts of gender and sexuality within the family actually shape the psychic structures of girls as part of their psychological development, facilitating the reproduction of these belief systems and practices of gender inequality within immediate and extended kin; this is exacerbated if she becomes a full-time housewife and mother completely in charge of household work and the care of children.[22]

In contrast, a man who was deprived of the same opportunity of emotional socialization and relationship bonding via fatherhood may not develop an internal protection from sexually abusive behavior with his own child, and by extension, with other children in the family.[23] Within the larger Mexican cultural context, he was also exposed to a gender socialization that revolves around sexual exploration and permissiveness as a man, involving in extreme cases dangerous rites of initiation into manhood as an adolescent (e.g., coercive sex with a sex worker).[24] In the end, the boy who was socialized to perceive his mother and sisters as inferior (and later, girls and women in his extended kin) soon feels validated by the men of all ages actively reproducing these belief systems and practices through the family genealogies of incest across and within their immediate and extended families.

Some Mexican families with rigid sex roles may raise boys and men who are controlling, demanding, and who exercise a strong sense of entitlement over the girls and women in their families but who would never cross the line and sexually assault, harass, or rape a sister, a niece, or a prima. Based on my previous research with immigrants and anecdotal stories I was exposed to while growing up in Mexico, I learned about some of these perplexing family patterns. Future research is needed to find answers to this and related research puzzles within the intricate labyrinths of gender, sexuality, and family life. Regardless, exploring alternative, nonpatriarchal models of motherhood, fatherhood, and family life may promote what some Mexican family studies and violence prevention scholars have identified as "family democratization" and become as well a protection from a wide array of forms of violence in the lives of girls, children in general, women, and gender and sexually nonconforming people.[25]

Between consent and coercion: Homophobia in the family. Men's narratives exposed a continuum between two extremes, consent and coercion, frequently involving a relative of the same sex. For instance, some men recalled voluntary sexualized encounters with primos close in age, which emerged as part of curiosity and playful seduction. The same men (or other men), however, shared experiences against their will, which occurred in situations involving fear and at times extreme violence, which may include older primos or uncles. However, this continuum is complex and far from being unidimensional. Many layers of pleasure and danger, seduction and fear, may take place between the extremes. *Kinship sex*, for instance, identifies the sexualized experiences involving the highest level of consent between the involving parts as both parts explore sexuality and the erotic within immediate or extended family. The rich stories of gay men like Uriel and Matías are an invitation to further research on youth gay cultures within families and family sexualization in these men's lives.

Mexican families historically organized around codes of honor and shame may grant boys some license to pursue their sexual curiosities within their families, more so than girls and young women. "Al primo me le arrimo" for instance puts a gay spin on the corollary that objectified primas within their families. Gay men reported being the sexual targets of primos close in age who sexually approached them to "test" their sexuality, that is, to prove that they themselves were not gay. And last, homophobia may use the family as a social institution in order to reproduce itself through the sexualized punishment and sexual terrorism of boys who do not comply with heteronormative expressions of gender and sexuality. Men who recall being effeminate during childhood were exposed to these forms of sexual violence at the hands of their fathers, and in other cases, by mothers and siblings who similarly used more "gentle" gender discipline to teach them how to change their body movement and mannerisms that were associated with being homosexual during childhood and adolescence. Homophobia is successfully used against heterosexual boys also, as part of sexual abuse by a male relative, as in the case of Valentín. Being haunted by the fear of being gay as a consequence of sexual abuse is a pattern that clinicians told me they have observed in other heterosexual men with similar histories of sexual abuse during childhood.

With its roots in both the Iberian peninsula and precolonial Mexico, homophobia is a form of gender and sexual "cleansing" within the family and becomes part of the genealogies of incest, affecting effeminate boys who share these family marginalities with girls.[26] In homophobic Mexico, a "performative gender survival" is the only way to be alive for a gay man like Helián, someone whose choices challenge and expand our understanding of transgender lives.

Homophobia within the family as part of gay men's experiences of sexual objectification and different forms of sexual abuse or molestation was more frequently reported by gay men when compared to the few women who self identified as lesbians (Dalia, Itzel, and Odalys). These women grew up embracing a wide variety of gender expressions. Unlike gay men who were gender nonconforming as boys, however, women who were gender nonconforming during childhood did not report being vulnerable to social stigma and thus potentially being sexually molested during that life stage.[27] That was the case as well for Elba, Maclovia, Natalia, Renata, and Sagrario, who did not identify as lesbians (or who openly rejected the label, or identified as heterosexual) but who candidly reported same-sex fantasies, sexual, romantic, and/or exclusive relationship histories with women.[28] In general, for all of them, two types of silence combined, that is, silence because of lesbophobia and silence about their wide variety of experiences of sexual coercion or abuse within the family. Both types of silence became conflated in intricate ways for some of them. Odalys illustrated this when she exclaimed, "Imagine, *violada y lesbiana!*—raped and lesbian!" She had crushes on girls before her uncle molested her. She came out to her family later, but never told anyone about him, as that would have been too painful for her mother.

Finally, sexual violence against lesbian women within their families may take unexpected twists and turns. A lesbian rights activist in Mexico City, for instance, shared different cases, including the moving story of a young lesbian woman whose parents hired a policeman as a way to "make her a real woman." Her parents set up a sexual encounter between both with this intention in mind. The daughter resisted and the man raped her. A clinician in Mexico City reported the case of a father who hired two men to rape his daughter as a way to "discipline" her after he learned that she was a lesbian.[29]

Secreto en la montaña (literally, "Secret in the mountain," and the title given to the movie *Brokeback Mountain* in Mexico) was released for the first time there when I conducted my fieldwork in 2006, and I came across gigantic billboards in Mexico City advertising the television series the *L Word*, which was aired through cable TV the same year. In 2010, a law approving same-sex marriage became effective in Mexico City, which is legally performed now in the states of Coahuila and Quintana Roo as well. Anselmo, a Mexico City informant, watched the movie with his parents and his younger brother. Anselmo—who said that "he did not know yet if he was homosexual"—was proud of his parents for respectfully answering his brother's questions about same-sex love and relationships while they watched the movie. Anselmo and some of the self-identified gay and lesbian professionals I met were hopeful about the future in Mexico; some reflected about the visibility of gay men (more so than lesbian women) in *telenovelas*, movies, and other Mexico-based pop culture productions.[30] Although contrasting regional differences exist in the nation and progress is uneven and contradictory, they believe that pop culture, new laws, and local, national, and global LGBTQ activism and visibility are already translating into less homophobic families and more safety and loving acceptance for a new generation of gender and sexually nonconforming Mexicans.

The Law, the Hetero-Reproductive Family, and Social Policy

Heteronormativity goes hand in hand with homophobia, and the institutionalization of both in the Mexican legal system was evident in Mariana's story. When Mariana from Ciudad Juárez learned that her brother-in-law had sexually molested her son from ages eight to fifteen, she did not wait long to seek legal aid to press legal charges against him. A beloved, college-educated, generous, and charismatic leader in their Jehova's Witnesses religious community, Mariana's brother-in-law was relocated to a different Mexican city when her son and other children reported the abuse of many years to their church representatives. When her son confided to Mariana, he was already a young gay man, but she had never anticipated what she was about to learn the day she assertively decided to seek legal help. When she reported her son's case at the office of *investigaciones previas* (or previous investigations) at the Attorney General office in Ciudad Juárez, a woman attorney that Mariana identified as *la licenciada* asked her if her son "was by any chance gay." When Mariana replied affirmatively, the attorney told her she could not help press any legal charges because the jury or the judge was going to say that "her son had liked it." Mariana left the scene immediately, feeling frustrated and fuming with rage. Mariana's experience resonated deep in the hearts of the gay men I interviewed: seeking justice for the pain they had experienced during childhood was not only unattainable but a dangerous possibility. In homophobic Mexico, justice for a young gay man raped as a boy was unthinkable. In the United States and other developed economies (i.e., England and Wales), gay men who have been raped by other men may also encounter negative attitudes while reporting to the police, official authorities, and the criminal justice system in general.[31]

Mariana's story reflects the homophobic social attitudes of the State and the ways in which they have negatively influenced legal responses to sexual violence within families. Historically, Mexican penal codes have perceived incest as sexualized exchanges that involve a man and a woman. Whether or not the power differential or age differences are identified in these heterosexual arrangements, incest laws have thus become "heterosexualized" legal prescriptions mainly interested in protecting the hetero-reproductive marriage and family. Although a few penal codes have associated incest laws with an individual's right to sexual freedom, sexual safety, or normal psychosexual development (beyond the idea of "protecting the family"), these legal prescriptions still assume a heterosexual arrangement. This form of institutionalization of heteronormativity in the State has automatically excluded sexualized exchanges taking place in the family that would not result in pregnancy, for example, same-sex exchanges. Incestuous sexual coercion or extreme force from an adult man (i.e., father, uncle, brother, cousin, or other) toward a boy or a younger man (as illustrated by Mariana's case and the men I interviewed) are therefore excluded from these legal definitions. These laws reflect hegemonic norms and ideals about marriage and family: marriage is an exclusive right of women and men engaged in heterosexual sex and romance, and family is for reproductive purposes through biologically procreative, coitocentric heterosex.

In sum, incest remains partially or totally invisible in these Mexican penal codes, mirroring the same family invisibility reported by the people I interviewed. In the end, the Mexican State is as complicit of these sex crimes as the incestuous families themselves. Feminist critics of the legal system told me that although additional laws exist to prosecute cases involving, for example, a girl or a boy being raped by a male relative (with consanguinity as an *agravante* or an aggravating circumstance that may increase the sentence or punishment), incest per se (with all of the intricacies discussed in the book) is lost in a patriarchal legal labrynth. Incest is punished only indirectly. The attorneys I interviewed insightfully asserted: incest laws in contemporary Mexico expose the contradictions, problems, and roadblocks that exist to legally prosecute sexualized contact within the family, especially where age difference and complex and nunanced power relations are part of the equation. The future of these incest laws is unpredictable.[32]

When I interviewed Mariana in Ciudad Juárez in 2005, her brother-in-law was working as a religious leader of his congregation somewhere in Mexico, living a life of comfort and privilege. He might still be a free man today, sexually abusing other minors. In the meantime, Mexico and the world seem to be changing, to an extent. For the first time, the Catholic Church in Mexico filed a criminal complaint against a priest in May 2014. Eduardo Córdova, a priest based in the state of San Luis Potosí, was at the center of this historical intervention that followed the Vatican's order to remove him; with Pope Francis stressing "zero tolerance" of clerical cases of child sexual abuse. News reports and TV news have identified Córdova as having sexually abused at least one hundred children and on the run, apparently out of the country. After becoming the new, progressive leader of the Catholic Church in 2013, Pope Francis eventually embraced this "zero tolerance" approach toward all of the scandalous clerical cases of child sexual abuse; on July 7, 2014, he asked these victims for forgiveness. According to some critics, this is too late, insufficient, and a far cry from the stronger actions and structural interventions that are needed. Social change, however, is unpredictable and comes from all directions. The presence of socially progressive priests, like the one disrupting women's feelings of self-blame during confession, as well as the courageous activism of former priest Alberto Athié, brave journalists, along with other activists who experienced clerical sexual abuse who are publicly denouncing, confronting, and publishing their writings about a flawed religious and legal system—all of them give me hope. Social and legal progress made may lead to legal prosecution of religious leaders who are sexually molesting children beyond the Catholic domain. My hope as well is that the reflections I offer about male religious leaders and sexual violence against girls and women, and my additional examinations of incestuous Catholic priests fathering children, may inform future research projects as well as the urgently needed social and legal reforms.[33]

The knowledge I have developed while working on this incest project and my previous research on sexuality and gender with Mexican immigrants has been of help to me as a consultant who has offered her professional expertise to attorneys working on migration cases involving girls, women, and gay men seeking legal residency in the United States. I wonder, could incest and sexual abuse within families be used as grounds for asylum some day? Legal and policy changes are as unpredictable as the future itself, especially as the legal apparatus (it is hoped) continues evolving in both Mexico and the United States. On August 29, 2014, as I worked on this Conclusion, journalist Julia Preston reported the groundbreaking news in the *New York Times*: "The nation's highest immigration court has found for the first time that women who are victims of severe domestic violence in their home countries can be eligible for asylum in the United States."

The ruling involved the case of a Guatemalan woman who escaped an abusive marital relationship that involved weekly beatings, a broken nose, bleeding from injuries, and rape. She sought help on different occasions in Guatemala but the police did not intervene. She moved to another Guatemalan city as a way to cope, but her husband found her. She fled to the United States with her two children in 2005 and currently lives in Missouri.

My hope is that this book will inform future scholarly contributions and debates exploring issues around these and future emerging legal developments nationally and within the context of migration, as well as the wide variety of related themes discussed in this book. In the meantime, work must continue via the important and sustained efforts of the tireless activists for social change in Mexico, who are working hard on education in general and sexuality education in particular, and by the critical family studies professionals who are essential to the promotion of critical and more democratic redefinitions and models of family life. Some of these include but are not limited to the socialization of children and family life that involve a discussion of the human rights of children and women, ideas of trust and love in connection to family justice, and sexuality education that involves a discussion of relationships, power, and control *within* the family, and not only reproductive and nonreproductive sex, sexual health, and sexual relationships *outside* the family. Valeria, for instance, was well trained by her young parents about sexual hygiene, reproductive health, and pregnancy, but she wished they had talked to her about relationships, and violence, so she would have been able to make sense of what her brother was so violently doing to her. May these sustained cultural and social changes continue taking place in the meantime far and wide in Mexico to facilitate the conditions for girls to feel safe, cared for, and protected enough to report a sexually abusive father, brother, uncle, or primo (or any other relative) and successfully find family justice, as in the moving resilience stories of Itzel and Nydia. Asylum from Mexico to the United States on grounds of sexual violence in the family then would not even be necessary.

"Because My Mother Believed Me:" Resilience and Family Justice

In our conversations, each one of these women and men taught me life-changing lessons about resilience, coping, and healing of the human spirit. For instance, I was deeply moved by women who shared excruciating experiences, and who, unlike those with similar (and even less physically or sexually violent) stories, came across and reported being less traumatized or damaged by their experiences. That was the case for Itzel and Nydia, from Ciudad Juárez.

Itzel's father sexually molested her the first time at the age of twelve or thirteen, and when her mother learned about it, she supported Itzel and gave him a warning. But a few days after her *quinceañera*, the unexpected happened. Itzel experienced a state of panic when he assaulted her, ripped off her clothes, kissed her by the force on the mouth, and left her bruised and bleeding after raping her violently, while telling her that she needed to "understand what was going to happen to her the day she get married." A day after she was raped, Itzel talked to a supportive school counselor who helped her decide to talk with her mother about it. Itzel also told me that even though it was a painful episode in her life, she became a happy adult who enjoyed a stable personal life, enthusiastically pursued her education and other professional plans, and enjoyed a committed lesbian relationship that her mother eventually approved and supported.

Itzel is a young intelligent woman with a joyful and peaceful presence; she has never been in psychotherapy. As I listened to her, I was deeply moved when I realized that although she was affected by the tragic event, her personal life had not been as damaged when compared to the other women with similar or less intense experiences of violence. I shared these observations with her and I asked her if she would be willing to go inside her heart and find out why that was the case. With tear-filled eyes she said, "Because my mother believed me." When Itzel's

mother learned about her father raping her, she was completely supportive, felt outraged, and decided to take immediate legal action against
Itzel's father. But Itzel asked her not to proceed legally as she felt safe
enough and validated to know that her mother had not only believed
her, but was affectionate and loving to her and immediately separated
from him as a way to protect Itzel and two younger daughters. Itzel's
mother died years later. When I met her, Itzel was fighting against her
father for the legal custody of her sisters.

Nydia, also from Ciudad Juárez, lived under the threats of a stepfather who told her he would kill her if she dared to say anything.
She has memories of the wet rope he used to hit her so she would
not resist and instead would surrender to his sexual demands. Every
time he forcefully penetrated her vaginally, he used a handkerchief
to clean himself and Nydia afterwards. He then pushed her away and
asked her to wash the wet handkerchief by hand. Nydia was between
six and nine and he was in his mid-forties at the time. He worked as a
truck driver, which gave Nydia a break when he traveled out of town.
One day Nydia touched the bottom of pain and did not care about his
threats anymore. She recalled with crystal clear memory the day she
finally talked to her mother.

> When I told my mother, I recall that she gave me a hug and we cried. I
> told her crying how I felt and, and I felt as if my mother was protecting
> me. She took all that away from me. Just imagine, she removed all that
> pain away from me. "And I will protect you," she said. From that moment
> on, you know, after I told my mother, some kind of courage came out
> of her and she immediately left to, you know, to a small police station,
> she went to a *comisaría*, they call it that way. So she went and came back
> with a police officer driving a patrol car, and got him. Then, at that mo-
> ment, when he left home I felt like, no more, it was so peaceful. And I re-
> member, that is the way I remember that. And that way I felt more, more
> relaxed, as if a huge burden had been taken away from me. From that mo-
> ment on my mother said, "Do not worry my daughter, I will protect you."

Nydia did not recall any details about the legal process that followed
her stepfather's arrest. Her parents separated and he stayed in prison. "I
never heard about him," she said. Years later, she learned about his death

from a health-related condition. When I asked her, "What did you do with the pain?" She said, "The pain? To forget about it . . . when I told my mother about it, I felt free." A younger brother, however, has resented Nydia for her father being sent to prison. Both siblings have tried to resolve and heal these issues recently.

Now in her late thirties, Nydia is currently married to a man and raising children. Her marital relationship of more than fourteen years is stable, with minor conflict and tension, mainly revolving around disagreements about finances and the children's education. Other than the experience with the stepfather, she did not report any other forms of sexual violence in her life. She described herself as *fría*—cold, with low sexual desire, which she associated with being raped by her stepfather. She said she is sexually happy, however, because her husband has never "forced" her. "I am happy," she clarified, "because I feel free in that regard. And I know what freedom is about, and I know what it is to have a traumatizing life."

Like Itzel and Nydia, other informants reported responses of emotional resilience as a result of being believed by a family authority figure, an adult who also took action. They associated their emotional reaction with the support received from a source of love, an adult who was a caregiver who believed them and who was supportive when they reported their experiences. Also from Ciudad Juárez, Alba explained that after her stepfather gave her a deep kiss on the mouth, he told her that it was "normal." Frequently, he also undressed her, fondled her, and vaginally penetrated her with his fingers. It did not feel right and Alba did not wait to tell her mother about it, but her mother did not believe her. An intelligent and curious child, Alba talked then to her stepfather's father about it, a man she identified as her "grandfather." He believed Alba, did not approve what his own son was doing, and formally pressed charges against him. Her mother eventually supported the initial part of the legal process, but the stepfather defended himself by arguing that he "never penetrated her." He paid a fine and was released. His case might have qualified for further prosecution but Alba's mother did not pursue the legal process. The couple eventually divorced. Although her mother did not believe her in the beginning and that hurt, her grandfather's intervention made a remarkable difference in Alba's life. Her grandfather died shortly after these events; he was deeply, morally affected by what had occurred, Alba said. As adult women, both daughter and mother are emotionally close, healing past wounds.

Men like Matías and Anselmo similarly described the emotional benefit that being believed by a parent who took action meant in their personal lives. In these two cases, a father who believed and took action also made a significant emotional difference for both men when they shared with both parents. For others, being believed by teachers, an older sibling or relative, or adults who inspire moral authority and trust may have a similar effect.

From Itzel, Nydia, Alba, Matías, and Anselmo I learned about a delicate dimension of these Mexican stories of humanity: pain and social injustice does not always come from the experience of sexual violence per se but from the family context and the social and cultural ideologies that shape family life. A mother or a trusted adult who believes and takes action when a girl or a boy reveals experiences of abuse becomes a source of love, trust, and family justice, which in turns helps the child to be stronger emotionally and resilient to the potentially damaging emotional impact. The emotional consequences are less traumatic even if the experience involved intense physical violence, bruises, and bleeding. In contrast, for a girl or boy who is not believed by a family authority but blamed for "sexually provoking" a brother or an uncle (even if the event did not involve physical force), the consequences may become deeply traumatic, as in the case of Rosana and her brother.

In short, families can do much more than heal themselves, they can actually prevent potential trauma. Families that promote gender equality and defend children's rights may facilitate healing and resilience in these children, while the opposite may have emotionally disastrous consequences for these girls and boys. This promising possibility validates the previously mentioned idea of "family democratization," which has the potential to transform families into sources of pleasure (i.e., love and protection) rather than danger (i.e., gender oppression and discrimination, and sexual violence).[34]

"Being believed does justice, and justice in turn is potentially healing" is one of the fascinating lessons of human resilience that Itzel and Nydia taught me as a sociologist and a feminist. The mothers of Itzel and Nydia lived motherhood rooted in love and compassion *in action*, thereby engaging in experiential feminism.[35]

Future Directions

Our lives begin to end the day we become silent about things
that matter.
—Rev. Dr. Martin Luther King

Writing the last pages of this book is like wrapping up a long and revealing
interview: There is a special feeling of satisfaction as well as the concern
that I might be missing something of relevance or that I could have done
more. In that spirit, I suggest specific themes that could be considered for
future research in this area of intellectual inquiry. My hope is that these
reflections will inspire and stimulate our intellectual curiosity and interest
in family studies, gender inequality, sexuality, and sexual violence, among
other related topics. Some of these include issues and concerns involving
U.S. Latino communities, Spanish-speaking nations across the Americas,
as well as other societies with well-rooted patriarchal histories and cultures.

Beyond Poverty

Socioeconomic inequality is like a kaleidoscope that we can turn in
different directions, and as we do, we see how it may create complex
and intricate shapes and patterns of sexual vulnerability in children's
lives. This is a threefold lesson I learned and that I barely examined
in this book. First, as in Sabina's story, informants from Ciudad Juárez
frequently reported engaging in or witnessing a pattern they identified
as *los niños encerrados*—locked up children—an image reflecting fearful working-class mothers who lack family and institutional support,
and live everyday life under pressure to make quick work-related decisions; these women may lock up their children at home before they go
to work at the maquiladoras, which lack child care services.[36] Second,
women and men from middle-, upper-middle, and upper-class urban
families, raised by parents with paid employment, hectic lives, busy
routines, and/or economic ambition used the expression *falta de cui-
dado y negligencia*—lack of care and negligence—to make sense of the
reasons why they had been sexually molested by a relative. And last,
incest is rampant and fairly institutionalized in some rural locations
in Mexico. Women like Maclovia and Rosana, other informants, and

professionals with generous familiarity with some rural areas of Mexico used expressions like *rancho incestuoso* and *pueblo incestuoso* to refer to small ranches and towns where sexual contact within the family is a common practice.

I use the concept of *political economy of incest* to refer to sexualized contact within the family context that is prompted, sustained or maintained, and/or reproduced by and through socioeconomic forces, which is potentially useful to explain the above patterns. Although one of the limitations of this study is the absence of ethnographic research in rural Mexico (and thus the need for more in-depth examinations of incest in such contexts), I hope this book will inform future feminist-informed research projects on incest in rural families, including those with an indigenous presence and long histories of pernicious economic, political, and state violence and neglect.

Secrets and Silence

Secrets and silence are critical aspects of the social organization of sexual violence within families. During childhood, sex as violence and violence through sex become a narrative limbo of complex, unformed experiences. Words cannot explain what does not make any sense, but in the meantime *uno se acostumbra*—one gets used to it. Silence is negotiated within oneself and within the family; a secret is both personally experienced yet socially organized. Silence has codes and arrangements, involves love and hatred, trust and distrust. A secret may become an individual and a family social performance, part of everyday life, or simply a way to survive. In the end, secrets and silence about anything to do with sex become complex and messy social constructions. How and why do cultural and sexual norms of gender and sexuality shape secrets and silence in the lives of children, adolescents, or adults with life experiences like those portrayed in this book? How and why do different forms of social inequality selectively shape the construction of collective secrets around sexual abuse or voluntary sexual adventures in families? What does a feminist sociology of sex secrets and silence in incestuous families look like? Beyond the confessional and Christian sexual morality, how and why are silence about incest and Christian religiosity interrelated?

Sexual Violence and Spanish-Speaking People with Disabilities

"And when are you going to interview Latina women with disabilities?" a Latina woman in a wheelchair assertively asked me in the year 2000. The conversation took place at the end of a conference at the University of California–Berkeley after a panelist had cited my work and generously commented about the revealing interviews I had conducted years earlier with Mexican immigrant women about their sex lives. As I listened to the young Latina in the wheelchair, I was deeply touched and remained speechless as I realized the long road in front of me as a feminist researcher concerned about conducting sexuality research with socially excluded groups. Years earlier, while living in Los Angeles, I recalled feeling similarly moved as I watched a counselor using sign language to animatedly communicate with the deaf women arriving for their support group session at a community-based organization. Back then I was a volunteer at an agency offering services to people who have been sexually assaulted or raped, discovering my limited knowledge about sexual violence in the lives of these marginalized populations. What do we know about the experiences of sexual violence in the lives of Spanish-speaking people with disabilities across the Americas? What are the urgently needed research questions for a further exploration of sexual violence in the lives of these marginalized populations, within their families and beyond?

Queering Incest

"He was the first man I felt attracted to, I loved seeing him, I loved being with him, and the fact that he was a man. In other words, that was one of the key points that told me, that helped me accept myself as a gay man," said Elías. Born and raised in a small Jalisco pueblo and college educated in Guadalajara, Elías reported a three-year romantic and sexual relationship with his first cousin. A self-identified gay man from Mexico City, Zacarías similarly reflected about the four-year romantic relationship that involved frequent sex with a first cousin as well, when both were adolescents. "I don't believe I would have learned with anyone else what I learned with him. And the truth is that it was something that left a deep imprint in my life, there is definitely a before and after this relationship," Elías said. Both men kept their respective relationships a family secret. Unlike Elías and Zacarías, women who talked about their same-sex erotic desire, sexual curiosity, or romantic interest did not experience the type of long-term sexual and romantic engagements with a prima, or any other women within the family. Is this a pattern in the life histories of women who love women, men who love men, and maybe those who love both women and men in Mexico? Beyond the family socialization of gender and sexuality discussed in chapter 5 (e.g., sexual permissiveness for boys vis-à-vis girls), what are the additional dynamics responsible for these patterns? What can we learn about sexuality, gender relations, intimacy, and relationships from further research on queer incestuous relationships in Mexico?

U.S. Spanish-Speaking Communities, Pop Culture, Sexuality, and Incest

"And soon we'll have the candidates of *Miss Colita* with the *galanazos* (attractive men, also well dressed, elegant men) of the jury," Don Francisco announced with a lively, animated voice. The festive sound of music and people applauding and cheering served as a background as the photographs of five women wearing bikinis and assuming seductive or flirtatious poses were shown on the TV screen. Miss Colita (literally, Miss little butt) has become a popular contest in *Sábado Gigante*, a live entertainment TV show that has been followed by millions of U.S. Latinas and Latinos every Saturday for more than twenty-five years through *Univisión*, a major U.S.-based Spanish-speaking TV network. On August 2, 2014, however, Don Francisco's announcement of Miss Colita was the intermission during a short but moving interview with Rosie Rivera, the sister of late Latina singer Jenni Rivera. Just a few minutes after the Miss Colita advertisement, Don Francisco asked Rosie directly about the experiences of sexual abuse that she and her niece (Jenni's daughter) had endured at the hands of Jenni's first husband. Rosie candidly responded to Don Francisco.[37] The interview, watched by millions of U.S. Latinas and Latinos as I wrote the last pages of this book, made me think of relevant issues and concerns about pop culture, U.S. Latino communities, and sexuality: How do U.S. Latinas and Latinos perceive and interpret the juxtaposition of these images and discourses on women and sexuality and sexual violence within families? To what extent, how, and why does this juxtaposition appear in a pop culture that has become part of the complex structures promoting sexual violence against girls and women in U.S. Latino families? To what extent and how do pop culture discourses in U.S. Latino communities make children and women vulnerable to live similar experiences to those described in this book?

As I wrote this concluding chapter, Univisión was also airing during prime time *La Malquerida* (The Unloved), a telenovela that revolves around the forbidden desire between a stepfather and his stepdaughter. It is a remake of a movie of the same name produced in 1949 during the golden age of Mexican cinema, which was based on a play written in 1913 by Spanish writer Jacinto Benavente.[38] So, how have these borderless and timeless pop culture productions romanticized this type of incestuous sex and romance within the family? Do these pop culture images facilitate sexual violence within contemporary U.S. Latino families? Or maybe openness to talk about it? If so, how and why? What other pop culture representations need attention for a critical examination of all of the above issues in U.S. Latino families?

The Masculinity of Men in Incestuous Families

"Nobody could ever imagine what he has done," said Marina, referring to her uncle who fondled her when she was seven, started to rape her when she was eight, and established a pattern of sexual and physical violence against her that stopped only a year prior to our interview. Marina's uncle was a hardworking man who behaved with a kind and respectful demeanor in a wide variety of family interactions and contexts. Marina, other women, and men in this study frequently commented about the good image of the men in their families who have affected their lives so deeply.[39] These men were beloved sons, brothers, or uncles, or successful, charismatic, resourceful, and generous within the family or with their friends and communities. This created not only confusion and disbelief, but also a shocking puzzle my interlocutors tried to make sense of their entire lives and later during our interviews. In fact, men who candidly reported sexually molesting a minor in this study, Pablo, Samuel, and Alberto came across as engaging, respectful, kind, and gentle before, during, and after our interviews. In sum (and as others have similarly discovered), the masculinities of these men seem to be sophisticated and complex.[40] Research has found revealing patterns about the masculinity of Catholic priests who have abused children (see Keenan 2012, for example), but what do we know about the masculinity of Mexican men who have sexually abused a girl or a boy within the families? What can we learn about the gender socialization of all of these men (as boys, adolescents, and adults) so we can explore ways to prevent and disrupt the very same patterns that promote sexual violence within families in Mexico and other Spanish-speaking communities across the Americas? What can we learn about the masculinity and sense of manhood of incestuous uncles, men frequently reported in the study, as well as previous research? What do we need to learn about the brothers, cousins, and uncles of the men in these incestuous families, men *who did not* engage in any of these patterns of sexual violence?

Rape and Women's Bodies

"When I looked at myself in the mirror, and I looked at my breasts, my butt, my legs and I told myself, 'this *panza* (belly) is not normal', it's like this big stomach does not belong to this body," reflected Rosana in retrospect about the day she had an epiphany. A self-identified *bulímica*, Rosana used to wonder why she felt so sick to her stomach when a former partner used to gently caress her belly and she pushed him away. One day everything finally made sense to her: her brother used to touch her belly as part of the routine of sexual abuse during her childhood. During our interview, Elisa pointed at her flat chest and her petite body while asserting, "My breasts stopped growing when my grandfather touched them." As an adolescent, she recalled telling herself in silence as she engaged in conversations with her friends about how their bodies were changing: "'I want to be happy, I want to be happy,' I used to think deep inside of me." She reflected, "It is like I wanted to have my breasts, but at the same time I did not want them to grow. So it was always like that for me." Rosana and Elisa lived sexualized suffering as an embodied experience: their physical bodies were literally transformed by sexualized trauma.[41] And so I learned from Rosana and Elisa: The body may remind you what the heart is trying so hard to forget. What other lessons about the body, gender, sexuality, and social inequality can we learn from Mexican women's stories of sexual violence? What do we know about the bodies of Mexican and other Latina women who have been sexually molested or raped? How can we use the emerging knowledge to facilitate healing in the lives of Mexican and other Latina women?

Negras y Güeras: Pigmentocracy and Sexual Vulnerability in Families

"I was never pretty," said Alfonsina as she explained that she is the one with the darkest eyes and skin color in her family. She described her parents and siblings as *blancos* and *blancas* (men and women with fair skin) with *ojos claros* (light or fair eyes). "Remember that I love you very much, *negrita*," Alfonsina paraphrased her sister's words with a tone in her voice that evoked tenderness as she explained that her sister suspected everything and held her in her arms when she found her sobbing in the bedroom the first time Alfonsina was vaginally penetrated by her brother. *Negrita* and *negra* are to this day Alfonsina's nicknames in her family. Both words carry diminutive but endearing as well as racist connotations that felt deeply hurtful to her, especially during childhood.

Resonating with Alfonsina's story, Inés associated her dark skin with being ugly, and Rosana explained that another half-brother used to spy on her oldest sister when she took a shower. Rosana's brother used to call her sister "negra." In Mexico, *prieta* is also a word used to denigrate dark-skinned girls like Alfonsina, Inés, and Rosana's sister.

"Maybe I am racist," Ofelia asserted as she explained that she has associated dark skin tone with the experience of abuse and the fact that "she does not like dark-skinned people." Ofelia has white skin, blond hair, and green eyes; a woman with her phenotype is frequently identified in Mexico as *güera*. Ofelia was raped by the loyal assistant of her grandparents—a dark-skinned man—an experience that she identified as being even more painful than the other repetitive incidents of sexual assault by three brothers and a maternal uncle.

I suggest that dark-skinned girls like Alfonsina, Inés, or Rosana's sister occupy a vulnerable position within the politics of pigmentocracy of incestuous families. Being the daughter with the dark skin in the family identifies and marks a girl socially as *la negra* or *la prieta de la familia*, which may further devalue and marginalize her within the family and potentially make her rape-able. At the same time, having the phenotype associated with beauty may objectify light-skinned girls like Ofelia and thus make them targets of sexual curiosity or desire of men in incestuous families. In the racialized labyrinths of family sexual politics, a dark-skinned girl and one with the opposite phenotype may paradoxically have the same fate through a contrasting process, as in, "I can rape you because you are *negra y fea*—dark and ugly," or "I can rape you because you are *güera y bonita*—light-skinned and pretty."

I hope these modest reflections become an invitation to further inquiry on incest, sexual violence, family life, pigmentocracy, skin color privilege, and racism within families, especially in a nation where long overdue social issues and concerns affecting the well-being of Mexicans who are indigenous and *afro-descendientes* have remained painfully unresolved to this day.

Incest and Patriarchy beyond Mexico

"I just have to delete 'Mexican' and insert 'Middle Eastern' and it would be practically the same," a graduate student with family roots in Lebanon and Palestine told me. She was commenting after she had read a couple of my publications on virginity, gender relations, and the sexual socialization of girls and women within Mexican families. I have frequently noticed as well the nodding heads and expressive faces of my college students from different regions and nations who have asserted that our class discussions on incest and sexual violence reminded them of their cultures of origin in Asia, the Middle East, or Central or South America. Some have immediately asked: "So, is incest a universal problem?" My students' reactions and my own research have left me with similar questions to be further explored: To what extent do my research findings (e.g., the paradigm of family genealogies of incest, the feminization of incest, among others) apply to other Latin American, Middle Eastern, or Asian countries? To what extent are these paradigms generalizable beyond Mexico, for example, to Latin America, China, or the Middle East? How about incest in different and contrasting European countries? How about Oceania and Africa, and their complex cultural and political mosaic?[42] And how about mainstream and culturally diverse communities in the United States? What is particular or culture/region/society specific, and what is universal about incest?

"¿Cuánto vale un niño en México?"

"¿Cuánto vale un niño en México?" "How much is a child (boy) worth in Mexico?" This rhetorical question was posed to me by a psychoanalyst working for more than three decades who is also a leading figure in family violence prevention programs in Monterrey. I never saw her again, but her question has echoed in my mind since. Throughout my research experience, in which I had the privilege of gathering stories from the remarkable people I met in four contrasting Mexican cities, her words became an echo in my heart.

At a stop sign or a red light, or as I walked down the busy streets of these urban locations, I could not escape the heartbreaking presence of countless children who live and/or work on the streets. "¿Cuánto vale *una niña* en México?" I thought about giving a gender-sensitive twist to her statement. Activists working with these children taught me a lesson: it is not unusual to learn that these boys and girls believe that the volatile and dangerous streets of the city will be a safer space for them than family life conditions they have run away from, conditions of sexual abuse, molestation, and other forms of violence.

My heartfelt hope is that this book will be of benefit to many audiences, including but not limited to the activists and other professionals who so fearlessly work in Ciudad Juárez, and to all of the remarkable human beings in Guadalajara, Mexico City, and Monterrey who work equally hard and have so much to teach us about sex, power, and patterns of violence in Mexican families.

This book is the individual commitment I made to each one of the women and men who opened up their hearts and souls so I could share their experiences with others and hopefully make a difference in the lives of those looking for answers to a complex social problem that needs to be voiced, rather than keeping it in agonizing silence as one of their painful family secrets, as *secretos de familia*.

Study Participants

Name	Age	Marital Status	Children	Religion	Education	Sexual and Relationship History
Ciudad Juárez						
Women						
Nancy	Late 20s	Separated	Yes	Pentecostal*	Finished Secundaria	Heterosexual (W)
Orquídea	Early 30s	Divorced	Yes	Catholic	College Degree	Heterosexual (W)
Mariana	Early 40s	Married	Yes	Jehovah's Witnesses*	Primaria, Academia*	Heterosexual (W)
Alba	Early 30s	Single (1)	Yes	Catholic	Secundaria (2 years)	Heterosexual (W)
Sabina	Late 20s	Single (1)	Yes	None	Primaria	Heterosexual (W)
Viridiana	Mid-40s	Single (1)	Yes	Creyente	None	Heterosexual (W)
Inés	Early 30s	Married*	Yes	Jehovah's Witnesses	Secundaria (1 year), Trade School (1 year)	Heterosexual (W)
Orlandina	Early 30s	Cohabiting*	Yes	None*	Secundaria (1 year)	Heterosexual (W)
Luisa	Mid-40s	Cohabiting*	Yes	Catholic	Primaria	Heterosexual (W)
Elisa	Late 20s	Cohabiting (2)	Yes	Catholic	Secundaria, Trade School (3 years)	Heterosexual (W)
Nydia	Late 30s	Married (1)	Yes	Catholic (Jehovah's Witnesses by force)	Secundaria (2 years)	Heterosexual (W)
Camila	Mid-30s	Married	Yes	Catholic	Primaria	Heterosexual (W)
Itzel	Mid-20s	Cohabiting	No	Catholic	Preparatoria	Lesbian
Men						
Alberto	Early 40s	Married*	Yes	Pentecostal*	Primaria	Heterosexual (M)
Valentín	Early 20s	Single (1)	Yes	Catholic	Student, Preparatoria Abierta	Heterosexual (M)
Guadalajara						
Women						
Marina	Early 20s	Single	No	Catholic	In College (2 years)	Heterosexual (W)
Úrsula	Mid-30s	Married (stays for the children)	Yes	Catholic	Secundaria	Heterosexual (W)
Juliana	Early 30s	Divorced	Yes	Catholic	College Degree	Heterosexual (W)
Esmeralda	Early 30s	Single	No	Catholic	Master's Degree	Heterosexual (W)
Rocío	Early 40s	Separated (legally married)	Yes	Catholic	College Degree	Heterosexual (W)

Name	Age	Marital Status	Children	Religion	Education	Sexual and Relationship History
Eva	Late 20s	Single	No	Catholic	In College (1 year)	Heterosexual (W)
Soraya	Mid-40s	Single	Yes	None (raised Catholic)	Master's Degree	Heterosexual (W)
Luz	Early 20s	Single	No	Raised Catholic	College Degree	Heterosexual (W)
Ileana	Early 30s	Married	Yes	Catholic (because of fear of stigma)	Preparatoria	Heterosexual (W)
Bárbara	Early 40s	Married	Yes	Catholic	Secundaria	Heterosexual (W)
Regina	Mid-20s	Single	No	Catholic	College Degree	Heterosexual (W)
Men						
Elías	Mid-20s	Single	No	Catholic	College Degree	Gay
Santiago	Mid-20s	Single	No	Raised Catholic	In College (final year)	Heterosexual (Q)
Samuel	Mid-30s	Married	Yes	Catholic	Preparatoria	Heterosexual (Q)
Isaías	Early 20s	Single	No	None (raised Jehovah's Witnesses)	Secundaria	Bisexual

Mexico City

Name	Age	Marital Status	Children	Religion	Education	Sexual and Relationship History
Women						
Valeria	Mid-20s	Single	No	None	College Degree	Heterosexual (W)
Alfonsina	Early 30s	Married	Yes	Catholic	Secundaria, Trade School	Heterosexual (W)
Rosana	Mid-40s	Single (1)	No	Catholic	College Degree	Heterosexual (W)
Ofelia	Mid-40s	Separated	Yes	Catholic	Preparatoria	Heterosexual (W)
Natalia	Mid-30s	Married	Yes	None, Santa Muerte devotee	Secundaria	Heterosexual (W) (Q)
Elba	Mid-30s	Single	No	Catholic	Attends College	Lifelong lesbian, but rejects "lesbian" as an identity
Sagrario	Early 30s	Single	No	Spiritualist, self-identified Catholic	College Degree	Lesbian (*)
Perla	Mid-30s	Married	Yes	Creyente	College Degree	Heterosexual (W)
Otilia	Early 20s	Single	No	Catholic	Attends College	Heterosexual (W)
Renata	Mid-30s	Married	Yes	Catholic	College Degree	Heterosexual (Q)
Men						
Leonardo	Early 20s	Single	No	Jehovah's Witnesses*	Trade School (studies Prepa Abierta)	Bisexual (but self-identification "undecided")
Anselmo	Late teens	Single	No	Catholic, Creyente	Preparatoria (finished, will start college)	Homosexual ("o no se aun,"—"I don't know yet")
Pablo	Early 50s	Single	No	Creyente	Preparatoria	Gay
Adolfo	Early 40s	Single	No	None (raised Catholic)	Technical degree; training as professional consultant	Gay
Zacarías	Early 20s	Single	No	None (raised Catholic)	Preparatoria	Gay

Name	Age	Marital Status	Children	Religion	Education	Sexual and Relationship History
Monterrey						
Women						
Odalys	Late 40s	Single (in a relationship)	No	Christian (raised Catholic)	College Degree	Lesbian
Maclovia	Early 30s	Married	Yes	Catholic	Primaria (3 years)	Heterosexual (W) (Q)
Maricruz	Early 20s	Cohabiting	Yes	None (raised 7th Day Adventist)	Primaria (5 years)	Heterosexual (W)
Adelina	Mid-20s	Married	Yes	None (raised Catholic)	Secundaria	Heterosexual (W)
Noelia	Late 20s	Married	No	None (raised Catholic)	College Degree	Heterosexual (W)
Ingrid	Early 30s	Cohabiting	Yes	None (raised Catholic)	Secundaria, Nursing	Heterosexual (W)
Paloma	Early 20s	Cohabiting	Yes	Catholic	Technical Career (3 years after Secundaria)	Heterosexual (W)
Ágata	Mid-40s	Married	Yes	Catholic	Primaria (4 years)	Heterosexual (W)
Dalia	Early 30s	Single (in a relationship)	No	Mormon*	College Degree	Lesbian
Miriam	Mid-30s	Married	Yes	Catholic	2 semesters short of graduating from college	Heterosexual (W)
Evangelina	Late 20s	Cohabiting*	Yes	Catholic	Secundaria	Heterosexual (W)
Men						
Helián	Early 40s	Cohabiting	No	Creyente, Jehovah's Witnesses*	Master's Degree	Gay man, self-identified as 'heterosexual woman'; M→F transition; Rejects "Transgender"
Uriel	Mid-20s	Single	No	Christian, raised Catholic and Muslim	College Degree	Gay
Matías	Early 40s	Single, Divorced	No	None (raised Catholic)	College Degree (3 semesters short of graduating)	Gay
Saúl	Early 40s	Single	No	Christian (previously Catholic and Jehovah's Witnesses)	College Degree	Gay

Religion Codes

Christian	Non-Catholic, Christian-based religion
Jehovah's Witnesses*	Previously Catholic
Mormon*	Previously Catholic
Pentecostal*	Previously Catholic
Creyente	Literally, "believer." Informant said "to believe in God," with no affiliation to an organized religion
None*	Left Jehovah's Witnesses, previously Catholic

Marital Status Codes

Single (1)	Cohabitation in the past
Married *	Married; previously married and divorced
Married (1)	Legally married for the first time, cohabitation in the past
Cohabiting*	Cohabiting; previously married and divorced
Cohabiting (1)	Cohabiting for the first time
Cohabiting (2)	Cohabiting for the second time (or more)

Education Codes

Primaria	Equivalent to elementary school; grades 1–6
Secundaria	Equivalent to middle school; grades 7–9
Preparatoria	Equivalent to high school
Preparatoria abierta	Preparatoria within a system equivalent to adult school
Academia	Trade school training to become a certified secretary
Academia*	Completed 2 years of Academia
Normal	Escuela Normal, Equivalent to teachers' college
Normal*	Completed 1 year of Escuela Normal
College*	Completed the equivalent to Associate Degree

Sexual and Relationship History

Gay, lesbian, bisexual	Informants who self-identified with those identities
Heterosexual (W)	Self-identified heterosexual woman with history of romantic and/or sexual relationships exclusively with men
Heterosexual (M)	Self-identified heterosexual man with history of romantic and/or sexual relationships exclusively with women
Heterosexual (Q)	Identifies as heterosexual, with a history of same sex romantic and/or sexual relationships
Heterosexual (W) (Q)	Self-identified heterosexual woman with a history of romantic and/or sexual relationships exclusively with men, and romantic, sexual interest, and fantasies about women
Lesbian (*)	She did not identify as a lesbian, or with any other sexual orientation. She has had attraction toward girls since childhood, has been in love and in casual relationships with women (with no sexual contact), and expressed an interest in having a stable relationship with a woman.

APPENDIX B

Methodological Considerations

Memory Work and Storytelling: A Final Reflection

With a challenging tone, a colleague in my discipline asked me if I had actually "believed" what people shared with me in this study. This reminded me of the "second assault" of women who are raped and who are not believed when they share their stories with official authorities, and who then become retraumatized instead of being supported and helped. Another sociologist warned me about the danger of "reconstructing memories" and suggested I needed to look more at theorizing in this area of intellectual inquiry. I am in fact familiar with the so-called sociology of story telling (Plummer 1995), that is, I am aware of the ways in which the sensitive, honest, and overwhelming stories that were told to me are not narratives or texts that exist in the abstract, these stories are social constructions as well. I am also aware of the ways we may tell lies to ourselves and to others as we access our recollections and tell stories (again, to ourselves and to others), and the ethical implications involved (Plummer 2001; Maynes, Pierce, and Laslett 2008). Pain may never leave completely and a person may give a different meaning through telling the story; while talking about it, the experience may acquire a new meaning.

The life stories that women and men shared with me (as well as my retelling of them), are both sociological phenomena (Plummer 1995, 167) as well as self-work (173). That is, these women and men carefully engaged in the attentive endeavor of doing "memory work" in my presence, looking back in retrospect to make sense of their individually lived experiences in a specific historical moment and socioeconomic contexts in patriarchal Mexican society. Interestingly, their heartfelt and honest stories expose their subjectivities in context, that is, their individual stories are collectively shared through common meaning, language, and all similarly shaped by specific contexts of social inequality.

In this study, I found myself frequently being interviewed by a potential informant, before she or he had officially accepted my invitation to share her or his life story with me. This became part of the process for a potential informant to assess my professional credentials and my human integrity and thus decide to participate (or not) and finally trust me with her or his life stories. These inquisitions in turn helped me trust in the stories as truth as well (see González-López 2010a, 571–72). Although I am aware of potential distortions and oblivion in these recollections, I listened and made sense of their stories from what I called "epistemologies of the wound." I trust this state of consciousness helped me, among other things, to become sensitive and receptive, and thus identify, for example, some inconsistencies in their narratives. I learned a lesson from participants: the interviews themselves became a vehicle they used to make sense of what they have lived, especially for those who were talking about it for the first time. Frequently, informants would say, "I had not thought about it until now that you are asking me about this," as they engaged in our interviews. This made me trust in their stories even more. And finally, I listened to their stories and analyzed them from my own subjectivity as a Mexican immigrant woman who has lived in the United States since the mid-1980s, and a self-identified feminist who was trained as a sociologist and a psychotherapist in this country.

Memory work and storytelling (and their ethical implications) have been examined in the social sciences as a revealing and powerful qualitative methodology that can give voice to disenfranchised communities, produce knowledge, and potentially promote change (see Haug et al. 1987; Pease 2000; Plummer 1995, 2001; Méndez-Negrete 2006; Maynes et al. 2008). I hope these individually yet commonly shared stories may not only become a form of knowledge production but also potentially inform social reform and justice in Mexico.

I discuss these and additional methodological-related concerns in the publications that emerged from this project, which I include in the References section of this book.[1]

A Note on Selection of Informants

When I recruited informants, I was frequently asked if I was interested in interviewing people who had been in psychotherapy. I heard stories about people who had been affected or retraumatized by what they identified as "poorly trained" psychotherapists, and thus, I decided to interview people who had been in psychotherapy. Of the sixty informants, about half have never received any kind of psychotherapy or psychological services for any reason, and about a third have been to a few sessions (2–4 sessions, average) of support groups for people with a history of sexual violence, with many of them frequently explaining that they have "only listened" to others but have not talked about their own experiences. The rest reported receiving some form of psychological counseling to help with other issues (i.e., a painful divorce, relationship problems, postpartum depression, self-esteem related issues, among others) and who frequently clarified as well that they had not disclosed about the experiences of sexual molestation or abuse as a child. Only a very few had been in therapy with the purpose of dealing with the events they shared with me, which involved a combination of positive and negative experiences, especially if they had gone from one therapist to the next with feelings of confusion and frustration. This was the case of Matías and Miriam. Matías, "a self-identified gay man who described to me the ways a therapist had placed electrodes in his genitals, nipples, fingers, and anus as he explained that electroshock therapy and hypnosis would help him 'cure' his homosexuality, which presumably had some connection to abusive sexual history" (2010a, 575). Miriam assertively stated, "I do not trust psychologists" as she talked about her feelings of discomfort and disgust while seeing a woman psychologist she and her two sisters saw regularly for about two years. "Tell your father that, that [what he is doing to you] should not be done because you are his daughter," paraphrased her words while talking about her "absurd interventions." As discussed in chapter 2, Miriam and her two sisters lived complex experiences of sexual violence at the hands of their father. In sum, I had the impression that people who had been in therapy before and decided to be interviewed might have selected themselves: they wanted to talk about what they never had the opportunity to disclose to a clinician for a variety of reasons, and reporting (when was the case)

specific situations of clinical malpractice. The above is only a preliminary assessment of this dimension of my study. An in-depth analysis of
these informants' experiences in the context of their professional relationships with these clinicians is beyond the scope of this book, but it
certainly deserves special attention and further critical examination.

Finally, although I have been exposed to a wide variety of expressions
of sexual violence as a young woman (with strangers, a former partner,
and in the context of work), I was blessed to grow up as a child who was
not sexually abused. Conducting these interviews led me to realize how
incredibly fortunate I have been just because of that fact. In some of my
methods related publications, I have similarly talked about the ways I
took care of myself while working on this emotionally challenging but
intellectually and politically rewarding project.

APPENDIX C

Incest in 32 Mexican State Penal Codes

States with Penal Codes That Are Family Centered	States with Penal Codes That Are Individual Rights Centered	States with Penal Codes That Are Marriage Centered	Other	States Where Incest Does Not Appear in the Penal Code
Aguascalientes	Campeche	Tabasco	Colima (1)	Puebla
Baja California	Chiapas		Hidalgo (2)	Tlaxcala
Baja California Sur	Chihuahua		Sonora (3)	
Coahuila	Distrito Federal			
Durango	Oaxaca			
Guanajuato				
Guerrero				
Jalisco				
Mexico, State of				
Michoacán				
Morelos				
Nayarit				
Nuevo León				
Querétaro				
Quintana Roo				
San Luis Potosí				
Sinaloa				
Tamaulipas				
Veracruz				
Yucatán				
Zacatecas				

Of the 32 Penal Codes, incest is legally conceptualized as:

21 Family centered, identified as a crime against the family, *la familia* (also identified as *el orden familiar* or *el orden de la familia*), only one case as a crime against the family and marital status

5 Individual rights centered, referring to sexual freedom, sexual safety (protection), and/or "normal" (meaning "healthy") psycho-sexual development

1 Marriage centered

1 Without a classification, below "Bigamy"

  1 As a crime against the right of family members to a life without violence

  1 As a sex crime

  2 Tlaxcala and Puebla have not criminalized incest as an offense in their respective penal codes.

Codes

(1) Without classification, below "Bigamy"

(2) Crime against the right of family members to a life without violence

(3) Sex crimes

A Legal Commentary

Alejandra de Gante Casas, a Guadalajara-based attorney, commented: "The *age of majority* or *'la mayoría de edad'* in the country is 18 years, with each state following the same norm. The *age of consent* or 'age to consent to start an active sex life' is also 18 at the national level but varies by state." That is, 18 is the age where there are no restrictions for consensual sexual activity.

Sources

On July 8, 2013, I found and consulted most of these penal codes through the Instituto de Investigaciones Jurídicas of the Universidad Nacional Autónoma de México website at info4.juridicas.unam.mx/adprojus/leg/.

I found and downloaded the penal codes of Campeche, Distrito Federal, and Querétaro through other Internet searches.

The cases of Puebla and Tlaxcala have received a lot of media attention due to the fact that they have not criminalized incest as an offense.

APPENDIX D

Uncle-Niece Cases

			Maternal Side				Paternal Side			
Name	His Age at First Incident	Her Age	Mother's brother	Tia's husband (mother's sister)	Mother's primo (cousin)	Mother's maternal uncle	Father's brother	Tia's husband (father's sister)	Father's primo (cousin)	Other (father's side) (*)
Ciudad Juarez										
Sabina	21	8		•						
Viridiana	mid-40s	6–7	•							
Elisa	30s	7–11	•							
Itzel	30s	16					•			
Guadalajara										
Marina	mid 20s	7–9		•						
Juliana	late teens	9–10	•							
Esmeralda	40s	early 20s	•							
Eva	14	10–11	•							
Eva cont.	30s	6				•				
Luz	20s	4–5			•					
Luz cont.	30s	7–8		•						
Ileana	19	12	•							
Ileana cont.	35	30	•							
Barbara	40s	8	•							
Barbara cont.	40s	8	•							
Barbara cont.	40s	8	•							
Regina	30s–40s	9						•		
Mexico City										
Alfonsina	teens	elem. school	•							
Alfonsina cont.	teens	elem. school	•							
Ofelia	late 40s	15			•					
Natalia	early 20s	6	•							
Elba	70s	3–4								•
Renata	40s	4–6					•			
Monterrey										
Odalys	late 30s	10–11		•						
Paloma	12–13	6					•			
Miriam	n/a	n/a					•			
Evangelina	25–30	7–8		•						
Evangelina cont.	18	10	•							

(*) Distant uncle (tío lejano)

21 women reported a total of 28 men they identified as their uncles.

NOTES

CHAPTER 1. *EN FAMILIA*

1 Some of these professionals included, for example, attorneys, physicians, priests, psychologists, psychiatrists, psychotherapists, social workers, and other professionals involved in human rights activism and sexual violence prevention programs with college degrees or professional training across a wide variety of disciplines.

2 All translations of text cited and originally published in Spanish are mine. For words and expressions with a special cultural meaning in Spanish, I have selectively chosen (1) not to translate them literally into English but instead let the narrative convey its meaning, and (2) to use the English translation of a word or expression only when it is introduced for the first time, but not in subsequent sections in the book.

3 See, for example, Guridi Sánchez 1961; Falconi Alegría 1961; Vidrio 1991; Floris Margadant 2001; Méndez-Negrete 2006; Gudiño 2011.

4 Russell 1997.

5 The Finkelhor (1994) study included these twenty countries: Australia, Austria, Belgium, Canada, Costa Rica, Denmark, Dominican Republic, Finland, France, Germany, Greece, Great Britain, Ireland, Netherlands, Norway, South Africa, Spain, Sweden, Switzerland, and the United States.

6 González-López 2013a, 403.

7 Elsewhere (2012), I offer a working definition of sexual violence:

> From a feminist sociological perspective, sexual violence can be defined from the subjectivity and positionality of those who live it, that is, it can be understood as the attitudes and behaviors (verbal and non verbal) that one or more people exercise toward other human beings and that invade, hurt and/or damage their sense of erotic-sexual integrity, safety and/or well being. Sexual violence possesses two fundamental characteristics: (1) it takes place within a wide variety of social contexts and circumstances under power and control dynamics (evident and disguised), and (2) it may acquire countless expressions, from the most subtle, nuanced, delicate, refined or sophisticated to the most grotesque and perverse, including (but without being limited to) sexual harassment, rape, genital mutilation, and different forms of sexual exploitation of minors and women (e.g., cyber-pornography of girls and boys), and sexual trafficking of human beings.

8 Dietrich 2008.

9 See for example the 1965 Moynihan Report.

10 See González-López and Gutmann 2005; González-López and Vidal Ortiz 2008; and Ramirez and Flores 2012 for further reflections on these issues.

11 In retrospect, I realized that I might have received these warnings in part because I was perceived as a researcher from the United States. Although I was born, raised, completed my undergraduate education, and lived and had paid employment in Mexico through my mid-twenties, I was in some ways like Oscar Lewis: a researcher from the United States "visiting" Mexico in order to do research on a sensitive topic. Elsewhere I discuss some of these issues and additional methodological implications (see González-López 2007b).

12 A popular tabloid, *Alarma!* shows graphic images of violent crimes. For about fifty years and until recently, it was frequently sold in newsstands with a wide coverage in the country.

13 Interestingly, Lewis captured nuanced and sophisticated feelings, attitudes, and situations related to brother-sister incestuous love and sex; however, this is not a central theme in his examinations (although some of his critics have offered interesting examinations of these incest-related issues. See for example Riviere 1967).

14 Mummert 2012.

15 Reese Jones 2011.

16 González-López 2013a.

17 Arrom 1985.

18 González-López 2013a, 405.

19 For more on this topic, see Escalante Gonzalbo, María Paloma (n/a) "El Abuso Sexual y el Uso Simbólico del Concepto Religioso del 'Padre,'" in *La Luz del Mundo: Un análisis multidisciplinario de la controversia que ha impactado a nuestro país.* Accessed June 3, 2014, at http://www.revistaacademica.com/tomouno.asp.

20 Joyce 2000, 165.

21 A. Castañeda 1993. Some priests inspected "the genitalia of married couples if they did not have children on a regular basis" (Miranda 2010, 97).

22 C. Castañeda 1989.

23 C. Castañeda 1989, 68–71.

24 González-López 2013a, 405.

25 C. Castañeda 1984; 1989, 143; Giraud 1988, 334–35, 339; Lavrin 1992.

26 Penyak 1993, 236.

27 Floris Margadant 2001.

28 Arrom 1985, 310. See Moro 1996 on children and adolescents in the genealogy of the law in Mexico.

29 García 1891.

30 González Ascencio 2007.

31 Saucedo González 1999, 79; Ruiz Carbonell 2002, 64.

32 In 1988, Asesoría y Servicio Legal S.A. de C.V. opened its doors to provide legal services in the area of sexual violence prevention, and it was the first one of its kind

in Guadalajara. In 1996, this organization became the Centro de Orientación y Prevención de la Agresión Sexual, A.C. and expanded its legal services to include psychological assistance and prevention education as well in the area of sexual violence.

In 1990, ADIVAC, or the Asociación para el Desarrollo Integral de Personas Violadas, A.C., was established in Mexico City. To this day, ADIVAC offers medical, legal, and psychological services to people who have been exposed to different forms of sexual violence. ADIVAC has its headquarters in Mexico City and offers services in other locations in the country, such as León, Guanajuato, and the city of Puebla.

33 Some claim that the first *Ojo Mucho Ojo* TV commercial was aired in the mid-1980s, while other sources say the first one was being shown in 1987 (see for example Martínez Rojas 2001, 19).

34 Alejandra de Gante Casas, an attorney and cofounder of the Centro de Orientación y Prevención de la Agresión Sexual, A.C., in Guadalajara reported that children participating in a self-care and prevention project taking place at the end of the 1990s voluntarily referred to the Ojo Mucho Ojo slogan in the exercises they engaged in, that is, without any of the professionals conducting the study making a suggestion about it. This project included 20,000 children attending third through sixth grade and living across different locations in Jalisco. I personally remember watching some of these TV commercials, and those I watched showed the potential aggressor as a stranger, not a family member or relative. Some of the informants I interviewed who were also familiar with this campaign shared the same reflection; they also mentioned additional reflections about these commercials. The ways in which this campaign has shaped views of sexual molestation during childhood in the population needs further analysis and goes beyond the scope of this book.

35 Guillé Tamayo 2007.

36 Senior professionals working with women and their families in the early 1960s and early 1970s, for instance, recalled the Instituto Nacional de Protección a la Infancia, a public institution established nationwide in 1961 where (frequently poor) families sought social services. This institution is the origin of the current DIF (Desarrollo Integral de la Familia).

37 Prolific scholarship and intellectual activism seeking answers to the brutal violence against women in the border city has resulted in abundant research across disciplines in both nations, for example Fregoso and Bejarano 2010.

38 These include the "Ley General para la Igualdad entre Mujeres y Hombres" and the "Ley General de Acceso de las Mujeres a una Vida Libre de Violencia" made official by the *Diario Oficial de la Federación* on August 2, 2006 and February 1, 2007, respectively. These laws are viewed by some as the State's effort to comply with commitments established with the Convention on the Elimination of All Forms of Discrimination against Women (or CEDAW, an international bill of rights for women adopted by the UN General Assembly in 1979), and the Inter-American Convention on the Prevention, Punishment and Eradication of Violence against

Women, known as the "Convention of Belém do Pará" (the place where it was adopted in 1994) (see Olamendi Torres 2007).

39 In the *Delitos contra las mujeres* report, the following are included under the category of sexual violence: *violación* (rape), *violación agravada* (aggravated rape), *violación por objeto distinto* (rape with a different object), *abuso sexual* (sexual abuse), *incesto* (incest), *estupro*(*), *hostigamiento sexual* (sexual harassment), and *aprovechamiento sexual* (similar to *quid pro quo* sexual harassment in the United States). (*) The table of penalties by state identifies estupro as "intercourse with a woman who is older than 12 and younger than 18, *with consent*, through seduction or deception" (51) (italics in original text in Spanish, *con consentimiento*). Olamendi explains, "In some *legislaciones* (laws), subjective elements such as chastity or honesty continue to be in effect to assess the victim; marriage between the victimizer and the victim continues to be considered as a way to repair the damage, and of course, excludes the aggressor from penal responsibility" (50).

40 See de la Garza-Aguilar and Díaz-Michel 1997. In a conversation in Ciudad Juárez in 2005, Esther Chávez Cano commented that incest statistics usually have been conflated with and get lost within the general domestic and sexual violence categories. Many times a person may identify domestic violence or rape as the reason for seeking therapy, for example. Then some history of incest eventually emerges during treatment; however, this is never documented in the statistical records.

41 From these professionals I also learned that although these efforts have increased the social awareness of these issues, it is difficult to assess the effectiveness of these campaigns. That is, it is difficult to know whether they have decreased the incidence of violence against girls and women, or have simply helped women speak up about what had remained hidden for too long.

42 The ENDIREH (Encuesta Nacional sobre la Dinámica de las Relaciones en los Hogares) was the first national survey on family relationships in Mexican households (highlighting violence) and it was conducted and published by the INEGI in collaboration with the Instituto Nacional de las Mujeres for the first time in 2003. The INEGI (Instituto Nacional de Estadística, Geografía e Informática—literally, National Institute of Statistics, Geography, and Information) is a government institution conducting major demographic research in the country. The INMUJERES (Instituto Nacional de las Mujeres) is also a government organization. The ENDIREH can be accessed through the INEGI website: www.inegi.org.mx.

43 See Elizabeth Velasco 2013.

44 "By proposing the term *regional patriarchies* I seek to explain how women and men are exposed to diverse, fluid, and malleable but regionally uniform and locally defined expressions of hegemony and their corresponding sexual moralities. While shaped by the socioeconomics of a local region, each one of these patriarchies takes myriad forms and promotes various levels of gender inequality" (González-López 2005, 6).

45 Based in Madrid, Spain, the Real Academia Española (RAE) is the official institution with a predominant influence in the use of the Spanish language. Visit the official website of the Real Academia Española at http://www.rae.es/.

46 For more on sexual trafficking of women in Mexico, see research by sociologist Sheldon X. Zhang and anthropologist Arun Kumar Acharya.

47 CIMAC 2014. Muere niña víctima de violación sexual [Girl victim of rape dies]. CIMAC: Comunicación e Información de la Mujer, May 28, 2014. Available online at http://www.cimacnoticias.com.mx/node/66614.

48 For more information, visit www.inmujeres.gob.mx.

49 See Acharya 2009, 152–53.

50 The CONAPRED has conducted large-scale research on different forms of discrimination, including but not limited to race and sexual orientation, for example.

51 Relevant parallels between *Family Secrets* and *Enduring Violence* by Cecilia Menjívar include for example: (a) women experiencing violence, including sexual violence, as a larger and complex process of interconnected factors including but not limited to gender and socioeconomic inequalities; (b) women perceiving violence as part of the routine of everyday life, thus facilitating a cognitive acceptance of violence as "normal"; (c) women embodying the social construction of gender inequality in the flesh, that is, illness and series of ailments are interconnected with humiliation and suffering; and, (d) women participating in the reproduction of the hierarchies that promote gender inequality, echoing Bourdieu's theorizing on "misrecognition" and women's introjection of and engagement in the structures and gender scripts that oppress them.

52 Although vergüenza is usually translated as "embarrassment," "shyness," "shame" or "to be ashamed," the term may have a wide variety of meanings, which are deeply gendered and socially contextualized. For example, for some women, vergüenza may have an important connotation with regard to sexuality and loss of virginity. Vergüenza in that case may be associated with a sense of worthlessness and failure, or *fracaso*. For men, it may have a different meaning as well. For more on this, see Riviere 1967, 576–77 and González-López 2005, 51, 55–56, 58, 114.

CHAPTER 2. CONJUGAL DAUGHTERS AND MARITAL SERVANTS

1 The English version of Delgadina is included in Dr. Américo Paredes's (2001, 14–16) examinations of folklore in the Lower Rio Grande Border, which shares important historical roots and cultural expressions with the Mexican states of Coahuila, Nuevo León, and Tamaulipas. For Spanish and English versions of Delgadina, see Pan-Hispanic Ballad Project at http://www.depts.washington.edu/hisprom/ballads/index.php.

2 Based on her research and clinical work with African American families, Nancy Boyd-Franklin (2006) uses the concept of "parental child" to explain the experiences of working single mothers who decipher survival and everyday life as they rely on the oldest child in the family by assigning her/him parental responsibilities. A parental child may become "overburdened" when the mother is physically ill or when she suffers from a psychiatric condition and/or drug or alcohol addictions.

3 See Carol Gilligan 1982 and Margarita Dalton 2010. Paid and unpaid forms of servitude are established through gendered practices and routine acts over time,

creating cultures that are highly stratified. See Ray and Qayum 2009 on cultures of servitude and paid domestic work in India.

4 Noelia's experience in commercial sex illustrates the tensions and contradictions in women's lives identified at the core of debates and dialogs among feminists who have explored both dangerous and pleasurable dimensions of commercial sex and pornography. See, for example, Lynne Segal and Mary McIntosh 1993 and Wendy Chapkis 1996.

5 Alcohol and/or drug use in the lives of men who assaulted informants was reported, which is a factor that may facilitate incidents of all types of violence and deserves further investigation in the case of incest in Mexico. However, I concur with sociologist Diana Scully's concern about the widespread idea of perceiving men who engage in sexually violent behaviors as men who are "sick" (i.e., alcoholics, drug addicts, or mentally ill). This has promoted "the medicalization of rape," which blames the individual for his sexually violent behavior rather than analyzing rape and other forms of sexual violence as complex social problems (Scully 1990, 74, 120). See also chapter 3.

6 Perla's perception of virginity echoes the narratives of other Mexican women with regard to virginity as a form of social capital (or capital femenino), family values associating obedience and family respect with virginity, and virginity as a "gift" for a husband, as I examined in the book Erotic Journeys (2005).

7 Herman 2000, 94.

8 See Herman (2000) on incest and marital discord (43), mothers who are full-time housewives (72), and a daughter's awareness of parents' marital problems (80, 81).

9 The "conjugal daughter" as an idea is inspired in the father-daughter incest literature that has identified girls in this incestuous arrangement as the "little mother"; see Herman 2000, 45, 79–80; and Russell 1997, 142.

10 "Traumatic sexualization refers to a process in which a child's sexuality (including both sexual feelings and sexual attitudes) is shaped in a developmentally inappropriate and interpersonally dysfunctional fashion as a result of sexual abuse" (Finkelhor and Browne 1985, 531). Traumatic sexualization is one of the four "traumagenic dynamics" that Finkelhor and Browne use in their model to examine trauma, including but not limited to sexual abuse. The other three traumagenic dynamics include betrayal (a child being harmed by someone she/he depended on), powerlessness (a child's body space being invaded against her/his will and experiences a sense of disempowerment), and stigmatization (a child internalizes feelings of "badness, shame and guilt" based on the negative messages she/he receives from the aggressor, the family, and/or community). The women in this study selectively reported all of the above.

11 See for example Margarita Dalton's reflections on women's responsibility of household work, child care, and patriarchal ideologies in Mexico as part of the ética del servicio (literally, ethics of service) while referring to Carol Gilligan's theorizing on ethics of care (2010, 33). In Mexico, daughters vis-à-vis sons are more than twice

as likely to be in charge of housework when the mother has paid employment outside the home (ENADIS 2010, 76).

12 In her analysis of religion and family life in colonial Mexico, historian Pilar Gonzalbo Aizpuru (2003) reflects about the ordinances that bishop Don Vasco de Quiroga established in the *hospitales-pueblo* in Santa Fe, which stated that "*las mujeres sirvan a sus maridos*" (the women serve their husbands), as "an expression of a natural law endorsed by canon and civil law." Gonzalbo Aizpuru elaborates, "His words provided a commentary to the succinct dogmatic Tridentine text exposed in Castilian in the catechism of Jesuit Jerónimo Ripalda, commonly used since the end of [the] 16th century which demanded women to treat their husbands '*con amor y reverencia*' (with love and reverence)" (31). See Arredondo (2003), for more on formal and informal education, family life, the lives of girls and women, and gender inequality in colonial Mexico.

13 Gutiérrez 1991, 209. See also Seed 1985 and Lavrin 1992.

14 See Tuñón-Pablos 1991, 51, 120–22; Kellogg 2005, 91; Esteinou 2008, 109.

15 Marcos 1992, 165.

16 Ibid.

17 See Marcos (1992) for comments and citations on pernada in Chiapas (Mexico) and Peru. More recently, anthropological research has documented a landlord's right to rape a woman before her wedding night in Zapatista territories in Mexico (see Mora 2008, 97). The historical origins of the derecho de pernada have been identified by some in the feudal practices of the Middle Ages, which shaped legal and cultural views of rape of women in different kingdoms of Spain, prior to Christopher Columbus's expeditions to what is now known as Latin America (see Barros 1993).

18 Herman 2000, 54. For more on the sexual division of labor in the family and the father-daughter incest, see Herman's reflections on the influential feminist psychoanalytical contributions of Nancy Chodorow, Helen Block Lewis, and Juliet Mitchell (55–56).

19 Armstrong 1978, 234–35.

20 Marcos n.d., 207.

21 Rural patriarchies and urban patriarchies are examples of "regional patriarchies." See note 44, chapter 1.

22 On role reversal between mother and daughter, see Herman 2000, 45, and Russell 1999, 323.

23 Chesler 1974, 76.

24 Cited in Barrett et al. 1990, 160.

25 Historians, anthropologists, archeologists, journalists, and scholars across related disciplines have extensively documented and examined witchcraft, sorcery, and a wide variety of practices associated with the supernatural, which have existed throughout history—from pre-Columbian times to this day—and across rural and urban contexts in what is now Mexican territory. See for example, Behar 1987; Lucero and Gibbs 2007; Romero 2011.

26 Although clerical celibacy is the rule for priests in the Roman Catholic Church, men like Otilia's father may establish romantic and sexual relationships with women, procreate children, and establish some alternative form of family life while still maintaining their status as priests within the Church. Soraya from Guadalajara years back sustained a similar relationship with a Catholic priest and had children with him.

I examined Otilia's story as a case study in an article titled "Incest Revisited" (2013a). This article studies Otilia's story and situates and examines her case from a feminist perspective that looks at gender, race, class, and family life as interconnected processes; incest, sexuality, and Catholic sexual morality within a historical context in Mexico; and the scandal of sexual abuse by Catholic priests, one that has rarely reported and examined incestuous priests who sexually abuse a biological daughter.

27 *Dios Habla Hoy: La Biblia*, Versión Popular. Segunda Edición. Canada: Sociedades Bíblicas Unidas, 1983.

28 "Pacto entre mujeres sororidad," Coordinadora Española para el Lobby Europeo de Mujeres. Madrid, October 10, 2006.

29 González-López 2005, 178–86.

30 González-López 2013a, 416.

31 See Kashyap 2004. The legal complexities involved in the cases I discuss here and in other chapters are beyond my area of specialty and beyond the scope of this book. I hope, however, that the cases I have presented will advance conversations and debates on policymaking and Mexican laws sensitive to women's rights, something I discuss further in the final chapter of this book.

32 For reflections and additional citations on motherhood and patriarchy in Mexican families, see González-López 2005, 117–22.

33 González-López 2013a, 416.

34 Gutiérrez 1999, 255.

35 Ibid.

36 Ibid.

37 See also David Herlihy 1991.

38 See Penyak 1993; and Giraud 1988.

39 Finkelhor et al. 1988, 8.

40 Lanning 1992, 18.

41 See Jane Caputi 1987 for a reflection on sex crimes, rituals, and violence against women. See also Catharine MacKinnon 1996, 28.

42 Erdely and Argüelles n.d., 12.

43 Ibid., 11.

44 As of the time of publication by Erdely and Argüelles (which I accessed online in 2014), formal legal convictions against La Luz del Mundo had not been presented. As they explain, it is not a surprise given the historical alliances between this religious denomination and influential political groups (12). Television news

reports have similarly presented testimonies of sexual abuse by Samuel Joaquín. See also Marcos n.d.

45 See for example the brutal expressions of ritualized sexual violence against Mexican women reaching extreme expressions in Ciudad Juárez. For more on sexual violence against women in Ciudad Juárez, see Monárrez Fragoso 2003, and Fregoso and Bejarano 2010.

46 Cited by Caputi 1987, 6.

47 Sanday 2007 and Quinn 2002. I personally witnessed and was exposed to a wide variety of expressions of sexual harassment as an adolescent and young adult while working in administrative jobs in Monterrey, Matamoros, and Saltillo. I actually quit a job in Monterrey because of fear of being raped after receiving sexually explicit and graphic anonymous messages and threats.

48 Goffman 1967; Collins 2004.

49 Collins 2004, 230.

50 For more on virginity as *capital femenino* and hymen reconstruction in Mexico, see González-López 2005.

51 In his research with women who are sexually trafficked and exploited as sex workers in Mexico City, Acharya (2008) has documented pimps' demands for younger single women and lack of interest in women who were divorced and married. Acharya found that the "majority of the trafficked women were therefore single. As one pimp said: 'I do not want to buy a married woman, even a divorced one, because for me she is just like a used cloth, where she does not have the same smell as a new one'" (84–85).

52 See Erdely and Argüelles n.d., 9–10.

53 See González-López 2005, 43.

54 I discuss this topic in more depth in 2013a.

55 Sexual violence perpetrated within families by non-Catholic religious leaders was frequently reported in my interviews. For instance, Mariana (whose story I discuss in chapter 3) left the Jehovah's Witnesses congregation after her oldest son confided in her about the sexual violence that he experienced from the age of eight until he was fifteen years old at the hands of his uncle, an *anciano* (a high-ranking representative known as an "elder" in English) within the Jehovah's Witnesses congregation in her natal Ciudad Juárez; the anciano was the brother of Mariana's husband. Professionals frequently shared with me, for instance, that they were working on family cases involving articulate, well-dressed, and respectful men representing the Jehovah's Witnesses (or other non-Catholic congregations) who have been accused of sexually abusing a child within their families.

56 In the end, for Otilia and Maricruz it was unthinkable to even consider the possibility of making a report to their respective churches about what their fathers (with the knowledge and participation of their mothers) have done to them.

57 Erdely and Argüelles n.d., 9.

58 Ibid.

59 For example, see the case of brujo involved in "ritual narcosatánico" and murder of a woman, in Domínguez Ruvalcaba and Ravelo Blancas 2003, 126.

CHAPTER 3. *A LA PRIMA SE LA ARRIMA*

1 For more on *vergüenza*, see note 52, chapter 1.

2 In Mexico, young men are socially trained to use sexuality as a way to construct and prove their sense of manhood, especially as adolescents and as part of their experiences of camaraderie with other men. For discussion on these issues, see my book *Erotic Journeys* (2005, 62–97).

3 See Connell 2005, 82.

4 Chapter 4 includes Maclovia's family genogram.

5 According to the 2000 Census in Mexico, "In Mexico, the fourth most important religious doctrine is the Jehovah Witnesses, more than one million people reported to be members of it, which represents 1 out of 100 people who are older than 5 years old" (INEGI 2005, 21). In the 2000 Census, 1,057,736 people were identified with this religion (20). This trend has remained fairly constant. According to the 2010 Census, 1,561,086 people were similarly identified with this religion (INEGI 2011, 3). Sources: *La diversidad religiosa en México: XII Censo General de Población y Vivienda 2000*. México: Instituto Nacional de Estadística, Geografía e Informática (INEGI); and *Panorama de las religiones en México 2010*. México: Instituto Nacional de Estadística, Geografía e Informática (INEGI).

6 A social phenomenon with its roots in the first half of the twentieth century in Mexico, the *porros* are organized gangs for hire who may strategically serve (and be paid for and protected by) university authorities, the government, or a political party. The groups have a well-established presence in institutions of higher education, most notably (but not exclusively) at the Universidad Nacional Autónoma de México (UNAM), a public university located in Mexico City. A common image of porro violence is illustrated by intense attacks and intimidation against student organizations and activism. For more on porros and violence in Mexico, see Lomnitz 1986; Sánchez Gudiño 2006; and Ordorika 2008.

7 Rosana completed her college education in Mexico City and became deeply familiar with psychoanalytical theory as part of her academic training. Alert and intelligent, Rosana offered this reflection during the interview as she worked hard to understand *why* her brother sexually approached her when she was only eight years old.

8 This important reflection has more than one side, and chapter 5 in this book examines the reasons why some of the men I interviewed explored sex with a sister as they came of age. None of them, however, explained that they did so in order to avoid sexual initiation under coercion, for instance, with an adult woman engaged in prostitution. This reflection is based on my research with Mexican men who migrated to the United States as young adults. For instance, I learned that some of them were forced by adult men in their families (i.e., uncles, brothers) and/or their peers to have their first sexual experience when they were adolescents with adult

women working as prostitutes. Men frequently recalled these experiences as emotionally traumatic and painful. See *Erotic Journeys*, chapter 3, for a discussion of these men's first sexual experiences and the social construction of masculinity, manhood, and the sexual initiation of young adolescent men under coercion.

9 MacKinnon 2002, 43.

10 For Kelly, this continuum is not a unidimensional clear-cut linear paradigm but "a basic common character underlying many different events and as a continuous series of elements or events that pass into one another. The common underlying factor is that men use a variety of methods of abuse, coercion and force in order to control women" (1987, 58). Kelly also explains, "women's experiences of hetero-sexual sex are not either consenting or rape, but exist on a continuum moving from choice to pressure to coercion to force . . . The concept of a continuum suggests that pleasure and danger are not mutually exclusive opposites but the desirable and undesirable ends, respectively, of a continuum of experience" (54-55).

11 These relevant issues in nonfamilial contexts deserve in-depth analysis, which is beyond the scope of this book.

12 See Connell 2005, 79.

13 See Siller Urteaga 2012 and Saldaña-Tejeda 2014. One of the largest national surveys on social discrimination, the ENADIS 2010 (Encuesta Nacional sobre Discriminación en México) has documented the experiences of sexual harassment of domestic workers. See ENADIS 2010, Encuesta Nacional sobre Discriminación en Mexico, Resultados sobre trabajadoras domésticas. México: Consejo Nacional para Prevenir la Discriminación.

14 Oré-Aguilar 1997–1998.

15 Saldaña-Tejeda 2011.

16 Lewis 1961, 26.

17 Renata explained that (a) her paternal uncle sexually molested her when she was a child; (b) her oldest sister was sexually abused by her father's youngest brother; (c) her oldest paternal uncle sexually abused all of his five daughters; and (d) another of her paternal uncles molested one of her primas during her childhood.

18 See González-López 2005. See note 44, chapter 1.

19 See Lavrin 1992 and Jaffary 2007 on incest and sexuality in Colonial Mexican society. The Pelayo family in Santa Rosalía (Jalisco) illustrates this pattern of romance and family formation; this popular case has received special media attention.

20 Sheffield 1989, 483.

21 Sheffield explains that, "All females are potential victims—at any age, any time, or in any place—and through a variety of means—rape, physical abuse, incestuous assault, sexual, prostitution, pornography," and "Many forms of sexual intimidation are perceived as common, that is, ordinary, everyday occurrences. They are often readily dismissed by the women themselves and by agents of social control, and are the least studied" (483).

22 Ibid., 483, 484.

23 Kissling 1991, 456.

24 Sanday 2007 and Quinn 2002.

25 Sheffield 1989, 488. See my *Erotic Journeys* (2005, 87–89), for additional reflections and illustrations of "A la prima se le arrima."

26 In 2003, Isabel Vieyra conducted a survey with 320 women living in Mexico City, ages 17 to 64. Vieyra learned that "approximately, 26% of these 320 women had their first sexual relation with a relative, in first place with a primo, and the rest with tíos" (Vieyra 2012). Vieyra did not have information about the ages of primos and tíos. Email communication with Isabel Vieyra, October 11, 2012. See also Vieyra Ramírez 2013.

27 I had this shocking realization at a conference I attended in the same city in 1998. In a publication discussing the findings of a different project with Mexican immigrant women, I wrote about it: "During a presentation I offered at a sexuality conference in Mexico City in 1998, I was questioned by a male Mexican about my definition of incest. According to him, a self-identified sex educator and physician, uncles and cousins should not be included in the definition. While passionately arguing that sex between a woman and her male cousin should not be considered incestuous, he used the saying 'A la prima se le arrima,' emphasizing that it was not unusual for Mexican males to experience sexual initiation with their female cousins" (2007a, 237). I recall at least one or two of the professional women attending the workshop being visibly angry by his comment. These women confronted him while referring to the sexism implied in both the saying and his commentary, a courageous intervention that turned out to be unsuccessful. This experience exposed to me some of the frightening ways in which Mexican society reproduces a belief system that continues to perpetuate gender inequalities within families.

28 Davis 2002, 223.

29 See Kissling 1991; Davis 2002.

30 Kissling 1991, 456.

31 Ibid.

32 See Scully 1990, 35. See chapter 2, note 5.

33 See Herman 2000, 89.

CHAPTER 4. NIECES AND THEIR UNCLES

1 In a large-scale study recently conducted by Chávez Ayala et al. (2009) on sexual abuse of children and adolescents in the state of Morelos (n=1,730; 1,045 women and 685 men; ages 12–24), women identified the figure of "the uncle" as the relative who more frequently engaged in both attempt and consummation of sexual abuse than fathers, stepfathers, and brothers. Similarly, the Secretaría de Seguridad Pública de Sonora conducted a large-scale survey with women and men living in fifteen of its municipalities and identified el tío as the one exercising sexual violence with the highest incidence, more so than any other men within the immediate and extended family, including stepfathers, cousins, grandfathers, brothers, brothers-in-law, and biological fathers.

Visit www.prominix.com to access the *Estudio sobre violación: Sonora 2008–2013*.

2 Russell (1999) addresses the scarcity of research of this distinctive expression of uncle-niece sexual violence and its traumatic consequences, and cites Karin Meiselman's study (published in 1978) as one of the few studies that includes uncles and nieces. See also Margolin 1994 and Gillison 1987 for research on uncles and incest, in psychotherapy and anthropology, respectively.

3 See Kinsey et al. 1953, 118.

4 Russell 1999, 323.

5 Ibid., 323–24.

6 Herman 2000, 60.

7 Of the 21 women, 15 reported 22 maternal uncles, and 6 women reported 6 paternal uncles. That is, seven out of ten women who reported at least one uncle identified these men as related to them through the maternal side of the family. Appendix D gives detailed information about these uncle-niece cases.

8 In a publication in progress, I offer an in-depth examination of "transnational incest" as a paradigm through a case study of Ileana's story.

9 See Scully on rape and revenge (1990, 137).

10 Children buying beer or cigarettes for family adults may not be common in all parts and socioeconomic strata of Mexican society. However, I personally witnessed that practice while I did my fieldwork in these four locations and while growing up in Mexico. For instance, I recall in my own childhood (ages 6–12) running errands to buy bread, milk, or sodas for my parents and going to the grocery stores coincidentally always located at the corner of the two working-class colonias where I lived in Monterrey as a child. I used to carry a little piece of cardboard where the store owner would record my family's purchases, to be paid on the weekend when my father received his paycheck. I saw other children running the same family errands.

11 "Un arrimón" comes from the verb "arrimar," which means getting physically close. "Un arrimón" is commonly used as slang to refer to groping and it has the connotation of sexual molestation. Un arrimón is used in colloquial language, for example, to identify the experiences of women in the bus when other people (men, usually) get close to fondle them.

12 Sabina's story resonates with the case of Laura, a Mexican informant in a study with women who work in cantinas in Los Angeles, California (see Ayala, Carrier, and Magaña 1996). "Laura's first sexual encounter, at the age of seven, occurred involuntarily with one of her adult cousins" (109).

13 Psychotherapists frequently use the concept of "dissociation" to identify this state of consciousness. Dissociation occurs when a person is exposed to psychological trauma or experiences causing intolerable emotions, feelings too painful to bear in a "normal" or "associated" state of mind (see Herman 1997, 12; 2000, 86).

14 Paloma couldn't explain her father's sudden decision not to force the couple to marry. It might have happened because her father wasn't sure the young man was the right man for his daughter. Also, Paloma wasn't pregnant, and they didn't have

their first child until after years of living with him. This suggests an interesting pattern of fatherhood and the sex education of daughters. Paloma's father belongs to a new generation, in which a father would not force his daughter to marry, especially if she isn't pregnant or he has doubts that marriage is in her best interests. My research with Mexican women and men suggests this was different for a previous generation of women.

15 See Russell 1997, 147; Méndez-Negrete 2006.

16 In a personal conversation and email communication with Ana Jaimes in May 2013, I learned that families living in some mestizo and indigenous communities in Guerrero and Chiapas use terms of endearment such as (1) *mamá* (literally "mom") to refer to all young maternal and paternal aunts, (2) *mamita* (literally, "mommy") to refer to the same maternal or paternal aunts as they become older, and (3) *mamacita* (another expression for "mommy") to identify grandmothers and great-aunts. In these everyday conversations, an aunt's first name would follow any of these expressions, as in for example, "*mamita María.*" Ana Jaimes works as a psychotherapist and college professor in Monterrey, and has been an expert witness there in legal cases of sexual violence against minors. A senior psychoanalyst also commented on the ways Mexican adults living in some urban areas use terms of endearment such as *papito, papacito, chiquita,* and *mamacita* for a partner, and some parents similarly use *papi* and *papito,* and *mami* and *mamita* with sons and daughters.

17 Hackstaff 2010, 658.

18 Sociologists studying family genealogy and inequality include Patricia Hill Collins (1998) and Karla Hackstaff (2010). Some classic feminist revisions of family therapy include contributions by Rachel T. Hare-Mustin 1978; Virginia Goldner 1985; Monica McGoldrick, Carol M. Anderson, and Froma Walsh 1991; and Carmen Knudson-Martin 1994. See Monica McGoldrick and Randy Gerson 1985 on genograms and intergenerational family patterns, and Kee MacFarlane and Jill Korbin 1983 for an illustration of these dynamics in a case study of incest within extended families. See Lynette M. Renner and Kristen S. Slack 2006 for additional reflections on intergenerational transmission of family violence. See Diana Russell (1997, 85) on three generations of incestuous abuse in South Africa.

19 See for example, Mary Joe Barrett, Terry S. Trepper, and Linda S. Fish 1990. For a feminist review of family studies, see Barrie Thorne and Marilyn Yalom 1992, and Greer Litton Fox and Velma McBride Murry 2000.

20 Diana Russell found that "Women who had been sexually abused by an uncle were significantly more likely than women who had never been incestuously abused to have been the victim of rape or attempted rape at some time in their lives (70 percent and 38 percent, respectively; significant at < 0.01 level)" (1999, 340–41).

21 See Saldaña Tejeda 2014; Siller Urteaga 2012.

22 Norandi 2010.

23 See also Saldaña-Tejeda 2014.

24 Herman 2000, 55.

25 These cases included, at its worst, (1) women who had been raped by their fathers (Itzel and Miriam), (2) a woman whose father protected his sexually abusive brother rather than believing and acting on behalf of his daughter or other girls abused by him within the extended family (Paloma), and, (3) a woman whose father had been emotionally abusive toward her (Regina). And at its best, the father-daughter relationship included the case of a woman who experienced tension and distance with him and while also witnessing rigid gender arrangements promoting gender inequality in the marital relationship of her parents (Elba).

26 Some of these findings are similar to what Leslie Margolin found in her research on sexual abuse by uncles in a survey-based study in a Midwestern U.S. county. Margolin found that "These parents' failure to attend to their children may be explained in part by the fact that some appeared highly protective of their brothers. Thus, a few refused to believe that their brothers could do what their children said they did" (1994, 221). This is reinforced by the fact that the men may have a good image within their families.

27 See Menjívar 2011, 227; Bourdieu 1996–1997, 2001.

28 Some were willing to participate in an interview with me, for example, in hopes of learning about ways to disrupt the family patterns or perceptions of sexuality that affected them as children, and thus protect their own daughters and sons from a similar fate. Like other Mexican women, they are exposed to certain forms of gender inequality that have been reproduced across generations and within larger social contexts, but they may experience cross-generational transitions with regard to perceptions of sexuality and relationships. See Módena and Mendoza 2001 on research exploring the latter with three generations of Mexican women.

29 See Russell for further discussion of the patterns of sexual violence, age differences between involved parties, and reported trauma, among other results in her analysis of the uncle-niece arrangement in the study she conducted in California in 1978 (1999, 323–42). I concur with Russell's concern about previous research by Meiselman "discounting the upset and long-term effects of this type of incest [uncle-niece]" (342).

CHAPTER 5. MEN'S LIFE STORIES

1 See González-López 2011.

2 In her ethnographic work with effeminate men, homosexual, and bisexual men in Ciudad Nezahualcóyotl (a working-class sector in the outskirts of Mexico City), Prieur found that machines (the plural of machín) was a term used to identify "men who are considered truly masculine, who look masculine and who are supposed to not let themselves be penetrated" (1998b, 289).

3 Research has documented the high incidence of child sexual abuse in the lives of U.S. Latino men who have sex with men (MSM)—regardless of how they identify themselves sexually—at similar or higher rates when compared to women, and heterosexual men (see Arreola et al. 2008; Díaz 2010). About 63 percent of the U.S. Latina/o population is of Mexican origin (U.S. Census 2010). Men used the terms

"gay" and "homosexual" interchangeably during our interviews, either to identify themselves or other men with these identities.

4 Seed 1985; Gutiérrez 1991; and Lavrin 1992.

5 This finding is consistent with the results obtained from a study I conducted in the late 1990s with a different group of forty Mexican women informants living in Los Angeles. Women's narratives of their first sexual experiences illustrated the "pleasure–danger" paradigm, with an overrepresentation of the "dangerous" side of the spectrum (see González-López 2005, 50–52).

6 Kelly 1987.

7 The stories of the other six men I interviewed are not included in this chapter, although I refer to them briefly and selectively. Zacarías and Elías, for example, talked about the voluntary sexual and romantic relationships they sustained with their primos during their adolescent years. Aside from those experiences, they didn't report any other relevant sexualized experiences within the family. Similarly, Adolfo talked about the first sexual experiences of pleasure while caressing his father's feet when he was three or four, or even five, a habit he developed while his father slept late every Sunday. Adolfo's habit emerged again when he was nine or ten, and he recalled feeling sexually aroused by the experience. (This echoes a story by Mario, a Chicano gay man, in Almaguer 2007.) Zacarías, Elías, and Adolfo, all self-identified gay men, didn't report any sexually coercive experiences. I will examine their unique yet parallel stories in a separate publication. I briefly refer to Samuel's and Isaías's stories in chapter 1 in chapter 3, respectively. I will discuss their unique stories, as well as Santiago's, elsewhere.

8 Journalist Lydia Cacho has documented scandalous cases of sexual exploitation and child pornography involving men in positions of power in Mexico. Visit www.lydiacacho.net.

9 The ambivalence and contradictory messages Pablo offered while telling his story came as no surprise, especially with regard to his oldest tío. Though in his early fifties when we talked, Pablo was in a lot of pain during our interview, recalling and sharing his story for the first time. So I didn't challenge him and I am presenting the story as it was told to me. His narrative also shows the blurry line between coercion and consent, as well as the challenges of recalling these experiences with precision, a pattern well documented in the literature (see Herman 2000, 228).

10 In my interviews with professionals working at NGOs serving children who live and work on the streets in Mexico City, I often heard stories of children who use the street as a space to survive after running away from home, as a way of coping with violence in the family. Research by Erick Gómez Tagle on sexual exploitation of children in México has identified a similar pattern, which may expose children to illicit activities, including drug trafficking, prostitution, and child pornography (2005, 115).

11 This resembles the pattern reported by some Mexican immigrant women after they have access to paid work in the United States. For instance, when a woman gets paid work and controls her income, this may reorganize power relationships within

marriage and the family. Two examples include a wife who develops some leverage and disrupts old patterns of marital rape, and a daughter who feels empowered to confront a mother with regard to her sexual freedom (see González-López, 2005, 188, 193).

12 The Seguro Social, also identified with the acronym "IMSS," is a governmental institution offering health care and medical services, a pension plan, and other social security related services.

13 A major study conducted at 285 hospitals and 88 family clinics within the public health system in Mexico surveyed 373 employees working at these institutions (staff included but was not limited to physicians, nurses, and laboratory technicians) who reported in 23% of these cases that homosexuality was the cause of HIV/AIDS in Mexico. (Infante et al. 2006)

14 According to a survey conducted with a national sample of 1,273 gay, lesbian, bisexual, and other sexual and gender nonconforming informants, three out of four young gay men in Mexico have been exposed to homophobic bullying. See *Primera encuesta nacional sobre bullying homofóbico*, conducted in 2011 by Youth Coalition for Sexual and Reproductive Rights and the Coalición de Jóvenes por la Educación y la Salud Sexual (COJESS). To access the study, visit www.enehache.com, or www.youthcoalition.org.

15 List 2005 and Carrillo and Fontdevila 2011 have similarly documented the sex cultures that young working-class gay men have established in the Mexico City subway system.

16 See Prieur on working-class biological men and the high-risk and unsafe ways they experience male to female transitions (1998a, 153).

17 See Prieur 1998a, 85, 87, 183, 215, 233.

18 See Herman 2000, 49.

19 See Brandes 2002; Wentzell 2013, 77.

20 Kimmel and Messner 2012; Kaufman 2012.

21 Keenan 2012.

22 These cases included Santiago from Guadalajara, who had a romantic and sexual relationship with a married first cousin. He and his prima had intercourse regularly for about a year. Also from Guadalajara, Isaías had a one-night stand with his tía, the wife of the uncle who sexually assaulted him when he was a boy.

23 In his groundbreaking research on gay men in Guadalajara and other locations in the Western region of Mexico, anthropologist Joseph Carrier (1995) reflects about the childhood of effeminate gay men: "Because of their early effeminacy, they were sexual targets for some of their older relatives, family friends, and neighbors. There is also evidence that fathers and effeminate sons become alienated at a very early age, and that the effeminate boy establishes a protective alliance with an older sister (who more often than not appears to be the eldest)" (59). See also Prieur 1998a, 92, 105, 116–26; List 2005, 176; Núñez Noriega 1999, 145, on gay men, sexual harassment, and other forms of sexual violence within the family. The *Informe de crímenes de odio por homofobia, México 1995–2008* prepared by Brito and Bastida (2009) refers to a study conducted by the Universidad Autónoma

Metropolitana-Xochimilco on health and oppression in the lives of lesbians, gay, and bisexual people: 21 percent of them identified brothers as the people exercising aggression against them (i.e., mocking and humiliation).

24 Hennen 2008, 51.

25 The homophobic expressions *mano caída* or *se le cae la mano* ("the fallen hand"— limp wristed) are commonly used in Mexico to refer to gay men, illustrating among other things the ways in which the assumed homosexuality of man may become an embodied experience of the "limp wrist" in this case, and suggesting it potentially can be corrected. See also Laguarda for more on homophobic language used to identify gay men as part of everyday life in Mexico (2007, 131).

26 A Mexican pioneer in anthropological research with gay men, Núñez Noriega has conducted and published his extensive ethnographic research with gay men living in different regions of Mexico.

27 Although homophobia is alive and well in Mexico, Núñez Noriega believes that sexual violence against gender nonconforming boys in Mexican families may have eased for a younger generation of gay men because of government-sponsored programs aimed at preventing discrimination and encouraging greater acceptance of sexual diversity in the country in recent years.

28 "The Enadis 2010 reveals that four out of ten Mexican women and men would not be willing to allow that a homosexual person lived there, in their home" (ENADIS 2010, 33). In other words, these four out of ten people would not welcome a homosexual in their homes. The *Encuesta Nacional sobre Discriminación en México, Enadis 2010, Resultados sobre diversidad sexual* is a major survey conducted in 2010 with 52,095 informants from all states in the country and has exposed a revealing assessment of different forms of discrimination and prejudice, including but not limited to sexual diversity. The CONAPRED conducted the ENADIS 2010, *Resultados sobre diversidad sexual*. The survey is available online at www.conapred.org.mx. Also, Brito and Bastida (2009) cite a second study conducted by the Segob/IFE: "66 percent of Mexicans would not share their roof with a homosexual person" (9).

29 See Kane 2006.

30 See González-López (2005, 50–52). Pleasure and danger are not merely static and extreme categories of a flat and unidimensional continuum. They are contrasting dimensions in a heuristic model that attempts to expose the wide, complex spectrum of sexualized experiences in patriarchal contexts. As I wrote in *Erotic Journeys,* "Danger and pleasure are not mutually exclusive and, at times, the former may enhance the latter" (52).

31 Carrillo and Fontdevila have identified the same dynamic as "homosocial sexual initiation" in their research with gay and bisexual Mexican men. These sexualized exchanges involve young adolescents close in age, including youth who are related by blood as well as neighbors and friends (2011, 1247).

32 In his demographic study of 250 gay men living in Mexico City, Gallego Montes (2007) found that for gay men who reported having their first same-sex experience with a relative, the highest reports of the incestuous arrangement was for men born

in the 1981–1989 period, (19.6 percent) when compared to previous cohorts, for example, men born in the periods identified as 1950–1970 (13.9 percent) and 1971–1980 (10.8 percent). Gallego Montes observes, "Sexual initiation with a relative (especially primos, although tíos and grandfathers are also reported) seem to prevail as a constant across generations, even though it gets 6 percentage points for a younger generation vis-à-vis an older adult cohort" (146). Echoing these patterns, Tomás Almaguer similarly found in a qualitative study involving fifty men who felt comfortable identifying themselves as gay or homosexual: "Uncles, cousins, brothers, and even grandfathers have all played a sexual role or had sexual contact with the men interviewed for this larger project" (2007, 148). Almaguer's study included all ethnic Mexican men, born in either Mexico or the United States, who lived in the San Francisco Bay Area when the life history interviews took place.

33 Gallego Montes discovered that gay men may perceive voluntary incestuous experiences beyond the idea of "prohibition" and redefine them as a "possibility and opportunity" to engage in same-sex practices (2007, 147). Based on anthropological research conducted in the late 1960s and early 1970s, Carrier (1976) documented cases of homosexual Mexican men who recalled their first same-sex erotic experiences as prepubertal boys who engaged in sexual encounters with postpubertal relatives while both slept in the same bed, activities they sustained during prolonged periods of time (116).

34 See Fausto's story in Carrillo and Fontdevila 2011, 1248. Elías and Zacarías, both self-identified gay men (and whose stories are not included in this book), similarly reported exclusively voluntary sexual exchanges with primos before and during adolescence. Both men established romantic relationships with their primos as part of these sexual experiences, which they enjoyed and kept for long periods of time, and in secret within the family. Zacarías confronted his primo and broke up with him after learning about the relationship he was having with a young woman. In both cases the relationship ended and the primo married a woman soon afterward.

35 Kimmel 1994.

36 Carrillo and Fontdevila similarly found the homophobic discourse in the lives of the gay and bisexual men they studied, some of whom had their first sexual experiences with adult relatives (mostly primos and tíos) during childhood or early adolescence, sometimes by force or without consent (2011, 1244). Other studies have similarly found the high prevalence of child sexual abuse by uncles and cousins in the lives of U.S. Latino men.

Sonya Grant Arreola (2010) explains in her comprehensive review of the literature on child sexual abuse (CSA), men who have sex with men (MSM) and U.S. Latino communities:

> For example, in a probability survey of 2,881 adult men who have sex with men residing in San Francisco, New York, Los Angeles, and Chicago, a significantly higher proportion of Latino MSM reported sexual abuse before age thirteen (22 percent) than did non-Latino MSM (11 percent). Other studies have also found that, compared to non-Latinos, CSA among

Latinos is generally more severe: Latino boys are more likely to have been sexually abused by an extended family member such as a cousin or an uncle, experienced more genital fondling, been exposed to more sexually abusive behaviors, and experienced more anal abuse. It is yet unclear how machismo may contribute to the increased risk for CAS among Latinos. (53–54)

Interestingly, Helián and Leonardo referred to "machismo" as an idea to make sense of the reasons behind their fathers' sexually violent behavior. Although both men as well as other Mexicans may use "machismo" as a paradigm to explain everyday life experiences and relational expressions of hegemonic masculinity and heteropatriarchal privilege within their families and communities, as indicated in chapter 1, "machismo" has been critiqued as an idea and a paradigm for a critical examination of men's lives and gender inequality.

37 A study conducted in Mexico indicated that for every ten boys and teenagers who have been exposed to homophobic verbal insults, only one is in fact homosexual (see Brito and Bastida 2009, 9).

38 Sociologist Tomás Almaguer (2007) discusses the first moments of awareness of sexual desire and discovery during childhood within the nephew-uncle context in the lives of gay men of Mexican origin (see Mario's story, pp. 140–43). The uncle-nephew relationship recently received attention in two influential and relevant bodies of knowledge: children sexual abuse literature and family studies. Two scholars stand out in this area—Leslie Margolin and Robert Milardo. Margolin (1994) addressed the relevance of the uncle in the family as one who would be more likely to sexually abuse a niece rather than a nephew; Milardo (2005) conducted ambitious research examining the lives of uncles and nephews living in New Zealand and the state of Maine, exposing the absence of high conflict or abuse in these relationships. In contrast, little is known about the uncle-nephew relationship in the social sciences literature in Mexico.

39 According to Connell and Messerschmidt, "the hierarchy of masculinities is a pattern of hegemony, not a pattern of simple domination based on force. Cultural consent, discursive centrality, institutionalization, and the marginalization or delegitimation of alternatives are widely documented features of socially dominant masculinities" (2005, 846).

40 See Jane Kilby's (2010) analysis of Judith Butler's theorizing on incest and the child's love.

41 In a large-scale study by Chávez Ayala et al. (2009) on sexual abuse of children and adolescents in the state of Morelos (n=1,730; 1,045 women and 685 men; ages 12–24), male informants identified the uncle as the one who most often tried to sexually abuse them, more than any other relative. Núñez Noriega observed that because of the authority relationship that exists from an older brother toward a younger one (and punishment for not behaving well, for example), the affectionate bonding and emotional closeness between primos close in age may facilitate their engaging in voluntary sexual encounters.

42 For an extensive analysis of the continuum of sexual violence, see Nicola Gavey (2005, 61–62, 171–72, 189–90, 228–29).

43 Isaías (who had an incestuous relationship with his sister) was sexually assaulted when he was seven or eight by his mother's brother (an 18-year-old adolescent at the time), and Samuel reported a long history of sexual experiences with female and male relatives during childhood and adolescence, varying in degrees (between voluntary to experiences under coercion and force) and age differences, including sexual molestation by an 18–20-year-old brother when Samuel was five or six years old, and Samuel as an adolescent molesting his two nephews, ages seven to nine years old.

44 See Almaguer 2007.

45 See Seed 1985; Gutiérrez 1991; and Lavrin 1992.

46 Simon and Gagnon 1986.

CHAPTER 6. TOWARD A FEMINIST SOCIOLOGY OF INCEST IN MEXICO

1 In recent years I have found myself in shock while becoming an active listener of the monologs of relatives and friends sharing horror stories after losing someone who was killed, kidnapped, or simply disappeared overnight. Some of my undergraduate and graduate students at the University of Texas at Austin have similarly lost relatives and loved ones, especially those with close family ties in northern states.

2 "Servir" in the Real Academia Española, http://lema.rae.es/drae/?val=servir. Accessed May 28, 2014.

3 Ibid.

4 Kelly 1987.

5 Gavey 2005.

6 See Blanca Vázquez Mezquita (1995, 12–13) for more reflections on children who are sexually abused as sexual transgressors. See O'Connell Davidson 2007 for a reflection on sexuality and children as innocent.

7 See Kaye 2005.

8 A major national survey analyzing discrimination against women in Mexico found that "A fifth of the population, female or male (who said to agree, strongly agree or depending on the circumstances), have a perception that assigns certain 'responsibility' to women who are raped, which represents an expression of gender discrimination to the extent that it justifies or removes responsibility from men when they rape a woman if she does not engage in socially accepted behaviors." (ENADIS 2010, 133). The survey was conducted in 2010 with a total sample of 13,751 households, throughout every state in the country, and offered information about 52,095 persons. See ENADIS 2010.

9 See González-López 2007c.

10 On blame-the-victim and incest, see publications by Judith Herman and Diana Russell cited in this book. For a sociological review of the blame-the-victim and women-as-seductresses ideas, see Scully 1990, 41–45, 102.

11 Priests may have more power in a small town than in a larger city. I suggest this based on the idea of "regional patriarchies," which examines how local and regional economies and cultures may shape gender inequality. A woman may have exposure to a wider variety of discourses on sexuality and morality in a larger urban context, for example. See Russell 1999, 121. See also Elden 2005 for reflections on the confessional and sexuality in Michel Foucault's celebrated works.

12 I interviewed four Catholic priests, three of them self-identified with left-wing ideologies, working mainly with poor families, frequently distancing themselves from Vatican politics. A second priest, for instance, who works with children who live and work on the streets, said that he usually "takes into account the social context" before giving moral guidance to anyone. He actively recommends condom use and contraceptive pills to the adolescent girls he works with. A third priest trained in the Jesuit tradition embraced similar values to the first and second priests, promoting gender equality and women's rights during the Mass homily; he was critical of some biblical texts for being read out of social and historical contexts. He has found himself being confronted by his parishioners after mass, frequently men (and women as well) who do not believe in equal rights for women. Similar to the first priest, he has been moved by the feelings of guilt and self-blame in women who have shared their histories of incestuous violence in different conversational contexts (i.e., in and out of confession); he identified about 20–30 incest cases while working for about seven years with his current community. And a member of the Opus Dei, a fourth priest working with upper-class families, came across as gentle and kind and contrastingly more conservative in his approach and explained that he could not share with me the general themes he heard in the confessional booth, not even for research purposes. He gave me an unsolicited lecture on homosexuality and his strong belief in conversion therapy. When I asked him about the scandal of sexual abuse by priests, he said not to trust the press and media. See Keenan 2012 on the masculinity of priests, sexual abuse of children, and the Catholic Church.

13 Menjívar 2011, 87.

14 Thought-provoking and highly acclaimed, *El castillo de la pureza*, literally "The castle of purity" (1972) is a Mexican production directed by Arturo Ripstein. The movie is based on a true story; the narrative takes place in Mexico City, and depicts an incestuous relationship between sister and brother. When I referred to "The castle of purity" movie, a Monterrey psychoanalyst nodded her head and used the concept of *familias aglutinadas* (enmeshed families) to describe families that may represent a risk for incest. She gave examples of wealthy Mexican families that cannot tolerate separation; parents may close the door to strangers and control children's decisions of romantic and marital choices. Some of these families may buy a large piece of land with all the homes of married children built on the same big lot.

15 See Kinsey et al. 1953; and Russell 1999 [1986].

16 See Segura and Pierce 1993.

17 See Menjívar 2011, 227.

18 See Bourdieu 1996–1997, 2001.

19 Only a few cases identified a woman as the one initiating a sexualized exchange with a minor, against the will of a girl or a boy. In this book, I discuss the case of Elba (chapter 4). Other informants who reported stories involving a preteen girl or an adolescent girl as the one sexually approaching a minor (either a boy or a girl younger in age) included Samuel and Soraya from Guadalajara, and Camila from Ciudad Juárez. I will examine these complex cases in a future publication. The clinicians I interviewed talked about the relevance of also conducting research on women who sexually coerce, harass, or rape minors within the family, a pattern they said is "apparently less frequent" but still exists and deserves special attention. The experiences of Mexican men like those I interviewed in Los Angeles who recalled being forced by an older male relative to have sex for the first time with an adult woman sex worker deserves attention as well (see González-López 2005, chapter 3). A priest, a law professor, and a clinician (all involved in violence prevention activism and education) who identified the above as a form of sexual violence against adolescent boys, shared with me stories of men who similarly confided their coercive experiences of sexual initiation during adolescence, and asserted these were "more common than what we could imagine," events frequently facilitated by an older male relative.

20 A 2012 INEGI report indicates that family households in Mexico have two characteristics: seven out of ten follow the nuclear family arrangement and 77.7 percent of the family households have a man as the head of the family. See INEGI, "*Estadísticas a propósito del día de la familia mexicana*," Instituto Nacional de Estadística y Geografía," March 4, 2012, available online at www.inegi.org.mx. Another study suggested that 63 percent of the women are in charge of housework and 54 percent are caregivers of their children (cited in Schmukler and Alonso 2009, 29).

21 Herman 2000, 55.

22 See note 18, chapter 2.

23 This resonated with the voices of the Mexican men I interviewed in the previous project on sexuality and migration (see González-López 2005). Men who were pro-feminist about women's issues (including but not limited to violence against women) had something in common: a sister, a daughter, or a mother had been exposed to pain in the past, and love and concern for them helped them develop some form of gender consciousness about these and other related issues affecting women's lives.

24 See González-López 2005, chapter 3.

25 See Schmukler and Alonso 2009.

26 Kimball 1993; Castañeda 1989.

27 Being a gender nonconforming girl does not mean automatically that she will be sexually or romantically attracted to girls later in life; and being a gender conforming girl does not mean that she will be sexually or romantically attracted to men. I interviewed women who recalled engaging in gender nonconforming activities

during childhood (e.g., playing rough sports and climbing trees) who were in exclusively heterosexual relationships as adults.

Also, it seems that a girl who is a tomboy in Mexico (i.e., *machetona*, a label I was personally given during my childhood) does not become a concern for a parent until she reaches adolescence. That is, when the girl becomes sexualized she is then expected to behave properly, like a señorita, a form of "emphasized femininity" (see Connell 1987).

This pattern needs further analysis for girls and young women in Mexico. Nevertheless, this pattern of gender nonconformity in girls resonates with research on gender and parents raising children in the United States (see Kane 2006, 157–58).

28 The stories of Dalia and Sagrario are not included in this book.

29 See Careaga 2012 for more on *lesbofobia* and sexual violence against lesbian women in Mexico, and see Bartle 2000 for a critical perspective on hate crimes against lesbian women vis-à-vis hate crimes against gay men.

30 See Carrillo 2003 for an analysis of telenovelas and cultural representations of gay men in contemporary Mexico.

31 See Rumney 2009.

32 See Bell 1993; and Kaye 2005.

33 See González-López 2013a.

34 See Schmukler and Alonso 2009.

35 In this study, mothers who did not support their children and/or intervene on their behalf seem to have one or more of the following characteristics: (a) they depend financially on a husband or a partner, feeling afraid of compromising that support for her and the children, paradoxically, at the expense of the well-being of the child or children being abused; (b) they feel emotionally incompetent, helpless, or fearful to confront a husband or partner; (c) they are emotionally wounded themselves, with their own unresolved histories of abuse and without inner resources to protect themselves, much less to protect or advocate for a child; (d) they feel disempowered and/or devalued emotionally, financially, morally, and/or sexually; (e) they have internalized sexist perceptions about themselves (and girls and women in general), including the normalization of different forms of violence in women's lives.

36 See Pulsipher and Pulsipher 2006; and Vega-Briones 2011.

37 Rosie and Don Francisco engaged in a conversation about the ages of the incest-related events, the reasons why she was silent about the abuse for many years, the legal prosecution and incarceration of her brother-in-law, the ways in which her life was deeply impacted as she grew up, her involvement in an abusive relationship, her suicidal attempts, and the ways she has transformed her own life while also helping others do the same through the workshops she facilitates in Los Angeles.

38 For more than one hundred years, incest and incestuous relationships have inspired fiction writers in the Spanish-speaking literary world. A comprehensive feminist examination of those publications and related productions in the particular case of Mexico is of high relevance but beyond the scope of this book. See Rosaria

Champagne's book *The Politics of Survivorship: Incest, Women's Literature, and Feminist Theory* (New York University Press, 1998) for an examination of incest in relevant U.S. and U.K. literary texts and U.S. popular culture.

39 See Herman 2000 on positive images of incestuous fathers (71, 72, 87).

40 This pattern also reminded me of the kind and respectful men I worked with on an individual basis as a clinician in training, men who were referred by a probation officer at one of the Los Angeles organizations where I completed a clinical internship in the 1990s and who had been legally arrested for raping or sexually molesting a minor.

41 See Menjívar 2011 for an in-depth sociological examination of the ways in which other women living in Guatemala may somatize their suffering as women, a consequence of multiple forms of violence.

42 Diana Russell's research findings on incest in South Africa (1997) resonate with what I discovered in Mexico, including but not limited to patterns of incestuous abuse across generations (85), perceptions of an oldest daughter as the "little mother" (142), and a father's sense of entitlement over his daughters (147).

APPENDIX B. METHODOLOGICAL CONSIDERATIONS

1 These publications include: *Mindful Ethics* (2011), "Ethnographic Lessons" (2010a), "Epistemologies of the Wound" (2006), "Engaged Research on Incest in Mexico" (2010b), "Crossing-back Methodologies" (2007b), and "The Maquiladora Syndrome" (2013b).

REFERENCES

Acharya, Arun Kumar. 2008. "Sexual Violence and Proximate Risks: A Study on Trafficked Women in Mexico City." *Gender, Technology and Development* 12, 1: 77–99.
———. 2009. "Tráfico de mujeres hacia la Zona Metropolitana de Monterrey: una perspectiva analítica." *Espacios Públicos* 12, 24: 146–60.

Almaguer, Tomás. 2007. "Looking for Papi: Longing and Desire Among Chicano Gay Men." In *A Companion to Latina/o Studies* edited by Juan Flores and Renato Rosaldo, 138–50. Malden, MA: Blackwell.

Armstrong, Louise. 1978. *Kiss Daddy Goodnight: A Speak-Out on Incest.* New York: Hawthorn Books.

Arredondo, María Adelina. 2003. *Obedecer, servir y resistir: La educación de las mujeres en la historia de México.* Mexico City: Universidad Pedagógica Nacional and Grupo Editorial Miguel Angel Porrúa.

Arreola, Sonya Grant. 2010. "Latina/o Childhood Sexuality." In *Latina/o Sexualities: Probing Powers, Passions, Practices, and Policies,* edited by Marysol Asencio, 48–61. New Brunswick, NJ: Rutgers University Press.

Arreola, Sonya Grant et al. 2008. "Childhood Sexual Experiences and Adult Health Sequelae Among Gay and Bisexual Men: Defining Childhood Sexual Abuse." *Journal of Sex Research* 45, 3: 246–52.

Arrom, Silvia M. 1985. "Changes in Mexican Family Law in the Nineteenth Century: The Civil Codes of 1870 and 1884." *Journal of Family History* 10, 3: 305–17.

Ayala, Armida, Joseph Carrier, and J. Raúl Magaña. 1996. "The Underground World of Latina Sex Workers in Cantinas." In *AIDS Crossing Borders: The Spread of HIV Among Migrant Latinos,* edited by Shiraz I. Mishra, Ross F. Conner, and J. Raúl Magaña, 95–112. Boulder, CO: Westview Press.

Barrett, Mary Joe, Terry S. Trepper, and Linda S. Fish. 1990. "Feminist-Informed Family Therapy for the Treatment of Intrafamily Child Sexual Abuse." *Journal of Family Psychology* 4, 2: 151–66.

Barros, Carlos. 1993. "Rito y violación: derecho de pernada en la Baja Edad Media." *Historia Social* 16 (Spring–Summer): 3–17.

Bartle, Elizabeth E. 2000. "Lesbians and Hate Crimes." *Journal of Poverty* 4, 4: 23–43.

Bartra, Eli. 1992. "Mujeres y política en México: aborto, violación y mujeres golpeadas." *Política y Cultura* 1: 23–33.

Behar, Ruth. 1987. "Sex and Sin, Witchcraft and the Devil in Late-Colonial Mexico." *American Ethnologist* 14, 1: 34–54.

Bell, Vikki. 1993. *Interrogating Incest: Feminism, Foucault and the Law*. London and New York: Routledge.

Bourdieu, Pierre. 1996–1997. "Masculine Domination Revisited." *Berkeley Journal of Sociology*, 41: 189–203.

———. 2001. *Masculine Domination*. Stanford, CA: Stanford University Press.

Boyd-Franklin, Nancy. 2006. *Black Families in Therapy: Understanding the African American Experience*. New York: Guilford Press.

Brandes, Stanley. 2002. *Staying Sober in Mexico City*. Austin: University of Texas Press.

Brito, Alejandro and Leonardo Bastida. 2009. *Informe de crímenes de odio por homofobia, México 1995–2008*. Mexico City: Letra S, Sida, Cultura y Vida Cotidiana, A.C.

Campbell, Rebecca. 2002. *Emotionally Involved: The Impact of Researching Rape*. London and New York: Routledge.

Caputi, Jane. 1987. *The Age of Sex Crime*. Bowling Green, OH: Bowling Green University Popular Press.

Careaga Pérez, Gloria. 2012. "Primero muerta que lesbiana: Violencia contra lesbianas." In *Diálogos interdisciplinarios sobre violencia sexual,* edited by Héctor Domínguez Ruvalcaba and Patricia Ravelo Blancas, 49–67. Mexico City: Fondo Nacional para la Cultura y las Artes, Centro de Investigaciones y Estudios Superiores en Antropología Social, Ediciones EON.

Carrier, Joseph. 1976. "Cultural Factors Affecting Urban Mexican Male Homosexual Behavior." *Archives of Sexual Behavior* 5, 2: 103–124.

———. 1995. *De los otros: Intimacy and Homosexuality among Mexican Men*. New York: Columbia University Press.

Carrillo, Héctor. 2003. "Neither Machos nor Maricones: Masculinity and Emerging Male Homosexual Identities in Mexico." In *Changing Men and Masculinities in Latin America,* edited by Matthew C. Gutmann, 351–69. Durham, NC: Duke University Press.

Carrillo, Héctor and Jorge Fontdevila. 2011. "Rethinking Sexual Initiation: Pathways to Identity Formation Among Gay and Bisexual Mexican Male Youth." *Archives of Sexual Behavior* 40: 1241–54.

Castañeda Antonia I. 1993. "Sexual Violence in the Politics and Policies of Conquest: Amerindian Women and the Spanish Conquest of Alta California." In *Building With Our Hands: New Directions in Chicana Studies,* edited by Adela de la Torre and Beatriz M. Pesquera, 15–33. Berkeley: University of California Press.

Castañeda, Carmen. 1984. "La memoria de las niñas violadas." *Encuentro* 5, Vol. II, 1: 41–56.

———. 1989. *Violación, estupro y sexualidad: Nueva Galicia 1790–1821*. Guadalajara: Editorial Hexágono.

Chapkis, Wendy. 1996. *Live Sex Acts: Women Performing Erotic Labor*. New York: Routledge.

Chávez Ayala, Rubén et al. 2009. "Factores del abuso sexual en la niñez y la adolescencia en estudiantes de Morelos, México." *Revista de Saúde Pública* 43, 3: 506–14.

Chesler, Phyllis. 1974. "Rape and Psychotherapy." In *Rape: The First Sourcebook for Women*, edited by Noreen Connell and Cassandra Wilson, 76–81. New York: New American Library.

Collins, Patricia Hill. 1998. "It's All in the Family: Intersections of Gender, Race, and Nation." *Hypatia* 13, 3: 62–82.

Collins, Randall. 2004. *Interaction Ritual Chains*. Princeton, NJ: Princeton University Press.

Connell, R.W. 1987. *Gender & Power*. Stanford, CA: Stanford University Press.

———. 2005. *Masculinities*. 2nd edition. Cambridge, UK: Polity Press.

Connell, R.W. and James W. Messerschmidt. 2005. "Hegemonic Masculinity: Rethinking the Concept." *Gender & Society* 19, 6: 829–59.

Dalton, Margarita. 2010. *Mujeres: género e identidad en el Istmo de Tehuantepec, Oaxaca*. Mexico City: CIESAS.

Davis, Deirdre E. 2002. "The Harm that Has No Name: Street Harassment, Embodiment, and African American Women." In *Gender Struggles: Practical Approaches to Contemporary Feminism*, edited by Constance L. Mui and Julien S. Murphy, 214–25. Lanham, MD: Rowman & Littlefield.

de la Garza-Aguilar, Javier and Enrique Díaz-Michel. 1997. "Elementos para el estudio de la violación sexual." *Salud Pública de México* 39: 539–45.

Díaz, Rafael. 2010. "The Psychological Impact of Childhood Sexual Abuse in Gay Men: A Review of Research." Unpublished paper.

Dietrich, David. 2008. "Culture of Poverty." *International Encyclopedia of the Social Sciences*. Accessed May 20, 2014. Encyclopedia.com.

Domínguez Ruvalcaba, Héctor and Patricia Ravelo Blancas. 2003. "La batalla de las cruces: Los crímenes contra mujeres en la frontera y sus intérpretes." *Desacatos* (Invierno) 13: 122–33.

Elden, Stuart. 2005. "The Problem of Confession: The Productive Failure of Foucault's *History of Sexuality*." *Journal for Cultural Research* 9, 1: 23–41.

ENADIS. 2010. *Encuesta Nacional sobre Discriminación en México: Resultados sobre mujeres*. Consejo Nacional para Prevenir la Discriminación. Available at www.inmujeres.gob.mx and www.conapred.org.mx, accessed March 15, 2013.

Erdely, Jorge and Lourdes Argüelles. n.d. "Secrecy and the Institutionalization of Sexual Abuse: The Case of La Luz del Mundo in México." *Revista Académica para el Estudio de las Religiones*. Available at http://www.revistaacademica.com/ToLive/luz-del-mundo-mexico.asp, accessed April 24, 2014.

Esteinou, Rosario. 2008. *La familia nuclear en México: Lecturas de su modernidad, siglos XVI al XX*. Mexico City: CIESAS and Grupo Editorial Miguel Ángel Porrúa.

Falconi Alegría, Federico. 1961. *El delito de incesto: estudio dogmático*. Mexico City: Universidad Nacional Autónoma de México, Facultad de Derecho.

Finkelhor, David. 1994. "The International Epidemiology of Child Sexual Abuse." *Child Abuse & Neglect* 18, 5: 409–17.

Finkelhor, David and Angela Browne. 1985. "The Traumatic Impact of Child Sexual Abuse: A Conceptualization." *American Journal of Orthopsychiatry* 55, 4: 530–41.

Finkelhor, David, Linda Meyer Williams, Nanci Burns, and Michael Kalinowski. 1988. "Sexual Abuse in a Day Care: A National Study." Executive Summary. Durham: Family Research Laboratory, University of New Hampshire.

Floris Margadant, Guillermo. 2001. *La sexofobia del clero*. Mexico City: Miguel Angel Porrúa.

Fox, Greer Litton and Velma McBride Murry. 2000. "Gender and Families: Feminist Perspectives and Family Research." *Journal of Marriage and the Family* 62: 1160–72.

Fregoso, Rosa-Linda and Cynthia Bejarano. 2010. *Terrorizing Women: Feminicide in the Américas*. Durham, NC: Duke University Press.

Gallego Montes, Gabriel. 2007. "Patrones de iniciación sexual y trayectorias de emparejamiento entre varones en la Ciudad de México: Una mirada biográfica-interaccional en el estudio de la sexualidad." PhD diss., Mexico City: El Colegio de México.

García, Genaro. 1891. *Apuntes sobre la condición de la mujer*. México: Compañía Limit. de Tipógrafos. Puente Leguísamo 3.

Gavey, Nicola. 2005. *Just Sex? The Cultural Scaffolding of Rape*. London and New York: Routledge.

Gilbert, Lucy and Paula Webster. 1982. *Bound by Love: The Sweet Trap of Daughterhood*. Boston, MA: Beacon Press.

Gilligan, Carol. 1982. *In a Different Voice: Psychological Theory and Women's Development*. Cambridge, MA: Harvard University Press.

Gillison, Gillian. 1987. "Incest and the Atom of Kinship: The Role of the Mother's Brother in a New Guinea Highlands Society." *Ethos* 15, 2: 166–202.

Giraud, François. 1988. "La reacción social ante la violación: del discurso a la práctica (Nueva España, siglo XVIII)." In *El placer de pecar & el afán de normar*, edited by Seminario de Historia de las Mentalidades, 295–352. Mexico City: Joaquín Mortiz / Instituto Nacional de Antropología.

Goffman, Erving. 1959. *The Presentation of Self in Everyday Life*. New York: Anchor.

———. 1967. *Interaction Ritual: Essays on Face-to-Face Behavior*. New York: Pantheon Books.

Goldner, Virginia. 1985. "Feminism and Family Therapy." *Family Process* 24, 1: 31–47.

Gómez Tagle, Erick. 2005. *La explotación sexual commercial de niñas, niños y adolescentes: Una aproximación sociológica*. Mexico City: Instituto Nacional de Ciencias Penales.

Gonzalbo Aizpuru, Pilar. 2003. "Religiosidad femenina y vida familiar." In *Obedecer, servir y resistir: La educación de las mujeres en la historia de México*, edited by María Adelina Arredondo, 27–43. Mexico City: Universidad Pedagógica Nacional and Grupo Editorial Miguel Angel Porrúa.

González Ascencio, Gerardo. 2007. "La igualdad y la diferencia en el estado constitucional de derecho. Una reflexión feminista a la luz del pensamiento garantista." In *Violencia familiar y violencia de género: Intercambio de experiencias internacionales*, edited by María Jiménez, 75–99. Mexico City: Universidad Autónoma de la Ciudad de México y Dirección General de Igualdad y Diversidad Social.

González-López, Gloria. 2005. *Erotic Journeys: Mexican Immigrants and Their Sex Lives.* Berkeley, CA: University of California Press.

———. 2006. "Epistemologies of the Wound: Anzaldúan Theories and Sociological Research on Incest in Mexican Society." *Human Architecture: Journal of the Sociology of Self-Knowledge* 4 (Summer): 17–24.

———. 2007a. "*Nunca he dejado de tener terror*: Sexual Violence in the Lives of Mexican Immigrant Women." In *Women and Migration in the U.S.-Mexico Borderlands: A Reader,* edited by Denise A. Segura and Patricia Zavella, 224–46. Durham, NC: Duke University Press.

———. 2007b. "Crossing-back Methodologies: Transnational Feminist Research on Incest in Mexico." *Forum,* Latin American Studies Association (LASA), 37, 2 (Spring): 19–20.

———. 2007c. "*Confesiones de mujer:* The Catholic Church and Sacred Morality in the Sex Lives of Mexican Immigrant Women." In *Sexual Inequalities and Social Justice,* edited by Niels F. Teunis and Gilbert Herdt, 148–73. Berkeley: University of California Press.

———. 2010a. "Ethnographic Lessons: Researching Incest in Mexican Families." *Journal of Contemporary Ethnography* 39 (October): 569–81.

———. 2010b. "Engaged Research on Incest in Mexico." In *The Routledge Handbook of Sexuality, Health and Rights,* edited by Peter Aggleton and Richard Parker, 309–15. London and New York: Routledge.

———. 2011. "Mindful Ethics: Comments on Informant-Centered Practices in Sociological Research," *Qualitative Sociology* 34, 3: 447–61.

———. 2012. "Desde el otro lado: reflexiones feministas para una sociología de la violencia sexual." In *Diálogos interdisciplinarios sobre violencia sexual,* edited by Héctor Domínguez Ruvalcaba and Patricia Ravelo Blancas, 69–89. Mexico City: Fondo Nacional para la Cultura y las Artes, Centro de Investigaciones y Estudios Superiores en Antropología Social, Ediciones EON.

———. 2013a. "Incest Revisited: A Mexican Catholic Priest and His Daughter." *Sexualities* 16, 3/4: 401–22.

———. 2013b. "The Maquiladora Syndrome." *Contexts* (Winter): 40.

González-López, Gloria and Matthew C. Gutmann. 2005. "Machismo." *New Dictionary of the History of Ideas* 4: 1328–30. New York: Charles Scribner's Sons.

González-López, Gloria and Salvador Vidal Ortiz. 2008. "Latinas and Latinos, Sexuality, and Society: A Critical Sociological Perspective." In *Sourcebook on Latinos/ as in the United States,* edited by Havidán Rodríguez, Rogelio Sáenz, and Cecilia Menjívar, 308–22. New York: Springer.

Gudiño, Jorge Alberto. 2011. *Con amor, tu hija.* Mexico: Alfaguara.

Guillé Tamayo, Margarita. 2007. "Las razones de los refugios. Protección a mujeres mexicanas en riesgo por violencia." In *Violencia familiar y violencia de género: Intercambio de experiencias internacionales,* edited by María Jiménez, 375–417. Mexico City: Universidad Autónoma de la Ciudad de México y Dirección General de Igualdad y Diversidad Social.

Guridi Sánchez, Jorge. 1961. *Ensayo sobre dogmática del delito de incesto en el derecho penal mexicano*. Mexico City: UNAM, Facultad de Derecho y Ciencias Sociales.

Gutiérrez, Ramón A. 1991. *When Jesus Came, the Corn Mothers Went Away: Marriage, Sexuality and Power in New Mexico, 1500–1846*. Stanford, CA: Stanford University Press.

———. 1999. "Crucifixion, Slavery, and Death: The Hermanos Penitentes of the Southwest." In *Over the Edge: Remapping the American West*, edited by Valerie Matsumoto and Blake Allmendinger, 253–71. Berkeley: University of California Press.

Gutmann, Matthew C. 1994. "Los hijos de Lewis: la sensibilidad antropológica y el caso de los pobres machos." *Alteridades* 4, 7: 9–19.

Hackstaff, Karla B. 2010. "Family Genealogy: A Sociological Imagination Reveals Intersectional Relations." *Sociology Compass* 4, 8: 658–72.

Hare-Mustin, Rachel T. 1978. "A Feminist Approach to Family Therapy." *Family Process* 17, 2: 181–94.

Haug, Frigga et al. 1987. *Female Sexualization: A Collective Work of Memory*, trans. E. Carter. London: Verso. (Original work published 1983.)

Hennen, Peter. 2008. *Faeries, Bears, and Leathermen: Men in Community Queering the Masculine*. Chicago: University of Chicago Press.

Herlihy, David. 1991. "Family." *American Historical Review* 96: 2–35.

Herman, Judith. 1997. *Trauma and Recovery*. New York: Basic Books.

———. 2000 [1981]. *Father-Daughter Incest*. Cambridge, MA: Harvard University Press.

Infante, César et al. 2006. "El estigma asociado al VIH/SIDA: el caso de los prestadores de servicios de salud en México." *Salud Pública de México* 48, 2: 141–50.

Jaffary, Nora E. 2007. "Incest, Sexual Virtue and Social Mobility in Late Colonial Mexico." In Gender, Race and Religion in the Colonization of the Americas, edited by Nora E. Jaffary, 95–108. London: Ashgate.

Joyce, Rosemary A. 2000. *Gender and Power in Prehispanic Mesoamerica*. Austin: University of Texas Press.

Kane, Emily W. 2006. "'No Way My Boys Are Going to Be Like That!' Parents' Responses to Children's Gender Nonconformity." *Gender and Society* 20, 2: 149–76.

Kashyap, Girish S. 2004. "Looking Abroad to Protect Mothers at Home: A Look at Complicity by Omission Domestically and Abroad." *Boston University International Law Journal* 22, 2: 425–47.

Kaufman, Michael. 2012. "The Seven P's of Men's Violence." In *Men's Lives*, 9th edition, edited by Michael Kimmel and Michael Messner, 543–47. Boston: Pearson.

Kaye, Kerwin. 2005. "Sexual Abuse Victims and the Wholesome Family: Feminist, Psychological, and State Discourses." In *Regulating Sex: The Politics of Intimacy and Identity*, edited by Elizabeth Bernstein and Laurie Schaffner, 143–66. New York: Routledge.

Keenan, Marie. 2012. *Child Sexual Abuse & the Catholic Church: Gender, Power and Organizational Culture*. New York: Oxford University Press.

Kellogg, Susan. 2005. *Weaving the Past: A History of Latin America's Indigenous Women from the Prehispanic Period to the Present*. New York: Oxford University Press.

Kelly, Liz. 1987. "The Continuum of Sexual Violence." In *Women, Violence and Social Control*, edited by Jalna Hanmer and Mary Maynard, 46–60. Atlantic Highlands, NJ: Humanities Press International.

Kilby, Jane. 2010. "Judith Butler, Incest, and the Question of the Child's Love." *Feminist Theory* 11, 3: 255–65.

Kimball, Geoffrey. 1993. "Aztec Homosexuality: The Textual Evidence." *Journal of Homosexuality* 26, 1: 7–22.

Kimmel, Michael S. 1994. "Masculinity as Homophobia: Fear, Shame, and Silence in the Construction of Gender Identity." In *Theorizing Masculinities*, edited by Harry Brod and Michael Kaufman, 119–41. Thousand Oaks, CA: Sage.

Kimmel, Michael S. and Michael A. Messner. 2012. *Men's Lives*, 9th edition. Boston: Pearson.

Kinsey, Alfred C., Wardell B. Pomeroy, Clyde E. Martin, and Paul H. Gebhard. 1953. *Sexual Behavior in the Human Female*. Philadelphia and London: W.B. Saunders.

Kissling, Elizabeth A. 1991. "Street Harassment: The Language of Sexual Terrorism." *Discourse & Society* 2, 4: 451–60.

Knudson-Martin, Carmen. 1994. "The Female Voice: Applications to Bowen's Family Systems Theory." *Journal of Marital and Family Therapy* 20, 1: 35–46.

Laguarda, Rodrigo. 2007. "Gay en México: lucha de representaciones e identidad." *Alteridades* 17, 33: 127–33.

Lanning, Kenneth V. 1992. "Investigator's Guide to Allegations of 'Ritual' Child Abuse." Behavioral Science Unit, National Center for the Analysis of Violent Crime. Federal Bureau of Investigation.

Lavrin, Asunción. 1992. *Sexuality & Marriage in Colonial Latin America*. Lincoln and London: University of Nebraska Press.

Lewis, Oscar. 1961. *The Children of Sánchez*. New York: Vintage Books.

List Reyes, Mauricio. 2005. *Jóvenes corazones gay en la Ciudad de México*. Puebla, Mexico: Benemérita Universidad Autónoma de Puebla.

Lomnitz, Larissa. 1986. "The Uses of Fear: *Porro* Gangs in Mexico." In *Peace and War: Cross-Cultural Perspectives*, edited by Mary LeCron Foster and Robert A. Rubinstein, 15–24. New Brunswick, NJ: Transaction Publishers.

Lucero, Lisa J. and Sherry A. Gibbs. 2007. "The Creation and Sacrifice of Witches in Classic Maya Society." In *New Perspectives on Human Sacrifice and Ritual Body Treatments in Ancient Maya Society*, edited by Vera Tiesler and Andrea Cucina, 45–73. New York: Springer.

MacFarlane, Kee and Jill Korbin. 1983. "Confronting the Incest Secret Long After the Fact: A Family Study of Multiple Victimization with Strategies for Intervention." *Child Abuse & Neglect* 7: 225–40.

MacKinnon, Catharine A. 1996. *Only Words*. Cambridge, MA: Harvard University Press.

———. 2002. "Pleasure Under Patriarchy." In *Sexuality and Gender*, edited by Christine L. Williams and Arlene Stein, 33–43. Malden, MA: Blackwell Publishers.

Marcos, Sylvia. 1992. "Indigenous Eroticism and Colonial Morality in Mexico: The Confession Manuals of New Spain." *Numen* 39, 2: 157–74.

———. n.d. "La Luz del Mundo: El abuso sexual como rito religioso." *Revista Académica para el Estudio de las Religiones*, vol. 3. Available at http://www.revistaacademica.com/tIIIenlinea.asp, accessed April 25, 2014.

Margolin, Leslie. 1994. "Child Sexual Abuse by Uncles: A Risk Assessment." *Child Abuse & Neglect* 18, 3: 215–24.

Martínez Rojas, Lorenza. 2001. "Diseño de un programa de prevención de abuso sexual infantil." Tesis de licenciatura en Psicología Social. Mexico City: Universidad Autónoma Metropolitana, Unidad Iztapalapa.

Maynes, Mary Jo, Jennifer L. Pierce, and Barbara Laslett. 2008. *Telling Stories: The Use of Personal Narratives in the Social Sciences and History*. Ithaca: Cornell University Press.

McGoldrick, Monica, Carol M. Anderson, and Froma Walsh. 1991. *Women in Families: A Framework for Family Therapy*. New York: W.W. Norton.

McGoldrick, Monica and Randy Gerson. 1985. *Genograms in Family Assessment*. New York: W.W. Norton.

Meiselman, Karin. C. 1978. *Incest: A Psychological Study of Causes and Effects with Treatment and Recommendations*. San Francisco: Jossey-Bass.

Méndez-Negrete, Josie. 2006. *Las hijas de Juan: Daughters Betrayed*. Durham, NC: Duke University Press.

Menjívar, Cecilia. 2011. *Enduring Violence: Ladina Women's Lives in Guatemala*. Berkeley: University of California Press.

Milardo, Robert M. 2005. "Generative Uncle and Nephew Relationships." *Journal of Marriage and Family* 67 (December): 1226–36.

Miranda, Deborah A. 2010. "'Saying the Padre Had Grabbed Her': Rape Is the Weapon, Story Is the Cure." *Intertexts* 14, 2: 93–112.

Módena, María Eugenia and Zuanilda Mendoza. 2001. *Géneros y generaciones: Etnografía de las relaciones entre hombres y mujeres de la ciudad de México*. Mexico City: EDAMEX, S.A. de C.V. y Population Council.

Monárrez Fragoso, Julia. 2003. "Serial Sexual Femicide in Ciudad Juárez, 1993–2001." *Aztlán* 28, 2: 153–78.

Mora, Mariana. 2008. "Decolonizing Politics: Zapatista Indigenous Autonomy in an Era of Neoliberal Governance and Low Intensity Warfare." PhD diss., University of Texas at Austin.

Moro, Javier. 1996. "La reforma a la ley de menores en México: ¿del modelo tutelar al modelo garantista?" *Alegatos* 34: 641–50.

Mummert, Gail. 2012. "Pensando las familias transnacionales desde los relatos de vida: análisis longitudinal de la convivencia intergeneracional." In *Métodos cualitativos y su aplicación empírica*, edited by Marina Ariza and Laura Velasco, 151–84. Mexico City: Universidad Nacional Autónoma de México.

Norandi, Mariana. 2010. *"Sin servicios médicos, 98% de empleadas domésticas.* [Without medical services 98% of domestic workers]." La Jornada. March 28, 2010. Available at www.lajornada.unam.mx, accessed April 12, 2014.

Núñez Noriega, Guillermo. 1999. *Sexo entre varones: Poder y resistencia en el campo sexual.* Mexico City: Universidad Nacional Autónoma de México.

———. 2013. Personal interview via Skype. November 14, 2013.

O'Brien, Jodi. 2009. "Sociology as an Epistemology of Contradiction." *Sociological Perspectives* 52, 1: 5–22.

O'Connell Davidson, Julia. 2007. *Children in the Global Sex Trade.* Cambridge, UK: Polity Press.

Olamendi Torres, Patricia. 2007. *Delitos contra las mujeres: Análisis de la Clasificación Mexicana de Delitos.* México: UNIFEM e INEGI.

Ordorika, Imanol. 2008. "Violencia y *porrismo* en la educación superior en México." In *Anuario educativo mexicano: visión retrospectiva, año 2005,* edited by Guadalupe Teresinha Bertussi, 459–75. Mexico: Universidad Pedagógica Nacional and Miguel Ángel Porrúa.

Oré-Aguilar, Gaby. 1997–1998. "Sexual Harassment and Human Rights in Latin America." *66 Fordham Law Review,* 631–46.

Paredes, Américo. 2001. *A Texas-Mexican Cancionero: Folksongs of the Lower Border.* 3rd edition. Austin: University of Texas Press.

Pascoe, C. J. 2011. *Dude, You're a Fag: Masculinity and Sexuality in High School.* Berkeley: University of California Press.

Pease, Bob. 2000. "Beyond the Father Wound: Memory-Work and the Deconstruction of the Father-Son Relationship." *Australian & New Zeland Journal of Family Therapy* 21, 1: 9–15.

Penyak, Lee Michael. 1993. "Criminal Sexuality in Central Mexico (1750–1850)." PhD diss., University of Connecticut.

Plummer, Ken. 1995. *Telling Sexual Stories: Power, Change and Social Worlds.* London and New York: Routledge.

———. 2001. "The Call of Life Stories in Ethnographic Research." In *Handbook of Ethnography,* edited by Paul Atkinson, Amanda Coffey, Sara Delamont, John Lofland, and Lyn Lofland, 395–407. Thousand Oaks, CA: Sage.

Prieur, Annick. 1998a. *Mema's House, Mexico City: On Transvestites, Queens, and Machos.* Chicago: University of Chicago Press.

———. 1998b. "Bodily and Symbolic Constructions among Homosexual Men in Mexico." *Sexualities* 1, 3: 287–98.

Pulsipher, Lydia M. and Alex Pulsipher. 2006. "NAFTA and the Maquiladora Phenomenon." In *World Regional Geography (without Subregions): Global Patterns, Local Lives,* 126–27. London: Macmillan.

Quinn, Beth A. 2002. "Sexual Harassment and Masculinity: The Power and Meaning of 'Girl Watching'." *Gender & Society* 16, 3: 386–402.

Ramirez, Hernan and Edward Flores. 2012. "Latino Masculinities in the Post 9/11 Era." In *Men's Lives,* 9th edition, edited by Michael Kimmel and Michael A. Messner, 32–40. Boston: Pearson.

Ray, Raka and Seemin Qayum. 2009. *Cultures of Servitude: Modernity, Domesticity, and Class in India*. Stanford, CA: Stanford University Press.

Reese Jones, Leslie. 2011. "La narración de historias en familias mexicanas." XI Congreso Nacional de Investigación Educativa, Universidad Nacional Autónoma de México, 7–11 de noviembre 2011.

Renner, Lynette M. and Kristen Shook Slack. 2006. "Intimate Partner Violence and Child Maltreatment: Understanding Intra- and Intergenerational Connections." *Child Abuse & Neglect* 30: 599–617.

Riviere, P. G. 1967. "The Honour of Sánchez." *Man*, New Series 2, 4: 569–83.

Romero, Laura. 2011. *Chamanismo y curanderismo: Nuevas perspectivas*. Mexico: Benemérita Universidad Autónoma de Puebla.

Ruiz Carbonell, Ricardo. 2002. *La violencia familiar y los derechos humanos*. Mexico: Comisión Nacional de los Derechos Humanos.

Rumney, Philip N. S. 2009. "Gay Male Rape Victims: Law Enforcement, Social Attitudes and Barriers to Recognition." *International Journal of Human Rights* 13: 2, 233–50.

Russell, Diana E. H. 1997. *Behind Closed Doors in White South Africa: Incest Survivors Tell Their Stories*. New York: St. Martin's Press.

———. 1999 [1986]. *The Secret Trauma: Incest in the Lives of Girls and Women*. New York: Basic Books.

Saldaña-Tejeda, Abril G. 2011. "Women and Paid Domestic Work in Mexico: Food, Sexuality and Motherhood." PhD diss., University of Manchester.

———. 2014. "Tlazolteotl: 'The Filth Deity' and the Sexualization of Paid Domestic Workers in Mexico." *Sexualities* 17 (1/2): 194–212.

Sánchez Gudiño, Hugo. 2006. *Génesis, desarrollo y consolidación de los grupos estudiantiles de choque en la UNAM (1930–1990)*. Mexico: UNAM and Miguel Ángel Porrúa.

Sanday, Peggy R. 2007. *Fraternity Gang Rape: Sex, Brotherhood and Privilege on Campus*. New York: New York University Press.

Saucedo González, Irma. 1999. "La experiencia de las ONG en el trabajo sobre violencia sexual y doméstica." In *Las Organizaciones No Gubernamentales mexicanas y la salud reproductiva*, edited by Soledad González Montes, 75–95. Mexico City: El Colegio de México.

Schmukler Scornik, Beatriz and Xosefa Alonso Sierra. 2009. *Democratización familiar en Mexico: Experiencias de un proyecto de prevención de violencia familiar*. Mexico City: Instituto Mora.

Scully, Diana. 1990. *Understanding Sexual Violence: A Study of Convicted Rapists*. Cambridge, MA: Unwin Hyman.

Seed, Patricia. 1985. "The Church and the Patriarchal Family: Marriage Conflicts in Sixteenth- and Seventeenth-Century New Spain." *Journal of Family History* 10: 284–93.

Segal, Lynne and Mary McIntosh. 1993. *Sex Exposed: Sexuality and the Pornography Debate*. New Brunswick, NJ: Rutgers University Press.

Segura, Denise A. and Jennifer L. Pierce. 1993. "Chicana/o Family Structure and Gender Personality: Chodorow, Familism, and Psychoanalytic Sociology Revisited." *Signs* 19, 1: 62–91.

Sheffield, Carole J. 1989. "The Invisible Intruder: Women's Experiences of Obscene Phone Calls." *Gender and Society* 3, 4: 483–88.

Siller Urteaga, Lorena. 2012. "Ni Domésticas Ni Putas: Sexual Harassment in the Lives of Female Household Workers in Monterrey, Nuevo León." MA thesis, University of Texas at Austin.

Simon, William and John H. Gagnon. 1986. "Sexual Scripts: Permanence and Change." *Archives of Sexual Behavior* 15, 2: 97–120.

Thorne, Barrie and Marilyn Yalom. 1992. *Rethinking the Family: Some Feminist Questions*. Revised edition. Boston: Northeastern University Press.

Tuñón-Pablos, Enriqueta. 1991. *El álbum de la mujer: Antología ilustrada de las mexicanas, Vol. I.* Mexico City: Instituto Nacional de Antropología e Historia.

U.S. Census 2010. *The Hispanic Population: 2010.* United States Census Bureau.

Vázquez Mezquita, Blanca. 1995. *Agresión sexual: Evaluación y tratamiento en menores.* Mexico City: Siglo XXI Editores.

Vega-Briones, Germán. 2011. "Hogares y pobreza en Ciudad Juárez, Chihuahua." *Papeles de Población* 17, 70: 151–81.

Velasco, Elizabeth. 2013. "De cada 100 mujeres víctimas de trata en México, 70 son indígenas: ONG [70 out of 100 women victims of human trafficking in Mexico are indigenous: NGO]." www.lajornada.unam.mx. Published June 24, 2013.

Vidrio, Martha. 1991. *Estudio descriptivo del abuso sexual en Guadalajara: violación, incesto, atentado al pudor y estupro.* Guadalajara: Editorial Universidad de Guadalajara.

Vieyra Ramírez, Isabel. 2012. Electronic communication. October 11, 2012.

———. 2013. "El encuentro con la otra. Consideraciones sobre el himen, el dolor y el sangrado en la primera relación sexual." MA in Anthropology, thesis report. Mexico City: Escuela Nacional de Antropología e Historia.

Wentzell, Emily A. 2013. *Maturing Masculinities: Aging, Chronic Illness, and Viagra in Mexico.* Durham, NC: Duke University Press.

INDEX

A la prima se le arrima, 24, 76, 79, 113, 122, 143, 226–227, 235, 286n25, 286n27
abortion, 21
abuso sexual (the term), 278n39
Acharya, Arun Kumar, 279n46, 279n49, 283n51
Al primo me le arrimo, 26, 182, 184–185, 224, 226–227, 244
Alarma! (newspaper), 9, 276n12
alcohol: informants and alcohol use, 42, 136, 162, 210; relatives who exercised sexual violence and, 43, 280n5; religion and alcohol use, 222; in romantic and family relationships, 140, 141–142, 212, 219, 279n2
Almaguer, Tomás, 290n7, 292n32, 294n38, 295n44
amigos de la familia, 15, 106
apariencias, las, 159, 174
Apodaca, Nuevo León, 20
aprovechamiento sexual (the term), 278n39
Armstrong, Louise, 5, 54, 281n19
Arreola, Sonya Grant, 289n3, 293n36
arrimón, 143–144, 166, 287n11
Arrom, Sylvia, 276n17, 276n28
Asesoría y Servicio Legal S.A. de C.V., 276n32
"*Así son los hombres, todos son iguales*" ("That is the way men are, all of them are the same"), 79, 123
"*Así son los muchachos, no les hagas caso*" ("That is the way young men are, ignore them"), 24, 123, 236

Asociación para el Desarrollo Integral de Personas Violadas A. C. (ADIVAC), 18, 276n32
Ayotzinapa, 232

Bartra, Eli, 18
Bell, Vikki, 298n32
Bible, the, 5, 63, 64, 67, 237–238
blame the victim, 8, 83, 96, 104, 221, 224, 236–238, 253, 295n10. *See also* self-blame
body, the: children, 169, 237, 280n10; men, 109, 224, 227–229 (*see also* gay men); women, 1, 49, 71, 77, 108–109, 241, 259–260 (*see also* conjugal daughter)
Bourdieu, Pierre, 68, 236, 279n51, 289n27, 297n18
Boyd Franklin, Nancy, 279n2
boys will be boys, 24, 123
Brito, Alejandro, and Leonardo Bastida, 291n23, 292n28, 294n37
brother-sister incest, 23–26, 29, 32, 39, 52–53, 76–79, 103–113, 168; daughter-father relationship and, 105; daughter-mother relationship and, 104; expressions and patterns of, 106; sister-brother emotional relationship, 104; women's interpretations of, 106; women's perceptions of her parents and, 105
brothers-in-law, 103, 246, 298n37
bulimia, 101, 162, 259
bullying, 21. *See also* homophobia
Butler, Judith, 294n40

Cacho, Lydia, 290n8
Campbell, Rebecca, 11, 13
cantinas, 155, 287n12
capital femenino, virginity as, 73–74, 280n6, 283n50
Caputi, Jane, 282n41, 283n46
Careaga Pérez, Gloria, 298n29
Casa Amiga, 19
Castañeda, Carmen, 16, 276n22–23, 276n25, 297n26
castillo de la pureza, syndrome, *el*, 239, 296n14
Catholic Church, 13–16, 53, 222–223, 237, 282n26; abuse of children by priests, 59–60, 74; celibacy, 282n26; confession, 238; guilt, 238, 296n12; liberation theology, 238; Opus Dei, 296n12; Pope Francis, 248; priest Eduardo Córdova case, 248; "zero tolerance" and abuse of children by priests, 248
Catholic priests, 59–60, 75, 296n12; masculinity of, 238–239, 259
Centro de Apoyo a la Mujer (CAM), 17
Centro de Apoyo a Mujeres Violadas (CAMVAC), 17
Centro de Orientación y Prevención de la Agresión Sexual, A.C., 18, 276n32
Champagne, Rosaria, 298n38
Chávez Ayala, Rubén, 286n1, 294n41
Chávez Cano, Esther, 278n40
Chesler, Phyllis, 57, 281n23
children: agency of, 27 (*see also* resilience); as desexualized and innocent, 25, 236, 295n6; as less-than-human, 10, 71, 121, 169; as property, 10, 54–55, 169, 241; as sexual transgressors, 236–237, 295n6; human rights of, 10, 17, 22, 249, 253, 262; in the law, 17, 276n28; working and/or living on the streets, 262, 290n10
Chodorow, Nancy, 128, 169, 281n18
Ciudad Juárez, 3–4, 11; informants, 263; migrant women and, 50; professional

services, 19; violence against women and, 19, 232, 283n45. *See also* maquiladoras
class, 9, 23, 32, 78, 174, 254; middle, 49, 51–53, 112, 254; upper, 55–58, 112; upper-middle, 49, 53, 57–58, 112, 174, 254; working, 7, 9, 55, 112, 254, 287n10, 289n2, 291nn15–16
Colectivo de Lucha contra la Violencia hacia las Mujeres (COVAC), 17
colonial society, 10, 16–17, 19, 31, 53, 71, 113, 184, 230, 281n12, 285n19
colonias populares, 238, 287n10
cómplices por omisión, mothers as, 69
conjugal daughter, 23, 28, 31–33, 48–52, 56, 59, 67–68, 75, 173, 234, 238, 280n9
Connell, R. W., 78, 284n3, 285n12, 294n39, 297n27
Consejo Nacional para Prevenir la Discriminación (CONAPRED), 22, 279n50, 292n28
continuum of sexual consent and coercion, 6, 26, 183–185, 224–225, 228, 243, 290n9
continuum of sexual violence, 78, 110–111, 120, 185, 235, 285n10, 295n42; family continuum of sexual violence, 185, 224, 229–230
Convention of Belém do Pará, 277n38
Convention on the Elimination of All Forms of Discrimination against Women (CEDAW), 277n38
conversion therapy (reparative therapy). *See* homophobia; lesbian women
cousins. See *primas* and *primos*
cultura de confianza, la, 239
cultura de la denuncia, la, 20
cultural scaffolding of rape, 24–25, 236
culture blaming, 8–9, 22
culture of poverty, 7–9, 26

daughters. *See* father-daughter incest
Davis, Deirdre, 122, 286n28

de la Garza Aguilar, Javier, and Enrique Díaz-Michel, 278n40
de Gante Casas, Alejandra, 272, 277n34
Delgadina, La, 31, 279n1
Delitos contra las mujeres report, 19, 278n39
derecho de pernada (right to the first night), 23, 33, 54–55, 234, 281n17
desexualization of children, 25, 121, 236
disability, 10, 256
dissociation, 287n13
domestic workers, 71, 111–112, 174, 235, 285n13
doncellas, 61
dowry (*la dote*), 16
drug trafficking, 232–233; father-daughter incest and, 240
drug use, prevention, 21. *See also* medicalization of rape
Durkheim, Émile 5, 73

El que golpea a una, nos golpea a todas (He who hits one [woman], hits all of us [women]) campaign, 20
Encuesta Nacional sobre Discriminación en México (ENADIS): report on domestic workers, 285n13; report on sexual diversity, 292n28; report on women, 295n8
Encuesta Nacional sobre la Dinámica de las Relaciones en los Hogares (ENDI-REH), 20, 278n42
endogamy, 113
Engels, Friedrich, 70, 235
enmeshed families, 296n14
Erdely, Jorge, and Lourdes Argüelles, 72, 74, 282nn42–44, 283n52, 283nn57–58
Esteinou, Rosario, 281n14
estupro, 278n39
ethics and research, 180–181, 299
ética del servicio, 280n11

familia, origin of the word, 70–71
family continuum of sexual violence. *See* continuum of sexual violence

family cultures of rape, 25, 129, 178, 236–237, 239–240
family democratization, 243, 253
family genealogies of incest, 25, 28, 67, 112, 127–129, 168–177, 185, 228, 230, 235, 240–244, 261
family justice, 30, 75, 249–253
family sex surrogacy, 23–24, 28, 77, 107–109, 120, 168, 235
family sexual harassment, 24, 28, 78, 120, 122–124, 129, 135, 168–169, 235
family sexual obligations, 32, 51, 234
father-daughter incest, 6, 21, 23, 25, 28, 31–33, 234–235; birth order, 49; daughter-mother relationship, 48; duration of incest, 49; frequency in the study, 25; kinship reassignments (wives as daughters, daughters as wives), 23, 33, 52, 56, 234; marital relationship, 48; serial incest, 48; sexualization of the parental child, 51–52, 234; silence, 49; social images of the father, 49; trauma, 50. *See also* conjugal daughter; *derecho de pernada*; gendered servitude; marital servant
feminicidio, 20
feminism in Mexico, 17–22, 68
feminization of incest, 25, 28, 127–129, 166, 168, 175, 240, 261. *See also* family genealogies of incest
Finkelhor, David, 4, 57, 72, 275n5, 280n10, 282n39
Floris Margadant, Guillermo, 275n3, 276n27
Fregoso, Rosa-Linda, and Cynthia Bejarano, 277n37, 283n45

García, Genaro, 17, 70
Gavey, Nicola, 24–25, 295n42
gay cultures within families, 185, 244
gay men, 2, 26, 180, 230; abused by male relatives, 183, 221, 223–224, 228–229; heteronormative compliance, 184, 224–226, 244 (*see also* homophobia);

gay men (*cont.*)
 pop culture, 245–246, 298n30; queer
 boys, 224–229; same-sex sexual
 contact within the family across generations, 292n32; sex between cousins,
 181–184, 293n36 (*see also* kinship sex);
 sexual objectification in the family,
 185, 244; the body, 224–225, 227–229,
 244; U.S. Latina and Latino communities and child sexual abuse of,
 289n3, 293n36. See also *Al primo me
 le arrimo*
gender, 10, 124, 255; discourses, 53; education on, 21; inequality in the family,
 68–70, 111, 126–128, 168–179, 185 (*see
 also* misrecognition); nonconformity,
 226–227; of incest, 22–27, 234–246;
 taken-for-granteds, 24–25, 122, 236.
 See also gendered servitude
gender helplessness, 24, 123, 236
gendered servitude, 23–24, 28, 32–33,
 52–53, 77, 107–108, 112, 127, 234–235,
 279n3
genograms, 170, 173, 231, 288n18
Giraud, François, 276n25, 282n38
Gonzalbo Aizpuru, Pilar, 281n12
González Ascencio, Gerardo, 18, 276n30
grandfathers, 25–26, 49, 52, 106, 127, 172–
 173, 286n1, 292n32
groping, 110, 143, 166, 212, 287n11. See also
 arrimón
Grupo 8 de marzo, 19
Guadalajara, 3, 11, 21, 73; informants, 263–
 264; professional services, 18, 276n32.
 See also La Luz del Mundo
Guatemala, 22, 68, 236, 249, 299n41
güeras, 260–261
guilt, 15, 78, 106, 237–238, 280n10, 296n12.
 See also blame the victim; self-blame
Gutiérrez, Ramón A., 70, 235, 281n13,
 282n34, 290n4, 295n45
Gutmann, Matthew C., 10, 276n10

hacienda. See *derecho de pernada*
hate crimes, 26, 29, 180, 298n29. *See also*
 homophobia; lesbian women
Haug, Frigga, 268
Herlihy, David, 70, 282n37
Herman, Judith, 6, 48, 53, 176, 242,
 280nn7–9, 281n18, 281n22, 286n33,
 287n6, 287n13, 288n24, 290n9, 291n18,
 295n10, 297n21, 299n39
heteronormative compliance. *See* gay men
heterosexuality: 77–78, 108–111, 224,
 235–237; compulsory heterosexuality,
 181–182, 227; heteronormativity, 223–
 226; heterosexual love and sex, 23–24,
 56–57, 73, 234; hetero-patriarchy, 78,
 109–110; the legal system, 246–247
Himno Nacional Mexicano, 232
history of incest laws. *See* incest laws
HIV/AIDS, 291n13
hogar como tierra de nadie, el, 239
hombría, 53
homophobia: gender and sexual cleansing
 in the family, 244; homophobic bullying, 182, 193, 209, 219, 291n14, 294n37;
 homophobic discourse, 182–184, 227,
 293n36; in the family, 26, 29, 223–228,
 243–244, 291n23; *mano caída*, 292n25;
 reparative therapy and gay men, 225,
 269; social change in Mexico, 292n27;
 surveys on homophobia in Mexico,
 292n28. *See also* lesbian women
honor and shame (*honor y vergüenza*), 23,
 53, 184, 230, 234, 244
hostigamiento sexual (the term), 278n39
hymen reconstruction, 73–74, 283n50
hypergamy, 57

immigration: U.S. laws, migration, and
 violence against women, 248–249. *See
 also* transnational incest
incest: definition-in-progress, 6; shifting
 definitions, 13

incest laws: hetero-reproductive marriage, 246–247; history of laws, 13–19; penal codes, 14, 271–272
indigenous women, 10, 16, 20, 60, 69, 71, 111, 261, 288n16
Informe de crímenes de odio por homofobia, México 1995–2008, 180, 291n23
Instituto Nacional de Estadística, Geografía e Informática (INEGI), 20, 278n42, 284n5, 297n20
Instituto Nacional de las Mujeres (INMU-JERES), 20–21, 278n42, 279n48
Instituto Nacional de Protección a la Infancia, 277n36
internalized sexism, 23, 68–69, 111, 127, 129, 177–178, 241, 298n35. *See also* misrecognition
investigaciones previas, 246

Jaffary, Nora E., 285n19
Jehova's Witnesses related cases, 85–88, 212, 214, 246–247. *See also* religion

Keenan, Marie, 259, 291n21, 296n12
Kelly, Liz, 78, 110, 229, 285n10, 290n6, 295n4
kinesthetic effeminacy, 225
Kinsey, Alfred, 127, 287n3, 296n15
kinship sex, 6, 26, 28, 183–186, 224–225, 243
Kissling, Elizabeth A., 121, 285n23, 286nn29–31

L Word, 245
La Luz del Mundo, 72–74, 276n19, 282n44
La Malquerida, 258
Lagarde y de los Ríos, Marcela, 20, 68
Lanning, Kenneth, 72, 282n40
Latinas and Latinos. *See* U.S. Spanish-speaking communities
Lavrin, Asunción, 276n25, 281n13, 285n19, 290n4, 295n45

laws regarding incest. *See* incest laws
lesbian women: lesbophobia, 226, 244–245, 291n23, 298n29; sexual abuse as children, 26; silence in the family, 244–245
Lewis, Oscar, 7–10, 276n11, 276n13, 285n16
"Ley General de Acceso de las Mujeres a una Vida Libre de Violencia," 277n38
"Ley General para la Igualdad entre Mujeres y Hombres," 277n38
Leyes de Reforma, 14
LGBTQ activism, 245–246
List, Mauricio, 291n15, 291n23
"Los muchachos nomás estaban jugando" ("The young men were *just* playing"), 24, 121, 236

machetona, 297n27
machín, 182, 289n2
machismo, 7–8, 22, 293n36
Maciel, Marcial, 15
MacKinnon, Catharine, 109, 282n41, 285n9
maquiladoras, 153, 254
Marcos, Sylvia, 54–55, 72, 281n15–17, 281n20, 282n44
Margolin, Leslie, 287n2, 289n26, 294n38
marital rape (laws), 20
marital servant, 23, 28, 31–33, 59, 67–75, 234
masculinity, 8, 26, 108–111, 122, 180, 185, 224–228, 235, 258–259, 284n8, 293n36. *See also* Catholic priests: masculinity of
Maynes, Mary Jo, Jennifer L. Pierce, and Barbara Laslett, 267–268
McGoldrick, Monica, 288n18
medicalization of rape, 123, 280n5. *See also* alcohol
Meiselman, Karin, 287n2, 289n29
memory work, 267–268

men abused as children: father-son relationship, 222; mother-son relationship, 222; reactions to the experiences of abuse, 223; relationship with person who exercised violence, 221; religion, 222–223. *See also* gay men

Méndez-Negrete, Jessie, 8, 268, 275n3, 288n15

Menjívar, Cecilia, 22, 68, 236, 239, 279n51, 289n27, 296n13, 296n17, 299n41

methodology, 7, 10–13, 28, 267–270, 276n11

Mexico City, 3, 7, 11, 233; activism and professional services, 17–22; informants, 264

"*Mi esposo me usó*," 53

misogyny. *See* rituals

misrecognition, 68, 111, 121, 178, 236, 241, 279n51. *See also* internalized sexism

Módena, María Eugenia, and Zuanilda Mendoza, 289n28

Monterrey, 3, 11, 20–21, 58, 232; informants, 265; professional services, 18–19

morality, 296n11; Christian moral values, 237–238, 255, 282n26; double standards of, 5, 10, 15, 74, 106, 111. *See also* Catholic Church

mothers: *cómplices por omisión*, 69; experiential feminism, 253; family justice, 250–253; infantilization of, 56; who do not intervene on behalf of their children, 298n35. *See also* father-daughter incest

multigenerational patterns and incest, 25, 170–171, 183–185, 230, 241. *See also* family genealogies of incest

Mummert, Gail, 276n14

narcofosas, 232

niños encerrados, los, 254

nuclear families, 126, 128, 169, 240, 242, 297n20

Núñez Noriega, Guillermo, 225–226, 291n23, 292nn26–27, 294n41

"*obedecerás a tu padre y a tu madre*," 239

O'Connell Davidson, Julia, 295n6

Ojo Mucho Ojo campaign, 18, 277nn33–34

Olamendi Torres, Patricia, 19, 277n38

parental child, 23, 32–33, 51–52, 234, 279n2

paterfamilias, 23, 33, 55–56, 68–70, 234

patriarchal dividend, 78, 111, 120

patriarchy. *See* regional patriarchies; underground patriarchies

Pelayo family, the, 285n19

penal codes and incest. *See* incest laws

Pentecostal Church, 74

Penyak, Lee Michael, 276n26, 282n38

Pérez Cruz, Mayra, 21

performative gender survival, 244

physical violence, 20, 24, 32, 48–50, 78, 92, 105–108, 111, 129, 166–167, 183, 185, 223, 231, 237, 240, 250, 253, 258, 279n51, 285n10, 285n21

pigmentocracy, 260–261

play: boyhood and heterosexuality, 108; erotic play, 226; sexual harassment and molestation as "play," 24–25, 106, 120–121, 168, 182, 185, 236; sexual play, 225; sexualized encounters between male relatives close in age, 183–185, 243. *See also* kinship sex

pleasure—danger, 78, 183, 226, 243, 253, 280n4, 285n10, 290n5, 292n30

Plummer, Ken, 267–268

political economy of incest, 255

popular culture, 23, 245–246, 257, 298n38

pornography, 106, 108, 275n7, 280n4, 285n21, 290n8, 290n10; in informants' stories, 79, 140, 151, 160–161, 194, 197, 199, 202, 209

porros, 98, 284n6

poverty, 7–9, 26, 106, 112, 232, 254–255

pregnancy and incest, 21, 173, 247

prehispanic societies, 11, 16, 244

primas and *primos*: incest, 23–24, 28–29, 76–79, 119–124, 172, 235. See also *A la prima se le arrima*; *Al primo me le arrimo*
private versus public, 123
prostitution, 285n21, 290n10; sexual initiation of adolescent young men, 243, 284n8, 297n19
Protestantism, 59–60, 125, 222
provocativa, 237. *See also* blame the victim
psychotherapy, 11, 250, 269
pueblos, 113, 281n12; incestuous *pueblos*, 50, 54, 254–255

queer boys. *See* gay men
queering incest, 256–257
quid pro quo, 278n39

racism, 279n50, 282n26. *See also* pigmentocracy
ranchos, 113; incestuous *ranchos*, 50, 54, 254–255
Real Academia Española, 20, 234, 278n45, 295n2
regional patriarchies, 20, 74, 113, 278n44, 281n21, 296n11
religion, 11, 16, 33, 60, 67, 221–222, 239, 281n12; religious diversity, 284n5. *See also* Catholic Church
resilience, 27, 29, 75, 250–253
rituals: interaction ritual, 73; *ritual narco-satánico*, 284n59; ritualistic abuse, 67, 72; ritualizing misogyny, 23, 33, 60, 68, 72–75. *See also* witchcraft
Rivera, Jenni, 257
role reversal, 52, 281n22. *See also* conjugal daughter
rural patriarchy, 55, 74. *See also* regional patriarchies
Russell, Diana E. H., 6, 127, 275n4, 280n9, 281n22, 287n2, 287nn4–5, 288n15, 288n18, 288n20, 289n29, 295n10, 296n11, 296n15, 299n42

San Salvador Atenco, 20
Saucedo González, Irma, 276n31
Schmukler Scornik, Beatriz, and Xosefa Alonso Sierra, 297n20, 297n25, 298n34
Scully, Diana, 280n5, 286n32, 287n9, 295n10
second assault, 267
Secreto en la montaña (film), 245
secrets, 4, 15, 26, 49–50, 104–105, 129, 178, 185, 224, 255, 257–258
Seed, Patricia, 281n13, 290n4, 295n45
Segura, Denise, and Jennifer Pierce, 128, 169, 296n16
self-blame, 30, 121, 238–239, 248, 296n12. *See also* blame the victim; guilt
serial incest, 48, 67, 106, 171, 241
servir, 234–235, 280n11, 281n12, 295n2
Seventh-Day Adventist Church, 64, 74–75
sex surrogates. *See* family sex surrogacy
sexual cleansing in the family, 244. *See also* homophobia; lesbian women
sexual harassment, 25, 78, 110–112, 121, 124, 129, 224, 235, 243, 275n7, 278n39, 283n47, 285n13, 291n23, 297n19. *See also* family sexual harassment
sexual initiation of men: with male relatives, 292n31–32; with sisters and female cousins, 23–24, 286n27. *See also* kinship sex; prostitution
sexual scripts, 230, 235–236, 242
sexual slaves. *See* marital servant
sexual terrorism, 78, 120–123, 168, 235
sexual trafficking of girls and women, 20–22, 71, 228, 275n7, 279n46, 290n10
sexual violence (the term), 275n7
sexuality: 4, 16; cultural perceptions, 10, 184; health and well-being, 52, 106; of incest, 22–27, 173, 230, 234–246 (*see also* kinship sex); in pop culture, 245–246, 257–258, 298n30; taken-for-granteds, 24–25, 122, 236; youth and education on, 21, 249. *See also* heterosexuality

sexualization of daughters. *See* conjugal daughter; marital servant
Sheffield, Carole J., 78, 120–121, 285n20–21, 286n25
silence. *See* secrets
Simon, William, and John H. Gagnon, 295n46
social-sexual attraction, 57
socioeconomic status. *See* class
Sonora, research on rape in, 286n1
sororidad, 68, 282n28
spiritual incest, 15
stepfathers, 15, 23, 25–26, 74, 172, 222, 231, 238, 241, 258, 286n1
stepmothers, 67–68, 71
storytelling, 11, 28, 170, 267–268

telenovelas, 246, 258, 298n30
Thorne, Barrie, and Marilyn Yalom, 288n19
tíos lejanos, 126, 129, 163, 273
tíos políticos, 126, 129, 140, 160, 167, 176, 182
transgender, 1, 220, 244, 265
transnational incest, 136, 287n8
trauma, 27–30, 50, 52, 178–179, 250–253, 259, 267, 269, 280n10, 284n8, 287n2, 287n13, 289n29
traumatic sexualization, 52, 280n10
Tu Futuro en Libertad, 21
Tuñón-Pablos, Enriqueta, 281n14

uncle-niece incest: 25–26, 29, 48–49, 52, 106, 125–130, 165, 168–179; adolescent uncles, 167; biological uncles, 166; distant uncles (see *tíos lejanos*); maternal uncles, 130, 166; maternal and paternal uncles-in-law (see *tíos políticos*); paternal uncles, 156; uncle-niece cases in the study, 273. *See also* feminization of incest
underground patriarchies, 33, 58, 234
Univisión, 257–258
urban patriarchies, 281n21, 296n11. *See also* regional patriarchies
U.S. Spanish-speaking communities: people with disabilities, 256; pop culture in, 257–258

Vázquez Mezquita, Blanca, 295n6
vergüenza, 279n52. *See also* honor and shame
Vidrio, Martha, 275n3
violación (the term), 278n39; *violación agravada* (the term), 278n39; *violación por objeto distinto* (the term), 278n39
virginity, 16, 279n52, 280n6; as a gift, 74; as *capital femenino*, 73–74, 283n50; Middle Eastern cultures, 261; rape of virgins, 54, 74; sex between cousins and, 122. See also *derecho de pernada*

war on drugs, 232–233
witchcraft, 59–60, 75, 281n25. *See also* rituals
women's rights. *See* feminism in Mexico

zócalo, 22

ABOUT THE AUTHOR

Gloria González-López is Associate Professor of Sociology at the University of Texas at Austin.